Labor in Akron, 1825–1945

SERIES ON OHIO HISTORY AND CULTURE

Series on Ohio History and Culture
Kevin Kern, Editor

Kathleen Endres, *Akron's "Better Half": Women's Clubs and the Humanization of a City, 1825–1925*
Russ Musarra and Chuck Ayers, *Walks Around Akron: Rediscovering a City in Transition*
Heinz Poll, edited by Barbara Schubert, *A Time to Dance: The Life of Heinz Poll*
Mark D. Bowles, *Chains of Opportunity: The University of Akron and the Emergence of the Polymer Age, 1909–2007*
Russ Vernon, *West Point Market Cookbook*
Stan Purdum, *Pedaling to Lunch: Bike Rides and Bites in Northeastern Ohio*
Joyce Dyer, *Goosetown: Reconstructing an Akron Neighborhood*
Robert J. Roman, *Ohio State Football: The Forgotten Dawn*
Timothy H. H. Thoresen, *River, Reaper, Rail: Agriculture and Identity in Ohio's Mad River Valley, 1795–1885*
Brian G. Redmond, Bret J. Ruby, and Jarrod Burks, eds., *Encountering Hopewell in the Twenty-first Century, Ohio and Beyond. Volume 1: Monuments and Ceremony*
Brian G. Redmond, Bret J. Ruby, and Jarrod Burks, eds., *Encountering Hopewell in the Twenty-first Century, Ohio and Beyond. Volume 2: Settlements, Foodways, and Interaction*
Jen Hirt, *Hear Me Ohio*
Ray Greene, *Coach of a Different Color: One Man's Story of Breaking Barriers in Football*
Mark Auburn, editor, *Hail We Akron!: The Third Fifty Years of The University of Akron, 1970 to 2020*
Deb Van Tassel Warner and Stuart Warner, eds., *Akron's Daily Miracle: Reporting the News in the Rubber City*
Joyce Dyer, *Pursuing John Brown: On the Trail of a Radical Abolitionist*
John A. Tully, *Labor in Akron, 1825–1945*

Titles published since 2006.
For a complete listing of titles published in the series, go to www.uakron.edu/uapress.

Labor in Akron, 1825–1945

John A. Tully

The University of Akron Press
Akron, Ohio

ISBN: 978-1-629222-00-4 (paper)
ISBN: 978-1-629221-98-4 (ePDF)
ISBN: 978-1-629221-99-1 (ePub)

A catalog record for this title is available from the Library of Congress.

∞The paper used in this publication meets the minimum requirements of ansi/niso z39.48–1992 (Permanence of Paper).

Cover: Image from the Goodyear Collection, University of Akron Archives. Used with permission. Cover design by Amy Freels.

Labor in Akron, 1825–1945 was designed and typeset in Adobe Caslon by Beth Pratt and printed on sixty-pound natural and bound by Bookmasters of Ashland, Ohio.

Produced in conjunction with the University of Akron Affordable Learning Initiative. More information is available at www.uakron.edu/affordablelearning/.

For the Akron Socialist firebrand Marguerite Prevey, Akron Abraham Lincoln Brigade volunteer Salaria Kee O'Reilly, and Wilmer Tate— "the father of the CIO in Summit County."

Contents

Acknowledgments

I was fortunate in researching for this book to make the acquaintance of a number of very helpful archivists and librarians in Akron and elsewhere in Ohio. Firstly, I must thank the staff at The University of Akron Archives for their help. These include the current director, Vic Fleischer, John Ball, and the former director, John Miller. Sadly, another UAA archivist, Craig Holbert, died far too young in 2017. I missed Craig's unfailingly helpful and courteous presence when I last visited the archives. Craig was the author of two books and had an encyclopedic knowledge of the local history of his city. I must also thank Jeffrey Franks of Bierce Library at The University of Akron for his help in suggesting readings when I was first gathering material on rubber and the labor movement in the city. Jeff also kindly provided me with details of the life of his grandfather, K. H. Andonian, who came to Akron as an Armenian refugee before World War I and worked for many years at the Goodyear plant. Nor can I forget Judy James and Mike Elliott at the Akron-Summit County Public Library; the staff of the Ohio Historical Center in Columbus, Ohio; and the staff at the Center for Archival Research at Bowling Green State University. Thanks also to Ann K. Sindelar and her colleagues at the Cleveland History Center, Ohio. I am especially indebted to Norma Hill, the librarian at the *Akron Beacon Journal* for helping locate material while I was in Akron, and for searching for material and sending it to me in Australia. Andy Blunden, Tim Davenport, and Marty Goodman of the Marxist Internet Archive also kindly helped to find a photograph of the Akron Socialist leader

Marguerite Prevey, and I thank them for this. Thanks also to the staff of the Tamiment Library and Robert F. Wagner Labor Archives in New York. Thanks also to Noah Carmichael, Field Representative of Local 7 of the Bricklayers' Union, who shared details of growing up in Goodyear Heights and made time to give me a tour of the rubber factory sites in Akron. Noah also kindly contacted Dr. Samuel W. White of the Institute for Labor Studies and Research at the University of West Virginia for information on US coalmining terms. Thanks, Sam for tracking them down. (Evidently, my request for the American equivalent of the British term "banksman" caused Sam's contacts in the United Mine Workers some merriment!) I should also not forget the UMWA.'s Tim Baker for his help in this regard. I have visited Akron on a number of occasions and have come to view the city with affection. The people have been unfailingly kind and helpful. Two I must thank for their hospitality are Jim Slowiak and Jairo Cuesta of the New World Performance Lab in Akron. The late Stan Ovshinsky, who spent his early life in Akron, also took time from his busy schedule to talk with me over lunch in a pleasant restaurant near his workplace in Detroit. I would also like to thank David Roberts, a rediscovered friend from my earliest schooldays, for reading some of the manuscript and making pertinent suggestions. I must also thank Jon Miller and his staff at The University of Akron Press for their invaluable help in bringing the manuscript to a publishable state, particularly Amy Freels and Thea Ledendecker. Nor should I omit mention of Elliot Linzer for the indexing. Lastly, I must not forget my life partner, Dorothy Bruck, for her unstinting support, including reading the manuscript and making suggestions; for tolerating my absences on research trips; and for putting up with my abstracted demeanor while I was writing the book—which she called "going to Akron." Naturally, any errors and omissions are my responsibility and all interpretations are my own and do not imply agreement with my ideas by any of the people I have listed.

Glossary

ABJ	*Akron Beacon Journal*
AFL	American Federation of Labor
AFL-CIO	Merger of the American Federation of Labor and the Congress of Industrial Organizations
ARWA	Amalgamated Rubber Workers Association
Big Three	The Firestone, B. F. Goodrich, and Goodyear Tire & Rubber companies
CIO	Congress of Industrial Organizations. Initially the Committee for Industrial Organization
CLP	Communist Labor Party
CLU	Central Labor Union (Peak body of AFL unions in a particular city. Thus, there were CLUs in Akron, Barberton, and Cleveland)
CP (USA)	Communist Party (of the United States)
CPA	Communist Party of America
CWL	Citizens' Welfare League
Comintern	Third or Communist International
FLP	Farmer-Labor Party
GNP	Gross National Product
Gummers	Vernacular for blue-collar workers in the Akron rubber factories, or "gum mines"
IA	Industrial Assembly

IAM	International Association of Machinists
IATSE	International Alliance of Theatrical and Stage Employees
IGWU	Independent General Workers Union
ISR	*International Socialist Review*
IWW	Industrial Workers of the World, or "Wobblies"
LNPL	Labor's Non-Partisan League
NAACP	National Association for the Advancement of Colored People
NIRA	National Industrial Recovery Act
NKVD	Russian abbreviation for the People's Commissariat for Internal Affairs
NLR Act	National Labor Relations (Wagner) Act
NLRB	National Labor Relations Board
NMTA	National Metal Trades Association
O&E Canal	Ohio & Erie Canal.
P&O	Pennsylvania and Ohio Canal.
SLP	Socialist Labor Party.
SP(A)	Socialist Party (of America)
Summit County	County in northeast Ohio, of which Akron is the county seat
TLA	Trade and Labor Association
UAA	University of Akron Archives
ULP	Union Labor Party
UMW(A)	United Mine Workers (of America)
UNIA	United Negro Improvement Association ("Garveyites")
URW(A)	United Rubber Workers (of America)
VJ Day	Victory over Japan Day (August 14–15, 1945)
WASP	White Anglo-Saxon Protestant
Western Reserve	Today refers loosely to northeast Ohio. Originally, it was part of Connecticut, but the land was sold and subdivided
WLB	War Labor Board
WPA	Works Progress Administration

Preface

I make no apology for writing partisan history, but I do of course acknowledge John Adams' insistence that "Facts are stubborn things; and whatever may be our wishes, our inclinations, or the dictates of our passion, they cannot alter the state of facts and evidence."

I have always identified with the cause of labor. I was born in a Durham coalmining village whose people remembered the 1926 British general strike as if it were yesterday, and for whom solidarity and cooperation were the sine qua non of life. I am at least a fourth or fifth generation unionist. The labor movement has declined in most advanced capitalist societies, but it is the only force with the potential to unite all marginalized, oppressed, and exploited people, regardless of creed or color, nationality, gender, age, or sexual preference in a struggle for a just, democratic, and ecologically harmonious world. The American working class has fought tremendous battles against a system that, in Martin Luther King Jr.'s words, "does not permit an even flow of economic resources" and serves the interests of "a small privileged few [who] are rich beyond conscience" and dooms "almost all others .... to be poor at some level."[1]

Yet the American labor movement has never managed to take the logical step of forming a labor party to fight for reforms in its own interests and for the ultimate goal of the democratic socialist system advocated by activists such as King. I cannot fault the logic of the American Marxist writer George Novack, who believed "opposition to capitalist parties and policies is as vital a principle of working class conduct as opposition to company unions in industry."[2] The American labor movement, however, has been wedded to a pragmatic outlook that can see no further than immediate, short-term gains within the context of the social and political status quo. Samuel Gompers, the founding President of the American Federation of Labor, even took pride in such myopia. The system has always been loaded in favor of the rich and the corporations, so as King argues, "since we know that the system will not change the rules, we're going to have to change the system."[3] Why this has not happened in America as a whole—and in Akron in particular—is the subject of this book.

Introduction

Akron's labor history is a tragic tale of great struggles, defeats, long periods of relative quiescence, and lost opportunities. This book is both a narrative history of the city's often tumultuous labor movement and an attempt to explain why its radical tendencies failed.[1]

Over one hundred years ago, the German writer Werner Sombart visited America and famously asked, "Why is there no socialism in the United States?"[2] Today, with the American labor movement at a low ebb and with US politics still dominated by two capitalist parties, the enigma of "American exceptionalism" continues to puzzle academics[3] and bedevil labor activists.[4] We may also pose a related research question: why has the American labor movement—despite episodic upsurges of extraordinary militancy—been generally so conservative? George Meany, the post-war head of the AFL-CIO, boasted that he had never been on strike, led a strike, ordered a strike, or "had anything to do with a picket line."[5] That he could brag about this without fear of losing his position speaks volumes. It follows that if Akron, the proud recipient of the the All-American City award, has been the quintessential Midwest industrial metropolis, an examination of its labor history should help explain these puzzles. In the 1930s, Akron was a seedbed of the industrial unionism movement and the associated movement for a labor party. It had earlier been a stronghold of the Socialist Party, and before that, Akron's artisans had married trade unionism with political action. What happened that radicalism never bore permanent fruit in the city?

Karl Marx and Frederick Engels were optimistic about the future of the US labor movement. They were convinced that the labor upsurge of the late 1880s amounted to a "revolution" that had "shake[n] American society to its very foundations."[6]

Karl Kautsky, the German Social Democratic Party's chief theoretician, cautiously agreed: "[t]he future which America shows us would be very cheerless if it did not reveal at the same time a growth of the Socialist movement."[7] In 1912, the Socialist Party of America presidential candidate Eugene V. Debs won almost one million votes, inspiring Lenin to enthuse that "the American proletarian has already awakened and taken up his post."[8] This optimism survived massive setbacks. Twenty years later, Leon Trotsky forecast that "American politics will be Europeanized in the sense that the inevitable and imminent development of a party of the working class will totally change the political face of the US."[9]

None of these predictions has proved true. In contrast, in other highly industrialized societies such as Britain, France, and Germany, the working class built mass socialist, communist, or labor parties affiliated to powerful trade union movements. The same was true of other "new world" colonial-settler societies, most notably Australia, Canada, and New Zealand.[10] In the US, vast struggles broke out episodically but failed to build mass workers' parties or to sustain militant industrial unionism—the two, as current labor party advocate Mark Dudzic argues, are inextricably interlinked.[11] There is no simple explanation for the enigma.

Werner Sombart argued that American workers eschewed socialist politics because they enjoyed lashings of "roast beef and apple pie," and might even have loved capitalism as a result.[12] "Above all," according to the historian Thomas C. Reeves, "socialism lost out to the American dream. It was a casualty of the high degree of prosperity, class mobility (both real and imagined), and individualism enjoyed by the great majority of the people."[13] The ex-socialist Seymour Martin Lipset cites Leon Trotsky on the prosperity enjoyed by workers in the Bronx in 1917:

> Workers simply did better here than in Europe.... [Trotsky] described, almost in awe, his experience of "an apartment in a workers' district" in New York ... "That apartment, at eighteen dollars a month, was equipped with all sorts of

> conveniences that we Europeans were quite unused to: electric lights, gas cooking-range, bath, telephone, automatic service elevator, and even a chute for garbage..." He did not draw any political conclusions; he was just reporting the living standards of people in East Bronx, comparing them with those in working class areas of Paris and Vienna.[14]

Trotsky would probably take a dim view of Lipset's attempt to enlist his support, for, on the following page in his autobiography, he gives an example of horrible poverty in the same city: "I once saw, through the window of my newspaper office, an old man with suppurating eyes and a straggly gray beard stop before a garbage can and fish out a crust of bread." After failing to chew the "petrified thing," the man "shambled along down St. Mark's Place."[15]

The man's suffering hints at another America—one in which millions of people have tasted little of Sombart's roast beef and apple pie. In 1959, the American socialist Michael Harrington revealed how

> [a]s many as 50 million Americans continue to live below those standards which we have been taught to regard as the decent minimums for food, housing, clothing, and health. These millions are, in fact, a predominantly urban, white population; they have scarcely been affected by the reforms of the past quarter-century; and as a group they have profited least from the striking gains in productivity which have characterized the American economy since World War II.[16]

Harrington was writing at the height of the long boom that Eric Hobsbawm describes only semi-ironically as capitalism's "Golden Age." Penury has always co-existed with riches in cities such as Akron. The grinding poverty of Akron socialist Jim McCartan's childhood was the norm in turn-of-the-century Ohio coalmining villages. Most likely, only the most highly skilled, white, American-born workers could afford the domestic wonders of Trotsky's New York. Thomas Reeves himself points out that for millions of immigrants, America was "a strange and baffling world of back-breaking jobs or chronic unemployment, grinding poverty, repulsive tenements, and discrimination."[17] The uneven distribution of prosperity meant that millions missed out. Clearly, Sombart's explanation of US exceptionalism is by itself insufficient, although the comparative material prosperity of highly skilled layers of the working class can help explain the conservatism of the American Federation of Labor, which was led in its formative years by the champion of craft unionism, Samuel Gompers.

A more compelling explanation lies in the all-pervasive influence of Lockean anti-statist liberalism on all sections of American society.[18] John Locke, "the apostle of liberty" who preached the virtues of limited government, was a dominant intellectual influence on the American Founding Fathers. The role of government, according to Locke, was the preservation of private property. With only a slight variation in wording, Thomas Jefferson made Locke's watchword of "Life, Liberty, and Property" the cornerstone of the American Declaration of Independence. According to Thomas Paine, "Government, even in its best state, is but a necessary evil; in its worst state, an intolerable one"[19]—as was the case under George III. Jefferson's ideal was an agrarian society of small, but equal producers, of sturdy, self-sufficient citizens. The ideology suited and was reinforced by the material conditions of late eighteenth- and early nineteenth-century America. After the industrial transformation of American society, the anti-collectivist ideology was hegemonic. Free enterprise was the heart of Americanism, later encapsulated in President Calvin Coolidge's declaration that "the chief business of the American people is business. They are profoundly concerned with producing, buying, selling, investing and prospering in the world."[20] The ideology, Leon Trotsky argued, was not

> a function of some immaterial national spirit, but [was] a product of material conditions. A nation growing rich has sufficient reserves for conciliation between hostile classes and parties .... America was free of [collectivism and class solidarity] only because it had a plethora of virgin areas, inexhaustible reserves of national wealth, and, it would seem, limitless opportunities for enrichment.[21]

It would seem that belief in the American Dream was a powerful factor working against radicalism even if it was unrealistic for vast numbers of working class people. By the 1890s, the limits of the frontier, with its ready availability of virgin land, had been reached. Nevertheless, it had acted as a safety valve for ambitious and disgruntled workers and the individualism this inculcated passed on to future generations. It was enshrined in the Homestead Act of 1862, which provided 160 acres free to anyone who settled on it and occupied it for five years, and to any foreigner who declared their intention to become an American citizen. Although Samuel Gompers and Adolph Strasser had flirted with socialist ideas before the formation of the American Federation of Labor, they subsequently accepted the permanence of capitalism, preached the virtues of strong, independent male workers, opposed socialism and labor parties, and were suspicious of state intervention.[22] Apparently, a slim majority of Americans still agree. A Gallup poll published in May 2019 found that fifty-three percent of Americans would not vote for a socialist president.[23]

Other historical factors also include the effects of breakneck economic expansion and the consequent mushroom growth of American Midwest industrial cities such as Akron on working class consciousness. Growth that had taken European centers decades if not centuries to achieve was telescoped into a timeframe of mere decades. Mike Davis sums up the effects of such growth:

> This 'boomtown' characteristic of American industrialization meant that the labour movement in the United States, with the partial exception of New England valleys and the older Eastern port cities, arose without those deep roots in the artisanal resistance to industrialism which many historians have stressed as a determining factor in the formation of militant unionism and working class consciousness.[24] [British spelling in the original.]

America, too, has been populated by waves of immigrants from different cultural backgrounds. In many cases, ethnic or racial identity cut across class consciousness.

Many observers—including Marxists—also believed that America, as a society lacking a feudal past, was the freest society on earth, at least for members of the white male working class. Male workers enjoyed the right to vote in Ohio, without property qualifications, from 1803, when the state was admitted to the Union.[25] In contrast, the European working class—both male and female—had to struggle hard to win the right of suffrage, to enjoy civil liberties, and to stand parliamentary candidates. Those struggles helped the formation of collective class consciousness and fostered a tradition of political as well as purely economic struggle that was stunted in America. If American workers won these rights without a struggle, they exercised them in a political environment that was institutionally and ideologically hostile to the idea of third parties and was thoroughly anti-statist in outlook.

Independent working class organizations also ran up against a political system based on winner-takes-all elections and federalism. The system was—and still is—dominated by wealthy capitalist interests. As Karl Kautsky observed over a century ago, "Nowhere are all the means of political power so shamelessly purchasable as in America: administration, popular representation, courts, police and press; nowhere are they so directly dependent on the great capitalists."[26] Pork barreling and bribery have always bought votes—in the 1830s, Akron's wealthy establishment enticed voters away from a nascent labor party with "a churn of egg-nog" (see Chapter 2). If they could not use their wealth and the voting system to ensure a monopoly of political power, the two great capitalist parties were happy to "borrow" parts of the platforms of third parties. The system was also able to buy off many workers' leaders, including some who began their careers as socialist militants, a fact that gives credence to Robert Michels' idea of "the iron law of oligarchy."[27] Although the tendency towards oligarchy is not unique to American parties and unions, it was a factor in the failure of the Farmer-Labor Party to establish itself in the late 1930s.

From its inception in 1884, the central leadership of the American Federation of Labor (AFL) was relentlessly hostile both to the idea of independent working class political action and to industrial unionism. Sombart contrasted the American experience with that of Europe, but Robin Archer argues that a better comparison is with Australia, another "new world," colonial-settler state.[28] Following a series of big defeats during the 1890s depression, the Australian Workers' Union—Australia's largest union—was instrumental in setting up a labor party in the continent's pre-federation colonies. The AWU, like many AFL affiliates, did not admit "colored" workers.[29] In Akron as elsewhere during the 1880s, the AFL leadership was able to crush the rival Knights of Labor, who had attempted to unite the working class in one big "army," and who were not averse to political action. Some AFL affiliates excluded Black and Asian workers, and even if this was not formally enforced, immigrants and people of color suffered under a racialized division of labor that confined them in less skilled occupations. They were therefore less likely to be organized. Racism was used consciously or otherwise to divide the US working class into hostile ethnic blocs. The Akron rubber companies, for instance, deliberately fostered anti-immigrant sentiment during the 1920s, and for a time during the same period, the Ku Klux Klan virtually controlled the city and fostered reactionary American nativism in the white working class.

The AFL also played a dishonorable role during the 1913 IWW rubber strike in Akron. The strike's defeat, coupled with the AFL's insistence on the craft union model, set back working class organization in the city for over two decades. Later, in the 1930s, the top leadership of the Congress of Industrial Organizations neutered the militant industrial unionism embraced almost instinctively by Akron's mass production workers. The same "labor skates" derailed the movement for a labor party and diverted the momentum for change behind the Democrats, arguably with dismal results to this day. One must also acknowledge the shortcomings and mistakes of radical leftism itself: not the least the propensity of socialist currents for fratricidal sectarian squabbling, which prevented united action. Above all, the malign influence of Stalinism from the mid to late 1920s led a whole generation of working-class militants into an historical dead end and allowed both the establishment and right-wing labor movement figures to equate socialists of whatever tendency with the Russian gulag.

A final, crucial factor is the fact that the State and Capital long worked together to crush militant—and even "moderate"—labor organizations. This was most certainly the case in Akron, as is set out below in chapters on the Industrial Workers of the World strike of 1913, and on the crushing of the Socialist Party in the Red Scare years following the First World War. While these might have been abnormally violent episodes, the city's big employers were implacably opposed to organized labor even in normal times. From the outset, they maintained droves of spies and strong-arm squads to crush the mildest expressions of trade unionism. Akron's big employers often combined coercive methods with "welfare-capitalist measures" designed to neutralize militancy.

Despite the employers' determination to keep Akron as an open-shop town, the appearance of class peace was periodically disturbed by bitter strikes, and in the 1930s, Akron's "gummers" virtually reinvented the sit-down strike as a potent weapon for American unionists.

Some time ago, I fell into conversation with a group of young people in an Akron bar. They were puzzled that I should bother to research the history of their city. "Nothing much ever happened here," one told me. "It's the most boring city in America." They knew, vaguely, that there had been a big strike at "the Goodyear," but "it was a long time ago," and they had no idea that workers in their city had once marched in huge May Day demonstrations. The idea of an independent labor party—once the dream of militant rubber workers—seemed bizarre to them. Alas, even those Akronites who are markedly sympathetic to labor tend to know little about their city's radical history. Few people I have spoken with have heard of the labor leaders Marguerite Prevey, Wilmer Tate, or Sherman Dalrymple, or of the viciously oppressed young women who shivered on the picket lines outside the rubber factories during the bitter IWW strike in the winter of 1913. Historical amnesia, surely, is one reason why the city's labor movement is a shadow of what it once was.

In retrospect, Akron's labor history is a microcosm of that of America as a whole. It resembles a roller-coaster ride, with long periods of apparent quiescence punctuated by exhilarating outbreaks of popular mass struggle. Alas, none of these struggles has resulted in either a continuing militant, social union movement, or its corollary of a permanent mass workers' party independent of the Democrats. The history has been one of defeats and lost or blocked opportunities due to a combination of the factors discussed above. Moreover, as Mike Davis warns, it is wrong to focus on "the 'temporary' character of obstacles to political class consciousness" because this obscures "*the cumulative impact of the series of historic defeats suffered by the American working class.*" [Emphasis in the original.]

Davis argues—with a nod to E. P. Thompson—that this melancholy history has resulted in the "*unmaking* of the American working class."[30] [Emphasis added.] Davis begins his 1980 essay by highlighting the "mute, atomized protest" of the American workers: "in no other capitalist country is mass political abstentionism as fully developed as in the United States, where a 'silent majority' of the working class has sat out more than half the elections of the last century."[31] Yet up to the late 1930s, Akron and adjacent centers were seething hotspots of workers' struggle. It was possible for the city's working people to spend their leisure time almost entirely within a myriad of labor movement activities. By the end of the decade, the proud hope of militant industrial unionism was largely dead, subsumed into what we might call industrial business unionism. So too had the labor party idea perished.

1.

Akron's First Proletarians

Akron's first proletarians—or wage laborers—were the so-called "canawlers,"[1] itinerant workers who dug the Ohio & Erie (O&E) Canal—a massive public works project, completed in 1832, which linked the St. Lawrence basin with that of the Mississippi. The diggers were members of "a class of labourers," who as Marx and Engels put it, "live only so long as they find work, and who find work only so long as their labour increases capital."[2] [British spelling in the original.] They were doubly uprooted people: rural in origin, Irish in the main, they had left their native soil to work across the ocean on industrial projects in the New World. These nomads were part of what Karl Marx called "the light infantry of capital, which moves them rapidly from point to point, as the need for them varies."[3] One of their camps was at "Dublin"—now North Akron—which the chronicler Sam Lane tells us was "thickly dotted over with log and slab shanties."[4] Their work was crucial for the economic and social development of Akron and of Ohio and America as a whole. The historian Peter Way describes them as "miners and sappers digging the earthworks of North American capitalism, agents of change burying the past and digging the trenches of a future world of industrial production with every spadeful of earth turned."[5] Their lives were Hobbesian: "poor, nasty, brutish, and short," but being human, they responded to their miseries by forming workers' associations of a kind and staging a number of strikes.

The canawlers were proletarians, but it is unlikely that they saw themselves as members of a distinct working class. Despite their common experience of wage labor, countervailing factors cut across the formation of class consciousness. What E. P. Thompson has to say about the making of the English working class has universal application:

> Class-consciousness is the way in which these experiences are handled in cultural terms: embodied in traditions, value-systems, ideas, and institutional forms. If the experience appears as determined, class-consciousness does not.[6]

The bulk of the canal laborers were poor Irish immigrants—*spailpíní fánach*[7]—who had fled famine and dispossession in their homeland—with a sprinkling of Germans who had left their native Rhineland and Alsace to seek a better life in the New World, and a minority of native-born Americans of British descent. Each of these groups existed within a separate cultural superstructure, cut off by walls of language, which inhibited class solidarity. In addition, the native-born all too often despised the Irish, particularly as they performed work that had traditionally been done by unfree labor in America. This ethnic division was a premonition of things to come in a nation that was to experience successive waves of immigration.

Their work was arduous and relentless. Let the reader imagine the scene—thousands of laborers are sweating in the humid heat, their picks loosening the dirt and their shovels dumping it on the berm that parallels the excavation. Snaking behind them alongside the Cuyahoga River is an immense ditch, forty feet wide and four feet deep. Forty miles south of Lake Erie, the land rises steeply and the work becomes more taxing. Work continues into the fall and on into bone-chilling winter. Between 1825 and 1832, up to five thousand of these laborers built the 309-mile canal. When work reached the Ohio River near Portsmouth, they had shifted at least thirty-seven million cubic feet of earth, most of it by hand.[8] It was no less an "epoch-making event" than the inauguration of the Erie Canal at the eastern end of Lake Erie seven years earlier.[9] The construction was the largest capitalist project undertaken in Ohio, and one of the largest in all of America. Rich men dreamed it up, but it took an army of poor men to build it. They performed backbreaking work in appalling conditions, often for dishonest contractors.

Decades earlier, George Washington and others had suggested possible routes to link the St. Lawrence and Mississippi basins, but obstacles to construction were too great for the fledgling American republic to overcome.[10] By 1825, the idea had come into its own. Financed by loans from American banks, private contractors undertook the construction under the supervision of the Ohio Canal Commissioners. When finished, the cost of construction including interest payments had ballooned from around $2.3 million to roughly $20 million, which translates to as much as $319 billion in today's currency.[11] Raising this astronomical sum was challenging, given that in 1825 the total combined authorized capital of all US banks was only slightly greater than $191 million.[12] Canal construction also required great technical skills and organizational expertise. As Way observes, "Canal construction at this time was more problematic than setting up the early manufactories." Apart from the huge capital investment, the work demanded the marshaling of thousands of workers ranging from navvies[13] to carpenters and masons: a difficult task given that early nineteenth-century America had a precapitalistic labor market.[14]

Fortuitously, the start of work followed on from the completion of the Erie Canal, which had also employed a mainly Irish and German immigrant workforce. Many of them had been recruited by shipping agents—gombeen men in Ireland and *Neuländer* in Germany—hustlers who sold shipping tickets on commission.[15] Although the O&E was built entirely by "free" labor, some of the Germans may have been among the last indentured "redemptioners" to land on the docks of New York and Philadelphia.[16] The immigrants were not necessarily passive and gullible victims. Many fled political or religious persecution, poverty, and starvation.

The *spailpíní fánach* were a common sight in Ireland: wandering the roads in search of work, drifting off to serve as mercenaries in France, or emigrating beyond the seas. The Great Hunger of 1847, which killed one million people, is well known, but the potato crop on which the Irish peasantry depended failed in many other years. In 1817, following bad harvests in the previous two years, there had been a terrible famine, accompanied by a typhus epidemic. Poor economic and social conditions also led many Germans to emigrate after the Napoleonic Wars. Many Irish saw their transplantation as exile or banishment rather than emigration. According to Kerby A. Miller,

> It may be significant that the Irish language had no equivalent for the English word 'emigrant' with its voluntary and emotionally neutral connotations. Rather the Irish word primarily used to describe one who left Ireland has been *deoraí,* the literal meaning of which is 'exile.'[17]

Irish folk music reveals a sorrow of separation from the homeland that is almost physical in its intensity. Although later waves of Irish emigrants adopted America as their own country, the canawlers' sense of separation may have prevented them from acquiring a sense of belonging to a common class with the Germans and the native-born.

While the canal advocates and investors are remembered today, the names of the laborers have been forgotten. Many were illiterate. Many spoke English badly if at all. They left no memoirs or fictionalized accounts of their lives. It was as with the Ohio writer Jim Tully's ditch-digging grandfather, "Old Hughie," who "was considered an educated man among the Irish peasants" because he could read and write.[18] Most of the Irish–and a fair proportion of the Germans–were Catholics, but while Irish priests began arriving occasionally after 1826, it was not until 1844 that the first permanent Catholic Church was built in Akron.[19] The Irish were a despised Other in a strange foreign land: aliens for whom poverty, isolation, and lack of spiritual comfort must have been hard to bear.

Although American wages were higher than their European equivalents,[20] the immigrants had not arrived in a land of milk and honey. Their work was relentlessly hard. Before they started digging, they had to "grub out" the forest along a line marked out by the surveyors. Today, we would use chain saws, bulldozers, and stump grinders to clear a path, but the laborers had only axes, iron bars, handheld crosscut saws, and perhaps fire for the Herculean task. They had to cut a forty-foot wide swathe for the canal itself, plus a twenty-foot cleared margin on each side. Only then could they begin digging the earth and rock.

Excavation was dirty work—"the filth of progress" in historian Ryan Dearinger's words—but by no means unskilled, for "in the muck lay complex tasks, demanding both brain and brawn."[21] An incompetent laborer would not last long, and navvies could take pride in their work. Old Hughie exclaimed in horror "It's not a job for a Tully!" upon learning that his grandson had taken a job washing dishes in a local restaurant.[22] While much of the ground was glacial drift and riparian alluvium, the laborers often cut and blasted through hard bedrock and gouged out massive stones. This involved drilling deep holes using sledgehammers and handheld star bits—"single jacked" if one man performed the task and "double jacked" if one man wielded the hammer and his buddy held the bit. The knack was to twist the star bit as the hammer hit it. Afterwards, if the drill did not shatter the holes, the navvies would fill the hole with blasting powder and tamp it with clay to concentrate the force of the explosion. Construction of the canal's 146 locks was the work of highly skilled masons and carpenters for pay of around $1.50 a day, or around $39.30 in purchasing power today.[23] They built the locks from mortared and dressed stone blocks, fitted with massive oaken sluice gates.[24]

The canal was forty feet wide at the top and twenty-six feet wide at the bottom, with a minimum depth of four feet. To prevent seepage, the workers lined the excavation with clay slurry, which hardened into an impervious barrier. The spoil dug from the canal bed was not wasted, but was recycled to build a ten-foot wide towpath for the boatmen's horses, and the remainder was piled up on the opposite side of the canal into a continuous protective berm. The boatman O. W. Petersen claimed, probably accurately, that the O&E was "the largest single engineering earthwork in the world at that time."[25] As the present author calculated elsewhere, "If the excavated earth was heaped up it would form a pile with the same ground level area of the Empire State Building, but over three times higher than that structure's 1,453 feet.[26]

Many laborers would not long survive the rigors of work and life on the canal. Marx's description of the hellish lives of navvies on British construction projects would seem to fit those of their nomadic counterparts in America. The arrival of the army of laborers was "A flying column of pestilence, [which] … carries into the regions in whose neighbourhood it pitches its tents, small-pox, typhus, cholera, scarlet fever, etc."[27] [British spelling in the original.] As late as the 1930s, fossickers occasionally disinterred laborers' bones from shallow graves at the site of the former Dublin shantytown beneath Akron's North Hill viaduct,[28] testimony to backyard burials. Folklore holds that canal construction claimed the life of one Irishman for every mile of canal, but this may be a conservative estimate, for William Donohue Ellis claims that there was a laborers' graveyard every ten miles.[29] Swarms of mosquitoes and black flies tormented them, and hundreds died of malaria or from "swamp fever."[30] One of the worst jobs was lowering the level of Summit Pond (now Lake) just south of the village of Akron, where the laborers stood up to their waists in mud and water and many fell ill and died from the "miasma." In the second summer of the canal's construction, heavy rains and humid heat made life intolerable. There was an outbreak of smallpox, but for every worker buried, three left the work.[31]

Matthew Carey estimated that fully fifty percent of America's canal laborers suffered occupational illnesses.[32] The workers' living conditions, too, could not but breed disease. Again, Marx's observations ring true of America—and the Dublin shantytown: "In undertakings that involve a large outlay of capital ... the contractor generally provides his army with wooden huts or something of the sort, improvised villages devoid of sanitary requirements, lying outside the control of the local authorities."[33] On the later Illinois and Michigan Canal works, the Catholic priest John Raho noted that "the diseases in this area are horrible, and so many die that there is hardly any time to give Extreme Unction."[34] White American males born in 1850 could expect to live on average for 38.3 years,[35] so it is safe to assume that most Irish canal laborers would not have survived into their thirties. Their tarpaper shanties provided little shelter, and this, along with poor food and sanitation, contributed to high mortality rates. A further hazard was snakebite—an especial dread for people from St. Patrick's serpent-free land. Early surveying parties encountered swarms of rattlesnakes in the Akron vicinity.[36]

Work on the canal ran from sunrise to sundown. For this, the men received between thirty and sixty cents per day according to Boryczka and Cary,[37] or $6.00 a month according to later Akron journalists,[38] a sum equal, perhaps, to $161 today.[39] This estimate is perhaps too low as laborers on the Muscle Shoals Canal in Tennessee in 1830 received $15.00 for a twenty-six-day month.[40] William Ellis reckons O&E laborers were paid thirty cents a day, plus rations of "slumgullion" and whiskey—"and the hope that in three years they would have repaid their passage from Ireland."[41] Since pay rates varied from locality to locality for without a union, there was little chance of employers along the canal paying a common scale. Contractors often stole payrolls, especially in the early stages of the project. Even after 1827, when the canal commissioners guaranteed pay rates after spontaneous strikes erupted, cheating continued, and contractors charged the workers exorbitant prices for essential supplies.[42] There was no pay for traveling time.[43] Popular wisdom has it that the laborers subsisted on a diet of bread and whiskey, and it was in fact usual for contractors to pay their men in part with alcohol. Canal superintendent Richard Howe's cash account book for March–December 1827 reveals that he bought one gallon of whiskey on August 15 from a Mr. Hammond for thirty-eight cents and another barrel of it for $8.37, followed by yet another for an unspecified price, and another consignment on August 28.[44] According to the physician Zerah Hawley, in the 1820s almost the entire rye and wheat crop of the Western Reserve was distilled into whiskey and was "drunk in great abundance";[45] even by children, according to an early diarist.[46] In one instance at Cuyahoga Falls, the canal laborers staged a spontaneous sit-down strike when cheeseparing contractors stopped the whiskey ration.[47]

The sit-down hints at a tendency towards spontaneous militancy by the workers and perhaps as Boryczka and Cary speculate, to the existence of "unions of a kind" on the canal.[48] When the contractors cut wages in 1827, further strikes erupted. It seems likely that expatriate Irish secret societies organized to right some of the wrongs done to the laborers.[49] However, it is probable that ethnic and even regional intraethnic animosities blunted incipient class solidarity. Boryczka and Cary believe that the Irish societies intrigued against the Germans and other ethnic groups.[50] Also, if the evidence from the Wabash & Erie construction projects of the era is anything to go by, the Hibernian workers may have feuded among themselves, with "Corkonians" intriguing against "Fardowners" from the Irish Midlands, for example.[51] Common experience of oppressive living and working conditions did not translate into a common class consciousness. As E. P. Thompson puts it, while "[w]e can see a *logic* in the responses of similar occupational groups undergoing similar experiences … we cannot predicate any *law*."[52] The transient nature of the work also helped to inhibit union organization, and it is even less likely that the laborers would have organized politically in a foreign land to which many felt no strong attachment.[53]

Echoing Bertolt Brecht, one may ask where did the workers go and what did they do when the canal was completed? Many canawlers stayed on in Dublin, overlooking the Little Cuyahoga River north of Furnace and west of High Street in Akron.[54] Peter Way tells us that others squatted in shacks on the marshes around the Cleveland docks, seeking casual laboring work or employment as longshoremen, barge hands, and canal maintenance men.[55] It was often a brutal life. "The working-class neighborhoods to which many ex-canallers were drawn," Way believes, "were fragile worlds of transiency, work shortages, ethnic bigotry, substandard living and working conditions, little hope of advancement, violence, crime, disease and death."[56] Many of these immigrant workers "knew little or no English, speaking only their Gaelic or German or French," writes Murray Powers.[57] After completion of the construction, most would have sought work not too different to their customary pick-and-shovel labor. Some "followed the work" to other construction projects. In 1835, work began on the Pennsylvania & Ohio Canal under the supervision of chief engineer Colonel Sebried Dodge. Again, German and Irish laborers carried out the work, with a sprinkling of local farmers seeking to augment frugal incomes with cash. On several occasions, there were outbreaks of malaria and cholera and many deaths.[58]

The work of the "light infantry of capital" linked Akron to the outside world in a way the crude dirt roads of the time could not. It encouraged modest industrialization and enabled farmers to seek distant markets.[59] It facilitated an expansion of coalmining in the little town and its environs. New industries such as sewer pipe manufacturing and china tableware demanded the digging of clay. Quarrying would also have attracted the former canawlers: sandstone was once quarried in downtown Akron along Main and High Streets, and East Bowery Street was once called Quarry Street.[60] Other laborers would have gravitated to the building trades, either as skilled men or as laborers digging foundations, carrying hods, and mixing concrete. Some would have also transferred to construction work on the railroads, which were to challenge and then eclipse the canals. The canawlers got little thanks or reward for their work. Dearinger writes that they "endured brutal working conditions, punishing state and company policies, and hostile community reactions that demarcated their experiences from those of the free laborers so romanticized in American history." "Respectable" folk regarded them as uncivilized;[61] a cruel calumny on hardworking people on whose labors civilization depended.

Without the toil of these forgotten wage laborers, Akron might never have existed as more than an obscure frontier village. Nevertheless, they left no labor organizations behind them, although it is entirely possible that those who settled in the Akron region participated in later union activity.

2.

Radical Artisans and Sweated Female Labor

The first white settler arrived near Summit Lake in 1806, three years after Ohio was admitted as a state of the Union. Twenty-one years later, the modest settlement that followed the pioneer homesteader became the village of Akron. After 1827, with the O&E Canal opened for traffic between Akron and Lake Erie, the village's growth accelerated, doubling to 3,254 by 1850, with over twenty-seven thousand in Summit County as a whole.[1] Akron's economy was precapitalist in its early years. Most of its population were self-employed, but by the late 1830s, there were small, but significant, numbers of wageworkers in the little town. Journeymen in the main, it is possible that some had worked in the more skilled occupations in canal construction, and one can trace the beginning of the town's trade unions to this period.

In Ohio, as in America as a whole, free white male workers did not have to fight for the suffrage as did their European counterparts. In 1819, for instance, English workers were massacred at Peterloo for demanding the right to vote and in 1832 the British parliament grudgingly extended the franchise but still denied it to the vast majority of the population. In the same period, artisans' unions in Akron regarded male suffrage and the right to stand in elections as their birthright. These unions organized on craft lines, but the fact that they engaged in politics indicates a level of class consciousness that had not existed among the workers building the Ohio & Erie Canal. Nevertheless, powerful social and economic forces were working against them and their relatively small numbers ensured that their political ventures were usually unsuccessful.

The population of Ohio grew rapidly during this time,[2] but the state remained overwhelmingly rural.[3] Although Akron was only thirty-two years old in 1837, settlers were pouring into the region, anxious to purchase land at cheap prices.[4] The ready availability of cheap freehold land was to have profound effects on the development of American society. Benjamin Franklin noted that land on the frontier was so plentiful "and so cheap … that a labouring man that understands husbandry can in a short time save money to purchase a piece of land for a plantation. . . ."[5] [British spelling in the original.] Akron's artisans, perhaps, worked with one eye on their tools of trade, and the other on advertisements for land sales. In 1825 when it was incorporated as a town, Akron boasted only a handful of stores, a tavern, and a scattering of solid houses and workshops.[6] Almost all consumable domestic products, including soap, candles, wooden items, textiles, and clothing were made in the family home.[7] Some products, however, could not be made domestically and were too expensive to import from the east coast. Joseph Hart's water-powered gristmill on the Little Cuyahoga River produced flour from 1815,[8] and other small enterprises made nails and sawn lumber. Sixty men and boys produced iron kettles in Laird & Norton's primitive foundry in what is today Akron's Old Forge precinct.[9] Eliakim Crosby and Simon Perkins built a plow factory, powered by the waters of the Little Cuyahoga—a humble precursor of the agricultural implement trade that later thrived in Akron.[10] The record is mute on the organization of production in these small factories and on what division of labor existed. The town's skilled journeymen artisans, however, did organize, as did at least some factory workers.

One May evening in the year 1837, small groups of workingmen converged on the South Akron schoolhouse, which was likely a single-story wooden frame structure, built by these same men or others very like them. Most of them arrived directly from their places of work, for in that era the working day began at dawn and ended at sunset. The scene combined both archaic and modern elements. The men's dress was fustian: narrow trousers and heavy jackets fashioned of homespun wool and shirts made of coarse linen, all laboriously hand-stitched by their "womenfolk." They gathered at the schoolhouse in response to a notice placed in the *Summit Beacon*—the precursor of today's *Akron Beacon Journal*—by Mr. E. N. (possibly Elisha) Bangs, the Secretary of the Carpenters' and Joiners' Society. He advised that the meeting would commence "on Thursday 16th inst. At early candle light."[11] Bangs did not stipulate a precise starting time, for this was a preindustrial age, and his approach to timekeeping was still premodern. In Akron, as in Thomas Hardy's Dorset, the streets were "laid out before inches of land had value, and when one-handed clocks sufficiently subdivided the day."[12] The lives of the Akron journeymen were regulated by diurnal and seasonal rhythms rather than by the remorseless ticking of the clock. Their meeting began when dusk faded into darkness.[13] The journeymen's society appears to have been the town's first regularly organized labor union. An earlier meeting, held on March 2, had endorsed a slate of candidates for the township elections. Disgusted with the corrupt practices of the existing Whig and Democrat parties, the meeting had condemned their bribery of electors with churns of "egg-nog" and barrels of spirits. Given the frontier population's predilection for strong drink, elections at the time must have been Hogarthian affairs. The workers' ticket was defeated by a combined slate of the other parties[14]—a premonition of the future, when American politics would be dominated by those with vast amounts of money at their disposal. The willingness of the established parties to bribe the electors was not the only problem facing Mr. Bangs and his fellow unionists.

In 1837, Akron was still a primitive place in comparison with the cities of the East Coast. Whereas the huge Lowell textile mills in Massachusetts[15] resembled the "dark Satanic Mills" of the English Industrial Revolution, the Akron carpenters' shops could have sprung from the pages of George Eliot's *Adam Bede:* smallish workrooms smelling of wood shavings, fitted out with heavy workbenches, and stocked with lengths of sawn lumber and gleaming, well-oiled tools. The majority of the village's population were self-employed farmers and artisans, with a sprinkling of journeymen and laborers, as was common across the

Republic—today, in contrast, only one in nine persons in the American labor force are self-employed.[16]

Many early journeymen fancied—not without reason—that they could become master artisans or farmers,[17] and this must have dampened their enthusiasm for class-based politics. The French Ambassador Guillaume Poussin believed that American workingmen were "stimulated" by "the hope of one day becoming a proprietor."[18] In Ray Allen Billington's words, "in the American West the hired hand was the potential farmer, the serving girl the future wife of the town's leading citizen."[19] In any case, nonagricultural workers formed a tiny minority of Ohio's population and the ready availability of cheap freehold land—the fruits of the dispossession of the American Indians[20]—encouraged workers to see themselves as potential independent farmers, not as permanent members of a class that existed by selling its labor power. John Commons wrote that "as long as the poor and industrious can escape from the conditions which render them subject to other classes, so long do they refrain from that aggression on the property rights or political power of others, which is the symptom of a 'labour movement.'"[21] [British spelling in the original]. This, arguably, is the root material cause of the pervasive individualistic ideology that still affects Americans of all social classes and blocks the development of the kind of class consciousness seen in Europe.

Nevertheless, Akron's carpenters and joiners were able to organize a union and act independently of the city's political establishment. In this, they were arguably far in advance of the later American Federation of Labor, which refused to support labor and socialist parties—and still does today in its AFL-CIO iteration.[22]

The socioeconomic system in which Bangs and his comrades lived and worked was precapitalist. Producers engaged in what Marx called "the simplest form of the circulation of commodities" in which they sold the products they made for money and in turn used this to purchase other commodities.[23] Many farmers existed largely outside of the cash economy, making and consuming their own produce with only a small surplus with which to sell to purchase essential goods they could not make themselves. These factors affected the relationships between masters and men. Labor historian Foster Rhea Dulles argues that the relationship between a master artisan and his journeymen was not "an employer-employee relationship in the modern sense."[24] Patriarchal and quasi-familial relations blurred class distinctions. Although class—or as it was termed *rank*—arrived with the *Mayflower* in 1620,[25] and earlier at Jamestown—it is a moot point whether the operatives in the early Akron enterprises saw themselves as members of a distinct working class with its own separate interests, rather than just a sectional interest group.[26] Nevertheless, American society was in a state of flux, and the development of class cleavages is shown by the activities of Akron's carpenters and joiners.

Their numbers, however, were too small for them to overcome the structural and ideological forces ranged against them. In 1787, Charles C. Pinckney had argued at the Federal Convention "there is more equality of rank and fortune in America than in any country under the sun; and this is likely to continue as long as the unappropriated western lands remain unsettled."[27] Leaving aside the gross facts of African slavery, indentured white labor, the dispossession of the American Indians, and women's domestic servitude, Pinckney's observation was apposite and almost certainly true of Ohio some decades later. Most nonagricultural workers worked in small workshops or as itinerant journeymen.[28] Masters often worked and lived alongside their employees. They enjoyed few comforts. Their food was basic and "often confined to the bare necessities of life" and "if the food of the artisan would be thought coarse, his clothes would be thought abominable."[29] Despite this, the Manx immigrant Thomas Kelly wrote encouragingly to artisans thinking of joining him in the Western Reserve in the late 1820s. Wages and prices for finished goods were attractive compared to those back home:

> Mechanics for work and board themselves, a joiner gets 1 ¼ dollar, mason 1 ¼ dollar, tailor, 1 dollar; shoemaker ½ dollar, a smith (by way they sell their wrought iron) can earn 3 or 4 dollars a day. Any man that could set up a tanyard would be a fine thing. Sadler is a very good trade....

This enabled workers to purchase domestic goods and livestock at reasonable rates.[30]

In 1835, the Welsh clergyman David Griffiths advised that, provided they brought their tools of trade, "Carpenters ... blacksmiths, masons, tailors, tanners, shoemakers etc., are almost sure of employment; and are well-paid for their work, although the English are apt to grumble because they cannot always get cash for their wages."[31] The hours of work were relentlessly long. The Akron newsman and chronicler Sam Lane informs us that workers "in all departments of mechanical labor" were required to work twelve hour days, which in winter meant toiling for two to three hours by candlelight.[32] Settlers from New England brought with them an outlook that viewed work "with the sacred character of a moral, if not a religious precept,"[33] and this translated into thrifty and pugnacious employers, many of whom traced their ancestry back generations in Connecticut or Massachusetts.

This helps explain the marked disparity in wages between the East Coast and Ohio. In 1819 for instance, bricklayers in New York and South Carolina received on average $1.50 a day and their counterparts in Pennsylvania and Washington, DC, could expect $2.00 and $3.00 respectively. Carpenters could expect $1.50 a day in Maine and New York, but bricklayers and carpenters received a mere $1.00 a day in Ohio.[34] Thomas Kelly attested that locally produced foodstuffs were cheap in the Reserve, but Sam Lane records that with wages "scarcely more than half" of what they were fifty years later, and with "many essentials cost[ing] about double,"[35] Akron was no Land of Cockaigne for the working class.

Journeymen's work was generally on a very small-scale, and often on a bespoke basis. An enterprise employing more than fifteen workers—such as the Crosby and Perkins forge and larger factories such as Akron's Laird & Norton—were atypical. Since colonial times, America had been home to the merchant-capitalist, who was largely a product of the British mercantilist system, which was a hangover into post-Revolutionary times. As Mary Ritter Beard explains, the merchant-capitalist was "not usually the owner of industries nor the employer of artisans." He was a trader and middleman, mediating between the producer and the consumer. He specialized in buying and selling, accumulating goods in warehouses, and selling to local storekeepers. Significantly, he competed "sharply with the local master and his workmen,"[36] thus inhibiting the development of full-blown capitalism and blurring class lines by throwing master and journeyman together against the trader who threatened their common interests. Nevertheless, from colonial times and afterwards, a skilled craftsman could combine "within his person the functions of merchant, master and journeyman."[37] It was only when the merchant-capitalists became industrialists (or were replaced by them) that modern American capitalism was born.[38]

The development of full-blown capitalism after the Revolution of 1776 was also inhibited by a chronic shortage of capital and labor. As for finance, British political power had been broken, but the hangovers of the mercantilist colonial past persisted. Before the revolution, banking had been a "detached activity of the state" via the Bank of England rather than "an ordinary agent of commerce."[39] In 1791, there were only three banks in the US, with a total capital of just under $90 million. By 1816, this had grown to 246 US banks with a combined capital of just under $204 million.[40] Such sums were insufficient to seed the construction of factories and communications infrastructure.

Although Marx and Engels claimed that America was "entirely without a feudal past,"[41] in late colonial times huge swathes of arable and virgin lands were owned by a handful of feudalistic grandees, notably the Penn family (eighteen million acres) and King George III (perhaps 380 million acres). Outside of southern New England, small farmers had to pay quitrents—permanent annual fees on top of the sale price for their land.[42] Investors put their money into shipping and trade rather than industry and the "Mother Country" legislated to block the American colonies from competing with British manufacturers.[43] The revolution introduced freehold land, opened up land west of the Appalachians, and abolished mercantilist restrictions on industry, but the effects of enforced underdevelopment lingered. Moreover, the abolition of the seigneurial estates and the provision of freehold land for small farmers contributed to a crippling labor shortage for the nonagricultural sector of the economy.

The Western Reserve, however, was a society in flux. The old colonial order established by British settlers was changing. Social and economic development that had taken centuries to unfold in Europe telescoped into decades once the revolution had begun to free the economic potential of America.[44]

During this period, changing economic conditions flowing from the new canal eroded the artisans' independence. As elsewhere in America, "the master workman faced the choice of becoming a merchant-capitalist.... or a journeyman... [and] hard-pressed by growing competition, the merchant-capitalist pressed his journeymen the harder, cutting his labor costs whenever he could." Moreover, the logic of this process led to an increase in the division of labor, which was a mortal threat to the craftsmen's autonomy.

Naturally, American journeymen, "in reaction to this threat to their long-standing independence, good living conditions and status, formed the first trade unions."[45] Thus the late 1830s saw the emergence of fledgling labor organizations such as the Carpenters' and Joiners' Society in Akron and its hinterland.[46] It was followed shortly afterwards in other trades and callings. A Summit County teachers' association appeared in 1841,[47] but whether it regarded itself as a union or as a vague "professional association" is unknown. Even earlier, the March 2, 1837, edition of the *Beacon* had published a notice that urged "the mechanics of Akron and vicinity" to meet "with a view to the formation of a Mechanics' association." The constitution and bylaws of the association state that the organization aimed to secure for artisans "by all honorable means" their interests and just rights and to acquire "that position in society to which we are justly entitled." The association provided a sickness and disability fund, and funeral benefits. Members were also entitled to attend lectures organized by the association and to use its library.[48]

The association did not restrict itself to the activities of a friendly and educational society. There was sufficient interest for it to run independent labor candidates in the township elections in April of that year. Perhaps the Akron Mechanics were inspired by the election of Ely Moore—the president of the New York General Trades Union—to Congress on the Locofoco ticket in 1834.[49] Alas, "through lack of harmony" a bloc of Whigs and Democrats were able to defeat the Akron union ticket. Differences between those parties did not prevent them from forming a common front against the labor upstarts. On November 23, 1842, a large body of working men from Portage and Copley Townships packed out a local hall to discuss the "deplorable" political and economic situation in the recently formed Summit County. A local mechanic called John Ayres chaired the meeting, and his colleague S. J. Welton took minutes. Akron's economy suffered cruelly from the Panic of 1837, which saw the closure of hundreds of banks across the nation. The effects of the crash lingered for half a decade, with wageworkers and artisans hit by high levels of unemployment. A number of local businesses had gone bankrupt,[50] and for five years, Akron functioned as a "truck and dicker" (barter) economy, with woolen cloth accepted almost as "legal tender."[51]

The workers' meeting slammed what they saw as a cabal of dishonest politicians, "blacklegs," "gamblers," and "lawyers" who had "almost ruined" the county. They resolved that "labor is the original and producing cause of all wealth and prosperity" and should receive the full support of government, which should operate on the principle of "the greatest good for the greatest number." The resolution echoed the utilitarian ideas of Jeremy Bentham, Cesare Beccaria, and Joseph Priestley and conflicted sharply with the ideology of American individualism. A further resolution called on Summit County's workers to vote only for candidates who would not "sell out" the electors. They decided to hold a follow-up mass meeting the following January.[52] Not surprisingly, President John Tyler—a Virginian states' righter, slave owner, and apostle of free enterprise—ignored the workers' plea for federal government intervention.

It seems that these early workers' associations were rather unstable combinations, and failed to weather the economic slump that set during the late 1830s. By the mid-1840s, after a period of "quiescence,"[53] Akron's workers again started to organize. Long working hours and payment in kind rather than wages had "created the most intense dissatisfaction among the laboring classes," Sam Lane writes. On November 11, 1845, Akron factory workers staged the town's first strike, demanding an end to payment in woolen cloth. Storekeepers had been short-changing them in the exchange for other goods.[54] Payment in kind or in scrip went back to colonial times and was a perennial source of dissatisfaction for American workers.[55] On May 28, 1845, too, there was what Sam Lane describes as a "general strike" of mechanics in Massillon, twenty-five miles south of Akron, in support of a demand for a ten-hour day and cash wages. The Massillon union sent "missionaries" throughout the region to spread the message of worker solidarity. Two Massillon agitators, Dodd and Mathews, addressed a "large meeting" of Akron mechanics in the town's Military Hall in late June, and the meeting voted to form a union, which "grew rapidly."

On July 4, the Akron association chartered a canal boat to take a one-hundred-strong delegation replete with banners and a brass band to celebrate with their fellow unionists in Massillon. Curiously, a local capitalist addressed the gathering, but three years later Akron mechanics drew a sharp class line, when on March 3, 1848, a workers' meeting resolved to form a "Working Man's Party" and to field candidates in forthcoming elections. Only those "who gain their subsistence by manual labor" were recognized as workingmen, and the aim of the union was "to unite for our mutual good and protection against the encroachments of wealth, aristocracy, and a few unprincipled office-seekers, who act only for their own aggrandizement." The office bearers included a K. N. Bangs, doubtless a relative of the first carpenters' union official, and the indefatigable John Ayres. Alas, the labor ticket was defeated in Akron,[56] perhaps because its wealthy opponents again doled out lashings of eggnog and whiskey to the susceptible electors, but met with more success in Portage County.

The growth of independent labor organizations spooked the *Summit Beacon*. In April 1850, the paper reprinted an op-ed piece from the *Ohio State Journal,* which supported the "general movement in the large cities to form Protective Unions" but warned against strikes, which it claimed, "oppressed" the owners of wealth.[57] The city's employers were to echo the caveat endlessly over the next century and beyond as the growth of large-scale industry surged after the Civil War. Employers were also determined to keep the open shop. Alexis de Tocqueville warned presciently that "The manufacturing aristocracy which is growing up under our eyes is one of the harshest which ever existed in the world. . . ." He urged "the friends of democracy" to "keep their eyes anxiously fixed in this direction; for if ever a permanent inequality of conditions and aristocracy again penetrate into the world, it may be predicted that this is the channel by which they will enter."[58]

In fact, the domination of American society by the rich was built into the US political and social system.[59] President James Madison had insisted that "the minority of the opulent" had to be protected "against the majority";[60] a view echoed by John Jay, the first Chief Justice of the Supreme Court, who said "the people who own the country ought to control it."[61] The full import of such views were to become apparent with the growth of fully-fledged capitalism.

By the fourth decade of the nineteenth century, Akron was still no more than a village of fifteen hundred people, but while the villages of Europe had remained static for centuries, the fledgling settlement had entered into a period of accelerated social and economic expansion. The opening of the O&E Canal had sparked an optimistic mood in Ohio. In 1835, work commenced on the Pennsylvania & Ohio (P&O) Canal, which when completed five years later would run for eighty-two miles to link Akron with Cuyahoga Falls, Kent, and Youngstown, and include fifty-seven stone locks, two aqueducts, three side canals, and nine dams. Horse-drawn boats hauled cargoes of New Portage whiskey, Akron flour, cheese, butter, and Turkeyfoot coal north to Lake Erie or south to the Mississippi basin and as far south as New Orleans. Settlements sprang up at the numerous locks. Sawmills and boat-building yards, distilleries, breweries, and a range of food processing, mining, quarrying, smelting, and other enterprises grew up to provide for the local and export markets. These enterprises called for greater numbers of workers, who boosted the population and increased the demand for agricultural and industrial products. Coal from the Akron region was barged along the canal to Cleveland, where it fired the boilers of Lake Erie Steamers, and later the blast furnaces.[62]

By the mid-1830s, Akron was importing $500,000 worth of goods per annum and exporting $400,000 worth. Recession struck in 1837 with factory and store closures,[63] but by 1840 business was booming again, and Akron boasted of being "the wheat center of the West."[64] The agricultural boom stimulated the growth of a thriving agricultural implement and machinery industry, and the thousands of sheep on the hills around Akron formed the basis for a prosperous woolen industry.[65] These developments slowly created a growing proletariat: a class defined by the American labor historian Chester W. Wright as "a group of hired workers who remained such throughout their life: in short a distinct laboring class such as had scarcely existed in colonial times outside the group of slaves."[66]

By the 1840s Akron boasted established agricultural implement and machinery factories, iron foundries, and engineering workshops, most of which serviced the region's expanding agriculture. The Mechanics' Association, which was reborn after the slump, campaigned to reduce the long-established sunup to sundown working day to ten hours. The union also rejected payment by "mechanizing orders" (or scrip), demanding cash wages. It also set up a circulating library and sponsored a series of public lectures on relevant topics for working people. At one of these, an unnamed speaker denounced "those purse-proud, lordly aristocrats who produce nothing and consume all, and who grow rich upon the labor and toil of the industrial classes."[67] If the speech is anything to go by, class consciousness was growing among the town's working-class population.

The Mechanics' Association also published their own newspaper, *The Roarer,* later changing the name to *The Tee-Total Mechanic,* which was edited by Sam Lane, a well-known newspaperman and campaigner against "the demon drink."[68] The union's emphasis on sobriety sounds strange to modern ears, but it should be remembered that whiskey was the favorite frontier tipple and that overindulgence had ruined the health of many a working man and destroyed the lives of his family.[69] Not so long before, even children in the Western Reserve drank whiskey "as though it was water."[70] Temperance, as the Mechanics' Association realized, was part of a battle to civilize the macho frontier. In 1858, an enraged mob of Cuyahoga Falls women armed themselves with axes, hatchets, and hammers and smashed up the town's saloons in a three-hour rampage.[71] While the mechanics might not have agreed with their methods, they would have sympathized with the women's plight.

Although the early unions spoke of "workingmen's rights," Akron's working- and middle-class women also began to organize for their rights. Famously, one cold winter's day in 1851, the Women of Ohio held their annual convention in the city's Universalist Stone Church, which stood at the corner of North High and Perkins Streets. Their central demand was the right to vote. A white woman called Emily Robinson chaired the assembly, but a former slave called Sojourner Truth dominated proceedings and forcefully drew attention to race and gender oppression. When preachers burst into the hall shouting that the idea of voting rights for women was sinful,[72] Truth stood up and silenced the black-coated obscurantists with a speech so powerful that it is enshrined forever in the lexicon of liberation. "I have borne thirteen children," she declared, "and seen most all sold off to slavery, and when I cried out with my mother's grief, none but Jesus heard me! And ain't I a woman?[73]

Working-class women were drudges, as was highlighted over twenty years later by a letter one of them wrote to the editor of the *Summit Beacon* to denounce the plight of "servant girls" in the city. Paid "the scanty sum of $2.00 a week," plus room and board for a working day that began at five a.m. and ended only at seven, eight, or even ten p.m., it would take two years for such a servant to save up for a simple calico dress.[74] Dressmakers on piecework would also have to scrimp and save to buy one, for they too received "a pittance." An official government report stated that the seamstress's life was "a tale of long hours, low wages, and exploitation." Conditions for Akron's dressmakers were akin to those of their sisters in Philadelphia in 1829, where it required "great expertness, unceasing industry from sunrise till 10 or 11 o'clock at night, constant employment (which few of them have) without interruption whatever from sickness or attention to their families, to earn a dollar and a half a week."[75] The radical Irish-American journalist Matthew Carey calculated that in 1833, an American seamstress might, by dint of the greatest industry, earn no more than $58.00 in one year. From this, she would need to pay $26.00 in rent, $10.00 in clothing and shoes, $7.80 for fuel, and $4.16 for soap, candles, and suchlike. This left $10.54 per annum for food and other essentials, and precious little for luxuries.[76] American male artisans' pay, in comparison, was around $1.00 per day, $6.00 per week, or around $300 per year.

In 1854, a group of women met and formed the Female Labor Association of Summit County to demand "better compensation for female labor." The focus of their concern was the plight of seamstresses. A Mrs. McConneaughty gave an "excellent address" to the meeting, the *Summit Beacon* informed its readers. The meeting elected a committee of nine women to coordinate its activities and passed three resolutions:

> That hereafter we will take no work from any clothing store that will not pay the prices agreed upon;

> That we recommend to the gentlemen of Summit County not to trade with any clothing store where our prices are not paid;
>
> That we also recommend to all our friends and seamstresses who reside in Akron, the neighboring villages, and the surrounding country, to aid us in carrying out the above resolutions.[77]

Some employers tried to trick the women into abandoning the association. The *Summit Beacon* mocked "the superlative meanness" of the Akron merchant tailors Koch & Levi and S. B. Hopfman, who were selling "nice linen coats made for twenty-two cents" at an enormous mark-up. These merchants had agreed to the prices demanded by the seamstresses, but had gone back to the old rates after their workers had naively quit the Association.[78] After the women called a boycott of their stores, the recalcitrant merchants capitulated and agreed to pay the new prices.[79]

It was a powerful demonstration of the power of collective action. The women had organized themselves, but they did not reject sympathetic men's help, nor that of the town's affluent women. Not only did the association thank local grandee General Lucius Bierce for "his liberal donation" to cover expenses, but John Teesdale, the English-born proprietor of the *Beacon*, was vocal in support. Teesdale reported that women's pay in the city had been "constantly decreasing" and that "work that was done a few years since for 50 cents is now done for 20 cents...." He urged that "the man that has not soul enough in him to help forward such a movement, ought to have a perfect vixen for a wife, be obliged to mend his own breeches, darn his own stockings, wash the dishes, and rock the baby, until he has learned to respect the rights of women."[80] Akron's women afterwards kept up a sustained campaign to win the right to vote, and they proved to be the equal of men in the city's trade unions. In later years, the city's rich and paternalistic people were not as supportive of rebellious female factory workers as they had been to the seamstresses.

Akron's people of all classes could not have known it, but their town was standing on the brink of an era of bewildering change. In 1861, America descended into the carnage of the Civil War that was to grind on for four bitter years and claim the lives of three quarters of a million soldiers.[81] According to the Akron historians Kern and Wilson, "Ohio sent nearly 347,000 troops, the third highest of any state, [to the war] and nearly 35,000 died from battle wounds or disease."[82] The war was terribly destructive, yet it smashed the Southern slave system and unleashed hitherto unrealized social and economic forces that changed the lives of Americans forever. In historian Louis Hacker's words, the war's "striking achievement was the triumph of industrial capitalism."[83]

Scholarly debates have raged over Louis Hacker's work,[84] but as Charlie Post points out, the war was "a powerful impetus to the expanded reproduction of capital."[85] The postbellum rate of increase in American iron and steel production, for example, was staggering. It rose from 19,643 long tons in 1867 to 198,796 long tons in 1873, then to 1,586,314 tons in 1881. By 1913, the US was producing as much steel as Britain and Germany combined, and although Germany exported more steel, the US had an incomparably larger internal market.[86] With America on the way to becoming the world's preeminent industrial power, the bulk of the nation's people became wageworkers, especially so in Akron.

3.

From Artisans to Proletarians

Labor historian Thomas R. Brooks writes that the "Civil War unleashed the demonic in American life.... Capital accumulated out of wartime profits searched for investments; the new trusts in oil, iron, steel, copper, coal and coke, sugar and railroads rose as giants of the land."[1] Capital invested in US manufacturing grew from $1 billion in 1860 to $10 billion in 1900, and the value of manufactured products from $2 billion to $13 billion in the same period. Increasingly, the American economy was dominated by "mammoth corporations such as General Electric, Westinghouse and International Harvester."[2] Ohio was already the third largest manufacturing state before the war and second only to Pennsylvania in production of coal and pig iron. The state's industrial production swelled by some 122 percent over by the end of the 1860s.[3]

Industrial expansion was epitomized in Akron by the activities of Ferdinand Schumacher, the "Oatmeal King," whose German Mills provided the Union's Civil War armies with an innovative breakfast food.[4] Schumacher's products became famous under the Quaker Oats brand. Setting up as a small grocer after his arrival from Germany,[5] he grew fat on profits generated by the Civil War and invested in a variety of industries, including oil refineries and coalmines.[6] The growth of the new mass production industries expanded the class of proletarians—people whose livelihoods depended exclusively on wage labor. The previous system in which four-fifths of Americans were self-employed artisans and farmers faded rapidly away.

American mineworkers organized an industrial union to fight for better wages and conditions, and in an economy increasingly dominated by large firms and trusts, their form of organization made sense for workers in other sectors. In Akron and other industrial cities, however, the development of industrial unionism was blocked until well in the following century. From its inception in 1886, the AFL organized along craft lines and defeated the rival Knights of Labor, who had organized on class lines. Akron's artisans had a history of organizing politically, dating back to the 1830s, but the AFL leadership was wedded to the idea of "pure and simple unionism" and refused to support independent labor or socialist parties. This conservatism acted as a powerful brake on the city's labor organization.

Socialists and anarchists dreamed of overthrowing the capitalist system; populists worked to reform it; and some hankered for the good old days of precapitalist production. In 1903, John Mitchell, President of the United Mine Workers of America, observed, "[t]he average wage earner has made up his mind that he must remain a wage earner. He has given up hope of a kingdom come, where he himself will be a capitalist."[7] The wage laborers did not simply "lack ambition" as some journalists believed. Rather, they recognized that they could not escape wage labor, which had become the predominant form of work in capitalist society. Prevented from seeking individual betterment, they came collectively into sharp conflict with the rapacious robber baron capitalists of the Gilded Age.[8] The ensuing class struggle was waged with singular ferocity in America, including Akron.

By 1863, Akron's population had grown to seven thousand, and the town officially became a city the following year.[9] The population increased to over nine thousand in 1867,[10] and by 1888, it had jumped to fifty-four thousand.[11] This mirrored the dramatic demographic shift from rural agricultural to urban industrial settlement across America. In 1800, almost ninety-eight percent of the non-slave American workforce was engaged in agriculture. The proportion declined steadily to 88.5 percent in 1820; 85.3 percent in 1840; 72 percent in 1850; 67 percent in 1860; 52.2 percent in 1870; and to 42.7 percent in 1890.[12] The number of wageworkers mushroomed both in raw numbers and proportionally: in the first part of the nineteenth century, around four-fifths of the American workforce was self-employed, but this fell to about one-third in 1870.[13] Union density in the nonagricultural workforce grew to five percent in 1873 and six percent in 1886, but fell to three-and-a-half percent in 1897 because of the serious trade depression.[14] Akron was vulnerable to the periodic economic crashes that swept the nation. Between 1837 and 1844, the city reportedly faced oblivion because of an economic depression. An economic upturn followed, and new industries sprang up, absorbing the unemployed and demanding fresh supplies of labor.

By the 1880s, Akron had become a major industrial center. In 1888, the New York *Daily Graphic* dubbed Akron the "Tip-Top City" and listed 320 locally manufactured products.[15] If Akron had a hallmark industry during this period, it was agricultural implements and machinery.[16] This industry stoked the demand for coal, iron, and steel, and in 1869, a large steel rolling mill opened in Akron.[17] Benjamin Franklin Goodrich moved his rubber factory to the city from Melrose in New York State in 1871, and this was a harbinger of things to come.[18] Coal-fired electrification came to the city during the same period. People would travel from miles around to see the "Electric Light City" and train crews would dim the lights of sleeper compartments so that passengers could marvel at the spectacle.[19] In the 1890s, business again went into free fall and remained in the doldrums for much of the decade, with drastic consequences for the city's unions.

The second half of the nineteenth century saw the establishment of a number of permanent national trade unions in America, including the International Typographical Union (1850) and associations of iron molders, mechanics, blacksmiths, and locomotive engineers. By 1870, there were about forty national unions in the US.[20] Many of these organizations set up locals in the Akron region. These unions organized along craft—as opposed to industrial—lines, with the notable exception of the mineworkers.

In 1886, a number of national unions met in Columbus, Ohio, to found the American Federation of Labor (AFL) under the leadership of a former cigar-maker named Samuel Gompers. The AFL, however, was arguably born obsolete as an organizing model for the vast majority of

American workers. Seeking to organize skilled workers in craft unions, the leaders of the new federation ignored the tide of history, which dictated that unions had to recruit all workers regardless of craft, skill, or calling. Craft unions may have been adequate for artisanal production in the early stages of capitalism—such as among the Akron potters, for example—but with the emergence of mass production and the division of labor within occupations, they became an impediment. Gompers and his lieutenant, Adolph Strasser, also rejected calls for the AFL to adopt a socialist objective and support an independent workers' party. Although both had once flirted with socialism, they had retreated into a crude pragmatism. Gompers declared, "I have no formula for [our] work and could not have expressed my philosophy in words. I worked intuitively." In 1883, Strasser told the Senate Committee on Labor and Capital: "We have no ultimate ends. We are going on from day to day. We are fighting only for immediate objects—objects that can be realized in a few years."[21] Despite these self-imposed restrictions, the hard-nosed and cash-rich leaders of the AFL first defeated the Knights of Labor, and then the Industrial Workers of the World (IWW).

As industrial production increased, so did the size and character of the city's working class. Whereas strikes had been rare in the old artisans' shops, they became common enough in the new factories and in construction and transport. By the 1870s, the employing class was alarmed with the "labor agitator … stereotyped as a shiftless, immoral loafer content to live off the toil of others."[22] In 1872, the city's coopers struck over wages. These workers were members of Martin Foran's Cleveland-based Coopers' International Union, which represented some 6,700 workers in 142 locals across the northeastern states and nearby parts of Canada.[23] Cooperage was no longer an affair of handcrafted barrels made in small shops. Ohio's first oil refinery had opened for business in Akron in 1860,[24] and as steel tanks and pipelines had yet to be invented, the oil had to be stored and transported in wooden barrels. The soaring demand spurred mechanization, with consequent deskilling and the heightening of class antagonisms.

The Akron unions were also campaigning for shorter hours at the time. In July 1872, the Eight Hour League agitated in the city. It "abandon[ed] hope" of success due to stagnant trade, but still planned strike action according to contradictory press reports at the time.[25] Retail clerks also waged a lengthy but unsuccessful campaign to secure the eight-hour day.[26] In response, the Akron Employers' Central Executive organized to prevent their employees from striking, with a rash of firings in retaliation against what the employers considered "high wage demands."[27] Nevertheless, on July 15, 1872, employers granted a wage increase to striking members of the Boatmen and Laborers' Union, which had formed an alliance with the local coalminers' union.[28] Akron's two canals still carried a great deal of freight, and the Boatmen's Union had the power to damage their employers because of stiff competition from the railroads, which had arrived in the city in 1852. The boatmen's allies, the coalminers, who had formed industrial unions in the district and across America by this time, were locked in a permanent, ferocious struggle with the coal owners.

Another locus of union struggle was the city's burgeoning pottery industry. Pottery was one of the largest industries in nineteenth-century Akron. Some industrial porcelain is still made locally,[29] but the industry had largely died out by the First World War. Summit County's first commercial pottery opened at Springfield in 1828 and by 1853, twelve potteries were operating in the township.[30] The early potteries were primitive affairs, but their products were often beautifully designed, thrown, and decorated by skilled craftsmen, many of whom were immigrants from the Staffordshire Potteries district in England. The immigrants were probably unionists, as potters' unions had existed in North Staffordshire since the 1790s,[31] and unemployed potters had been encouraged to emigrate to America by William Evans, the Secretary of the English potters' union.[32] They brought with them a hybrid form of labor organization known as the Staffordshire "helper system." The skilled potter hired his own unskilled assistants and paid them from the price given him per piece for finished goods by the capitalist, who owned the premises. The craftsman was trained to perform all of the tasks necessary for the production of pottery. Armed with what Braverman calls "the power of conceptual thought,"[33] he could make products to his own original design if necessary, and was able "to imagine how things would appear in final form if such and such tools and materials were used."[34] In the helper system, the assistants worked under the craftsman's supervision.

It was possible for them to become artisans and even masters,[35] but the early artisans' unions jealously restricted the availability of skilled labor to ensure full employment and the highest prices and wages.

The immigrants were to find that new technology had followed them across the ocean. Muscle power was giving way to steam power and, perhaps more importantly, the craftsmen would gradually lose control over the work processes, which would be broken down into a myriad of detail tasks. The helper system shared similarities with what Eric Hobsbawm has called the "co-exploitation" of boilermakers' helpers in British shipyards,[36] but the potters were able to control the methods and pace of the work.

The old system of artisanal production was, however, increasingly obsolete. It hampered production and profits, and it did not outlast the increasing mechanization and division of labor that characterizes large-scale capitalist production. This demanded the ever-increasing division of work processes into smaller and smaller segments, ostensibly for greater efficiency, but also with the effect of cheapening labor power by taking away control by deskilling the workers.[37] Thus, in the Akron potteries, the skilled potter was replaced by a multiplicity of semi-skilled workers, each of whom would and increasingly could only perform one task out of the many required to produce the finished goods. Mechanization accelerated deskilling and in the process, the worker became an appendage of the machine. Nevertheless, the workers stubbornly resisted encroachments on their autonomy, as is evidenced by one Akron worker's statement to a journalist in 1894 that it still took between seven and ten years for a man "to be called a journeyman [i.e. skilled] potter."[38]

By 1870, a new steam-powered pottery at Mogadore was employing seven hundred workers to make a variety of goods including "crocks, churns, pie plates, jugs, vases, flower pots, jardinières, urns, [and] umbrella stands." In 1883, the annual production of the city's potteries amounted to 9,350,000 gallons (or 1880 railroad cars) of chinaware. From the 1890s, the new electrical industry created the demand for porcelain insulators and acid-resistant stoneware.[39] In 1878, the average rate of pay for semi-skilled pottery workers in Akron was thirteen cents an hour,[40] or $1.30 for a ten-hour day. This was during a prolonged downturn in trade that sapped the workers' ability to resist the employers' demands.

The rate was not much more than that paid to artisans half a century earlier, and increased living costs had further eroded real wages.

The pottery industry was the site of a number of bitter industrial disputes during the harsh economic climate of the 1870s. In January 1875, representatives of dozens of pottery firms met in Akron to plan joint action to cut wages. Interestingly, some of these employers were still paying their employees in merchandise rather than cash.[41] Another cause of conflict was the employers' practice of charging potters for the steam used in mechanized production. The Wetmore, Robinson & Co. factory in Middlebury charged the turners $1.80 per week for the privilege, for example. In the winter of 1876, following rumors of an impending miners' strike, which would have raised the price of coal, the company unilaterally raised the price of steam to $2.70 per week, causing the turners to walk off the job.[42] It seems that remnants of the helper system imported from Staffordshire still existed, with the skilled potters continuing to control important aspects of production. Payment must have been on a piecework basis, and the dispute was triggered as much by the owners' desire to exert greater control over production as by direct financial considerations. In the winter of 1877–1878, pottery proprietors in Mogadore attempted to cut wages by five cents a day, bringing down rates to between seventy-five and eighty-five cents a day depending on skill (which suggests day wage payment rather than piecework in those factories). They claimed that the pay cut was the only alternative to shutting down for the winter. Indeed, a number of potteries, including the Myer & Hall firm had already done so, and others had gone bankrupt.

In these circumstances, it was difficult for the union to make strikes effective. There were considerable numbers of unemployed nonunion potters in the district, and some of them had little compunction about strikebreaking.[43] It appears that the potters' union in the district collapsed during this period because in early 1894, a reporter for the *Akron Daily Democrat* reported that the workers had formed a new union. One potter told the reporter that he did not know why no union existed, which indicates that the workers had been unorganized for many years. A meeting of several hundred potters in the Inman's hall in Akron resolved to send delegates to the Akron Central Labor Union and to affiliate with the American Federation of Labor.[44]

The pottery industry had started during an era of small-scale commodity production based on artisanal methods. The Civil War accelerated a change towards greater scale of production and mechanization. This also meant the creation of a larger proletariat with some awareness of its existence as a distinct class. That this awareness existed to some degree from the 1830s is apparent from the activities of the Mechanics' Association and the Potters' union, as well as in the struggles of the coalminers in the Akron region. Looking back today, one cannot but regret the fate of the potters, proud craftsmen whose complex skills were devalued by the ruthless drive for profits. The historian of the Summit County potteries laments that mass production "brought an end to the beautifully designed and decorated ware of the individual potters."[45] It also ended the worker's autonomy and thus leached away at his humanity.

Between 1873 and 1878, the American economy again plunged into recession, and although this dampened militancy to an extent, Akron's workers still made some gains. In June 1876, for example, workers in the railroad repair shops in nearby Kent won the eight-hour day as part of a six-day working week.[46] The 1870s were years of stagnant trade across America. Countless workers were unemployed or on short hours, and living standards fell sharply. In the summer of 1877, goaded by the constant erosion of their living standards and the high-handed behavior of the employers, millions of workers across the nation took spontaneous strike action. The nationwide strike began in July at Martinsburg, West Virginia, when Cornelius Vanderbilt slashed wages on the Baltimore & Ohio railroad, and spread rapidly. In many centers, it took on an insurrectionary character as working people lashed out against a system that had condemned them to hopeless poverty.[47] Nevertheless, although the effects of the great strike on Akron were "quite manifest"[48] the city did not experience violent upheavals. It seems likely, however, that local workers employed on the Pennsylvania Railroad and the Pittsburgh, Fort Wayne, and Chicago line[49] did take action to protest a ten percent wage cut imposed on them by their employer.

The strikers' actions perhaps would not have mattered much in Akron, as few scab trains were running the length of the lines from the East Coast. Although the strike spread from the railroads to rolling mill, foundry, and refinery workers in neighboring Cleveland, and other major centers in Ohio were strikebound, it seems that Akron workers generally remained aloof. In neighboring Kent, fourteen miles across the Portage County line, track and workshop employees of the Atlantic and Great Western line were reportedly "unenthusiastic" about taking action, probably because the company had not imposed Vanderbilt's ten percent pay cut and had granted the eight-hour day the previous year. While "a few excited ones," clamored to take solidarity action, mass meetings of local railroad men decided to stay at work. Indeed, attendance dwindled rapidly after the first meeting to discuss the strike.

The strike hit Akron's businesses hard. Local ironworks, rubber mills, and the Barber match factory closed for lack of raw materials and inability to transport finished goods. "Oatmeal King" Schumacher's profits dropped sharply for he declared that "he would like to choke that old Vanderbilt for causing all this trouble."[50] In the end, the strike burned itself out due to lack of leadership and coordination, and savage government repression, including the use of federal troops.

The 1880s were a period of economic boom and frenetic expansion for Akron. Not for the first or last time, journalists noted that there was "fearful pressure" for rental housing and commercial premises, so there was a shortage of carpenters and other skilled workers in the city to build more,[51] and this gave the building unions considerable bargaining power. In the decade to 1890, real estate values shot up by between fifty and seventy-five percent.[52] Business was booming at Seiberling's Excelsior (or Empire) Mower & Reaper works, which had undergone big expansion in 1868.[53] Six years later, the Seiberling firm was turning out twenty-four Excelsior mowers a day,[54] a considerable achievement in pre-Fordist days when craftsmen assembled individual machines by hand. Wages, however, do not appear to have increased much. Daniel Brown recalled that Peninsula quarrymen received $1.07 to $1.14 a day during this period.[55]

In 1883, the Ohio State Trades & Labor Assembly was formed at Cincinnati, and local peak union bodies were set up in major centers across the state. In 1889, the city's carpenters spearheaded a renewed movement for the eight-hour day.[56] Building trades workers were well organized and had spearheaded the creation of a Central Labor Union, which in 1883 affiliated to the Ohio State Trades & Labor Council.

Akron's printers first organized in January 1880, when, on a "cold, blustery" day twelve workers gathered at the Central Labor Union building at Twelve South Howard Street—sometimes called the Carpenters' Hall—to set up a typographical union local.[57] Three months later, printers struck work at the *Daily Beacon* to protest the dismissal of a unionist and his replacement with a nonunionist. The strike fizzled out, and work continued with the scab still in the print room. According to the journalist Howard Wolf, this was the first and only strike at the staunchly Republican *Beacon*.[58]

In late March 1885, a significant strike erupted at the Diamond Match Company's Akron factory. The city's match industry had started in the late 1850s, when the Middlebury farmer George Barber made matches in his barn. Business was so good that in 1860, Barber took over a former blacksmith's shop[59] before moving to a small factory in Middlebury.[60] The following year, his son Ohio Columbus Barber took over the business. In 1881, Barber Junior created the Diamond Match Company after taking over and amalgamating twenty-eight smaller firms. Barber also had interests in strawboard, sewer pipe, iron tubing, sprinkler systems, cartridges, boilermaking, and aluminum smelting.[61] By 1885, he was employing hundreds of "match boys and girls" on piecework in his downtown Akron factory. A Trump-like figure "as obstreperous and vain as his name,"[62] he later shifted production to the eponymous Barberton, just south of Akron, possibly because he resented paying city taxes.[63] He was a harsh employer who hated unions and socialism but strangely, he praised the island of Guernsey for its "cooperative culture." As a writer in the leftist *People* remarked, "as a blind leader of the blind.... he cannot see that the soul and essence of labor unions and Socialism are identical with the soul and essence of Guernsey society."[64]

At one o'clock on March 27 of that year, forty teenage boys and one hundred teenage girls from the Barber packing department "arose from their work and left the shop," demanding a twenty-five percent increase in piecework rates.[65] Although Barber insisted many employees wished to return to work, and hinted at intimidation by "ringleaders," the *Daily Beacon* reported that the plant was "practically shut down in consequence of the strike."[66] If any of the workers opposed the strike, they kept quiet about it. One of the strikers wrote, "Be it remembered that there are plenty of honorable places for every girl to work without standing on our feet from early morn till night for 2½ cents per gross." Barber had refused to provide chairs because the young women could not work as fast sitting down, she said. She also demanded "the officers of the Match Company should not employ little girls under 14 years of age during the strike...."[67]

Barber's refusal to grant the demand for chairs hinted at a deadly occupational health and safety hazard for match workers. He was keen to avoid public scrutiny of a terrible industrial disease. Physicians advised that sitting down would bring the workers' faces "so much nearer the phosphorus than when they were standing up."[68] The fumes from yellow phosphorus, the key component of matches at the time, caused "phossy jaw" or osteonecrosis, a hideous disease that rotted match workers' jawbones. "Phossy brain," "phossy lung," and other horrors could often follow and end in agonizing death. Barber was well aware of the dangers, but deliberately chose not to use safer alternatives in order to keep his product competitive. In 1850, an Austrian chemist had developed a relatively benign but comparatively expensive substitute, red phosphorus, but industrial safety legislation and enforcement was weak, and the employers' appetite for profits was immense. The first recorded instance of the disease occurred in Vienna in 1838, and fifty years later in London, Bryant & May's famous striking "matchgirls" sought the elimination of yellow or white phosphorus.[69] The 1885 Akron strikers did not mention it,[70] perhaps because of their age (thirteen to sixteen years) and inexperience. Nor did they have a union or articulate supporters to take up the matter. In 1906, the Berne Convention banned yellow phosphorus in match making and similar industrial processes, but it continued in use in the United States until 1913 when the federal government forced the Diamond Match Company to relinquish its 1910 patent on a substitute made with phosphorus sesquisulfide.[71]

Barber continued to use yellow phosphorus in his Akron and Barberton plants for at least twenty years after the 1885 strike. He refused to negotiate with the teenage strikers and after ten days, they returned to work without any significant gains.[72] Perhaps had the strikers been able to publicize the "phossy jaw" question as their London sisters did three years later, they too might have beaten their employer. One wonders at the fate of Barber's youthful employees, some of whom must have contracted the dreadful disease. Twenty-eight years later, the Diamond Match workers walked off the job in solidarity with Akron's rubber workers in their ill-fated 1913 IWW strike.[73]

Cases such as the match strike highlighted the need for an independent labor press. The American media, then as now, largely served the interests of the capitalists and slanted press reports were a perennial problem for the labor movement. Journalists blatantly editorialized in "news" articles and were seldom in sympathy with strikers. *Beacon* editor Charles E. Wright did organize food and clothing for striking Summit County coalminers and their families,[74] but he was fired in March 1896, "apparently because he ... [had] not been partisan enough in supporting the Republicans."[75] Akron's first labor newspaper was *The Roarer*, edited by Sam Lane, which merged with a larger Cleveland publication in the late 1840s. In 1883, Akron again had its own independent workers' publication, *The Labor Unionist*, which declared itself the organ of all "Without Regard to Creed, Color, Nation, or Party."[76] Proudly class conscious and aware that disunity helped only the employing class, the paper also tried unsuccessfully to bridge the gulf between the Knights of Labor and the craft unions organized in the American Federation of Labor.

The Knights of Labor appear to have arrived in Ohio in 1875,[77] but they made slow progress: there were only eight hundred members across the state by 1880. By 1887, however, their statewide numbers had grown to seventeen thousand.[78] The organization appears to have gained a foothold on the coalfields to the south and west of Akron in early 1879, with miners' assemblies in Wadsworth, North Lawrence, and Canal Fulton.[79] The *Summit County Beacon* reported that a delegation of Akron Knights attended a New Year's Eve "ball and oyster supper" in North Lawrence in 1880.[80] In February 1883, a Knights' organizer named Ralph Beaumont spoke at a public meeting in Akron's Phoenix Hall and reportedly held the attention of the audience for one-and-half hours.[81] The Knights were the only national labor organization in America and, after a period of phenomenal growth, they boasted around one million members.

Founded in 1869 as a secret society by journeymen tailors in Philadelphia, they had emerged as a more open organization in 1878 following the bloody class battles of the preceding year. The Knights were a contradictory force. Frederick Engels described them as "an immense association spread out over an immense extent of country in innumerable assemblies, representing all shades of individual and local opinion within the working class."[82] Despite what he saw as their "medieval mummeries," programmatic "indistinctness," and their (theoretical) rejection of strikes in favor of arbitration of disputes, other aspects of their program were remarkably progressive. They were much in advance of the program of their emerging rival, the American Federation of Labor, and the Knights' rank-and-file were often considerably more militant than their officials were. In time, impatience with Terence V. Powderly, the "somewhat bumbling head of the Knights,"[83] who boasted that he had never organized a strike, was a salient factor in the organization's demise. Powderly dabbled in business at the same time as he led the union and the labor historian Thomas R. Brooks suggests that "perhaps his failures as a businessman and as a labor leader can be ascribed to these divided loyalties."[84]

Whereas the AFL sought in the main to organize only the most highly skilled workers—the "aristocracy of labor"—the Knights sought to organize the entire working class in one big union regardless of trade or occupation, race, religion, ethnicity, or gender. They demanded equal pay for equal work for women and were internationalist in outlook to the point of organizing overseas branches. Rejecting socialism and anarchism, the Knights nevertheless aimed to educate the working class to abolish the wages system and replace capitalism with a vaguely defined cooperative society.[85] The Knights did not always live up to these ideals, but their insistence on organizing all employees chimed with working-class needs at a time when the mass production industries were supplanting the old craft shops.

Ralph Beaumont's earnest speech at Akron's Phoenix Hall meeting bore fruit. The *Stark County Democrat* reported that in June 1883 Akron Knights joined with members from Cleveland, Canton, and other centers in a seven-thousand-strong "grand picnic" at Cuyahoga Falls.[86] By January 1886, an Akron Knights' coopers' union, Local Assembly (LA) 2903, was in existence along with three other Knights' affiliates, and these sent delegates to the Akron Trades & Labor Assembly. There were also reports that the Knights were in the process of setting up a further three local assemblies in the city, including one covering plasterers. At the same time, a German-speaking organizer was recruiting from Akron's numerous German workers.[87] Nine months later, the *Beacon* reported there were fourteen Knights' local assemblies in Akron, along with eight other labor unions, with a combined membership of around two thousand.[88]

The Knights were able to cooperate with other labor organizations in the city, but not all craft unionists shared this ecumenical approach. The year 1886 appears to have been the high-water mark for the Akron Knights. If the memberships of the assemblies and the other unions were roughly equal in size, this would mean branches of around ninety members each, or a total of perhaps 1,260 Knights in the city as a whole. They did not reject political action—Powderly himself served as mayor of Scranton in New York State in 1878, elected on a Greenback Labor ticket. In April 1886, the Akron Knights were said to have "caused the election" of a striking unionist called William Anderson as a police justice.[89] Three years earlier, the Akron Trades & Labor Assembly had endorsed the candidature of the Knight Lewis C. Parker for the Ohio legislature. The *Labor Unionist* approvingly quoted Parker's election speech in which he declared,

> You [the workers] had bravery enough to fight the battles of the Republic [in the Civil War against the Confederacy], but you are not brave enough to fight your own. On with the armor then. Prepare for the struggle, and as victory is in the end with the right so it shall certainly be yours.[90]

Parker's election bid was not successful. He moved to Los Angeles in 1888 and seems to have dropped out of radical labor politics.[91] During his politically active years in Akron, despite Powderly's example, he does not seem to have joined the Greenback Labor Party, which was strong in Summit County and surrounding districts at the time.

Labor parties of the "Locofoco" type[92] had come and gone across America for many years. This was certainly the case in Akron, where workers had fielded independent candidates for public office since the late 1830s. The Greenbackers flourished across America in the years following the Great Upheaval of 1877. Although the movement predated those events, it had been primarily based on farmers: afterwards, common grievances united small farmers and workers against the growing power of the big industrial trusts. The Greenback Party itself emerged in February 1878 and the following year it won one million votes and elected fourteen members to Congress across America.[93] It thrived in Ohio, and held its 1884 national convention in Canton, close to Akron. Following the convention, the local Greenbackers nominated a slate of candidates for the state and federal elections, including Joseph Rogers, who stood unsuccessfully for the Twentieth Congressional District. Resolutions passed at the convention attacked "the cruel indifference to the wants and needs of an oppressed, unemployed and suffering people" and condemned both the Democrats and Republicans for supporting the monopolies and corporations.[94] The party called for the introduction of the eight-hour day, opposed monopolies and trusts, and supported the right of workers to take strike action. Its main plank, however, called for a return of the "greenback," the $1 bill introduced during the Civil War, which had lost over half of its value because of a return to the gold standard. This had created abject poverty, as many farmers, workers, and small businesspeople were unable to pay crippling debts.

As elsewhere in the US, the Akron party faded away when the Democrats and Populists "borrowed" its policies. However, the increasingly sharp divergence of their interests from those of the employers caused Akron's workers to form branches of similar parties in the following years. The fact that the courts and politicians generally sided with the employers was an added impulse for working-class political organization. One such party was formed in March 1887, when "between 65 and 70 enthusiastic friends of the Union Labor Party met in Emmett Hall on South Howard Street" to nominate candidates for city office. The meeting endorsed the principles set out at the ULP convention held in Cincinnati the previous month.[95] It is likely that many of the attendees of the Akron meeting doubled as members of the Knights of Labor as this had dominated the party's Cincinnati convention.

Although the party's central executive insisted on the ULP's independence from the established parties, advocated shorter working hours, and sought to extend its platform beyond "the old Greenback idea," the party suffered from a lack of unity, vagueness of program, and recruited small numbers of industrial workers compared to small farmers. Its ideological mentor was Henry George, the "single taxer," who was at odds with the adherents of socialist theory.[96] "Ticket Number Two," as the Akron ULP election slate was known, was unsuccessful, and the party soon went the way of its predecessors—both nationally and locally. Most likely, its adherents drifted back into the Democratic Party's orbit or dropped out of political activity from disillusionment. Others, possibly, turned towards the nascent socialist movement.

The Knights of Labor, meanwhile, were prominent in a number of industrial disputes in and around Akron in the 1880s. This was despite the national organization's avowed opposition to strikes. One of these was a lengthy molders' strike for higher pay, which began at the Seiberling & Co.'s Empire works in March 1886, and ended ten months later. The Knights' executive board endorsed the stoppage (which involved 175 workers including forty nonunionists) and announced a boycott of all of Seiberling's extensive businesses in the city.[97] The boycott included a refusal to load the firm's products onto trains passing through the city. When the company brought in scab labor to replace the strikers, the Knights persuaded the city's boardinghouses to refuse to house them. "Oatmeal King" Schumacher offered to accommodate the strikebreakers in his two city hotels,[98] but the strike and boycott continued. The boycott, which was subsequently endorsed by the Akron Trades & Labor Assembly (TLA),[99] was not lifted until a member of the Knights' general executive board visited the city the following January to negotiate with the employer. Although he probably planned to starve the strikers back to work, Frank Seiberling was instead worn down by the strike. He agreed to the pay raise and reinstated all the strikers.[100] The settlement must have stuck in his craw, and in his subsequent career as a rubber manufacturer, he distinguished himself a ruthless enemy of trade unionism of any stripe.

The boycott proved a useful industrial weapon for Akron's unionists. The TLA, which included Knights' organizations, organized many boycotts of employers during these years. In early 1886 for example, the TLA boycotted the Akron Milling Company after it fired union bricklayers and coopers and replaced them with scabs. The TLA lifted the boycott after two weeks when differences were "amicably and fully adjusted."[101] The TLA also boycotted one of the city's cigar makers for employing nonunion labor.[102] Militant actions such as these prompted the Republican State Assemblyman Marshall J. Williams to introduce an unsuccessful bill "to punish boycotters" later that year.[103] Industrial unrest continued into the next decade, with reports of strikes by masons and carpenters, bricklayers and hod carriers, printers at the Werner Printing Company, potters, quarrymen, retail clerks, and wire workers. Glassworkers also struck in a number of Akron factories. Although many of the strikes were in support of wage claims, carpenters and retail clerks also raised the demand for the eight-hour day.[104]

Akron's glassworkers also campaigned against the widespread use of child labor in their industry. Children received less than half of the adult rates of pay, and although they were supposed to work solely on light tasks, they were often expected to produce as much as adults. The city's glass manufacturers were determined to continue employing children and were prominent in agitation against the Haley Bill, which was introduced into the Ohio legislature in 1889 to forbid the employment of minors under the age of fourteen and to require them to attend school.[105] Passage of the legislation in 1890 caused the firing of a number of children at the city's glass works and the Diamond Match Company.[106]

The Labor Unionist also drew attention to the alarming frequency of industrial accidents in Akron, particularly on multistory building sites in the city center. There had been a number of scaffolding collapses, including one at the five-story Buchtel Hotel on Main and Mill Streets and another at the Kohler Block on the avenue of the same name.[107]

Holding to its pledge to support workers of all colors and creeds, in 1883 the *Labor Unionist* also took up the case of a meeting of "colored men," who had voted to support the Knight Lewis Parker and rejected the Democrats' candidate, J. A. Kohler. The meeting had taken the resolution of support for Parker to the *Beacon Journal* office, and although the paper initially promised to publish it, it reneged and "took it upon itself the right to steal the property of the colored men."[108]

The *Unionist* also vigorously opposed the employment of convicts in industrial enterprises. The convict labor system had existed in Ohio for over thirty-five years, and it was a deadly threat to working-class interests. The state authorities sold cheap convict labor "not always to the highest bidder, but to gentlemen with the most influence," including a "contractors' powerful ring." This, the newspaper pointed out, undercut "the labor of honest artisans" and drove competitors out of business. Some branches of industry were "entirely monopolized" by the convict contractors, who made "enormous profits." Certain articles such as pitchforks, hoes, baby buggies, saddlery, and hardware were made only by convict labor in the state. The *Unionist* blasted the Republican Party, which, it said, "paraded as champion of the working class," periodically promising to abolish the convict contract system while refusing to stop it. The convict contractors undercut competition because they could get labor at a quarter of the cost of free labor. They did not have to invest any capital in buildings, and paid no insurance, rent, or taxes because "the State assumes the entire expense."[109] Moreover, the system did not reform the criminal, argued the *Unionist,* but "hardens and embitters him." The convict laborer became "the personal property of the contractor," and was driven harder even than Southern slaves were, the paper believed. Whereas slave owners had to buy their slaves, the contractors did not have to purchase the convict. "If he falls by the wayside, the contract calls for so many men, and his place is taken by another," the paper reported.[110] The system was a throwback to the bonded and convict labor system in colonial times, mimicked slavery in the South, and foreshadowed the widespread use of convict labor in the bloated private prison system of America today. The employers clung tenaciously to what provided them with a profit bonanza. Despite its activism, the labor newspaper did not last. It waged a spirited fight for workers' rights for a few years, only to fold, perhaps for financial reasons, in mid-1886.[111]

In December 1886, craft unionists set up the American Federation of Labor (AFL) in Columbus, Ohio. The new federation and the Knights were soon locked in bitter conflict, and while both organizations lost bargaining power and members with the onset of the 1890s trade depression, the AFL weathered the storm, whereas the Knights perished. In January 1889, Knights of Labor District Assembly 38 held its annual general meeting in Akron with representatives from eight counties in attendance. The officers elected included T. T. O'Malley of Canton,

John B. Fitzgerald and F. M. McKnight of Akron, and M. J. Beatty of Crystal Springs. The business discussion included a campaign to elect friends of labor to the State Legislature. The meeting also appealed in vain to the AFL for cooperation and common cause.[112] The Assembly seems to have collapsed shortly afterwards, for the only mentions of the Knights in the local press for the next six years are concerned with their activities elsewhere in the country. According to a former local official, the Knights had "existed here several years ago, but … [it] went to pieces because of disagreement among its members." The AFL, on the other hand, had "secured quite a foothold in Akron," including in the powerful carpenters' local.[113] Early in 1895, a Knights' organizer returned, charged with rebuilding the organization. The Knights' new recruiting drive came to nothing, mirroring the organization's terminal decline across the country. According to the 1930s rubber unionist John D. House, the Knights attempted to organize his industry in the late nineteenth century, but this fizzled out when the Knights' Executive Board refused to grant a charter.[114]

Information that might help explain the Knights' demise in the Akron district is sketchy. Apart from the lack of unity hinted at by the former local official, ingrained conservatism in sections of the working class appears to have played a part. This was the case with the Massillon barbers' union, which disaffiliated from the Akron district Knights' Assembly in 1893. A letter from the barbers expressed outrage that the Assembly had commended Illinois Governor John P. Altgeld "for pardoning the anarchists" convicted in 1886 of throwing a bomb in Haymarket Square in Chicago during a labor rally. The barbers repudiated the Knights for "dabbling in politics" and declared that they wanted no truck with anarchism or socialism.[115] A certain "Pendragon" expressed similar ideas in a letter published in the *Daily Beacon* in February 1887. It was, he claimed, "an American's privilege to be free to work for whom and what he pleases" and blamed strikes and boycotts for the deteriorating economic situation.[116] Conversely, many other workers appear to have left the Knights because they considered its official anti-strike policy to be too conservative.

A further factor in the Knights' decline was the fact that the depression had deprived organized labor of its bargaining power. Huge numbers of workers were unemployed. Many were desperate enough to take strikers' jobs, and those still in employment were naturally reluctant to do anything to jeopardize their positions. The final reason—and this appears to have been crucial in Akron—was the intense rivalry between the Knights and the AFL. The AFL was able to appeal to conservative craft instincts of the more skilled layers of the working class and cut out the Knights, who were committed to building general labor unions encompassing workers in all occupations. In this, the Knights were perhaps ahead of their time, although they might have retained more members if they had jettisoned their dogmatic insistence on arbitration.

The American Federation of Labor prevailed, but whether or not it better served working-class interests is debatable. The years following the end of the Civil War had seen a huge expansion of manufacturing industry: by 1890, American manufactures were worth half of much as all of Europe and double that of Britain, the cradle of the Industrial Revolution. The proportion of the workforce employed in agriculture[117] and in artisanal labor had steadily declined since the beginning of the century, and there were huge leaps in industrial employment after 1860. America had become an industrial juggernaut, producing goods and services on a scale never seen in human history. To organize in the interests of a thin and relatively privileged layer of the working class that some characterize as a "labor aristocracy" and to divide workers into unions organized by craft increasingly made little sense.[118] With the arrival of Fordist mass production in the late nineteenth century, the AFL's stubborn craft fetishism became an impediment to effective union organization. The idea of industrial unionism was not dead, however, for it was vigorously promoted after the demise of the Knights by the socialists. The AFL leadership also refused to endorse the socialists or other working-class political formations.

In 1893, a devastating global slump buffeted the city's unions. This followed the collapse of the Philadelphia and Reading Railroad and the National Cordage Company and caused some fifteen thousand bankruptcies across the United States. The slump hit Akron hard: whole industries went bust, and unemployment levels soared to unprecedented levels. The city's thriving agricultural machinery industry collapsed. J. F. Seiberling's Excelsior (formerly Empire) Mower & Reaper Works went to the wall, followed by most of the city's smaller fry. The industry never recovered, as it had already suffered from the shift of grain production westwards. While there were some fierce industrial battles during the slump years, these were primarily defensive in character. Frank Seiberling later recalled that the city had experienced few labor disturbances "since 1886, the period of the Powderly [Knights of Labor] wave."[119] Unemployment rates in Ohio reached fifty percent among industrial workers.[120] National unemployment statistics were only calculated from 1929, but anecdotal evidence suggests that by 1893, half of Akron's workforce was unemployed. The slump eased a little in mid-1894 but returned the next year, and it was not until mid-1897 that the economy revived. For five or six consecutive years, national unemployment levels never fell below ten percent. Real GNP declined by around six percent in the years between 1893 and 1894 and did not rise above 1892 levels until 1899.[121]

It is puzzling that recessions always seem to surprise people.[122] They may as well be surprised that the sun rises in the mornings and sets in the evenings as that capitalism goes through cycles of boom and bust.

The depression did not automatically result in an upsurge of working-class militancy. While there is no direct, mechanical relationship between the economic slump and the weakness of the city's labor movement, there is no doubt that unions were hit hard. Nationally, union density declined from six percent of the nonagricultural workforce in 1886, to 3.5 percent in 1897.[123] In Akron, whole industries went to the wall, putting thousands out of work and forcing them to rely on charity to survive. The slump was a watershed event in American history, and it profoundly altered the social, economic, and political face of Akron. If times were hard for captains of industry such as J. F. Seiberling, they were appalling for those thrown out of work by the crisis. Even before the slump began to bite, a widow insisted that with some exceptions the local capitalists did not treat their workers as human beings.[124]

While the Great Depression of the 1930s etched itself into American popular consciousness, there is little memory of the 1890s catastrophe. In 1896, there were reports of destitution and even famine on the Ohio coalfields.[125] The following year, the Akron unemployed created a scrip system, which they called "Labor Exchange" to obtain the necessities of life. Organized by Pat O'Neil and J. W. Beckwith, this was a barter system in which people traded goods or labor for scrip that could be exchanged in a number of stores or sold for legal tender. The scheme ran for over two years until improved conditions rendered it redundant.[126] With half of the city's workforce unemployed, the Akron Central Labor Union agitated for the creation of public works relief schemes to provide the unemployed with an income. The CLU also opened its reading room and library to the unemployed.[127] At a mass meeting chaired by CLU vice-president Philip Breillatt, L. Schunk, a former member of the Knights of Labor, declaimed that "receiving alms helps to lose one's manhood ... [so] We must force the city to furnish employment for the idle, and not at wages of $1 a day either, but wages that are above the starvation limit." Schunk threatened, "If it can be done in no other way we must shoulder guns." He later claimed to have been joking, but his rhetoric hints at the desperation of the times.[128] In the same month, Local 182 of the Typographers' Union held a "Hard Times Ball" in the Germanic Hall to raise funds for unemployment relief.[129] In nearby Cleveland, on May 1, 1894, the local unemployed rioted because the local authorities failed to provide adequate relief,[130] but the Akron unemployed were quieter despite Schunk's incendiary rhetoric.

The American working class suffered cruelly during the depression as there was no publicly funded social security. Poor relief was modeled on the English poorhouse model. Governments and a substantial slice of the population remained ideologically hostile to regular, state-funded social security measures. These attitudes continued throughout the nineteenth century—and indeed up to the present. As late as 1915, only twenty-five percent of the money spent on "outdoor relief" came from public funds.[131] Alleviation of the sufferings of the poor would lead to dependence and a proliferation of "work-shy" paupers in the opinion of the establishment—and some craft unionists.

Hard times did not always prevent Akron's unions from striking for improved wages and conditions. The *Beacon* grumbled about a rash of building strikes throughout 1893[132] and called on unionists to oust their "lawless" leaders.[133] Three years later, Akron's retail clerks waged a long-running campaign for shorter hours with the CLU's support,[134] and the Diamond Pottery Company attempted to break a three-month strike with scab labor.[135] In January of the same year, Akron quarrymen struck over nonpayment of their wages.[136] The city's municipal workers scored a major victory in March 1897 when they won the eight-hour day,[137] although the worst of the depression was over by that time. The campaign for shorter hours by municipal and retail workers was more than just a demand for their own better conditions; it was an act of solidarity with the city's unemployed, who would benefit by the sharing of the available work.

By the turn of the century, modest if uneven prosperity was returning to the city, and soon it would soon ride an enormous boom. In 1899, twenty-five Goodrich Rubber women workers went on strike,[138] causing company representative J. W. Kelley to grumble, "These little strikes occur quite often." The women had downed tools to demand the reinstatement of their spokesperson, who had attempted to negotiate a pay raise with plant superintendent B. G. Work. Although Work said the dispute "could hardly be called a strike," he dismissed the women and brought in scabs to do their work when they refused his ultimatum to return to work within twenty-four hours.[139] Although they could not have known it, the women had probably fired the first shots in a class war that was to last for over fifty years in one of the world's greatest manufacturing industries. As for attempts by the city's workers to organize politically, these had come to nothing.

4.

They Treat Horses Better Than Miners

In 1890, American mineworkers formed what was among the first of the nation's industrial unions, the United Mine Workers of America (UMW). Instead of organizing workers separately by craft or calling, which was the model adopted by the American Federation of Labor, the nation's mineworkers enrolled all of the workers in their industry, including skilled artisans. The UMW, significantly, resulted from an amalgamation of the existing National Progressive Miners' Union with the Knights of Labor miners' assembly. Mining was an important industry in the Akron district from an early time. The city's industries depended on it, and it was widely used as a domestic fuel. Curiously, books on Akron's labor history have little to say about the mineworkers and their struggles. This reflects, perhaps, the relative insularity of the miners, who lived in separate communities, many of them immigrants from the British Isles or their direct descendants, with a fierce sense of solidarity. Miners lived in a world apart, doing work that was—for most people—utterly strange. For these reasons, they are the subject of this stand-alone chapter.

There is very little evidence today that the Summit County coalmines ever existed. Once, however, winding gear towers and gob piles dotted the skyline, and tunnels honeycombed the earth. Locomotives huffed and puffed from the mines, hauling their cargoes through

Akron to waiting barges. Sons followed their fathers and grandfathers down the mines. It was a whole world and way of life and work for thousands of miners and their families, and society depended on them to dig the black flammable stone. As George Orwell wrote after visiting a British colliery, "it is only because miners sweat their guts out that superior persons can remain superior." "Down there where coal is dug is a sort of world apart which one can quite easily go through life without ever hearing about.... Yet ... practically everything we do, from eating an ice to crossing the Atlantic, and from baking a loaf to writing a novel, involves the use of coal, directly or indirectly."[1] By the 1880s, with the massive expansion of industry and population, coal became America's largest source of energy. Until the 1940s, it accounted for half of the nation's energy production.[2] Despite this dependency, John Miller, who worked down a mine near Akron for over thirty years, observed bitterly that the coal owners treated their horses better than their miners.[3] The fiercely competitive industry was a byword for desperate class struggle. H. G. Wells modeled his outré Morlocks in *The Time Machine* on coalminers, but being human, the real-life colliers resisted their oppressors, built a powerful industrial union, carved out communities, went on strike, and in the process earned the special hatred of the ruling class.

"Mining is simple, but very laborious," a *Summit Beacon* journalist wrote in 1849 following a visit to the Tallmadge coalmine. "The miner lies down on his side and with a pick and other instruments undermines the coal."[4] Had he known more, he might have added that mining is perilous work[5] that requires specialized knowledge and skills. In 2009, the US Department of Labor reported that mining was the nation's second most hazardous industry, with a fatal work injury rate of 12.7 per one hundred thousand equivalent full-time workers. Given coal's importance, the exploitation of the seams that underlie eastern Ohio was inevitable. In 1834, the Upson Coal Company commenced mining operations in Tallmadge,[6] starting an industry that lasted in Summit County for one hundred years. From the mid-nineteenth century onward, Summit County's mines produced huge amounts of coal. By 1872, the district's coal owners were shipping over 171,000 tons of coal annually on the local canals.[7]

The old collier William R. Hillier was perhaps typical of his fellow miners. Arriving in Ohio from Nova Scotia in 1868 as a twenty-year-old, he found employment at Canal Fulton, twenty-three miles south of Akron, and worked down the mines until his retirement. He and his fellow miners were paid twice a month, and on paydays they would head into Akron "to make merry." Their entertainments were simple: Hillier recalled they organized foot races and boxing matches.[8] Many miners were fond of a drink, as a party of local journalists found when they toured the Middlebury mines in 1872,[9] but a miner's life was not all fun and games. The coal trade was precarious. The domestic demand for coal fell during the warmer months, so seasonal unemployment and penury haunted the miners and their families. Mining was also acutely sensitive to downturns in the business cycle. While industry could not get by without coal, mining depended on steady markets, and as more mines opened, competition shaved profit margins. Naturally, the mine owners compensated for their lost profits by undermining the workers' wages and conditions.

According to Raymond Boryczka and Lorin Lee Cary, the attitude of the Ohio coal owners to their workers was "almost feudal."[10] Many owners lived in seigneurial mansions overlooking their domains. The Tallmadge coal baron Dr. F. W. Upson lived "about a mile and a half from the mines, in one of the finest farms, in one of the richest townships of land, and among happy, intelligent, wealthy and prosperous a body of farmers as can be found in the whole weal." The writer did not comment on the living conditions and well-being of the "begrimed and blackened miners" he had observed in the "gloom" of the doctor's mine.[11] Welsh miners in Tallmadge lived in unattractive tenements, and few outside their community grieved when lightning destroyed their homes in 1898. Some managed to save enough money to buy their own homes.[12] The Akron printers' union president Jim McCartan was born into an Irish coalmining family in New Philadelphia, fifty miles south of Akron, and started work in the summer of 1897 as a thirteen-year-old "trap door boy" in a local mine.[13] The miners called their settlement Slabtown, he recalled,[14] mocking its pretensions to being a new "city of light." Save for the less rugged topography, the miners' villages could not have been very different from the "coal camps" James Green describes in his history of the West Virginia miners' union:

> Miners' houses were clustered together on bottomland or perched precariously on hillsides.... Some rows of miners' cabins sat only a few yards from the railroad tracks, so close that dishes crashed to the floor when trains rumbled past. These Jenny Lind houses—named for the coal town where the prototypes appeared—were made cheaply without wall studs, horizontal siding, or insulation.... They were rough places to live, because they lacked amenities and were isolated from the larger world, but also because they were occupied by large numbers of single men living together in a raw new environment.... [15]

Wages were at subsistence level, so it was difficult for miners to save money and layoff in slack times meant destitution. Mining communities often existed in remote places, so the miners were doubly tied to their place of work, living in company houses from which they could be evicted almost at whim. Payment was often in the employer's scrip, exchangeable only in the company store where essential commodities were so overpriced that miners could end up owing the boss money on payday.[16] The preamble of the 1890 constitution of the UMWA demands the right "to establish as speedily as possible, and forever, our right to receive pay, for labor performed, in lawful money, and to rid ourselves from the iniquitous system of spending our money wherever our employers see fit to designate."[17]

The Middlebury Coal Company's offices sat on the P&O canal near the old coal loading chutes in downtown Akron.[18] Full production began in 1866. One summer's day in 1872, a party of Akron newspapermen traveled in open cars along the three-and-a-half-mile company railroad line as guests of the mine's owners. One found the rail trip was itself a minor ordeal "through a blinding shower of cinders, smoke from the 'dummy' [engine] and dust...." They did not mention the irony of miners' families scavenging for spilled coal along the tracks. Kitted out in overalls, rubber top boots, coats, and miners' lanterns, the party stood at the top of the pit shaft, underneath the soaring tower of the eighty-horsepower winding engine. When the doors of the cages rattled open, the car operator packed them inside the six by eight feet platforms suspended on steel ropes over the abyss. The platforms—one rising and the other falling simultaneously—moved at great speed: descending "100 feet in *ten seconds*" breathlessly emphasized the man from the *Daily Beacon*. Shortly before the bottom, the cage slowed and bounced giddily on its cables before the doors rattled open, and the party stepped out into the gloom.

It was a strange place, with the warm, pungent air full of the shrill voices of "sooty imps of darkness"—the journalist's fanciful description of the teenage "car boys" who drove the teams of mules that pulled the carts from the coalface. The boys found the visitors' clumsiness amusing: above ground, they were adults and fine gentlefolk but down the mine, they were as helpless as fish gasping on a riverbank. The men's ordeal was only just beginning, for they still faced a long walk to the coalface. "Tall persons can realize the situation when we say that we walked what seemed to us several miles, through passageways which in most places were not more than four feet high, with our bodies at an angle of 120°," recounted the "pencil pusher." When they reached the coalface, their backs had "almost given out from stooping."[19]

The following year, a party of thirty-two men toured "Oatmeal King" Schumacher's Wadsworth mine. When they returned to the surface, they were "all bespattered with mud..." [with] "wet feet, their hats stove in," and, partly scalped "by the low roofs of the tunnels."[20] Pausing from their work, the miners first demanded money for beer but then took pity on the party and proposed to take up a collection for them instead. Bruised and begrimed, the visitors made haste to the sunlight, leaving the miners deep below to finish their shifts. Perhaps they had acquired a new respect for the miners, for one observed:

> People who live above ground have no idea of the amount of toil and labor which these men accomplish daily. Seated on the wet rock the miner strikes, strikes, strikes the whole day, extracting the coal from its natural bed and without any company to relieve the monotony of his work by conversation.[21]

The hot darkness, the damp, and the claustrophobic confines that had startled the visitors were the stuff of everyday life for the miners. In winter, they seldom saw the sun. Long periods spent underground could lead to miner's nystagmus, the symptoms of which included the involuntary oscillation of the eyeballs, headaches, insomnia, spinal disorders, tremors, photophobia, and depression.

Mining has always been a hard, dirty, and dangerous occupation.[22] Miners never knew when they left for work whether they would come home alive. Death lurked from cave-ins, falls from heights, suffocation, and gas poisoning. Explosives, widely used in mines, were a hazard in themselves no matter how skilled the shot firers. If pumps failed, the miners might drown. Buildups of firedamp or methane gas often led to fires, and the danger of coal dust explosions was omnipresent. Carbon monoxide, which was colorless and odorless, was a silent hazard. The work itself, with constant contortion in confined spaces, was relentlessly hard on the human frame. Coalminers were easily recognizable from the blue-black scars on their faces, hands, and bodies. Their blackened hands were thickly callused, with the nails torn away to regrow like horn. Cuts and bruises were the daily price of their labor, and they suffered from "beat knee" and painful swellings on their elbows from constantly lying or kneeling on hard and often wet rock. Mining left men old and often crippled before their time—or worse, prematurely dead.

From the 1880s, mines were increasingly mechanized, and while this lightened the work, it added new dangers. Men—and unwary child trapper boys—could be struck by runaway coal cars, crushed by locomotives or frightened horses, or pulled into fast-moving conveyors. Temperature normally increases by about 1° Fahrenheit per seventy feet of depth, or 25° Celsius per kilometer of depth into the earth and the high temperatures in mines that burrowed thousands of feet underground could cause fatigue, cramps, chronic skin conditions, and fatal heat stroke. Rats infested the pits, and their urine could spread Weil's disease or infective jaundice.

Mines are noisy places; the noise increased with mechanization. Exposure to drilling, blasting, cutting, and the noise made by ventilators, conveyors, and other machinery often caused hearing loss. The introduction of electric lights, pumps, motors, and other such equipment led to the risk of electrocution, especially from the proximity of cables to water. Most insidious of all was pneumoconiosis, or black lung, in which coal dust set hard as cement in the miner's lungs and left the man gasping for breath. Chronic pulmonary obstructive disease increased the strain on the heart and often led to an early death.[23]

Akron's miners faced all of these perils. In 1871, there had been a spate of deaths in the Middlebury mineshaft.[24] That year, miners in Alexander Brewster's mine struck over poor safety, and although the management installed an improved ventilation system, another fire broke out the following year.[25] One of the worst pits at this time was the Atwater mine, twenty-three miles east of Akron just over the Portage County line. In early July 1871, a massive explosion killed seven miners in that pit, and another fire broke out shortly afterwards.[26] On the Fourth of July the following year, a new Atwater mine caught fire, killing ten miners. Those who were not burned to death perished of suffocation when the fire sucked all the oxygen from the mine. The oldest among the victims was a thirty-five-year-old Welsh miner called Evans who had just arrived in America. Mr. Evans had left his wife and seven children behind in Wales, intending to bring them to America as soon as he could pay for their passage. The youngest victim was Georgie Hofford, a nine-year-old trapper boy who opened and closed doors for coal cars in the mine, twelve hours a day.[27]

Tragedies such as this ensured that abolition of child labor was a central aim of the union. Forty-four years after Georgie Hofford suffocated to death, the US Congress passed the Keating-Owen Act to restrict (but not prohibit) child labor. The Act banned the transport of coal or ore across state lines from mines that employed children under the age of sixteen. Two years later, the US Supreme Court declared the act unconstitutional over the dissent of Judge Oliver Wendell Holmes. There had been a number of attempts at state level in Ohio to restrict child labor. One of these was the Haley Act, passed by the state legislature in 1889 over the employers' vociferous protests. To its credit, the Republican *Daily Beacon* editorialized in favor of the bill, which appears to have been moderately successful in restricting the employment of children under the age of fourteen years.[28] By 1903, Akron's deputy inspector of workshops and factories claimed that there was no child labor in the city.[29] Yet nine years later the Socialist orator Ella Reeves Blair declared at the Akron Grand Opera House that "[w]e have tried to have .... [child labor] abolished by trying to have bills passed in our legislatures regulating it, but all have failed."[30] It was not until 1938 that real progress was made to stamp out child labor in America.[31]

America's miners suffered grievously in the new industrial age, but they never passively accepted their fate. Their songs of struggle and protest still stir hearts today and became a byword for industrial militancy. In 1920, desperate coalminers in West Virginia came the closest American workers have ever come to armed insurrection.[32] While the Ohio miners never went that far, their communities fought bitter struggles against hard-fisted employers. From the mine-owners' point of view, heavy capital investment and small profit margins gave them little choice but to keep wages low if they were to make a profit in a highly competitive industry.

The miners could seem a clannish and insular lot. They worked and lived together in villages close to the mines. The utter strangeness and danger of their work marked them from those who spent their days above ground. Miners depended on each other for their safety and their lives. Specialist mining jargon peppered their speech, and many late nineteenth-century American miners spoke with the accents and tongues of the British Isles. Many "spoke Welsh in the mines, on the streets, in the homes and in the churches" as retired miner Levi Morgan recalled as a ninety-two-year-old at East Akron in 1931. Morgan had arrived in the US from Wales in 1863, and upon reaching Akron, walked five miles through the mud to begin work at Brewster's new mine at Middlebury.[33] Tallmadge was Little Wales, with many of its Welsh inhabitants unable to speak English.

Judy Anne Davis scrutinized the census figures of 1850, 1860, and 1870 and concluded "the vast majority of those who gave 'miner' or 'digger' as their occupation had been born in the United Kingdom" and that most of these were Welsh. She writes of "a whole community of Welshmen who not only labored in the mines but also built churches, held festivals, opened businesses. Fought in wars, and generally embraced their new home."[34] Likewise, Thomastown, long since subsumed into South Akron, was a Welsh mining village during the 1880s. Fifty-eight percent of the village's population were born in Wales, and a further twenty percent had Welsh-born parents or a Welsh spouse.[35] Eisteddfods were more popular than the national fad of "jubilee singing" on the local coalfields at the time.

The common danger of miners' work forged camaraderie, solidarity, and comradeship: a collectivist practical philosophy that was sharply at variance with the dogmas of American individualism. Small wonder that miners built one of America's first industrial unions at a time when craft unionism was the norm. The United Mine Workers enrolled not just miners and laborers, but all except bosses and managers who worked in the mines, including machinists, firemen, blacksmiths, electricians, engine drivers, and carpenters. Had they not done so, the rapacious coal owners would have taken advantage of the disunity to drive down the wages of all mineworkers regardless of occupation. It is therefore puzzling why William Green, the Mineworkers' official, should have been such a resolute supporter of craft unionism after he took over as AFL President after the death of Samuel Gompers. One wonders the same about mineworkers' official John L. Lewis, who attempted to split the Akron rubber workers during the big strike of 1913.

Boryczka and Cary recognize that the American "gospel of success" and individualism did hold some appeal and that solidarity was undercut to some degree by ethnic animosities and economic insecurity. There were clashes between native born and immigrant, white and Black, Protestant and Catholic, Irish and English.[36] In 1874, there were disturbances on the Ohio coalfields over the hiring of Black miners.[37] The national union, however, enrolled all mineworkers, regardless of color or creed, and would have no truck with racism.[38] Class solidarity usually prevailed, and most miners lived by a strict code that included not working for less than the going rate, not scabbing, and solidarity with workmates and their families in accidents, economic downturns, and strikes.[39] By 1870, upwards of one-third of Ohio's coalminers were British-born, and they brought with them their traditions of militant class struggle unionism.[40]

If the immigrants believed they would get a fairer deal in America than in hidebound, class-ridden Britain, they were soon disillusioned. In the fall of 1870, fifty British miners arrived at the strikebound Wadsworth mine fifteen miles west of Akron. Labor recruiters in New York had engaged them to work in the mine, but when the newcomers realized they would have to scab on strikers, they refused to work, despite the hardship this entailed. A journalist reported,

> They had lain in the open air two nights and some of them just over from England were suffering already from fever and ague.... They know nothing of the laws, but wanted to get back to New York. They would not go to work for eighty cents per ton and thus take bread from the mouths of the strikers who had told them their families were starving.

Later, penniless, sick, and homeless in a strange land, they threatened to hang the coal company officials unless they paid their fares back to New York. It seems they were successful.[41] Such incidents were common. Mine owners often made false promises to lure foreign miners, particularly after 1870 when the coalfields were strikebound for months at a time. That year, the Tallmadge coal owners George Steese and Alexander Brewster brought in what a journalist delicately called "replacements," and there were fierce battles when strikers picketed the loading chutes on the P&O canal.[42] In the same year, a Canton coal owner called Cohnert recruited fifty miners aboard an emigrant ship at the New York docks. He promised to pay them $1.00 a ton in his new mine. When they arrived on site, however, they discovered that the going rate was eighty cents a ton and that the owners had recently broken a strike for an extra twenty cents. The new men demanded the full $1.00 rate or, failing that, transportation back to New York. Cohnert refused, whereupon the miners threatened him with "summary vengeance." He escaped when the local mayor "quietened the matter," and a US marshal placed him in protective custody. It seems that the coal owner shipped the "troublemakers" back to New York.[43] Five years earlier, the National Guard quelled a riot following the arrival of nonunionists in the Massillon mines and the arrests of a number of strike leaders.[44]

The 1870s were years of bitter struggle on the coalfields of America. The booming economy slowed and then went into the long wave of recession that was to linger on and off until the late 1890s. Dwindling prices caused numerous attempts to cut wages, which were already at subsistence levels. In May 1870, a general strike erupted on the coalfields of the Akron area, with all mines except that of Alexander Brewster closed. Miners picketed "the mouth of every pit with starving families yet refusing to work," noted a reporter, and anyone who tried to push through faced "stern and riotous opposition."[45] In August, a miner called William Forrest was arrested on charges of threatening Brewster's life after he imposed a wage cut. A further seventeen men and women, including Forrest's wife, were also arrested.[46] The miners reserved a particular hatred for Brewster, a former carpenter, whom they regarded as a class traitor.[47] Sheriff Curtiss issued a proclamation on law and order in Summit County and local notables urged the unemployed to take the miners' jobs.[48] Around the same time, the Tallmadge mine owners began to evict strikers' families from company-owned housing.[49]

Further south in Massillon and Canal Fulton, between ten and a dozen mines were idle for "a year or more" according to the local press.[50] Nothing was resolved, for a savage struggle broke out in 1876 when miners downed tools in support of a claim for $1.75 a ton. The Akron City Guard camped near the mines in an effort to quash unrest. It was an unequal struggle, with the miners' families reduced to a diet of potatoes as the strike dragged on. In desperation, some of them turned to sabotage, and four dozen miners were charged with mine burning—an act the *Summit Daily Beacon* attributed to the influence of the Molly Maguires, a militant, semi-clandestine Pennsylvania coalminers' union led by Irish immigrants.[51] Anthony Moran, whom the *Beacon* described as "the notorious ringleader," was convicted of shooting and wounding a scab called Reinhardt Keller during the strike.[52] Respectable opinion clamored for a stiff sentence, but Judge Frease sentenced him to two years.[53] Moran and ten comrades had been arrested "on a general charge of riot." "Mansfield Blues" had dragged them from their beds at dawn and lodged them in the Canton jail. During the raids, a striker named Abram Williams died after being shot in the abdomen while allegedly resisting arrest.[54] Discontent simmered, and in the winter of the following year, the miners at Brewster's again walked off the job after a union member's pay was docked, although some old miners apparently remained at work.[55] Strikes continued and reached crisis point in 1876, when there was an explosion of industrial action across the entire Ohio coalfield.[56] In early January of the following year, following the execution of a number of Molly Maguires in Pennsylvania, the *Daily Beacon* attacked the militant union organization as "a bloodthirsty order" that had written "a dark and disgraceful page in the history of our country."[57] Jim

McCartan's Irish immigrant father, who worked in the Slabtown mines, had been a Molly Maguire, which indicates that the organization had roots in Ohio.[58] Anthony Moran, too, was probably a Maguire.

If the judicial murders of the Molly Maguires were meant as a warning, they failed. Strikes raged across the Ohio coalfields until well into the following century. In the summer of 1880, many mines in the Akron district were idle; there were bitter clashes when scabs entered the mines, and troops were called in to protect them from angry picketers.[59] In July, Judge Seward ordered the striking Middlebury miners and their families to vacate their company-owned houses, with two weeks' notice to find alternative accommodation.[60] Evictions from tarpaper shacks and barracks were a common occurrence on the coalfields. A few days later, the Middlebury miners returned to work, only to strike again less than two weeks later when the company tried to fire a checkweighman. Many mines paid on a piecework basis, and the checkweighman made sure that the miners were paid correct weight, so it was a serious provocation. Although attempts by employers to cut pay were often the cause of strikes—or they were staged in support of demands for pay increases, such as in the Summit Mine strike for a twenty-five-cent raise in 1890[61]—a recurring grievance was payment in company scrip, which was redeemable only in company stores for exorbitantly priced goods. This was the case in 1896–97 when strikes dragged on for so long across the bituminous coalfields that mining families faced hunger and even famine.[62] A report noted that the employers had constantly reduced wages for several years before the strike and that this had already brought the miners and their families to the verge of starvation.[63] Strikes over payment in scrip continued into 1898 and beyond.[64]

The Canton miner John Miller summed up the causes of the coal strikes, and the methods used by the bosses and local authorities to suppress them. While horses were treated better than miners, the mine owners were "rolling in riches and splendor." Miller was not a natural radical, but he believed that strike action was inevitable because as the Bible stated, "oppression maketh a wise man mad." Confronted with intransigent employers, the miners had no choice but to resist, but time after time, a sad story repeated across the coalfields. The bosses brought in scabs to render strikes ineffectual and "force.... [the miners] to a starved compliance." Moreover, Miller complained, the State authorities never inquired into the reasons for the unrest, but "they send out the military, establish martial law; [so] no wonder .... [the miners] become lawless when their grievances are ignored, and their rights trampled on."[65]

Today there is little to indicate that Akron was once a great coalmining center, and there can be few retired coalminers still living in the city or its surrounds. Summit County's first mine, at Tallmadge, closed in 1887 because of dwindling reserves and stiff competition, but reopened briefly as a nonunion business during big strikes in 1922.[66] The geologist Ann Harris has counted thirty-two abandoned mines in Summit County,[67] and a journalist claimed seventy-one and counted many hundreds more in nearby Tuscarawas and Stark counties.[68] Yet Akron could not have thrived without the miners. As Orwell observed, "[I]n the metabolism of the Western world the coal-miner is second in importance only to the man who ploughs the soil. He is a sort of caryatid upon whose shoulders nearly everything that is not grimy is supported."[69]

The human cost aside, there was also another—ecological—downside to the industry. Until well into the twentieth century, coal-smoke blackouts rendered Akron "gloomier than Pittsburgh."[70] A smoke abatement campaign led to a sixty-two percent decrease in air pollution between 1921 and 1928, but the onset of the Great Depression saw people switch from gas-fired home furnaces to cheap soft coal and the problem flared again.[71] Just after the end of the Second World War, a journalist quipped, "Akron saw the sun this afternoon—and liked it." Earlier in the day (as was often the case) traffic had been slowed, public transport delayed, airplanes grounded, and no school buses were in operation. Thousands were late for work or school as a result.[72] The local Chamber of Commerce estimated that air pollution cost Akron two million dollars a year in damage to merchandise and cleaning bills for houses, but nothing was done because of the perception that "where there's smoke there's prosperity"; a variation on the Yorkshire adage of "where there's muck, there's money."

However, while the belching smokestacks of the city's factories were partly to blame, another culprit was the coal used for domestic heating.[73] The days of King Coal were ending, however. Oil, gas, and electricity would soon drive him from his throne and replace coal as the direct source of energy for domestic and industrial purposes. The confident prediction by a Kent State Masters' student in 1950 that coal would continue to be important for the next thirty to forty years was to prove false. Even as he wrote, many local "snowbird" mines were closing. The closures of these marginal enterprises, which produced very low-grade coal at very low prices with nonunion labor,[74] were soon followed by shutdowns of the larger, unionized mines. In any case, the coal was running out, and the producing area was moving south from Akron.[75] Indeed, a number of key coalfields had closed some years earlier. Coal mining had started in 1863 at Wadsworth, for example, but the industry there slowly declined after the 1880s. In 1890, most of the mines closed and threw hundreds of men out of work. A small number of mines limped on until the 1930s.[76] What was true of Wadsworth was true of the Akron district as a whole. By the 1960s, the industry had died, and the miners had retired or moved elsewhere. A whole way of life had vanished. It had been a relentlessly hard life. The coalminers were at the raw end of industrial capitalism, having to fight for every last dime from their employers. Their working lives bore out Marx and Engels' observation that "as the repulsiveness of the work increases, the wage decreases."[77]

5.

Open Shop Town

By the early twentieth century, Akron had become a sprawling industrial metropolis of over two hundred thousand people and was dominated by the rubber industry. Goodrich employed three thousand workers in 1900, making it around one-third the size of the nation's largest firms.[1] The Akron rubber industry surfed a colossal wave of production and profit; by the end of the Great War, the Big Three rubber corporations were among the world's first multinational corporations. By 1909, Akron was manufacturing two-thirds of the nation's tires and employing seven thousand workers.[2] The *India Rubber Journal* dubbed Akron—home to thirteen rubber companies with a total investment of over four million pounds—"the rubber capital of the world." In 1911, between twenty-two thousand and twenty-five thousand people were working in the rubber mills and half of the city's population was dependent on the industry.[3] Akron had become, famously, "Rubber's Home Town."[4] The industry benefited from the breakneck expansion of the American automobile industry, which was turning out millions of cheap motorcars. They needed tires, and Akron was keen to provide them. Expansion was chaotic and came at unprecedented speed—it was capitalism on steroids. In 1903, Goodyear's capitalization stood at $100,000 and by 1913, it had grown to $10 million. Firestone's capitalization rose from $500,000 in 1910 to $4 million in 1912, making a thirty percent profit on that latter sum.[5] Outsiders, many of them Southerners, flocked to Akron to seek work in the rubber mills. John House left rural Georgia because "I had watched my father work harder [on the small family farm] than any man should have to make a decent living."[6] The mills promised steady work and good wages despite the volatile labor market of the time.[7]

However, while the wages must have seemed high to Southerners, other American mass production industries paid better money. As Marx and Engels had foreseen as early as 1848, it was a situation in which "labourers, who must sell themselves piecemeal, are a commodity, like every other article of commerce, and are consequently exposed to all the vicissitudes of competition, to all the fluctuations of the market."[8] [British spelling in the original]. On the eve of the First World War, worker discontent was building up like steam in a blocked boiler. Gummers joked that "You don't have to die to get to hell. Just come to Akron, Ohio, and get a pass to enter any one of the many rubber shops."[9] The rubber firms were among the most ruthlessly anti-union employers in the country and were able to block effective union organization for many years after the industry arrived in town. If American working-class organization lagged behind the rest of the industrialized world, this sheer ruthlessness cannot be ignored.

In 1902, the Goodrich pay scale ranged from sixteen to twenty cents an hour for millmen, and from fifteen to sixteen-and-a-half cents an hour for calendar men.[10] Junior males and women of all ages worked for much less. When future union leader Sherman H. Dalrymple started at Goodrich as a child laborer in 1903, he was paid ten cents an hour, or $6.00 for a sixty-hour week.[11] Wage levels averaged twenty percent less than those paid in northeastern factories. Single men had a shortfall of $37.00 per year.[12] By 1909, rubber workers' average annual earnings of $562 trailed the $613 for Detroit autoworkers, $614 for Pittsburgh ironworkers, and $627 for operatives in the Cleveland machine shops.[13] Karl Grismer argues that much of the industrial unrest before the First World War resulted from rising but unmet expectations created by a new consumer goods boom. To buy such goods, workers needed higher wages than rubber bosses were prepared to pay,[14] and rubber workers' wages fell before the outbreak of the war. Whereas adult male gummers "could

[once] make $3.50 to $7.00 a day," by 1913 "skilled workers ... [were] forced to work ten hours at high speed in order to make from $2.25 to $2.50 a day." This was due to new laborsaving machinery and the relentless speed-up of production. Employment was often seasonal, which added to the gummers' grievances.[15] House's recollections bear this out. Two weeks after starting at Goodrich, he and 50 others were laid off. He was rehired two months later, worked for two weeks, was laid off again, and then rehired ten days later.[16]

A further cause for discontent was relentless regimentation and surveillance. Marx and Engels could have been describing the Akron rubber mills when they wrote:

> Modern Industry has converted the little workshop of the patriarchal master into the great factory of the industrial capitalist. Masses of labourers, crowded into the factory, are organised like soldiers. As privates of the industrial army they are placed under the command of a perfect hierarchy of officers and sergeants. Not only are they slaves of the bourgeois class, and of the bourgeois State; they are daily and hourly enslaved by the machine, by the overlooker, and, above all, by the individual bourgeois manufacturer himself.[17] [British spelling in the original].

In 1913, over one hundred plant supervisors oversaw the Firestone factory,[18] and spies were omnipresent. The immigrants and farm boys and girls who arrived in Akron hoping for steady work with decent pay and conditions soon faced disillusionment. Half a century later, Sherman Dalrymple recalled the foremen's tyranny:

> We worked 10 hours a day, 6 days a week. Sometimes the foreman would come around on Saturday without any previous notice and tell us to work Sunday—and of course no overtime pay. If you refused you would get reprimanded or laid off or maybe even fired. The foreman always had his way and the worker didn't have a chance.[19]

There were fines for trivial mistakes; punishments were arbitrary and sometimes collective. Mike Flynn, the superintendent of the tire department at Diamond Rubber, once fired fifty men because "someone threw a small piece of rubber out a window."[20] The tragic case of Daniel Hirschberger highlights the despotic regime at Goodyear. When asked to operate an unfamiliar calendar machine, he begged the foreman to wait until he was properly trained. The foreman ordered him to do the job or be fired. Two hours later, Hirschberger's arm was crushed in the machine's massive rollers. Goodyear awarded him $75 in damages[21] and promised him a job for life at a salary $75 a month if he would sign a paper absolving them of blame. He signed, but they fired him anyway, and he was lucky to find low-paid work as an elevator man at Firestone.[22]

Women workers had extra reason for dissatisfaction. House tells of "deliberate discrimination against female employees" and gives the example of a woman being paid ten cents an hour less than he was, despite her greater proficiency at the same job.[23] The entrenched sexual division of labor excluded women from higher paying "male" jobs, so their average pay was half that of men. Nettie and Jennie Lee quit their jobs on the eve of the big strike in 1913 because of dissatisfaction with their pay. The sisters were on piecework at Goodrich, and each sometimes earned as little as thirty-eight cents a day. Jennie had never made more than $10 for two week's work, and sometimes she made as little as $7 for the same time.[24] Eighteen-year-old Annie Fejtko worked in Department 17-B, Goodrich's rubber bulb branch. On piecework, she took home between $4 and $4.50 for a sixty-hour week. Her weekly board bill was $3, which left $1 to $1.50 for all expenses, including clothing, medicines, and leisure. "I can't save anything and I haven't seen my papa or mamma or the little brothers and sisters since I came here," she said. The last day Annie worked before the big 1913 strike, she made seventy-five cents and often made less. Once she had made two dollars but had gone home that evening with blistered hands from wielding scissors all day cutting packing paper for the bulbs. She also said that the "girls" in her department received nothing for down time, but had to remain on the job for the full shift.[25] Without a union to protect them, adult women rubber workers in Akron earned a maximum of ten cents an hour for a ten-hour day, six-day week: the same rate as child laborers. At the time, many unmarried women had to pay up to four dollars a week for room and board: around two-thirds of their weekly income exclusive of overtime.

Mary Riley, an eighteen-year-old Goodyear employee, testified at a State Senate enquiry to a culture of sexual harassment in the plant. "A foreman frequently turned out the lights in the room," she said, "and would sit on the tables with the girls in the dark, hugging and kissing them .... He would stuff paper down our necks and then try to take it out again."[26] Working-women had few champions during this period. The Knights of Labor had supported the principle of equal pay, but AFL leader Samuel Gompers, although on record as in favor of female suffrage,[27] believed women's place was in the home.[28] Eugene Debs' Akron comrade Marguerite Prevey resigned her position as Socialist Party national women's organizer after a few months because of lack of cooperation from the party locals.[29] Formally, the Socialists had a more progressive policy for women than any other party, but many of its leaders and members were not interested in campaigning for women's equality.[30] In February 1906, Prevey delivered a powerful address on prostitution. There were, she claimed, twenty thousand prostitutes in the city of Cleveland, many of them unable to make a living any other way. "Factory girls," she pointed out, averaged thirty-eight cents a week less than they can live on,[31] but one wonders how many male party members were listening.

Discontent often boiled over into wildcat strikes, but more usually took the form of high labor turnover rates and absenteeism, which affected twenty percent of the Firestone workforce.[32] On one day in 1912, Goodyear hired 1,405 new workers but lost 461, and by 1913, Firestone was hemorrhaging 113 workers a day.[33] It cost "at least $25 to break in a new man,"[34] so the companies' losses were considerable. Despite unsatisfactory pay and conditions, the industry was notoriously difficult to unionize. According to a left wing journalist, "every applicant for a job was investigated and catechized in order to make sure he came clean of any taint of unionism."[35] The Knights of Labor had failed to organize rubber workers in Akron and the North East as far back as 1889. In 1899, twenty-five women walked out at Goodyear; there was another strike by men and women at the smaller India Rubber Company mill in Akron.[36] In 1900, a brief sit-down strike protested a cut in piecework rates at Goodyear but was unsuccessful.[37] Workers in Goodyear's solid tire department downed tools when the company demanded that they fill in time cards with personal details, but the company soon replaced them.[38] According to House, the Allied Metal Mechanics' union also made an unsuccessful effort to unionize the mills around the turn of the century.[39]

Two years later, the Amalgamated Rubber Workers' of America (ARWA), chartered an Akron local. It organized five hundred workers at Goodyear and Diamond Rubber but suffered a big reversal when burglars stole its records. All union members were fired shortly afterwards, but the police refused to investigate, thus demonstrating their contempt for the law when it interfered with the prerogatives of Capital.[40] In September 1902, the *Beacon Journal* reported a "stormy" meeting of ARWA Local 147. The local had experienced a modest influx of gummers angered by the firing and blacklisting of unionists. President John Boyle and others gave "fiery speeches" slamming the low wages paid in the industry. "We will shut up those places tight," declared one gummer, who saw the AFL's three million-strong membership as a guarantee of solidarity.[41]

On paper, the AFL was a formidable force, but in practice it favored class collaboration even in the face of ferocious repression or chicanery by the employers. Thus, James J. Mahoney, President of Akron's Central Labor Union (CLU), entered the Local 147 hall and proceeded to "throw cold water on everything." His message was to stay calm and leave it to the CLU to settle the dispute "peaceably" without recourse to strike action.[42] ARWA President Mulholland visited Akron a few days later and assured the *Beacon* that "we are not a striking organization, we do not intend to cause any trouble at all." Nor, he added, was the union demanding higher wages. Nevertheless, he assured Local 147 members that a settlement was at hand.[43] Incredibly, Mr. Mulholland declared a self-limiting ordinance: "we have to be careful not to organize too fast and take in too many men."[44] After this, matters descended to low farce. Although Mahoney claimed to have reached a settlement with the employers, with the fired unionists allegedly "back at their old jobs without any discrimination," the companies denied making any deal and refused to reinstate the men. Indeed, Goodrich plant superintendent E. C. Shaw "emphatically denied" even meeting with the union.[45]

Not surprisingly, Local 147 did not prosper. The ARWA held a national convention in the Akron Carpenters' Hall the following year,[46] but Local 147 was dead, and it seems that no local gummers attended the convention. Mahoney, a former bricklayer, became a pillar of the local Republican Party, and the ARWA limped on with no more than two thousand members nationally.[47] By 1906, it had "disintegrated completely" in Akron,[48] helped on its way by the employers' decision to grant a ten percent wage increase without any union involvement.[49] Although the AFL had moderate success in organizing craft workers, this incursion into mass production industry was a disaster.

The union made a further brief foray into Akron in 1910–11, but it was again unsuccessful.[50] This time, it operated secretly for fear of spies, and recorded members by number as safeguard.[51] The CLU donated $150 for organizing expenses, and the union enrolled between four hundred and fifteen hundred members. Alas, according to the Socialist Party journalist Leslie H. Macey, the AFL organizer absconded with $1500 he had collected from the members.[52] Wildcat strikes broke out occasionally in Akron despite the fiasco, but they inevitably collapsed. Between fifty and three hundred tire builders at the Diamond Rubber Company went on strike in 1908, for instance, but scabs took their jobs.[53] The same thing happened in 1911 at Swinehart Rubber when the company slashed piecework rates for three-inch tires from 41 to 35 cents, and from 52½ to 43 cents on three-and-a half-inch tires.[54] Even talking union was enough to get gummers fired, as the mills were "honeycombed with labor spies," with "likely-looking workers ... offered $85 a month to serve as snoopers."[55] For a gummer earning perhaps $45 a month, this was tempting bait. Local 147 "slid quietly into oblivion" after infiltration by company spies reportedly made workers reluctant to mention the word union.[56] The gummers hated the snoopers, as was shown in May 1908, when William "Big Bill" Haywood, the charismatic socialist leader of the Western Miners' Federation, ridiculed them at an overflow meeting at the Gayety Theater in Downtown Akron. Haywood declared that "nothing that creeps or crawls is as mean or contemptible as a detective," adding that "they get so low they have to get a ladder to get into hell" and joking that "the souls of 40,000 detectives would get into the small end of nothing with a hole punched into it." Many people came up at the end of what a reporter called "his harangue" to shake his hand.[57] Words alone, however, could not move implacable employers.

One of the companies' most effective anti-union ploys was the deliberate creation of a "reserve army of labor" in the city. "Standing advertisements of 'Men Wanted' at Akron were kept in the newspapers of neighboring cities," a Socialist journalist noted and the *Beacon Journal* corroborated the claim.[58] Even in early 1914, when the mills were laying off thousands of workers, they continued to advertise for labor outside of Akron. A CLU delegate told the press that he had spoken with a man from West Virginia who had arrived in response to the advertisements with $4 to his name and a wife and two children at home to support. The CLU inserted counter-advertisements in Southern newspapers,[59] but the influx continued unabated. When eighteen-year-old John House arrived from the South in 1922, he saw lines of job seekers stretching for a whole city block from the gates of the Goodrich.[60]

In the early days, many of the rubber workers were highly skilled and could make good wages. Tire builders had been the aristocrats among production workers, proud of their strength and skill. Working ten hours a day, they could make between six and nine medium-sized tires for pay of thirty to thirty-five cents an hour. Mechanization, however, turned them into semi-skilled machine operators who could produce between fifty and 110 tires a day, and despite the vast increase in productivity, they suffered pay cuts and large redundancies.[61] Workshop-style production could not meet the huge demand for tires and other rubber goods. After 1900, Paul Litchfield began to reorganize the Goodyear plant along Fordist mass production lines, and this forced the company's rivals to follow suit or perish. Fordist principles demanded standardized products. Nothing, if possible, was to be hand-made: everything was machine-made in long production runs on assembly lines staffed with semi-skilled or unskilled workers. Moreover, shiftwork kept the factories running twenty-four hours a day, seven days a week.

In 1909, Goodyear's master mechanic, William State, built a tire-making machine capable of producing high quality, standardized tires, with a five hundred to six hundred percent increase in output over the old hand-made products.[62] This spurred competition between the manufacturers, all of whom had to invest in the new technology. On

September 1, 1912, Firestone also began production of machine-built tires. The tires were still finished by hand, but the new classification of tire finisher received only one-third of the previous pay for hand tire makers.[63] New stock-cutting machines did the work of ten men and the beading machine, invented in 1909, wiped out the jobs of hundreds of hand bead workers. The new machines allowed Diamond Rubber to slash its tire building staff from 510 to 112.[64] Mechanization tended to make work lighter, but it intensified work tempos. The workforce was radically deskilled and wage rates slashed.[65] Tire builders who once averaged $4.20 a day saw their earnings cut to $2.70 and had to work much faster for it.[66]

In 1911, the American engineer Frederick Winslow Taylor published an influential book expounding the principles of what he called "scientific management."[67] The rubber companies seized on his methods. In the Taylorist system, wages were performance-based, as in existing piecework schemes, but the new system rested on the detailed "scientific" division of labor. Time and motion studies allocated a specified time for each task (often down to fractions of a second), tools and equipment were simplified and standardized, and tasks were broken down into smaller and smaller units. The workers performed the same task repeatedly so that they could do it with almost machine-like speed and efficiency. Taylor's aim was maximum production in the shortest time with the minimum number of employees. His professed aim was to reconcile capital and labor and eliminate any need for trade unions. He even claimed endlessly—and falsely—that "there has never been a strike of men working under scientific management,"[68] and his famous example of the prodigious output of a pig iron handler named Schmidt was more fiction than fact.[69] He also alleged without evidence that scientific management allowed a general shortening of hours.

Taylor was a former machinist, but he never displayed any solidarity with the workers. Despite his claim that his methods aimed "to secure maximum prosperity for the employer, coupled with maximum prosperity for the employee,"[70] critics contended that scientific management was an inhuman system, the apotheosis of the deskilling that had begun with the Industrial Revolution. Taylorism viewed workers as intelligent apes, and wherever implemented, it led to an unbearable and degrading pace of work in which workers performed mindless tasks ad infinitum. To the workers, it was the hated speed-up. In 1914, Lenin gave an example of the time and motion studies and their effects:

> An electric lamp was attached to a worker's arm, the worker's movements were photographed and the movements of the lamp studied. Certain movements were found to be to "superfluous" and the worker was made to avoid them, i.e., to work more intensively, without losing a second for rest....

In another example, after a few days a mechanic was able to perform "the work of assembling the given type of machine in *one-fourth* of the time it had taken before!" This was, Lenin conceded, "an enormous gain in labour productivity," but

> The worker's pay is not increased fourfold, but only half as much again, at the very most, and *only for a short period* at that. As soon as the workers get used to the new system their pay is cut to the former level. The capitalist obtains an enormous profit, but the workers toil four times as hard as before and wear down their nerves and muscles four times as fast as before.[71] [Emphasis and British spelling in the original.]

The Akron rubber companies were quick to embrace Taylorism. Men with stopwatches and slide rules appeared in the factories, timing every movement and making runic calculations. The workers complained that the experts based time allocations on the performance of the youngest and strongest workers, creating a "rawhide" system that pitted worker against worker. Previously, tire builders had been on piecework, but they had informal agreements among themselves to limit individual production.[72] They knew that working to the limit of endurance could only lead to accidents, burnout, and early death. Firestone workers nicknamed a stopwatch man called Holmes "Sherlock," but he had the last laugh. After months of prowling around the mill, he disappeared, and gradually the men forgot about him. Sherlock, however, was writing his report on eliminating inefficiencies and bottlenecks, and speeding up the work. Pacesetters appeared by the machines—fit, strong, well-paid young men who set production norms as high as they could make them. The companies introduced a new piecework wage scale, under which "the men would have had to travel at the speed of the pacesetters to make $3 to $3.50 a day." For most them, however, "$2.50 became the limit permitted by their skill and endurance."[73] This was, as was planned, a wage cut, and without a strong union there was nothing the workers could do about it. Strikes would see scabs brought in, and the old tactic of resentful workers—the go-slow—was counterproductive.

Even if the workers could not meet the production norms set by the pacesetters, the work was vastly speeded up, and there were big job losses and wage cuts. Tire curers who had once received five dollars for five tires now had to produce fifty for the same sum. The female employees in the hot water bag and rubber goods departments were offered a temporary bonus if they could glue a large quota of bags. The vastly increased number of bags was then set as the basis for piecework rates, and the bonus was not renewed. In 1913, Leslie Macey reported time checks showing that women in the bag department were getting as little as forty-five cents a day—equivalent in purchasing power to about $11.50 today.[74] This sweated labor system burned out workers by an early age. Goodyear President Paul Litchfield later privately admitted as much when he agreed that the new techniques allowed young workers "to command earnings equal to or greater than their elders." Moreover,

> A situation has been reached where a man in the factory reaches the peak of his earning power at a much earlier period of life than formerly. His usefulness on this kind of work starts to diminish at a much earlier age, thus making it more difficult for those who have passed the prime of life.[75]

Akron's housing crisis was a further cause of workers' discontent. Much of their pay disappeared into the pockets of rapacious landlords, who rented out substandard houses for exorbitant rents. Owning their own homes was for most gummers an impossible dream. Diamond Rubber worker Leonard Gowin made bricks on wasteland at Barberton to build a modest family home but with his dwindling paycheck, finishing it seemed an impossible dream.[76] An unsigned opinion piece in the *Beacon Journal* confirmed what the gummers already knew—"low wages prevent men from building homes."[77]

For many rubber workers, the speed-up made the already poor working conditions intolerable. They were already working for low to moderate wages in an unsafe environment. Depending on occupation and task, working in the rubber mills could amount to a slow death sentence. White male Americans born in 1890 had an average life expectancy of 42.5 years and white females 44.5 years,[78] but for factory workers it was well below forty years. According to the *Gale Encyclopedia of US Economic History,* working conditions in American factories were "considerably more dangerous than in Europe. This, the *Encyclopedia* ådds, "was largely due to the American system of manufactures, a method of mass-producing goods that involved a semiskilled labor force operating large machines that were often poorly maintained." Management ignored safety because "accidents were ultimately cheaper than slowdowns in production." By 1900, the United States had the highest worker fatality rate in the industrialized world.[79] Only the very strong and fit among the gummers could endure such conditions until middle age—if they lived that long. Health and safety conditions were poor and even deadly. Machinery lacked guards and override switches were absent, poorly located, or were badly maintained. Fume hoods and ventilation were virtually unheard of. Among the worst workplaces were "the hot, black, stinking environment called the mill room" and the enervating heat of the tire curing floor, dubbed with infernal overtones as the pit.[80] The hydrogen sulfide stench that wafted from the rubber mills was so strong that newcomers to the city searched their houses for dirty diapers.[81] John House, who did a stint in the Goodrich curing pit, recalls that his colleagues would often pass out from the heat.[82] Firestone admitted that only the very strongest could endure the pit, and then not for long.[83] In March 1913, a Goodrich pit worker wrote to the *Akron Press* to testify to the horrible conditions he had to endure:

> We work thirteen hours on the night shift and eleven hours on the day shift, with no noon hour to rest and eat. We are allowed to eat anytime between 10 a.m. and 2 p.m. if the work permits. If the work comes out so that we are not able to eat our lunch during those hours, we are not permitted to finish the meal at any time during the rest of the day. If we

> are caught eating we are liable to discharged, even though we might be idle at the time. We would not be eating on the company's time for we work piecework.

He went on to describe the work the pit men were required to do:

> The cores on which the tires are built are solid iron and a great many are so heavy they are all one man can lift. The cores are so hot that the men are compelled to wear two pairs of canvas gloves, one over the other in order to handle them at all.

The work took a terrible toll on the workers' health:

> Some men have been there two years; some have to be changed because they are worn out in eight months. Some come down, look at the men and say 'I don't want that job' and leave.... One night, I saw a "stripper" walk over to the night foreman and ask to be "fired." The foreman told the man that he knew just how he felt, and advised him to go back to work and try and stick it out until morning.

In conclusion, he wrote, "We are too tired to even get out of bed at all during the day; it wears a man down; he has very little time to spend with his family and his life is a cheerless, endless struggle."[84] Incredibly, Goodyear advertisements romanticized workers in the pit in words that adumbrated the Stakhanovite "heroes" of Stalinist Russia:

> Stripped the waist, his huge torso streaming with sweat, a workman swings the heavy iron core to an iron table, and wrenches off a tire which has just come steaming from the heater. His eye falls on the legend over his head ['Protect Our Good Name'] and he smiles.... His thoughts are—as they should be—chiefly of himself, of his little home, and of his family.[85]

What the pit workers thought of this was probably unprintable.

In 1913, a female rubber worker called Belle Myers complained of soapstone dust thick as flour on her clothing, the oppressively acidic atmosphere, and the lack of ventilation. Others told of how they routinely suffered headaches, dizziness, and nosebleeds.[86] The heat and chemicals used around the plant with scant ventilation also caused dermatitis, chronic rashes, and even unconsciousness. When workers complained of "rubber poisoning," the company doctors declared there was no such thing, but there could be little doubt about the injuriousness of the stinking solvents commonly used in the mills,[87] which included benzene, toluene, xylene, and naphtha. Experts attest that "any odor [of aromatics] means that concentrations are above safe levels . . . ." High concentrations of aromatic hydrocarbons can destroy bone marrow, induce leukemia and other cancers, and damage chromosomes and genetic material. Ominously, "people who work with aromatics gradually lose their ability to smell them."[88] In 2018, the International Agency for Research on Cancer published a compendium of the various cancers and other occupational diseases prevalent in the twenty-first century rubber industry.[89] The effects of exposure to the rotting radish reek of impure carbon bisulfide, which was used in the process of cold vulcanization, had been known for decades, but this made little difference to employers' attitudes.[90] The atmosphere in the Akron mills was thick with other toxins such as hydrogen sulfide (rotten egg gas) and sulfur dioxide—gases that irritate the eyes and upper respiratory tract and can cause pulmonary edema, a condition in which the victims drown in their own bodily fluids. Prolonged exposure to these gases can also cause brain damage. Another toxin widely used in the rubber factories was lead, which built up in the vital organs and could cause permanent damage to the central and peripheral nervous systems.[91]

Decades after medical journals described the effects of such toxins, including benzene, the Akron companies could not claim ignorance as an excuse. Despite this, as late as 1941, three claims for death and twenty-two for disability from benzene poisoning in the Ohio rubber factories were filed in the Ohio Industrial Committee.[92] The Firestone Company still denies using benzene at Akron, despite evidence that tire builders routinely used "benny" to add "tack" to rubber.[93] Most bizarre were the "blue men," workers whose skin turned blue from cyanosis[94] because of exposure to aniline dye, a chemical that was used to strengthen rubber products and speed up the vulcanization process.[95] After trials with unwitting human guinea pigs, company researchers found that although most workers could tolerate only limited exposure to the chemical without falling sick, a select few blue men were apparently immune.[96] Aniline dyes were in use in the Akron mills as late as 1930,[97] for despite the industry admitting that they were serious health hazard, they were much too profitable to discard.[98]

Years later, despite company safety campaigns and union scrutiny, the mills remained dangerous places. Goodyear's Frances Golliday told of how she rolled glue onto the seams of rubber barrage balloons during the Second World War, and how "You'd get drunk in there–from the fumes."[99] Dorothy Chevin, who worked in the company's dope room at the same time, wondered how long workers lived after exposure to the poisonous fumes.[100] Akron memoirist Joyce Dyer describes the Xylos recycling plant in South Akron, where her father worked for thirty-seven years as superintendent of Firestone's most dangerous factory. Not only was there a witch's brew of caustic chemicals at Xylos, but there were hog mills with rotating rolls, giant mechanical scissors, and tottering piles of tires stacked everywhere under a three-story digester plant that "belched ... sour air into South Akron twenty-four hours a day."[101] Roger Shuy, a linguistic researcher, recorded the difficulties he encountered talking with Firestone workers because of the high levels of noise inside the plant.[102] Rubber factories are also very hot places and continual exposure to high temperatures can be injurious to health. Working in the hot and ill-ventilated parts of the rubber factories, particularly during the summer months, must have been hellish, particularly as there was little understanding of the necessity to accustom workers gradually to high heat and to constantly rehydrate.[103] It is unlikely that the time and motion men factored in the need to pause to drink water.

A US Department of Labor pamphlet published in 1915 lists scores of poisons used in rubber mill operations. It makes for disturbing reading.[104] According to Dr. Alice Hamilton, the pioneer of industrial health in the US, it was possible to build safe plants, but the manufacturers were not interested, and were reluctant to let physicians into their factories.[105] The pamphlet concludes as follows:

> American rubber factories, even those that are in other

> respects admirably constructed and managed, are, almost without exception, lacking in the proper protection of workmen against poisons. In consequence, the industry is much more unhealthful in this country than it need be.[106]

Perhaps the final insult and injury was a report by the city chemist in July 1913 that Goodyear employees had been drinking diluted sewage drawn from a polluted company well.[107]

The prevalence of wildcat strikes worried the city's employers and other well-off folk—many of whom had lucrative rubber shares. When a predicted strike at the Diamond Rubber mill failed to eventuate before Christmas 1912, they must have breathed a collective sigh of relief.[108] Matters, however, were coming to a head. In early 1913, Akron's rubber industry slumped. Price wars erupted between the different companies, and as usual, the workers would have to pay for shareholders' shrunken dividends in reduced earnings and worsened conditions. The competition was ferocious. In 1913, Firestone undercut Goodyear's bid for the Ford Motor Company contract. It could only do so by intensifying the speed-up and cutting wages.[109] What this meant in human terms is illustrated by the testimony that Mary Riley, an eighteen-year-old former Goodyear employee, gave to a State senatorial inquiry into the city's rubber industry. The *Akron Press* edition of March 17, 1913, reported that Riley told the committee that she had worked ten hours a day for eight months in an "unlighted, unventilated attic, in which the benzine [sic] fumes were so strong that the girls frequently were sickened and were taken to the factory hospital. Other girls, she said, worked in the basement where the dirt and bugs were so thick that even the sweepers refused to stay in the place." Riley testified that she might make perhaps seventy-five cents for a ten-hour day working in that place. She elaborated thus:

> On piece work, my highest pay for two weeks was $20. My lowest was $6. On one day I made only four cents for half a day's work. I was not able to pay my board out of the wages and my father frequently had to help me out.[110]

Leonard Gowin, a forty-seven-year-old hard tire stuffer at Diamond Rubber, gave poignant testimony of how he could never make enough money to provide for his large family. In 1913, he was earning perhaps four dollars a day on piecework, but in winter, when there was a reduced demand for tires, his earnings could be as low as $2 to $2.50 a day, and he had to pay more for warm clothing and coal for his family. He could not keep his oldest girl at school, and she had to go to work in the mills. Times, however, had not always been so hard. "Back under the day work system," he said, "men made $4 to $7 for skilled labor.... But this piece work speeding has hit them all about like me." He admitted that his family was larger than most, but insisted that all of his fellow workers were suffering under the rawhide system.[111] To put the earlier day work wage in context, one might recall that Henry Ford famously introduced the $5 daily rate in his Detroit factory in 1913, and this was considered high pay. In comparison, Akron's rubber workers had suffered a huge fall in wages.[112]

On the eve of the First World War, frustrated with poor wages and conditions, fed up with layoffs and speed-ups, denied the right to bargain collectively, and goaded by high-handed supervisors, the "gummers" were ready to revolt. Akron was a notoriously anti-union town, but by the end of the first decade of the twentieth century, the AFL's Central Labor Union (CLU) was well established. Although it was craft-oriented in line with the Federation's rules, it had fallen under the influence of the Socialist Party.[113] Whereas Mahoney and his ilk had preached class collaboration, the CLU now gave priority to organizing the city's unorganized and unskilled workers, the bulk of whom were in the rubber factories. Akron's rubber industry was facing a perfect industrial storm. At the time, there were between twenty-two thousand and twenty-five thousand gummers in the city and they suffered intolerable conditions, not the least because of the Taylorist system. As the Italian Marxist Antonio Gramsci understood, "the fact that ... [the worker] gets no immediate satisfaction from his work and realizes they [the employers] are trying to reduce him to a trained gorilla, can lead him into a train of thought that is far from conformist." Unfortunately for the employer, Gramsci continues, "the worker remains a man."[114] [English spelling in the original.] Thus it was in Akron.

The final straw came in January 1913 when the $2,000,000 Ford Automobile Company tire contract came up for tender. Goodyear,

Buckeye, Goodrich-Diamond and Firestone all bid for the contract. Firestone's bid was accepted, and the company set about cutting wages by thirty-five percent in order to supply the product at a profit. The previous year, Firestone had paid a dividend of eight-hundred percent, and it was determined to squeeze the last drop of profit from its employees.[115] It is difficult to square the facts of the gummers' lives with the thesis that there was no socialism in America because living standards were so high. On February 10, 1913, twenty-five Firestone tire finishers walked off the job and set up picket lines outside the huge plant. Their immediate grievance was the cut to piecework rates.[116] Tire finishers on other shifts joined them, bringing their number to 150.[117] The first gust of wind in an industrial tempest had struck Rubber City. Meanwhile, political labor was growing in the city with the rise of the Socialist Party.

6.

The Heyday of Socialism in Akron

Akron's working class had a history of organizing independent labor parties dating back to the late 1830s. These parties sometimes started with great promise. The Union Labor Party, for example, began with fanfare in the city in 1887, only to disappear shortly afterwards. Its demise created a vacuum, which socialists of different hues were happy to try to fill. In this, they competed with the Democrats. Although the Democrats are a capitalist party, they have sought to portray themselves as friends of labor. Explicitly socialist ideas appeared in Akron and surrounding districts in the 1890s, a couple of decades after Marx published the first volume of *Capital*. The most important socialist current was the Socialist Party of America (SPA), which had been formed in 1901 from a fusion of the Social Democratic Party and a breakaway faction of the Socialist Labor Party. By the end of the first decade of the twentieth century, the SPA was growing rapidly in size and influence, including in Akron and other Midwest industrial cities. It appeared that Werner Sombart's pessimistic claim that there was no socialism in America was mistaken. The Akron Socialist local was also intimately involved with the gathering crisis in the city's rubber mills.

One of Akron's earliest explicitly socialist groups was the Commonwealth Club, which from 1894 met weekly in Kramer's Hall at 176 South Howard Street. Speakers such as the progressive Cleveland educator J. M. H. Frederick and his comrade Rousseau Hess addressed the club on questions of socialist theory.[1] According to a *Beacon* journalist, the "club seems to have sprung into popular favor among Akron workingmen, as the hall is filled to overflowing at each meeting." In January 1894, Frederick and Rousseau debated the Reverends Williard and Elliott on the question "What can the church do for bettering present social conditions?"[2] The fact that they spoke on behalf of the Akron Central Labor Union suggests that socialist ideas had taken root in the city's labor movement. The club folded, but five years later, local socialists met in the Carpenters' Hall on South Howard Street and formed the "Coming Nation Club" to debate leftwing ideas. The club's aims, again, were purely propagandist, because motions to become part of the "industrial brotherhood" (presumably the unions) and to contest elections were defeated.[3] It is possible that the club had come under the influence of Daniel De Leon's Socialist Labor Party, which was hostile to unions affiliated with the American Federation of Labor, and sectarian in its approach to other socialist currents. The SLP had earlier sent a national organizer, the Frenchman B. F. Keinard, to Akron, no doubt because the vibrant industrial city seemed fertile ground for recruitment.

In August 1897, Keinard spoke to a small crowd at the corner of Main and Market streets about putting the party back on the Ohio ballot. The party had stood in recent elections but received less than one percent of the vote. Keinard's speech, according to a hostile reporter, was "a tirade against labor-saving machinery" combined with a call for "the collective ownership and control of all lands and instruments of labor." Keinard warned prophetically that "more complete machines" would destroy jobs.[4] Despite its feeble showing in elections, the SLP was convinced that it could succeed in northeastern Ohio. The party held its national convention in Canton in the same year and continued its efforts to gain a foothold in Akron, but without much success. On one occasion, it advertised a "mass meeting" on "blood red dodgers," but fewer than twenty-five people attended.[5] Keinard and others were dedicated organizers, but the party's narrow ideas acted as a brake on its activities. The SLP insisted on strict doctrinal purity and tried to create separate "red" unions in opposition to the existing AFL affiliates, which it regarded as hopelessly reactionary. These were self-limiting ordinances. Frederick Engels regarded the party as being "to a certain extent foreign to America, having until lately been made up almost exclusively by German immigrants, using their own language...."[6] In 1886, Marx's daughter Eleanor visited the US with her partner, Edward Aveling, and they recorded their thoughts on the SLP and the prospects for socialism in America in a book published in London. They were moderately hopeful that the SLP leaders were "beginning to reap at last their deserved reward," but did note the "the distrust of Socialism held until recently by the average American working man," including members of the Knights of Labor. Another "impediment," they believed,

> lies in some of the German Socialists themselves. A few of these, as already hinted, not understanding the movement generally, and still less understanding it in America, are anxious to 'boss the show' in that country. As long as that is possible, the movement in America will not be American. Socialism, to be effective there, must be of native growth, even if the seeds are brought from other countries.[7]

Because of this, the party was something of an exotic growth in a city such as Akron, which at the time was largely populated by people who could trace their ancestry back to the British Isles, and who were imbued with a pragmatic outlook that did not sit well with the single-minded zeal of men such as Keinard. Morris Hillquit, who left the SLP in 1899 when it embraced "red" unionism, characterized the party leader, Daniel De Leon, as a "fanatic"—a zealot who was "carried away beyond the realm of reality by the process of his own abstract and somewhat Talmudistic logic"—and an autocrat who "for his opponents ... had neither courtesy nor mercy."[8] While such a rigid, authoritarian party made in De Leon's quarrelsome image might take root in a dictatorship such as Tsarist Russia, it had little hope of success in the more open society of America.[9]

In contrast, the SLP's rival, the Social Democratic Party, which was founded in 1898, was a broad, inclusive, multi-tendency organization that welcomed open debate and could tailor its message to the needs of different strata of the working class. It was founded with high hopes. Its foremost leader was Eugene V. Debs, a seasoned mass activist who had been jailed in 1895 for leading the great Pullman strike. In 1901, the SDP became the Socialist Party of America after it amalgamated with the so-called "kangaroo" faction of the SLP.[10]

In 1900, the SDP chartered its first Akron local. Max L. Hayes from neighboring Cleveland addressed "about a dozen wage workers" in the Carpenters' Hall and urged the creation of an SDP local. Hayes was an official of the Machinists' Union and Secretary of the AFL's Central Labor Union in Cleveland. He was a long-time critic of AFL leader Samuel Gompers' advocacy of "pure and simple unionism," but rejected the SLP's call to form breakaway unions. Hayes' comrades were in favor of industrial unionism wherever possible but chose to work from within the AFL unions rather than shouting from the sidelines. The policy made sense to militant trade unionists who were thinking seriously of embracing socialism.

The meeting elected J. M. Bowers as president, M. Beckwith as secretary and R. E. Nevin as treasurer of the new local.[11] Only a handful of Akronites attended, but it was a start. The SDP (shortly to change its name to the Socialist Party) was soon recruiting significantly among workers and intellectuals across America, especially in the industrial cities of Ohio such as Akron, Canton, and Cleveland.[12] Although the *Beacon Journal* dismissed the party's 1904 electoral performance as "insignificant,"[13] this smacked of whistling in the dark. The party's Akron street meetings were soon attracting hundreds of people, who gathered in all weathers to hear orators such as the Reverend Charles H. Vail speak of William Morris, Karl Marx, Frederick Engels, and Ferdinand Lassalle. H. Gaylord Wilshire, "the millionaire socialist" from California, also spoke at the corner of Main and Market Streets to several hundred people, many of them curious to hear a tycoon denounce his own class and call for justice for the workers.[14]

In 1904, the celebrated agitator Mary Harris "Mother" Jones spoke in the city in support of striking Colorado coal miners.[15] When she returned to Akron in 1910 and spoke on the same platform as AFL national organizer Emmet Flood, the meeting dissolved into chaos. Flood "took exceptions [sic] to Mother Jones' speech in which she introduced socialism and politics in a very direct manner." The Central Labor

Union showed its socialist colors by deeming Flood to be "an undesirable citizen."[16] At root of the clash was the Socialist Party's advocacy of industrial unionism as opposed to Flood's stubborn support for craft unionism, and the AFL's rejection of independent working-class political action. Nevertheless, because the Socialist Party rejected the sectarian "red" union schema of its SLP rival and was prepared to work within and strengthen the AFL, it was able to build a "small but dedicated base in the [established] union movement," particularly in the Mine Workers' and Machinists' unions[17] and in the Akron and Cleveland CLUs. In July 1905, party member Frank Prevey spoke to two hundred workers in the Akron streetcar barns[18] as part of an outreach to the city's working class. This kind of thing was something the rival SLP could only dream about. However, despite the Socialist Party's advocacy for industrial unionism, its relations with the newly formed Industrial Workers of the World (IWW) were not always smooth. In 1906, the IWW's Canton organizer was refused permission to speak at a party picnic at Springfield Lake, although this was rescinded following the intervention of a "prominent local member,"[19] perhaps Marguerite Prevey.

Although the mainstream press belittled the Socialists' appeal, the Democrats were compelled to plagiarize the milder parts of the SPA's program to prevent the erosion of their working-class electoral base.[20] The program included both the "maximum demand" of socialism and immediate reforms, including municipal ownership of utilities and improved sanitation, welfare, and workplace safety—pejoratively labeled "sewer socialism" by the hard left. A local reporter observed that the Socialist vote rose in Akron when the established parties fielded reactionary candidates and fell when they stood progressives who borrowed parts of the Socialists' "minimum" program.[21] In 1912, the Socialist Party boasted a national membership of 113,000, over seven thousand of them in Ohio not counting those in its large foreign language affiliates.[22] It published 323 English and foreign-language periodicals with a probable circulation over two million, including the weekly *Appeal to Reason's* three-quarters of a million or more. In the same year, 1,039 party members held public office in America, among them fifty-six mayors, including those of the Ohio towns of Canton, Lima, Cuyahoga Falls, Lorain, and Barberton.[23] In 1912, Eugene V. Debs and his running mate

Emil Seidel, the perennially popular Socialist mayor of Milwaukee, received six percent of the popular vote in the presidential elections, or almost one million votes,[24] in the face of press hostility and undemocratic voting procedures. In Summit County, Debs received a creditable 3,936 votes as opposed to Teddy Roosevelt's 7,473.[25] Debs was one of only three third party candidates in the twentieth century to receive more than five percent of the national popular vote. His total campaign expenditure was $66,000—a fraction of that spent by the three establishment candidates—and he faced several other constraints peculiar only to third party candidates.[26]

The Akron Socialist local replicated these successes. By 1908, fired up by what a reporter dismissed as some "rabid, rampant" rhetoric from the miners' leader "Big Bill" Haywood in the Gayety Theater, the Akron Socialists were gaining confidence. They stood Frank Goodenberger for the Nineteenth Congressional District,[27] and Prevey by now was speaking to large gatherings and attracting big audiences as far away as Columbus. In October 1908, the party moved into new headquarters in the Wilcox block on South Main Street, opening the premises with singing and music provided by the Woodsmen's Orchestra. The party's activities were intensely worrying for the city establishment, which stepped up the anti-Socialist rhetoric. Dr. F. J. Bauer interrupted Prevey at a large meeting in Mogadore to ask what would happen to a widow with children dependent on shares if the trusts were nationalized.[28] In 1910, George P. Smith, the Socialist mayoral candidate, polled almost three thousand votes, just a few hundred short of the Democrat, Henry Cronan, and a couple of thousand behind the winner, the Republican Frank W. Rockwell.

The Socialists' successes came about because of objective social conditions. Akron was an overwhelmingly working-class city. Some seventy-thousand of its inhabitants worked in the giant rubber mills, which in 1913 accounted for eighty percent of the city's trade.[29] Thousands more worked in ancillary industries and in engineering, mining, chemicals, matchmaking, and so forth. Class divisions were stark. The manufacturers made huge profits but little trickled down to workers on the factory floor. Eugene Debs provided charismatic leadership at a national level. By all accounts, he was among the finest orators

America has ever produced, but the party also had other talented mass leaders.

In Akron, the Canadian-born ex-farm girl Marguerite Prevey filled the role. The "vivacious [and] matronly" Prevey[30] moved to Akron in 1901, when she was thirty-two years old, and quickly established herself as a party stalwart and set up in business as an optometrist. She shared her work premises with her jeweler husband Frank in a building, long since demolished, at 162 Main Street. They bought a large house nearby at 140 High Street, which became a center for the city's radicals. Prevey could have lived a comfortable bourgeois life, and, with her fierce intelligence, risen to prominence in the Democrat or Republican parties, but she had dedicated her life to working-class emancipation.[31]

The Socialist Party's membership was overwhelmingly working class, but Prevey did not hesitate to recruit other "prominent and wealthy citizens," including the former Bishop William M. Brown and his wife, from Galion in Crawford County, Ohio.[32] Such was Prevey's strength of character that she was a national figure in a resolutely patriarchal age. A formidable woman, "[s]he looks out from faded drawings and photographs with the fierce determination that was her hallmark," wrote Daniel Nelson.[33] She sat on the SPA's National Executive Committee and in 1908 and 1909 headed its national women's committee. In adulthood, her youthful Catholicism transmuted into a passion for earthly justice, and she proved to be a holy terror to the establishment.[34] She was greatly concerned with the plight of working-class women, condemned to poverty by the sexual division of labor, which she saw as the direct cause of prostitution.[35] In 1915, street and brothel prostitutes could earn between one and five dollars a trick, which compares with an average weekly wage of $6.67 for female employees in department stores and light manufacturing.[36] To her comrades, she was never the zealot of her enemies' imagination.[37] She was impressively courageous. George Kirkpatrick, the party's 1916 vice-presidential candidate, related that during the rubber strike, "a great mob came to her home, filling the streets before it, led and violently urged on by a preacher whose mouth was actually frothing with anger." She did not flinch but guarded her door with a loaded revolver in each hand, "facing the raging brutes without fear" and forced them to disperse.[38] She was a superb orator and an indefatigable organizer and under her leadership, the Akron local emerged as a powerful force.

With leaders of Prevey's caliber, an intelligent and dedicated membership, and a program that could appeal to the city's workers and sections of the middle class, the party local seemed assured of success. On the eve of the First World War, less than two decades after its inception, it appeared that the party could say—*pace* Sombart—that there *was* socialism in the United States. After the first decade of the twentieth century, the party's Akron local had strong links to the labor movement. When in 1913 the workers in the city's giant rubber mills sought help to wage a strike against their employers they turned, perhaps naturally, to Prevey and the Socialist Party for advice and assistance.

7.

Revolution in The Gum Mines?

Although the novelist Margaret Alison Johansen claimed that Akron's 1913 rubber strike came as "a violent storm from a cloudless sky,"[1] it had been brewing for many years. Wealthy citizens were horrified by what they saw as "a revolution in the gum mines,"[2] but the Socialist journalist Leslie Macey welcomed the strike. "There is no fire under the boilers," he reported, "nor smoke issuing from the hundreds of industrial spires; the belts are on loose pulleys and even the wheels refuse to run .... Thus the class lines have been drawn and the class struggle is on in Akron."[3] The strike began, as so many stoppages had done, as a walk-off by workers in one small section of the Firestone plant. Every previous attempt to form a union had failed, so the 150 tire finishers who picketed the massive Firestone plant at the corner of Miller and Sweitzer avenues on February 10, 1913,[4] must have been apprehensive. Most gummers did cross the picket line that morning, but the plant was buzzing with debate. Two days later, the strikers' ranks had swollen to 600,[5] and from there the strike "spread like wildfire" to other Firestone departments and then to the rest of the city's giant mills, including Goodrich and Goodyear.[6]

A first, heady strike parade and meeting was addressed by the Rev. W. M. Davis and Industrial Workers of the World (IWW) general organizer Walter Knox. Asked whether the strikers had a permit to

Industrial Workers of the World strikers, Akron, 1913, with placards in English and Italian. *Reprinted with permission of the Akron Beacon Journal and Ohio.com.*

march, Knox replied, "the Constitution of the United States is my permit."[7] Thus began a six-week struggle, with up to seventy-five percent of the city's twenty-two thousand rubber workers downing tools at the strike's height.[8] Red banners fluttered on the gray winter streets, with huge parades, militant speeches, and mass pickets in the snow and fog.[9] It began as a tremendous carnival of revolt. It was bitterly cold on the picket lines,[10] but the strikers were warmed by faith in the justice of their cause. They were in a good position to win. Firestone had just won a huge contract from the Ford motor company, and all the city's rubber manufacturers stood to lose massive profits if the strike continued for any length of time.

The strike outraged the rubber companies and their supporters, who alleged that it was "not a strike for better wages or working conditions, but an attempt .... [by] a left-wing group to seize power."[11] Goodyear's C. W. Seiberling claimed that the IWW had engineered the strike because they saw the "the contented, well-paid workers" as "a fruitful field for [financial] contributions to their cause."[12] Seventeen years after the strike ended, novelist Margaret Alison Johansen described it as an bacchanalia of violence and arson engineered by "Reds" with "bulging wallets."[13]

None of this is true. Far from milking the strikers for money, the cash-strapped union had to find the money to support them, and as the staunchly Republican *Akron Beacon Journal* later admitted, "No strike ever started more peacefully or with less excitement,"[14] and that "Quiet reigns as the third week of the strike opens."[15] The paper also reported that the strike committee had banned three IWW organizers from addressing further meetings after they made "incendiary" speeches.[16] Any real violence on the strikers' part appears to have come later, in response to brutality by police and vigilantes, and in desperation as the strike crumbled. When George Speed arrived from Pittsburgh to direct the strike, he was at pains to ensure that it remained peaceful and the legendary "Big Bill" Haywood urged the strikers to "keep the peace at all costs."[17]

Claims that the Socialist Party had orchestrated the strike or had advocated violence are also unsustainable. The evidence indicates that the strike was a spontaneous rebellion of rank-and-file workers against intolerable conditions and dwindling incomes. The Cleveland-based IWW organizer Walter Glover had set up Akron Local 470 in 1912,[18] but it had no more than fifteen to twenty members at the outbreak of the strike[19] and was riddled with spies. David M. Goodrich's claim that the strike "was really a battle of the IWW vs. the AFL,"[20] is also a distortion. The AFL did try to undermine its rival, but a mass meeting called by the Federation could only muster two hundred and fifty gummers, some of whom may have only attended out of curiosity.[21] For all of its revolutionary rhetoric, the IWW behaved like an orthodox union throughout the strike[22] and "merely fanned the smoldering fire into roaring flames."[23]

The immediate detonator of the strike was Firestone's thirty-five percent cut to piecework rates and their arbitrary reclassification of jobs. The business historian Alfred Lief lists around twenty non-craftsman classifications, introduced by Firestone without consultation on the eve of the strike as causes of discontent.[24] The reclassification took place against a background of simmering resentment over unhealthy conditions and the Taylorist speed-up of work tempos. An Ohio State Senate investigation identified these factors, which combined with the lack of grievance procedures and a growing awareness of the disparity between wages and profits, as the root causes of the strike.[25]

The strike had begun spontaneously, but the strikers realized that they could not win unless they had an organization behind them. They needed to clarify their demands, elect negotiators and spokespeople, organize picketing and other essential activities, raise and distribute strike funds, and propagandize for their cause. They had few material resources. Few strikers had saved money to tide them over during the dispute. It was winter and they needed to heat their houses and feed and clothe their families. Against fabulously wealthy and ruthless opponents—who had the ear of government, most of the press, the police, the judiciary, prominent clergymen, and other notables—the strikers' only chance of victory lay in well-organized collective action and the solidarity of other workers. They turned to the Socialist Party, which had been growing in size and influence in the city. A delegation called on the party's headquarters in the Reindeer Hall and met with the leader of the Akron Party local, the redoubtable Marguerite Prevey, who urged solidarity, sobriety, and nonviolence as essential for victory. She advised the strikers to join the IWW,[26] as the party favored industrial as opposed to craft unionism where possible.

IWW Akron Local 470 was too weak to run the gummers' strike. Formed in 1912, it had distributed multilingual leaflets to the gummers, but had made little headway.[27] Nationally, too, the IWW's resources were overstretched. Since late January 1913, the IWW had been leading a massive strike of silk workers at Paterson, New Jersey.[28] Less than two weeks later, the first Firestone workers walked off the job in Akron. The IWW center in Chicago dispatched "a flood of agitators" to the city, further straining its resources.[29] The Wobblies, as the IWW men and women were known, were now fighting on two fronts. Despite establishment claims of a red conspiracy, the Wobblies did not attempt to take over the strike, despite funding it. The IWW believed that liberation had to come from below. Since its formation in 1905, the IWW had won some impressive victories, including at Lawrence, Massachusetts, where they led thirty thousand women textile workers to a huge triumph in a struggle forever associated with the unforgettable song "Bread and Roses." The IWW was at first unable to handle the flood of recruits as the Akron strike spread, peaking at between 16,000 and 20,000 out of the city's 22,000 rubber workers. Gradually, however, they imposed discipline, with picket rosters, soup kitchens, and a propaganda section to put the workers' side of the dispute, all operating from the strike headquarters in the Reindeer Hall. Marguerite Prevey served throughout as the union's treasurer and chief fundraiser and traveled widely throughout Ohio and beyond, drumming up support.[30] Late in February, the union was able to open a relief tent to provide food on a disused lot on Buchtel Street.[31] IWW leaders inspired the strikers with some vintage oratory.

Yet you cannot eat words, no matter how uplifting. The rubber companies refused to negotiate and swore that they would never allow a union to organize the Akron mills. Secretly, they were prepared to go to any lengths to achieve this. Caught flat-footed when the strike erupted, they quickly marshaled their forces, and they had one great advantage—they had already placed spies and agents provocateurs inside the IWW and Socialist Party locals. They were also prepared to use physical force to intimidate the strikers and could rely on the city and county police to back them. Both the Wobblies and the Socialist Party counseled nonviolence, aware that the employers would seize on violence by the workers to undermine the strike's legitimacy in the court of "public opinion." Shortly after the IWW arrived, George Speed and Walter Glover met with representatives of the State arbitration board and gave assurances that the strike would be peaceful.[32] They knew that the manufacturers would use any pretext to draw on the National Guard, city and county police, special deputies, Baldwin-Felts detectives, plant police, and vigilantes. Curiously, E. C. Shaw, the manager of B. F. Goodrich, downplayed reports early in the strike that "some foreign strikers" had stoned his plant from the banks of the nearby canal and stolen scabs' lunch pails. "Shaw reported" to the *Beacon* "that he did not propose to answer fool questions from newspapers every 15 minutes."[33]

Later, the rubber firms were happy to use violence. Establishment accounts of the strike give the impression that the employers won because management fortitude, the steadfastness of the worker "loyalists" who kept up some production during the strike, and the dawning realization among the "gullible" strikers that outsiders were misleading them. Nevertheless, the companies admit to "being aided materially by the organization of a citizens' group,"[34] which helped control "mobs of men wearing red badges" who were "terrorizing the populance" [sic].[35] The reference was to the Citizens' Welfare League, vigilantes organized by the pugnacious Episcopalian priest George P. Atwater. Known to the strikers as the "Cut-throats' Warfare League," the CWL had originated in 1908 as the Citizens' Alliance, with a brief "to crush the trade union movement in the city."[36] The CWL enrolled one thousand men, many of them "rubber stock gamblers"—shareholders with a direct interest in breaking the strike according to the Socialists.[37] The vigilantes included the staff of the Akron YMCA, tycoons such as Michael O'Neil—the Downtown department store owner and soon-to-be boss of General Tire & Rubber, Goodyear founder Frank Seiberling, members of the Akron Chamber of Commerce, and gangs of muscular young men anxious for excitement. Deputized by Sheriff David Fergusson, they carried heavy police nightsticks and drove out in automobiles at dawn to patrol the streets and intimidate strikers.[38] They enjoyed the full support of the Republican mayor, Frank Rockwell, and worked closely with the city police force.

Soon, the vigilantes and police were roughing up any strikers they encountered on the streets.[39] A particularly brutal affray occurred on March 7, when Sheriff Fergusson ordered a five-hundred-strong picket outside B. F. Goodrich to move back from the factory gates. When the picket failed to move quickly enough for the sheriff,[40] he ordered his "bulls" to attack the strikers. In the ensuing mêlée,

> the vigorous wielding of clubs soon had a telling effect. Steadily the clubs of the officers rose and fell as the excited mob was slowly battered back. As the strikers were unarmed, they could not long endure the severe punishment. Some of them seized bricks and stones and threw them. Mostly they fought with their fists.

A striker carrying the Stars and Stripes was "floored by a billy club," and sixty other strikers were injured,[41] including Hungarian immigrant Csikos Gyorgy, who was hospitalized with a fractured skull. Millie Harley, a twenty-year-old Firestone striker, was struck in the face and eye.[42]

Throughout the strike, the police arraigned many strikers before police judge Vaughan, of the legal firm Vaughan, Voorhies & Vaughan, which also acted as attorneys for the rubber companies. The glaring conflict of interest did not worry the local establishment. Arrested strikers were denied trial by jury[43] and could not expect a fair hearing from Vaughan, who had rubber shares.[44] Three days after the Goodrich affray, Judge Vaughan fined eight strikers sums varying from $20 to $50—huge sums at the time for wage workers—and imprisoned one of them, a gummer called Adolph Porosky, in the Cleveland workhouse for refusing to pay.[45] The workers must have gained grim satisfaction from the misfortune of Detective Marino, who was knocked unconscious by a special deputy who mistook him for a striker. Sheriff Fergusson, too, was accidentally bashed by one of his own men and was said to be "going about minus a few front teeth and wearing a face that looks like a piece of raw liver."[46]

Usually however, the strikers suffered most from the violence. The police and auxiliaries knew that they could act with complete immunity. On March 13, Atwater's *squadristi* clubbed a group of young women strikers as they were going up the stairs into the Reindeer Hall. The following day, the police chief and a delegation from the CWL met Bill Haywood as he left his train at Union Station. They demanded that he refrain from delivering "revolutionary speeches," but stepped aside when they could not produce a warrant to keep him from entering the city.[47] Vigilantes also broke into the strike headquarters, "stopped up the water pipes and flooded the hall."[48] The socialist printer Jim McCartan later recalled an attack by vigilantes on a peaceful procession of strikers:

> One evening we were marching up Main Street from the Firestone and Goodrich and when we reached where Main, Bowery and Howard converge this army of service club members came at us from all directions. We had no weapons and they were able to disperse us. I went up the alley back of the Second National Bank pursued by an insurance agent.

McCartan later chased the agent out of the Gothic Barbershop at the corner of South High and Main.[49] McCartan's friends joked that he "probably *could* start a fight in an empty house." [Emphasis in the original.][50] The Hungarian Wobbly Paul Sebestyen recalled that the police would single out strike leaders for special treatment:

> We went to John Brown's memorial, marching up there. [William] Trautmann was in front of me and I was lucky. The cop came along without any provocation, hit him in the head. He fell down, bleeding. He didn't hit me.... I suppose he knew he was one of the leaders of the strike. They knew who to hit.... [51]

The IWW's *Akron Strike Bulletin* recorded further examples of police thuggery:

> On Tuesday last the police without provocation clubbed and beat strikers who were in the picket line and parade. Mary Bryant, a 17-year-old girl, was clubbed about the head and shoulders when she was entering the socialist hall.... Shots were also fired by the police, thereby endangering the lives of all who might pass by on the street. All these crimes are committed in the name of law and order.[52]

The police and vigilantes ran amok in what Karl Grismer describes as "mob rule."[53] In one case, reported in the IWW Strike Bulletin, "a girl striker when pushed off the sidewalk said, 'I am an American citizen; let me alone.' The cop replied, 'Sure you are an American citizen, but get off the sidewalk.'"[54]

The police and auxiliaries could get away with violence because middle-class "public opinion" supported the rubber firms, who frightened them by depicting the strike as a "Red" conspiracy against democracy and public order. Indeed, the share-owning middle class formed the backbone of Atwater's CWL. Most of the city's clergymen opposed the strike, including Ira Priest of the Universalist Church, who doubled as President of Buchtel College, the precursor of The University of Akron.[55] There were some exceptions to middle-class support for the rubber magnates. The Rev. W. M. Davis of the United Evangelical Church in Akron backed the strikers from the beginning, and often spoke on the strikers' platforms.[56] A number of well-heeled Akron women also organized a relief committee to help "girls" on strike.[57]

Although the *Akron Times* and the *Beacon Journal* backed the rubber companies, the *Akron Press* was sympathetic to the strikers. The *Press* demanded to know "Why haven't workers the right to organize" if the CWL could do so, and noted that "companies prepare for war as strikers talk peace."[58] In retaliation, CWL goons invaded the newspaper's offices to intimidate the staff.[59] They knew that Mayor Rockwell, Sheriff Fergusson, and Judge Vaughan would look the other way. The Socialist alderman Esch's motion to condemn police violence was lost by eight votes to two at an Akron city council session immediately after the bashings at the Goodrich gates.[60] The small number of middle-class people who supported the strikers or demanded respect for their legal rights were outnumbered. As Big Bill Haywood pointed out,

> The Constitution has been trampled under foot. [sic] the Declaration of Independence scattered to the winds, the Bill of Rights forgotten, all because the rubber bosses wanted to drive their slaves back to work.[61]

The Socialists quoted in vain the Ohio Constitution, which gives

> The people ... the right to assemble together, in a peaceable manner, to consult for their common good ... [and gives] Every citizen [the right to] ... freely speak, write and publish his sentiments on all subjects, being responsible for abuse of the right, and no law shall be passed to restrict or abridge the liberty of speech or the press.[62]

An alliance of rubber companies, local authorities, police, and private individuals had illegally suspended the rule of law insofar as it applied to the strikers and their supporters. In doing so, they foreshadowed the Red Scare of 1919–20, in which the Left across America was the target of a wave of private violence and officially sponsored persecution. The IWW vainly appealed to the Governor of Ohio, the Democrat James M. Cox, to call out the National Guard to protect the workers from "the mob of the rich."[63] Cox did appoint a State Senate commission of inquiry to look into the causes of the strike and placed it under the control of William Green, Secretary of the AFL and a Democrat State

Senator. However, by the time the commission handed down its report, the strike was over. The brutal, tyrannical, and illegal behavior of the authorities and the vigilantes had contributed heavily to the strikers' defeat. Violent repression, however, was not the only weapon in the establishment's armory. Two of Akron's three daily newspapers sided openly with the employers and the authorities, peddling the myths of union violence, and ignoring the routine flouting of the strikers' constitutional rights. The *Akron Times* praised the vigilantes, declaring that "not since the Civil War had local citizenship and patriotism been in such thorough accord."[64] The rubber companies also had another very sinister and effective weapon in their anti-union arsenal.

8.

The Supreme Mistake of the IWW

Akron's rubber strikers would have agreed with Balzac that "a murderer is less loathsome ... than a spy. The murderer may have acted on a sudden mad impulse; he may be penitent and amend; but a spy is always a spy, night and day, in bed, at table, as he walks abroad; his vileness pervades every moment of his life."[1] On the eve of World War I, American industry was riddled with spies and company gun thugs. By the 1890s, the Pinkerton Detective Agency's staff was bigger than the US military.[2] Undermined from within by spies, the great Akron strike began to crumble. An allied factor was that—as the IWW organizer Frank Dawson explains—"a spontaneous strike is a spontaneous tragedy unless there is a strong local organization on the spot or unless a strong force of experienced men [sic] are thrown into town immediately."[3] Some years before the great strike, the rubber bosses had planted spies in the IWW and Socialist Party locals, and in the city's Central Labor Union.

Historians have not always understood the effectiveness of the spies' work in breaking the 1913 strike. In the early days of the strike, the workers celebrated in an almost carnival atmosphere, but as the strike dragged on, it became a war of attrition. The authorities acted with determination and brutality, and the strike took on an increasingly grim character. The employers adamantly refused to negotiate, and the strikers could not look forward to an early breakthrough. By mid-March, many families were destitute and there was a trickle and then a flood back to work. On March 31, 1913, forty-nine days after the strike began, the IWW conceded defeat. The spies could be satisfied with their dark work to keep the mills nonunion.

As the burglary of the AFL rubber workers' union offices back in 1902 had shown, the mill owners were not squeamish about the methods they used to enforce the open shop. The burglars were "industrial experts" employed by the Cleveland-based Corporations Auxiliary Company (CAC). At that time, the spooks also bribed an AFL official to hand over the names of union members and they signed a bogus agreement with 350 rubber unionists "simply to find out WHO were union members in order to get rid of them." [Capitals in the original.] Another spy, John E. Sebree or Sebre, had served as president of the Molders' Akron local and secretary of the Central Labor Union, and had worked full-time as an organizer for the Carpenters' Union before he was exposed and forced to flee.[4] The CLU's financial secretary H. E. Ellis and corresponding secretary B. Furey were also outed as spies. Ellis made a full confession and implicated a further twenty-five men and seven women as "provocateurs."[5] In January 1914, *The People* (the newspaper of the Akron unions) and the Cleveland IWW's *Solidarity* published further sensational stories of espionage and intrigue.[6] John W. Reid, secretary-treasurer of IWW Local 470 in Akron, had sworn an affidavit that he had been a professional spy for the rubber companies since his arrival in the city in 1908. Previously, Reid had worked as a motorman in Buffalo, and doubled as a spy. He told the Socialist journalist John K. Turner that the CAC had fired him because he had refused to steal the IWW's $3000 treasury, which he considered a step too far.[7]

IWW organizer Walter Glover had launched Local 470 at a meeting in Barberton on August 12, 1912. Glover believed that meeting semi-secretly in the nearby town would minimize the risk of infiltration. He was dead wrong. According to Reid, half of the Local's charter members were spies. Reid also revealed that the CAC had a mole at the IWW national headquarters in Chicago. When the Akron strike broke out in February 1913, "the Big Four" of Reid, V. G. Williams, Ed Dickerson, and G. A. Miller controlled Local 470. Even if Reid exaggerated, his

Strikers picket office of Motz Tire & Rubber, Akron, 1913. Courtesy of the Goodyear Collection, University of Akron Archives.

revelations were grim for organized labor. Although CAC operated against all unions, including those affiliated with the AFL, Reid claimed that CAC's vice-president and general manager had told him that the firm was "spending thousands of dollars a year to down the IWW."[8] The CAC was not the only detective agency in the rubber companies' employ, but it was the most effective. Goodyear also used the services of Edwin L. Reed & Co., which cost the equivalent of the wages of 1,100 tire builders during the strike. Frank Seiberling later complained that this was exorbitant, as he could learn about the union's activities in the daily press. However, we know that Seiberling learned much more than the press reported.[9] His complaints also ignore the spies' disruptive activities, which did much to break the 1913 strike.

Two years after the rubber strike, the CAC's district manager claimed to have "have handled many strikes and [we] have yet to lose a single one of them."[10] He was making a sales pitch, but he had every reason to be confident in his "product." Unlike the infamous Pinkerton and Baldwin-Felts agencies, the CAC did not rely on strong-arm methods, but specialized in what it called "industrial inspection" to bring about the "gradual disintegration" of labor unions.[11] The rubber companies did not need the Pinkertons because Atwater's vigilantes and the city and county police provided them with free "muscle."

The CAC's method was to penetrate the workforce in order to control it. They employed both "outside" and "inside" men and infiltrated a number of unions from bottom to top. CAC operatives sometimes spent years in a factory to win the workers' confidence. The aim was not merely to feed information to the employers, but to head off nascent union organization and if necessary to act as provocateurs. A company sales prospectus spells this out:

> Our man will come to your factory and get acquainted ... [and] will engineer things … to keep organization out. If, however, there seems a disposition to organize he will become the leading spirit ... [If] the union spirit may be so strong that a big organization cannot be prevented … our man turns extremely radical … he will be the loudest man in the bunch, and will counsel violence … The result will be that the union will be broken up.[12]

The agents had been in place in Akron for many years before the strike erupted, Reid since 1908 and Miller for ten years. Reid admitted that as "the rubber workers were determined to have an organization of some kind …. we [the spies] had orders to keep the [IWW] local alive, but to hold it in our hands."[13] They were so convincing that their activities might have remained secret save for Reid's belated attack of conscience.

The work of H. E. Pollack, the twenty-three-year old Goodyear tire builder who initially chaired the strike committee, was particularly damaging. He gave the impression of being an "honest," apolitical, rank-and-file worker thrown into activity by the strike, but he used his position to warn the employers in advance of the strikers' every move. His sister, who worked as Frank Seiberling's stenographer, typed up the union's minutes and gave the carbons to her boss. Pollack was exposed as a spy when he testified at the Ohio Senate inquiry that his main grievance with his employer was that shortages of materials prevented him from working as fast as he would have liked to do. The union expelled him, but by then it was too late to undo the damage he had caused.[14]

The spies' brief had been to prevent the looming strike, but if this proved impossible, to make a fiasco of it, and to turn over the names of all new union members to the employers as quickly as they were recruited. According to Reid, the Big Four met nightly in secret to evaluate developments and to plot further disruption. They quietly advised strikers not to join the union, because there would be "plenty of time when the strike was won." Not all of the strikers joined the IWW, so it is probable that some heeded the spies' honeyed words. The snoopers also conspired to get outside IWW organizers drunk and make fools of themselves and were apparently successful in some cases. They also stirred up racial and ethnic animosity and spread gossip "calculated to split the strikers up into factions." If they could waste the union's precious funds, they did so; according to Reid they put Dickerson and Miller on salaries of $12 a week for the duration of the strike. Reid also claimed that the spies had helped the AFL to set up a rival rubber workers' union during the strike. The AFL did indeed dispatch Carl Wyatt and John L. Lewis to Akron in an unsuccessful bid to undermine the IWW.[15] The pair were not spies, but a man called Neal, who served as the AFL union's president, was in the companies' pay. The purpose of this maneuver, an *Appeal to Reason* journalist noted, was to foster "the usual AF of L vs. IWW controversy," the age-old formula of divide et impera.[16]

These methods were effective to one degree or another, but the spies' most damaging intrigue was to delay the formulation of the strikers' demands. The strikers needed a quick victory, and this was entirely possible given the huge losses the companies stood to make because of the stoppage. Instead of moving swiftly to draw up a list of claims, the strike committee dithered. Daniel Nelson ascribes some blame for this to the Socialist Party's Marguerite Prevey, claiming that she saw the strike as a vehicle to build the union but ignored the vital question of formulating immediate demands.[17]

The same criticism, if warranted, also applies to the IWW, an ultra-democratic organization that left this task to the strikers themselves, rather than seeking to impose its ideas on them. Nevertheless, it is important to ask why experienced outside organizers did not see it as part of their job to advise clearly inexperienced workers in these matters. Nor can one overlook the crucial factor of the company spies' disruption. Reid testified that as the CAC operatives controlled the strikers' wage-scale committee, they were able to delay framing a set of demands until three weeks after the start of the strike.[18] This would not have been too difficult. There were few if any experienced unionists among the rank-and-file leaders and the spies could easily manipulate the unwieldy one-hundred-strong strike committee. Formulation of demands would have been difficult even without the spooks' disruptions, for there were a huge number of different classifications in the factories.[19] The agents knew that the union had few resources and that unless they could make a quick breakthrough, the strikers could not hold out. Without a list of claims, there could be no resolution, swift or otherwise. When the committee did produce a set of demands, they were so inadequate that the AFL's Lewis and Wyatt laughed at them. The strikers also were not impressed. Finally, a viable list of claims was worked up, including the following: reinstatement of all strikers, a general wage increase with a graduated scale of hourly pay, an eight-hour day, abolition of piece work, overtime pay at 22½ cents an hour, and recognition of the IWW local as the bargaining agent for the workers.[20]

By this time, the strikers were desperate. Between ten and twenty-five percent of the workforce had refused to join the strike, and there was a slow trickle of strikers back to work. After a further three weeks, the strike was practically broken, and the employers, who were kept informed by the spies, knew that they could sit back and wait for its inevitable collapse. By March 14, nearly fifteen thousand were back at work in the mills.[21] After six weeks, although George Speed denied it, the strike was over. On March 24, forty-two days after the initial walk-off at Firestone, the *Akron Press* reported long queues outside the factory employment offices.[22]

Like so many of the IWW's battles, the Akron strike was a noble failure. The organization of the strike was fatally flawed, in part because the workers had not been able to build up an effective shop floor network before the strike began. Many workers were young men with no firm roots in the city, and thousands of them left town once the strike began.

The ubiquitous spies also made workers reluctant to "talk union" on the job or even in bars and other places after work. Professional spies supported the stoolpigeons and between them, they undermined union organization. Once the strike began, the spies sabotaged it, and at the same time, the authorities and vigilantes viciously repressed the strikers. Nor was the IWW the powerful and sinister octopus of establishment propaganda and petty bourgeois nightmare. Although the rubber companies and their hired pens claimed that the Wobblies were awash with funds, the IWW was thinly spread and chronically impecunious. Nor was it a rigid bureaucracy acting on the orders of some kind of American Kremlin. Rather, the IWW held to the philosophy of working-class self-emancipation and abhorred hierarchy and bureaucracy. The ideal Wobbly organizer was "footloose and fancy-free," reflecting the IWW's origins among itinerant workers.[23] The Akron failure also stemmed from the fact that the IWW was heavily involved in the New Jersey silk strike and unable to throw in the resources necessary to win the rubber strike. It is also possible that the IWW did not realize the significance of the events in Akron until it was too late. There is also some truth in the assertion by Goodyear management that nonunionists "broke the back of the strike"[24] because although production was severely disrupted, the mass pickets were unable to shut the plants down completely, and this sapped the strikers' morale.

A further problem for the strikers was that whereas the employers and the state forces acted in concert, there was very little class solidarity on the workers' side. Jim McCartan recalled many years later that he traveled to nearby Massillon and Canton, giving speeches and soliciting strike funds, but "I wasn't very successful."[25] Although the Socialists called for a sympathy strike to counter vigilante violence, the CLU dithered, possibly because of the influence of AFL national organizers Carl Wyatt and John L. Lewis. The CLU leaders were also frightened—and not without reason—that their members would be fired if they supported the gummers. It is true that the Bricklayers' Union donated $500 to the strike fund,[26] but craft unionists harbored a distrust of industrial unionism in general and of the IWW in particular, and some were happy to see the strike collapse. Kevin Rosswurm considers that the AFL "did a grave disservice to the labor movement, to the IWW and to the workers themselves" because of its "half-hearted attempt" to enroll rubber workers [into AFL Rubber Workers Union Local 14407] in the midst of their strike.[27] Some local AFL officials were guilty of outright sabotage of working-class interests. Chief among them was the CLU's recording secretary, Ernest E. Zesiger, who conspired with Atwater's CWL to break the strike.[28] The local Republican Party later rewarded Zesiger with a judgeship,[29] and during the 1920s, he served as Exalted Cyclops of the Akron klavern of the Ku Klux Klan.[30] These factors, combined with the activities of the company spies, the inexperience of the strike leaders, and the fact that the CWL goons ran some of those they labelled as "undesirables" out of town,[31] caused the strike to crumble and collapse. The strikers crept back humiliated, with the militants blacklisted.

On April 17, 1913, the Ohio state commission of inquiry into the rubber industry handed its report to Governor Cox. The defeated strikers could find some consolation in the enquiry's conclusion that their complaints were justified. In fact, the commission amassed an enormous amount of damning testimony against the rubber companies, but it was too late for this to have any effect.[32] Although the union claimed late in the day that "50 more scabs have quit the Goodrich plant" because conditions were so bad that "even scabs cannot stick ... hellholes,"[33] this was a fantasy. Increasing numbers of strikers had given up and returned to work on the bosses' terms. There was also a steady drift of up to five thousand strikers out of the city—particularly young single, itinerant men without support networks—who left to try their luck elsewhere. By March 14, there were perhaps only three thousand strikers left.[34] On March 31, the IWW officially ended the strike, because by then only "pathetically small picket lines" shivered at the factory gates.[35] On Sunday, March 23, and for a number of days following, the greatest rainstorm the city had ever known hit Akron,[36] drenching the pickets in freezing water. In the last hopeless days of the strike, organizers Speed and White allegedly called on the workers to sabotage production.[37]

If as the adage "nothing succeeds like success" holds, then failure breeds apathy, fear, and despair. Wildcat strikes still broke out from time to time, but there was no mass strike in the mills for the next twenty years. Seven years after the strike ended, the IWW admitted that "Akron remains, to this day, the supreme mistake of the IWW ... Never in the history of the IWW has a strike that opened with such alluring prospects led to such a crushing disillusionment." The Wobblies recognized that the rubber workers would need to build a strong and stable local union, with an experienced and honest leadership,[38] and admitted that spontaneous strikes were almost certainly bound to lose against intractable employers. Many years later, the United Rubber Workers' of America (URWA) reached the same conclusion, noting that "Big Bill Haywood ... came to Akron in 1913 to inspire the striking rubber workers. But fiery speeches and militant parades were not enough. There was no strong union to back up the strikers. They were defeated."[39] Jim McCartan added that "the Rubberworkers were starved and had to go back to work."[40] Their defeat bears out historian Eric Loomis's assessment that "[t]here is simply no evidence from American history that unions can succeed if the government and employers combine to crush them. All other factors are secondary: the structure of a union, how democratic it is, how radical its leaders or the rank-and-file are, their tactics."[41] It would be over twenty years before the gummers recovered sufficiently to be able to organize in earnest. The strike's defeat was a terrible setback for organized labor, and it also contributed to the decline of the Socialist Party in the city.

9.

The Eclipse of the Socialist Party

In 1915, the Socialist Party lost all of its Akron council seats and its decline accelerated in the following years. Increasingly, the party's support was limited to circles of the most educated and highly class conscious and politically aware workers[1]—and fearless ones given the increasingly ferocious repression against the Left. Radical ideas lost their appeal, partly because the established parties took over some of the milder Socialist policies advocating for improved municipal infrastructure. The city's right-wing forces had been emboldened by the success of their brutal and illegal attacks on the rubber workers and their supporters. The Red Scare proper did not begin until after the end of the war, but private violence against Akron's party members continued after the collapse of the rubber strike. In 1919, the party split three ways, with a majority in northeast Ohio joining one of two new Communist parties. In Akron itself, party leader Marguerite Prevey chose to join the Communist Labor Party and was elected to its National Executive Committee, although she did not stay long. None of the successor parties ever regained the numbers or influence of the prewar Socialist Party.[2]

Immediately after the end of the 1913 IWW strike, the Knights of Pythias[3] expelled the Socialist Frank Prevey "on account of ... [his] activities on behalf of the IWW," and the next day, a self-styled "Committee of Seven" ordered him to leave town and never return. The Seven

Marguerite Prevey, Akron socialist firebrand and close friend of Eugene Debs

comprised Buchtel College President Ira Priest, vigilante leader Rev. George Atwater, County Treasurer William Kroeger, Street Commissioner Edward Dunn, banker George D. Bates, hardware dealer Crandall Morgan, and realtor William C. Hall. According to the Socialist press, Dunn returned the following day and warned, "We mean exactly what we said. If you don't obey, put a valuation on your property, as something is going to happen to it." He added without irony, "Law and order must prevail in Akron." Meanwhile, the rabblerousing Rev. Howard S. MacAyeal urged a one-hundred-strong meeting at the YMCA to "clean out the Prevey home."[4] MacAyeal later reemerged as a leading light in the Akron klavern of the Ku Klux Klan. The Preveys refused to budge. Frank Prevey lodged a $50,000 damages suit against Atwater and his friends in the Common Pleas Court, stating that on March 12, 1914, the defendants conspired to drive him from his home and force him to sell his property against his will. In what presaged the outcome, the Clerk of the Court refused Prevey's first attempt to file the suit.[5]

The suit never stood a chance, despite a witness testifying that he had seen Prevey "shoved against a post and threatened with tar and feathers if he didn't leave town," and "grabbed by Atwater and Priest and forced into a room."[6] Atwater's propensity for violence was well known. Earlier, the Rev. Irvine, a strike supporter, had declared, "It is incongruous to see a minister of the Gospel [Atwater] … walking about with a club in his hands."[7] An attempt by Judge Ahern to find Prevey's witness guilty of perjury failed when a jury found the man had no case to answer.[8] Nevertheless, in May 1915, Cleveland Appeals Court Judge Carpenter found in favor of Atwater and his codefendants, ruling that "no damage had occurred since Prevey is still here."[9] If Prevey had fled, perhaps he would have won the case.

The failure of the Prevey lawsuit proved that radicals, no matter how peaceable, could not expect justice. Yet the Socialists' agitation did not slacken. Audiences still packed the Reindeer Hall to hear the party's speakers verbally roast the city's rich and powerful for twisting local government to suit their ends, and in April 1915, the party launched a local chapter of the Young People's Socialist League, the "Yipsels."[10] At the same time, there were ominous signs of impending schisms in the party. In 1916, "Mother" Jones provoked Marguerite Prevey's ire by campaigning for the reelection of the Indiana Democrat Senator John Kern, and thus for the return of the Wilson administration.[11]

Party members might not have known it, but they were standing on the edge of a political precipice. Despite his professed noninterventionist stance, President Woodrow Wilson was covertly preparing for US entry into the war. Wilson had a reputation as a liberal, but he introduced an ugly strain of ethnic hatred into political discourse and was to preside over what was probably the greatest assault on constitutional rights in American history. In 1915, he harangued against "certain hyphenates" (i.e. German-Americans) whom he claimed had "poured the poison of disloyalty into the very arteries of our national life."[12] His speech lit the fuse for an explosion of hatred against "aliens" and "un-American activity." It dovetailed with increasingly rabid sentiments against the Left, partly because German-Americans had been over-represented in socialist organizations.

Two years later, the Department of Justice sent Agent W. A. Garrigan and three hundred volunteers to raid Akron's German clubs and Boy Scout troops. The agents stormed into the Liedertafel clubrooms and "fearlessly seized" the Kaiser's portrait, the *Beacon* reported, after which mobs threatened to tar and feather C. L. Knight, the newspaper's proprietor, for his alleged pro-German sentiments.[13] Fearing a pro-German uprising, the Rev. Atwater organized a thousand-strong "Akron Home Guard," which patrolled the Kent Dam armed with Springfield rifles and hickory clubs.[14]

Wilson's increasingly hawkish stance brought him into collision with the Socialists, who opposed US entry into what they regarded as the imperialist war raging across the Atlantic. Although isolationist sentiment was widespread, ever-larger slices of the population came to view Germany as the aggressor. On February 3, 1917, the Wilson government broke off diplomatic relations with Germany. In response, the Socialists' Akron local organized a protest meeting of some 250 people, chaired by Marguerite Prevey, in the city's Kiser Hall. The Central Labor Union agreed with the party's anti-war sentiment but advised workers to avoid "street wrangles or discussions likely to cause trouble."[15] The Council's caution did not augur well for labor movement resistance to anti-leftist repression. In fact, the Gompers' leadership of the AFL threw its weight behind the war effort and entered "into an alliance [with government] to crush radical labor groups" such as the IWW and the Socialist Party.[16]

On April 6, Congress declared war on Germany, and the Akron Socialist local threw itself into anti-war agitation. The police stopped the Cleveland party leader Charles Baker from speaking out against the war at a rally in Akron's Main Street, claiming that a riot would have broken out had he continued. Baker was able to finish his speech at an overflow indoor meeting attended by over a thousand opponents of the war. He declared rather melodramatically that he would rather die with a smile facing a firing squad than commit murder on the battlefield, and meeting chair Marguerite Prevey demanded that the government concern itself with jailing food speculators rather than hounding young men for speaking out against the war.[17] Baker was arrested a few months later for delivering another "subversive" anti-war speech in Akron and was sentenced together with two other Cleveland Socialists, Charles E. Ruthenberg and Alfred W. Wagenknecht, to one year's imprisonment in the Canton Workhouse.[18] The three were badly mistreated for refusing to perform menial prison labor—in one instance being hung by their wrists from the rafters for two days.[19]

Not all of the local Socialists agreed with their anti-war stance. James McCartan, who had become a convinced Socialist in his teens, agreed that the war was imperialist, but felt that it was his duty to support "the boys in the trenches" regardless of his own opinions.[20] Mother Jones, who had earlier crossed swords with Marguerite Prevey, felt the same way. It seems likely that after the main body of "Doughboys" began arriving in France in 1918—and some returned in coffins—that many others began to agree. The Republican and Democratic Party machines fell into line with President Wilson. Democrat Congressional candidate Martin L. Davey, who lived over the Portage County line in Kent, declared, "I am young, rich, virile and 100 per cent American and will be found in the ranks when the time comes." Later, regretting his impetuosity, he sent goons to vandalize bound volumes of newspapers in the Akron public library to destroy evidence of his boast.[21] Meanwhile, the city honored mothers of soldiers killed in France by putting gold stars in their windows.[22] Davey later became Governor of Ohio and was later dubbed "the Duke of Kent" by rubber workers' leader Sherman Dalrymple for redbaiting the rubber union.[23]

Meanwhile, on November 7, 1917 (October in the old Russian calendar), the Bolshevik Revolution broke out in Russia. Many American Socialists believed that for the first time since the brief interlude of the Paris Commune in 1871, the working class had seized power. The revolutionary government sued for peace with the Central Powers at Brest-Litovsk and published a list of secret treaties and protocols that exposed the flimsiness of the antagonists' claims to be fighting a just war. Today, with the Soviet Union thirty years dead, it is difficult to grasp the electrifying atmosphere that the revolution generated in the world's labor movements—and the dread and horror it generated in equal measure on the other side of class politics. It seemed to Marguerite Prevey and her comrades that American revolutionaries, like their Russian comrades, could storm the heavens, install a workers' and small farmers' government, and begin the socialist transformation of society. Despite the formidable forces arrayed against them, and despite anti-socialist persecution on a scale unseen in America, Prevey believed that "everywhere the field is rotten ripe" for the "emancipation for the workers of the world."[24]

The severity of the impending anti-socialist repression in northeast Ohio and America as a whole had already been shown by the arrest and jailing of Baker, Wagenknecht, and Ruthenberg. In June 1918, the authorities moved against the party's national leader, Eugene V. Debs. Debs, who had just returned from visiting his comrades in the Canton Workhouse, delivered a fiery speech attacking the war as one of conquest and plunder. The speech outraged federal government agents lurking in the hall, but electrified the twelve hundred party supporters in attendance.[25] "The truth," Debs declared, "will make the people free,"[26] but the authorities arrested him for speaking it. He was charged with breaching the Espionage Act, which, passed by Congress on June 15, 1917, was amended by the Sedition Act of May 1918, which made it illegal to write or speak against the American war effort. Marguerite Prevey chaired the Canton meeting, it was at her house in Akron that Debs received the indictment, and she posted his bail. His indictment was followed by that of several other prominent Socialists. The Act violated the First Amendment of the US Constitution, which states, "Congress shall make no law ... abridging the freedom of speech, or of the press" and acknowledges "the right of the people peaceably to assemble," but few dared speak out.

Debs did not back down. He returned to Akron and gave a blistering Labor Day anti-war speech to several hundred people in the city's Music Hall. He admitted proudly that he had shaken hands with Lenin and Trotsky and was cheered to the rafters when he mentioned his indictment for the Canton speech. Ominously, however, the party's support was slipping away, as shown when it failed to collect the requisite number of signatures to get on the ballot for the Ohio elections. A *Beacon* writer noted with some satisfaction: "those who formerly boasted of belonging to the party are backward about signing petitions, especially since some government investigations are being made."[27] The establishment's blows against the party were coming thick and fast. In August, the Ohio legislature passed legislation that provided

> That no red or black flag, banner, sign or ensign having upon it any inscription opposed to the organized government or which is sacrilegious or which may be derogatory to public

> morals may be carried in parade within the state or displayed on any street or building within this state.

Offenders faced fines of up to $100 or imprisonment for up to six months, or both.[28]

The war ended in November 1918, but the repression intensified. America was entering into the period of the Red Scare. The American establishment had long hated the socialist movement and the Socialist Party's opposition to the war effort, and support for the Russian Revolution gave it the excuse to launch ruthless repression against the leftists of all stripes. Theodore Kornweibel Jr. considers that

> The First World War and the subsequent Red Scare years establish two benchmarks in American Civil Liberties. At no time in the nation's history, before or after, was the Bill of Rights so freely transgressed … the years mark the birth of modern political surveillance in the United States.

The authorities repeatedly and massively violated the Bill of Rights.[29] In the toxic atmosphere generated by fear of Bolshevism, the government infested America with spies and gave confidence to lynch mobs, whose criminal activities against leftists and people of color multiplied during the years between 1918 and 1922.[30] A highly organized official intelligence network had mushroomed during the war years. This included the Office of Naval Intelligence, the Military Intelligence Division, the Justice Department's Bureau of Investigation (the predecessor of the FBI), and the Treasury Department's Secret Service. Even the US Postal Service and the US Food Administration maintained battalions of snoopers. Although the networks' initial purpose was to guard against enemy spying and subversion, they soon turned their attentions to civilians, starting with the German-speaking communities and moving seamlessly on to radicals of whatever description. The state surveillance apparatus was massively augmented by private organizations of "patriotic" citizens, including, for instance, the YMCA. Huge numbers of people were involved in these networks. As Ann Hagedorn writes in her book *Savage Peace,*

> Even more vast in numbers … than any of the federal intelligence staffs was a mammoth web of patriotic organizations

> enlisting thousands of volunteer spies, all of whom reported their findings to … [official intelligence agencies].… The most powerful was the American Protective League, a clandestine 'club' of volunteers.… By the autumn of 1918, there were at least three hundred thousand APL spies hidden in the folds of American society.[31]

To some Akronites, spying was perhaps as American as mom and apple pie, and justified by the need to win the war. The press supported the gathering witch hunt. The *Beacon Journal* editorialized at length about the Central Labor Union's "deplorable" support for Tom Mooney, the radical labor activist convicted on flimsy evidence of the 1916 Preparedness Day bombing in San Francisco.[32] Whenever radicals were under attack, the press would spin reports against them. Thus, the *Beacon* justified a police raid on a farm near Akron because the Socialists were meeting there to "plan … a demonstration"[33]—an activity supposedly guaranteed by the First Amendment. The *Beacon* also approved of the 1920 dragnet and deportation of "Reds," who had allegedly stockpiled rifles and bombs. The raids, the *Beacon* claimed, had broken "the backbone of incipient revolution in the United States." Intriguingly, it added that some male students at an unnamed "Soviet College" in the Midwest had long hair and beards, while the co-eds had short hair.[34] Such violations of established gender roles were guaranteed to scandalize "decent" citizens.

The Socialists were vastly outnumbered by the huge number of spies who augmented the regular apparatus of state repression. Their less courageous members, too, were quietly retreating into private life. A sign of the times was the defeat of a motion at the Akron CLU in July 1919 that called for a general strike in defense of striking machinists in the city.[35] Two months earlier, a "patriotic" mob had trashed the Socialist Party's Cleveland offices and drunken soldiers and armed businessmen had violently attacked its May Day parade, which was headed by a returned soldier carrying a red flag. One marcher died after his throat was cut, but instead of arresting the murderers, the police joined in the assault. Cleveland's leading newspaper, the *Plain Dealer*, blamed the riot on the Socialists and applauded the "prompt and vigorous" response of the vigilantes and police. Although it admitted that "the right of the people to assemble is not to be abridged," the paper justified the "abridgment" by insisting that "carrying the red flag of anarchy ... is an incitation [sic] to violence [and] an insult to every patriot." Thereafter, the police banned all left-wing parades and stopped the Socialists from holding election rallies,[36] using the Criminal Syndicalism Act, which Republicans and Democrats had united to push through the Ohio legislature. The Act, which remained on the statute books until 1969, allowed the authorities to criminalize any leftist activity in the state.[37]

Two weeks before the May Day fracas, Eugene Debs arrived at the Atlanta Penitentiary to start a ten-year sentence for breaching the Espionage Act. A former railroad union leader, he "rode to prison in a union train with not so much as a whisper of protest from his former coworkers."[38] Four months later, with Debs behind bars, the Socialist Party suffered a devastating blow when an Emergency National Convention, held in Chicago between August 30 and September 5, resulted in a three-way split. The majority of the party's organized leftwing walked out to form the breakaway Communist Labor Party, and a smaller number created the Communist Party of America. The CLP merged with a minority faction from the CPA in 1920 to form the (United) Communist Party of the United States. In northeast Ohio, the majority joined the CPA.[39] but Akron's Marguerite Prevey went with the Communist Labor Party. Already reeling from state repression and hemorrhaging large numbers of members, the Socialist party was badly weakened by the split.

By late 1921, the Red Scare persecution was beginning to ebb. When President Warren Harding pardoned Eugene Debs late that year, the *Beacon Journal* ran an editorial congratulating him for his kindliness in releasing a "clean, fearless man," while distancing itself from Debs' politics.[40] Six years later, the Cleveland *Plain Dealer*, for its part, admitted that "instead of arresting those who had attacked the [May Day 1919] parade, the police attacked the marchers."[41] Looking back it is clear that America had descended into a kind of collective madness akin to the Salem witch hunts, but on an incomparably greater scale. A *Beacon* letter writer opined that future generations would remember the Red Scare as "the darkest era in American history."[42] During the Palmer Raids of

1919–20, the police arrested tens of thousands of leftists. Attorney General Palmer deported over twenty-one thousand of them to Russia in one fell swoop. Palmer claimed that his agents had discovered that on May Day 1920, America's radicals would arise as one and overthrow the government. Whether Palmer believed this nonsense was beside the point; as millions of citizens did, it gave him the pretext to step up repression. The press joined in the clamor. In July 1919, the *Beacon Journal* published the sensational claim that "Debs is now opposed to radicalism; former Socialist leader undergoes change of heart behind prison bars; wants no bloodshed." Debs "who was ready to use machine guns," it added, was "a changed man." The article cited the Warden of the Atlanta Penitentiary as its source.[43] Marguerite Prevey riposted that she had been Debs' friend for nineteen years and knew that "he had always opposed violence." "In fact," she continued, "he is now in prison because he is opposed to violence as a method of settling disputes between nations." His aim, she continued, was to educate and organize the working class so that it could use its numbers to abolish capitalism.[44]

The Red Scare and the three-way split reduced Akron's party local to a ghost of its former self. The Preveys' marriage broke down under the strain, and Marguerite moved from her High Street residence to a small cottage at Springfield Lake. Local business boycotted Frank's realtor firm, forcing him to work for wages in Cleveland. By 1921, the Akron local was so weakened that it failed to organize anything to celebrate May Day. The rival Socialist Labor Party organized a small rally, which was heavily surveilled by detectives and armed representatives of the city safety directory. The Communist Labor Party was by this stage present in the city, but it suffered heavy repression. Detectives had earlier seized quantities of its literature produced for rubber workers—again in violation of the First Amendment.[45] Refusing to be intimidated, Marguerite Prevey threw herself into the work of the new party. Earlier, the police had kidnapped her at revolver point, and took her to Chicago to answer an indictment for conspiracy to overthrow the government.[46] A judge quashed the indictment.[47] She did not stay long in the Communist movement and resigned from the National Executive Committee of the United Communist (Workers') Party after only five months.[48] In his tribute to Prevey, Joseph Sharts (who stayed with the Socialist Party in the split) argued that "her shrewd common sense and quiet breadth of vision soon disillusioned her concerning the Communist Labor and Communist parties."[49] The Socialist Party had been an open, multi-tendency party, so the intensely disciplined, hierarchical Bolshevik style of organization must have been too narrow for Prevey's taste. She may also have begun to doubt the optimistic predictions of Bolshevik supporters that "the path of the Soviet dominion will lead from the harsh and cruel reality of dictatorship to the beautiful and realized dream of democracy."[50] She withdrew from all political activity for some time to study "all political expressions of American Labor."[51] It is also possible that Bishop William M. Brown, who knew her in the Socialist Party, was right when he opined that she "had never strayed away from her Catholicism,"[52] and this conflicted with the Communist Party's militant atheism.

Nevertheless, it is indubitably the case that she always worked to build a mass, democratic workers' party and that she found the Communist Party too narrow. Two weeks before her sudden death on April 14, 1925, at the age of fifty-two, she attended a convention of the Farmer-Labor Party in St. Paul, Minnesota. It is unclear why she did not rejoin the Socialist Party, but perhaps she shared Eugene Debs' private view that her old party was virtually extinct. In fact, the party did not perish, but its heyday was over. The Left as a whole never recovered from its earlier losses. Much of the Socialist Party membership went over to the Communist organizations so that in 1919 there were almost seventy thousand Communists in America, but in 1924, only thirty-six thousand people voted for the Communist presidential candidate, William Z. Foster. By 1927, the Communist Party had only eight thousand members.[53] The national decline of the Left was mirrored in Akron. Alfred Winslow Jones estimates that by the 1930s the Socialist Party had perhaps twenty members in Akron. In the same period, the Communist Party boasted perhaps seventy-five members in the city and the Trotskyists could claim no more than twenty-five.[54]

10.

Labor in a Boomtown

The great flood that inundated Akron in February 1913 achieved what the IWW could not. It completely shut down Goodyear's sprawling factories on the banks of the Little Cuyahoga River.[1] Ten inches of rain had fallen on ground frozen hard by winter. Forced from the rubber factory gates by the relentless rain, the few remaining pickets contemplated an uncertain future. With the outbreak of war in Europe in 1914, US industry entered into a spectacular boom, but a new slump hit Akron hard in 1921. East Coast banks stepped in to save Goodyear from bankruptcy, but within a year or so Akron entered the rip-roaring boom of the Roaring Twenties. With full employment, full lunch pails, and faith in the "American Dream," many workers felt they had no need of unions. On the other hand, in 1921 a Communist gummer declared that he had "been up against the game of wage-slavery in many places in my time, but I never saw anything to compare with Akron."[2] The Bedaux system constantly sped up the work and caused frequent wildcats.

The American economy was booming, but investigations commissioned by US President Hoover found that new wealth generated went disproportionately to Capital and that while workers' incomes were rising, they did not keep pace with increases in productivity.[3] In Akron, repression combined with "welfare capitalist" measures and "yellow unions," along with other factors generated by boomtown conditions, kept independent unions out of the rubber factories for over twenty years. The Socialist Party had virtually disappeared, crushed by the federal government in the Red Scare following the war and weakened by splits. A handful of left-wing activists kept the dream of industrial unionism and independent labor politics alive, but at times, they must have despaired that things could ever change.

The IWW strike had achieved nothing positive. The speed-up continued and "ringleaders" were blacklisted, depriving the city's working class of a whole layer of rank-and-file leaders. Among their adversaries, a triumphalist mood prevailed: vigilante leader George Atwater crowed about a "victory of the moral forces of the city over lawlessness,"[4] and Goodrich presented him with "a fine automobile" for his services.[5] Goodyear rewarded "loyalists" with two weeks' paid vacation,[6] and Goodrich donated $2000 to the police pension fund.[7]

Further upheaval was to come. In the fall of 1913, a short, but sharp slump hit America. Markets were glutted with rubber goods and vicious price wars broke out.[8] The price of Goodrich stock rose by only one cent to fifty-five cents.[9] The experience of Henry Pfaff is typical of the plight of the city's single workingmen. As work was impossible to find and there was no public relief, Pfaff lived in a flophouse with a group of other unemployed men, paying $2 or $3 a week for their shared rooms, pooling their money to buy food and beer in bulk to ride out the economic storm.[10] One rubber factory laid off up to 1500 workers in a few weeks, but the companies continued to advertise for labor in Southern newspapers.[11] James Thompson's experience was not atypical. Arriving in the city with his wife and three children in response to the advertisements, he wandered the streets with dwindling hope. Drenched by rain, the family sought refuge in the County Jail, where "to satisfy technicalities they had to be charged with vagrancy."[12]

The slump was short-lived. Laid-off workers were reemployed. Goodyear hired Henry Pfaff as a core assembler in their tire curing plant. It was relentlessly hard, sweaty work but like many others who had been subsisting from hand to mouth, he welcomed it.[13] The mills' renewed appetite for labor was enormous. When the war and subsequent immigration restrictions curtailed the supply of European labor, the rubber companies recruited huge numbers of poor Southerners. The

Diamond Rubber Company, for example, advertised for "Strong, active men for automobile and bicycle tire making and press work. Millmen and laborers. Steady work and good pay. Apply at Falor St. gates."[14] Thousands took heed. Akron was a destination of one of the greatest mass migrations in history. Between 1910 and 1917, the city's population swelled by 202 percent,[15] from 70,000 in 1910 to 208,000 in 1920, of whom 70,000 worked in the rubber mills.[16] The process was unplanned and chaotic, spawned a myriad of social evils, and gave self-appointed moral guardians constant employment. Akron lived twenty-four hours a day, its downtown packed with shoppers and waves of gummers coming off shift. The Kenneth Albee Palace and Loew's theaters on South Main put on elaborate vaudeville performances, and the city's movie houses did brisk business. The Colonial Theater on Mill Street's repertory company played to rapt audiences.[17] In 1921, WOE, the city's first radio station, commenced broadcasting.[18] Embers Restaurant on West Market Street, staffed by bunny type girls, did a roaring trade.[19] The press deplored an epidemic of vice, and denounced the "the grill houses," which it regarded as brothels. During Prohibition, Akron's gangsters made fortunes selling bootleg liquor to thirsty citizens—and bribed police to look the other way.

Across the Atlantic, Europe was sliding inexorably towards war. Although the US remained neutral until 1917, the conflict was a bonanza for business; with American manufacturers selling to whomever would pay the highest price. Between 1914 and 1917, American industrial production increased by thirty-two percent and GNP by almost twenty percent. America had become quartermaster for the warring armies.[20] Akron's rubber mills hired five thousand new workers in 1915 and a further ten thousand in the first two months of 1916. Factory payrolls ballooned out by $25 million to $40 million in 1916, and the rubber workforce increased from just under 40,000 to 57,000. In the same period, the total value of the city's rubber production soared from $150 million to $226 million.[21] In 1914, the US rubber industry was consuming two-thirds of the world's raw rubber,[22] much of it by this stage grown on the newly established plantations in Southeast Asia. By 1917, Akron consumed about half of the world's raw rubber and the US merchant marine could not handle the volumes.[23]

America's entry into the war in 1917 created a further profit bonanza for the Akron rubber industry. By 1918, Akron was gobbling sixty percent of America's raw rubber imports and filling sixty-five percent of US government orders for rubber goods. At Goodrich, "one day's production represented 60 miles of insulated wire, 15 miles of rubber hose, 60,000 pairs of rubber heels, 15,000 pairs of shoes, 4,000 water bottles, 18,000 battery jars and 11,000 golf balls, a ton of rubber bands, 7,000 bulbs, and 20,000 automobile tires."[24] The war also sparked a transport revolution, which further sent rubber profits skywards. In 1904, there had only been seven hundred registered trucks in the US, and these ran on solid rubber wheels. By 1920, there were one million, mostly running on pneumatic tires.[25] Production for private automobiles had also soared. The *Cleveland Plain Dealer* reported in mid-1915 that there were Goodyear tires on five hundred thousand American automobiles.[26] With one Ford car rolling off the assembly lines every ten seconds by 1925, the appetite for tires was insatiable.[27]

The boom outlasted the war, and rubber profits soared to ever-giddier heights. Goodyear's business rose by 59.3 percent in the first half of 1920, and stock dividends soared by 150 percent.[28] Its fortunes mirrored those of American capitalism as a whole, and the US ended the war as the world's preeminent industrial and financial power, overtaking its European rivals in the process.[29] However, in the second half of 1920, the bubble burst. The Akron manufacturers had huge stocks of unsold tires, and Goodyear avoided bankruptcy by accepting massive loans from East Coast banks. The Akron rubber workforce fell from seventy-five thousand in June to twenty thousand in December.[30] Southern workers went home, and those who could not "roamed the streets."[31] However, while recovery was slow, the new boom of the Roaring Twenties was just around the corner.

Booms of this size were unprecedented. Nothing in Europe could compare with the colossal expansion of US industry and the social and demographic changes it generated were likewise unparalleled. The newspaperman Hugh Allen arrived in Akron "one cold day in February 1914" aboard the Cleveland streetcar and observed that "[t]he town didn't look too good.... From the second floor window at the *Beacon Journal* office ... the view ... took me back to certain mining camps of the far west."[32]

Akron was the architectural incarnation of laissez-faire individualism. Little thought was given to the living conditions of the wage-laborers and their families, nor to civil aesthetics. "Akron was experiencing the hectic life of a boomtown," the socialist Chalmers K. Stewart wrote of his boyhood in the city one hundred years ago. "Rooming houses, where workers slept in shifts, and boarding houses proliferated." Major roads were still paved with wooden blocks, "which swelled up after several seasons of wet weather into alarmingly big bumps."[33]

Boom-time Akron was a city of stark contrasts of wealth and poverty. The manufacturers made huge profits and built grandiose mansions. Some of the wealth trickled down to the Akron population. In 1914, according to the journalist H. Earl Wilson, the city boasted no less than eighty millionaires. Rents were sky high as landlords cashed in on a housing crisis. Rooming houses became "lucrative temples of Morpheus," with "three beds to the room and each bed rented on an eight hour basis, three shifts a day."[34] Hotels seldom had rooms after 6:00 pm, and fifty men slept on cots in the YMCA auditorium and gym, and others slept on lobby chairs.[35] In 1906, CLU President T. J. Mumford uncovered a case in which fifty-three Hungarians and Poles were living in one room.[36] Landlords rented out basements and attics for $35 to $80 a month.[37] One enterprising family rented the mansion of a rubber baron who had moved out to leafy Fairlawn and ran it as a rooming house with cots crammed into every available bit of space, and rented beds at $1 a shift or $3 a day.[38] Given that tire builders and finishers received $3.50 for an eight to ten hour day in 1913, this was extraordinary price gouging. Just as the great rubber strike was beginning, the *Akron Press* reported that Italian construction workers were paying $5 a month to live in windowless railroad boxcars and working in conditions akin to "peonage."[39]

Water supplies ran short, and the city's sanitation was in a horrible state. The main trunk sewer was leaking into the O&E Canal near Lock 2 in the Downtown area,[40] and in the summer of 1913, a "water famine" caused an outbreak of typhoid in Barberton.[41] Overcrowded living conditions, with laborers sleeping in shifts in the same beds, were "exactly what was needed" to turn the influenza epidemics that struck Akron in waves from 1917 into a "great death-dealing machine." Entire families died, people fell ill on streetcars, jitneys, and buses, and "the victims died quicker than the undertakers could bury them.[42] Gang violence declined sharply in the "Hell's Half Acre" of South Akron because so many "gang bangers" died.[43] Akron's Health Officer concluded that,

> No city in the United States has a greater problem in health conservation than Akron, where the enormous transient population and inadequate housing facilities present extraordinary opportunities for the disease.[44]

Akron had "natural advantages of topography, climate, and water supply" but these could not counteract its inefficient sewer system, insufficient garbage collection and disposal, and the "inadequate supervision of milk and food processing." The overcrowded houses were deathtraps.[45] Little had changed since 1828, when a water-borne epidemic almost killed off the town's population.[46] There were periodic outbreaks of cholera, dysentery, and smallpox, and a report on the city's hospitals in 1877 branded them as "horrible dens, unfit for people to live in, a disgrace to the humane people of Ohio."[47] In 1903, city engineers traced another typhoid epidemic to contaminated water from Summit Lake, the city's main water supply, but G. W. Smith, the manager of the water company, blustered, "If the people of Akron get typhoid fever let them hire physicians."[48] Much of the city's water was "befouled by drainage from the local Goodrich and Firestone plants."[49] By 1918, Akron's sewers, which could service a population of fifty thousand, were unable to cope and threatened to make the city (with a population over four times larger) uninhabitable.[50] Sewers designed for a small Western Reserve town could not cope with the galloping increase in population.

The Socialists had campaigned to improve public health and sanitation, forcing the city authorities and establishment politicians to take heed. In 1912, the city hired Gale G. Dixon, a distinguished engineer, to take charge of upgrading Akron's water and sewerage works, including a new dam on the Cuyahoga.[51]

In 1903, the city limits contained forty-five thousand people.[52] By 1910, the population had risen to over 69,000[53] and by 1917, there were some 157,000 people in the city, or over 200,000 if the outlying districts were included.[54] By 1920, there were 208,000 people in Akron proper; one-third of whom worked in the rubber mills,[55] and the rest were to one degree or another dependent on the industry. Akron's surging population growth mirrored the galloping population increase of America as a whole. By 1930, the US population had doubled to 123 million and of these one in ten were foreign born and an additional twenty percent had at least one parent born overseas.[56] In 1910, Firestone opened a downtown employment office to enroll incoming laborers.[57]

By 1907, over two hundred foreigners were arriving at Union Station every day[58] and ten years later, half of Goodrich's workers were foreign-born.[59] One of them was K. H. Andonian, an eighteen-year-old Armenian, who arrived in Akron in 1913 from Sivas in Turkey. He had boarded a sealed railroad car at the Central Railroad of New Jersey Terminal after processing at Ellis Island. The authorities did not bother to provide the men with food. The train zigzagged across Pennsylvania, distributing workers in industrial towns along the way like so many commodities. Eventually, the car was shunted into the rail yard between the General Tire and Goodyear factories in East Akron. Andonian's grandson writes, "my grandfather went straight to work [in the summer heat] carrying bricks up and down a ladder at the Goodyear plant." "He became dizzy and began to stagger about … [so] a foreman thought he was drunk and began to shout at him." Andonian tried to explain that he was just tired and had not eaten since the train left New Jersey. Luckily, Frank Seiberling was nearby and he asked another man from Turkey to translate what Andonian was saying. "Mr. Seiberling gave the man money," the grandson relates, "and told him to take my grandfather home, feed him, and when he had slept bring him back and he would have a job waiting for him."[60] Andonian was fortunate for this random act of kindness on Seiberling's part and "when he returned he was put to work indoors and remained employed at Goodyear for about 25 years." He raised an American family in what must have been at first a bewildering and often hostile environment. Many other new immigrants were not so lucky. As many as half of the Italians, and more than half of the Greeks, Russians, Romanians, and Bulgarians went home, disillusioned with life in America.[61]

Akronites often scorned Appalachian immigrants as hillbillies and "snakes," but at least recognized them as fellow Americans. Eastern and Southern European immigration had alarmed the nativists, and rampant xenophobia infected the Akron press. Fourteen million immigrants had arrived in America between 1860 and 1900 and continued at the rate of around one million per annum.[62] In 1905, a *Beacon* writer scorned the "long lines of ignorant immigrants [who] line up at the various employment agencies and ask for work." He quoted an employment agent who said it was "thoroughly disgusting" that a "class of person" who supposedly reckoned time in terms of "so many Sundays and moons" was allowed into the country in the first place.[63] At the time, eugenic ideas were hegemonic and Americans regarded immigrants as threats both to the purity of the WASP gene puddle and to American jobs. Then, as now, American business could not function without immigrants, and they were scapegoats for most social ills. The *Beacon* journalist reproduced what he claimed was a typical question and answer session between a rubber agent and an immigrant:

> *Can you write?* No.
>
> *Can you read?* No.
>
> *What country are you in now?* Don't know.
>
> *What can you do?* Pick, shovel.
>
> *Any trade?* No.
>
> *Have you any money?* No. Come here with enough money to pay my way.
>
> *How old are you?* Don't know.[64]

Such prejudices reflected the "scientific" opinion of the time and IQ tests "were sure to produce grave concern in the minds of thoughtful citizens ... [for they] established that 83 per cent of the Jews, 80 per cent of the Hungarians, 79 per cent of the Italians, and 87 per cent of the Russians were 'feeble-minded.'"[65] The prominent psychologist Carl C. Brigham reckoned that "the American Negroes, the Italians and the Jews" were "born morons and imbeciles" and thus "genetically ineducable [sic] as a result."[66] Company psychologists even allocated jobs according to ethnicity—not surprisingly as the division of labor in America had historically been racialized.[67] Nativist ideology culminated in the

Johnson-Reed Act of 1924, which banned Asian immigration and restricted that of Eastern and Southern Europeans to small yearly quotas.[68] Immigrants from northwest Europe more favorably treated, but the Americanization policy of the 1920s targeted all foreigners and was enforced by Akron's rubber companies.[69]

The economic boom, population explosion, and large-scale influx of foreign immigrants and Southern incomers had profound implications for organized labor. As the historian and leftwing activist Mike Davis writes,

> The new Western industrial cities ... were built up almost overnight, with little continuity with pre-industrial traditions or social relations. This 'boomtown' characteristic of American industrialization meant that the labour movement in the United States, without the partial exception of New England valleys and the older Eastern port cities, arose without deep roots in the artisanal resistance to industrialism which many historians have stressed as a determining factor in the formation of militant unionism and working-class consciousness.[70] [British spelling in the original.]

This analysis fits boomtown Akron. The city housed tens of thousands of proletarians: men and women who lived by selling their labor power to the factory owners, and who owned little if any property. They were, in their relation to the means of production, a working class, but as E. P. Thompson reminds us, class is a cultural as well as a structural category. The breakneck speed with which the city had industrialized and expanded gave little time for the consolidation of traditions of struggle and for conscious identification on the part of the incomers that they were part of a class with its own distinct interests. The old artisanal layers of Akron's proletariat had been swamped by a huge influx of immigrants with varying levels of experience and education, and with different religions, languages, customs, and outlooks. Many were peasants from Eastern and Southern Europe, with scant experience of mass production industry or labor organization. A substantial and growing tranche of the newcomers hailed from the Appalachian hills and hollows—internal immigrants driven by the push of poverty and the pull of steady work and good wages—or at least the promise of them. Some of these "hillbillies" had had prior experience of union struggles, but many others arrived with the ideological/cultural baggage of rugged individualism, hard shell, fundamentalist religion, ingrained racism, and intolerance for human difference. There was also a high turnover of labor, both because of periodic economic downturns, and because many workers voted with their feet when conditions proved too onerous in the Akron factories. Blacklisted union militants would have looked elsewhere for work. It would take time to weld together this hastily assembled human gallimaufry into a class with consciousness of its common interests arising from common experience. Over everything, too, the specter of the 1913 defeat hovered as a warning to would-be militants.

The effects of the business cycle were contradictory. Wildcat strikes flared up across the industry. In November 1915, thirty Goodyear tire buffers struck when their piecework rates were cut from $1.75 to $1.25 per hundred. The strike did not spread, partly because rates in other departments were increased, at least temporarily, to isolate the strikers. It was clear that the radical mood of the city's working class had not completely abated when sixty young children went on strike at the Grace Elementary School on West Exchange Street, angered that the direct route to school took them along a busy road without sidewalks. The Board of Education agreed to build a new sidewalk, and the victorious children returned to school.[71]

Such little victories were unusual. The defeat of the Goodyear buffers' wildcat highlights the power of Cliff Slusser's sixty-strong Flying Squadron of "master rubber workers." The squadron was a kind of Praetorian Guard, which the company's in-house organs portrayed as medieval knights.[72] High school and college graduates were preferred.[73] Recruits received three years' training in all aspects of rubber production and the promise of permanent employment on good wages. Immediately that the buffers downed tools, management rushed in the *squadristi* to do their work.[74] Two years later, Goodyear formed an "engineering squadron" capable of doing all of the skilled work in the factory.[75] The squad broke strikes, overcame production emergencies, and acted as pacesetters to set production norms. It was so successful that Goodyear exported the model to its other North American and overseas plants.

Litchfield realized that stoppages in key departments could paralyze a whole factory. According to an IWW gummer, the squadron was "mainly effective as a moral influence or threat and would be powerless in case all the workers in the shop were organized so as to make possible a shop-wide strike."[76] The problem, however, was to organize a union capable of taking united action, and the squadron was a powerful barrier against one forming.

Wage cuts imposed at the start of the wartime boom mocked assumptions that conditions lost during a recession would be restored when trade picked up. This sparked a wave of wildcats, as when the Falls Tire & Rubber Company cut tire finishers' rates from forty-five to forty cents per tire, a symptom of the intense competition in the industry. In 1916, machinists staged a massive stoppage in support of a demand for an eight-hour day and other concessions.[77] They were partially successful at Firestone after intervention by a conciliator from the federal Department of Labor, but lost at Goodrich.[78] The strike at Goodyear collapsed after two weeks when the Engineering Squadron took over the machinists' jobs. Conservative elements on the city's Central Labor Union blocked a call by radicals for a general strike to support the machinists.[79] Goodyear rehired the strikers only if they passed a "vetting process" organized by the company union.[80] Simultaneously, a streetcar strike flared up and faded away without any gains for the strikers.[81] Smaller strikes over pay cuts continued into 1917 at Kelly Springfield in East Akron and 1918 at Goodyear.[82] In response, the rubber companies often selectively granted concessions, which they could afford because of soaring demand for their products. So great was the demand that by June 1918, there was a shortage of some 3,577 workers in the mills. The labor shortage saw increased numbers of women taken on.[83]

The labor shortage gave the rubber workers more bargaining power and the idea of forming a union once again gained traction. In June 1918, more than one thousand rubber workers gathered in the CLU hall to hear AFL organizer Carl Wyatt's call for a permanent union.[84] Nothing seems to have become of this, however, and the same was true of further efforts in 1923 during a rash of wildcats by thousands of gummers across the industry. In January, Samuel L. Newman, the business agent of the Machinists' Local and a former CLU president, called a mass meeting of rubber workers, but nothing eventuated.[85] In part, this was because of the employers' implacable opposition to unions. Henry Pfaff recalled that in 1919 he "pulled unauthorized strikes" in two rubber mills and signed up hundreds of workers to a (presumably secret) union.[86] The militant mood did not lead to permanent organization. As late as 1925, the only unionized rubber factory was at Carrollton, almost fifty miles south of Akron. The huge profits generated by the war boom enabled the rubber companies to grant wage increases and reduce working hours unilaterally. Although Akron was not the workingman's paradise painted by star-struck journalists and boosters, families had food on the table and a roof over their heads. As the boom continued, they might have imagined that the good times were permanent. However, the companies bestowed such raises on a "grace and favor" basis and could take them away on a whim. Full employment also meant that if individual workers were dissatisfied, they could find work elsewhere. The future union leader John D. House, for instance, often moved between employers during the boom years.[87] As a result, absenteeism and labor turnover continued to frustrate the rubber firms. The workers also resented the housing shortage, which forced them to pay exorbitant rents for "attics, sheds" and "every conceivable nook and cranny" of available space. Firestone responded by building a barracks for fifteen hundred single men, but it was a stopgap measure.[88]

The rubber companies were aware that repression alone would not keep out the unions and that labor turnover and absenteeism was not going to improve in the short term. The petty tyranny of the supervisors, who could fire workers for minor infractions of discipline or small mistakes in their work, had long created resentment. Evidence given to the 1913 Ohio Senate investigation also revealed widespread sexual harassment of female workers. After the 1913 strike, Firestone put the right to hire and fire in the hands of personnel managers and brought in industrial psychologists[89] whose brief was to fit human beings to the needs of mass production. They were ancillary to the speed-up, which continued and even intensified. According to the Akron Communist organizer John Williamson, the "poundage output" in tire making increased from an index figure of 100 in 1914 to 250.56 in 1922 and 506.25 in 1929. By 1930, it soared to 581.03 and to 681.05 the following year.[90] Although dressed up in humanistic language, the aim of the industrial psychologists was to supplement scientific management, not to replace it. Harry Braverman argues that industrial psychologists and personnel managers act as a "maintenance crew for the human machinery" of the factories with a brief of weakening "the hostility of workers to the degenerated forms of work … forced upon them."[91]

The "human machinery" functioned in a Taylorist system that had taken the division of labor to unheard of extremes. Goodyear boasted that its production system was one "of continuous supervision over *small groups of workers.* [Emphasis in the original.] It is not new. We have merely applied to ten thousand tiremakers, an old law. The law is, that if you take care of the small things, the big things will take care of themselves.… [Each worker] is a specialist in one or more operations."[92] Mill workers spent their lives on human treadmills; respite came only during layoffs or when, weakened by incessant toil, they quit or were fired. House considered that the system "sucks out … [a worker's] life and leaves him broken at forty."[93] It was the task of the psychologists to make industrial drudges "satisfied" with their condition. "Employee dissatisfaction" expressed itself in a whole spectrum of "behaviors" from wildcat strikes to grumbling and timewasting, to absenteeism and simply quitting—sometimes in the middle of a shift.

To counter these disruptions—and to cut across the appeal of unions—the employers introduced a raft of welfare capitalist measures. They were not the first to do so. Industrial paternalism had a long history in America, but it was stepped up during the first two decades of the twentieth century. In "an era characterized by unprecedented industrial strife and violence," writes Andrea Tone, "welfare work seemed to herald the advance of a new age in industrial relations, one that would be guided by the gentle hand of management rather than by the big stick."[94] Although some employers may have had a sincere desire to improve employees' working and living conditions, it would be naïve to imagine it was not part of a carrot and stick approach.[95] Moreover, as Tone points out, "employers [were] eager to check and repel the tide of governmental regulation" by introducing their own welfare reforms voluntarily.[96] This approach chimed with longstanding American anti-statist traditions and contrasted sharply with the European idea that welfare was government business.

Shortly after the 1913 strike, Firestone built a four-story employees' clubroom and opened a works canteen to provide meals at cost. A voluntary workers' compensation scheme, free life insurance, a savings bank, and a baseball park followed. In 1916, the company opened Firestone Park, which offered six hundred brand new houses to selected employees at cheap rates, along with churches, the Garfield High School, and a shopping center. Firestone sold the mass-produced Sears-Roebuck houses on the installment plan for between three thousand and seven thousand dollars, deducting a portion of the purchase price if the buyer stayed with the company for a specified length of time. This, commented a Wobbly gummer, ensured that "purchasers are careful to do nothing to bring about dismissal," and the debt was a good way of "keeping the workers' noses on the stone."[97] Nevertheless, because many gummers were paying up to one-third of their income in rents to private landlords, which at an average of $390 per annum, were some fifty percent higher than in other Midwestern cities and greater even than in East Coast cities, one imagines that the Firestone houses were coveted. Firestone also introduced an employee stockholder scheme,[98] and by 1929, claimed some seventeen thousand employee-shareholders and in the same year granted paid vacations.[99] Goodrich introduced similar measures. These, "sought to give Goodrich employees a sense of belonging to one, big, contented family," and included a clinic, insurance, free legal advice, a regular news magazine, and athletic and sporting facilities.[100]

Meanwhile, Goodyear was planning an even more radically ambitious welfare scheme. Declaring that "if Goodyear takes care of its workmen, its workmen take care of Goodyear," the company set up sporting, musical and technical clubs, a legal advice department, a plant hospital, a factory library, and published the *Wingfoot Clan* newspaper, all free of charge to employees. A plant canteen provided cheap meals and employees had access to workers' compensation, insurance, and retirement benefits schemes. A Goodyear advertisement explained that the company wanted a stable workforce "rather than itinerant workers," and that the welfare schemes would ensure this. Goodyear also set up "schools for the advancement of competent workmen [and] for the Americanization of aliens."[101] The company housed these activities in the brand new Goodyear Hall, which opened in April 1920, and featured a large auditorium decorated with mural of Vesuvius and a South American rubber loading dock, an orchestra pit, and sixty-five classrooms for the newly inaugurated Goodyear Industrial University.[102]

There appears to have been disagreement at top management level over some aspects of the welfare program because Paul Litchfield initially opposed plans for a company housing estate as "paternalistic."[103] Company housing schemes had overtones of progressive social engineering along the lines of the British "garden city" movement headed by Ebenezer Howard and this conflicted with the laissez faire ideology of men such as Litchfield. In fact, only a minority of US capitalists established welfare schemes during the Progressive era.[104] Nevertheless, the great 1913 strike perhaps changed Litchfield's mind, and construction of the Goodyear Heights estate began in May 1913 on vacant land half a mile from the factory. Ownership of the houses mirrored the racial division of labor in the rubber factories and made a distinction between deserving and undeserving employees. Only white people of "good character" could purchase homes:

> The Goodyear Heights Sales department wishes to correct the impression that there are no restrictions to sales on Goodyear Heights. One of the restrictions provides that no sales shall be made to colored people and this is rigidly carried out. This is not done with any view to discriminate against the colored man, but because it is thought best for the more rapid and thorough development of the section.

White nonemployees, however, were however free to apply. Although Firestone did not explicitly bar Black employees from purchasing homes, it is probable that that purchase of houses was beyond the means of Firestone's Black employees because they were confined to the lowest paid jobs in the factories. Firestone also excluded "aliens," although around one-sixth of the workforce were foreign-born.[105]

While gummers probably vied with each other for the chance to buy into the company housing precincts, organized labor viewed them more critically. An IWW member employed in the mills sneered that the houses were jerry-built and would soon fall down, but his view was founded more on hope than fact as they still stand today. The IWW detested welfare capitalism and warned that its purpose was to buy off the workers and put salve on the wounds inflicted by their chains. Likewise, according to Andrea Tone, the Socialist Party believed that "welfare work masked capitalism's most egregious symptoms without eradicating the structural source of workers' woes." The Socialists wished to place industry in public ownership under the control of the workers themselves, which, they felt, would assure decent working and living conditions for all.

The policy of the American Federation of Labor was rather more equivocal. Under the guidance of its long-time leader, Samuel Gompers, the Federation was suspicious of welfare and believed that it would lead to the "emasculation" of the red-blooded (male) American worker—who was almost invariably a skilled craftsman. In this, there was a curious symmetry with the anti-statist views of Akron's captains of industry, but Gompers was also suspicious of "handouts" from capitalists. In practice, however, because he accepted capitalism as a permanent system, he endorsed capitalist welfare for the benefits it gave to workers. At the same time, he worried that it might smother workers' independence: and emasculate them. As a result of this ambivalence, he came under sustained attack from the Socialists and spent a great deal of ink defending his position, no doubt because he himself was uncomfortable with capitalist paternalism.[106] Today, almost a century after these debates, the US can boast only a rudimentary public social welfare and public health net and without doubt one of the reasons for this melancholy state of affairs is the AFL's antipathy to statism and its refusal to support an independent labor party.

The centerpiece of Goodyear's social engineering scheme was the Industrial Assembly (IA), an elaborate "yellow union" set up after the big machinists' strike in 1919 and pitched as "a great blessing conferred ... by a benevolent employer."[107] Goodyear President "Old Man" Litchfield appears to have been a "true believer" in the IA scheme, which had great similarities to the corporatist model imposed by Mussolini in Italy after 1922. Goodyear called its employees "Industrians" and expected them to vote for "Senators" and "Representatives" in the IA's two "Houses." The "House of Representatives" consisted of forty members, who served one-year terms and had to be at least twenty-one years of age. The twenty "Senators" served five-year terms and had to be at least twenty-five years of age. All "Assemblymen" had to be US citizens in line with Goodyear's commitment to "Americanization" of aliens—and they attended meetings paid at the rate of 110 percent of individual hourly earnings.[108] Voting was not compulsory, but a recalcitrant radical claimed that after he failed to cast his ballot he was "doing all the most disagreeable work ever since."[109] Paul Litchfield served as unelected President of the IA, with the right to veto all "legislation." Although in theory a two-thirds majority of both Houses could override his veto, leftwing critics believed that "names would be recorded" and dissidents would be "marked men" thereafter.[110] To radicals, Goodyear had created the IA to undercut the appeal of independent union organization. Goodyear admitted as much in different language but insisted that the system was beneficial for both Labor and Capital. A Goodyear booklet admitted the anti-union motivation behind the Assembly:

> not only is it the object of the present effort to democratize industry, to promote harmony and to reduce labor troubles, but also to make the workers better off under "open shop" conditions than they would be under the control of unions.[111]

In February 1920, Litchfield announced at an IA meeting that "all of the American male employes [sic] in the factory will be paid a minimum wage of $6 per day, and all female employes $4 a day." He added that "pay increases of approximately 10 per cent on hourly rates and from five to twelve per cent on piecework rates will become effective Feb. 15." Some twenty-five thousand Industrians would benefit. The remaining five thousand employees included foreigners who had not taken out US citizenship.[112] The company employed devious methods to bolster the IA's image. Supervisors sometimes imposed some "petty tyranny" on their charges knowing that the IA would take up the matter, "thus giving the Assembly a great deal of credit."[113]

Alas, the minimum wages decreed in 1920 came a matter of months before the bottom fell out of the market for rubber. Only the intervention of big East Coast banks saved Goodyear from bankruptcy.[114] In January 1921, the Industrial Assembly voted for a 12.5 percent cut in factory workers' wages,[115] effectively wiping out the raises granted the previous year. The cuts were so unpopular that some IA Representatives protested, particularly as Goodyear had responded to the slump by speeding up production to cheapen its products. The dissidents asked that the 12.5 percent pay cut be restored, pointing out that both productivity and the cost of living had increased. The company's labor department tried to dampen down dissent, but it continued to smolder across the factory.[116]

The slump hit the city's working class hard. Journalists later recalled "beggars in silk shirts" on Akron's streets.[117] Yet with a revival in trade, wildcats again flared throughout the rubber mills. Pit workers at Mason Tire & Rubber in Kent walked off the job in May 1922, followed two weeks later by a strike at Swinehart, where workers protested a twenty-five percent pay cut.[118] A few days later, three hundred employees in the Goodrich tube department won a new wage scale of 77½ cents an hour following a three-day strike.[119] Perhaps wishing not to be outflanked, the Goodyear IA unanimously requested a raise of 12.5 percent for white-collar employees and ten percent for blue-collar workers. Goodyear conceded a raise of five and ten percent respectively, but it was not enough to satisfy the gummers.[120] In early December 1922, the IA requested a further raise of fifteen percent.[121] Litchfield vetoed the bill, whereupon the Assembly overrode him by the required two-thirds majority, only to have the raise vetoed by the Goodyear Board of Directors, whose decision was final.[122] Before the year's end, another strike of up to six hundred workers erupted at Goodrich over cuts to piecework rates. The company abandoned the cuts and the workers returned to work. Apparently satisfied, they told the *Beacon Journal* that they were not forming a union. However, the company must have double-crossed them because the strike broke out afresh and continued into the New Year. By January 4, about 750 strikers were holding regular meetings at the CLU hall. One week later, they claimed that ninety-five percent of the workers in the cord tire department were on strike, and pickets with banners and large signs confronted police at the factory gates.[123] Sensing greater possibilities for organizing than at any time since the 1913 strike, gummers were talking union. Sam Newman of the Machinists called a mass meeting of rubber workers, which at least a thousand workers attended.[124] The upsurge ebbed away but strikes continued to hit the various rubber companies. In mid-December, 1923, for instance, calendar operators at Miller Rubber struck following a pay cut and a week later one thousand workers—or one-third of the company's workforce—were on strike.[125] In total, there were nine strikes at Goodrich in 1922–23 in response to pay cuts.[126]

It is puzzling why the grave discontent did not lead to permanent union organization. The gummers were combative to a degree unseen since 1913 and the strike wave caught the rubber firms flatfooted. Although pay cuts were the direct cause of the strike wave, another factor was resentment over the speed-up and mechanization, which vastly increased production at the cost of the workers' health and slashed the workforce. In 1916, Goodrich introduced the Bedaux speed-up system in the machine shop and gradually extended it to the entire plant, spending hundreds of thousands of dollars in the process in order to save an even greater amount.[127] The other firms followed suit. Many of the strikes involved substantial numbers of workers, who elected strike committees and threw up picket lines. The degree of organization was much greater than had been the case before the 1913 IWW strike. The 1921–23 strikers also obtained the assistance of the CLU, which in January 1923 launched an organizing drive involving its thirty-three affiliated unions in Summit County, coordinated by Sam Newman of the Machinists.[128] Newman was not able under the AFL's strict rules to enroll production workers, so he requested a charter for a rubber workers' local and AFL general organizer Thomas J. Conboy came to set it up.[129] Conboy boasted at a mass meeting of eight hundred strikers that the AFL's rubber affiliate would be soon among the largest unions in the US.[130]

Conboy was a member of the AFL's conservative old guard, and he soon clashed with the CLU and the strikers, who had elected "progressives" to their strike committees. Despite its AFL affiliation, the CLU favored inclusive, industrial organization for the gummers in preference to Conboy's craft union approach, which would have divided the workers into different locals according to occupation. Leftist militants were scathing about Conboy but praised Sam Newman as "sincere and honest." Indeed, Newman would have supported *any* move to organize the rubber mills, even by an independent union or the IWW In the end, Conboy called the police "to oust some reds" from union premises, and "thus it was that the union exploded," an IWW man reported.[131] Militants accused Conboy of diverting strike funds and doing "everything possible ... to disrupt the union."[132] The differences were irreconcilable. Sam Newman's assistant, a former Iowa farm boy and socialist called Wilmer Tate, was to prove a lifelong advocate of the industrial union model despite being an artisan himself. Conboy, on the other hand, believed in the cooperation of Capital and Labor. The union collapsed, helped on its way by an unasked-for ten percent bonus at Goodyear. The company had given the bonus to head off the union and later took it away after the union collapsed.[133] John House records that a further attempt in 1926 to form a rubber workers' union failed, and that the leaders were sacked and blacklisted.[134] Curiously, the Trotskyist journalist B. J. Widick claims that members of the small Proletarian Party of America—a splinter of the Communist Party—briefly captured control of the Industrial Assembly in 1927 and led a strike that failed when only two hundred workers downed tools.[135]

There was no further serious attempt to unionize the mills for some years, but the idea of industrial unionism never disappeared. With militants such as Wilmer Tate prominent in Akron's AFL unions, Daniel Nelson considers that there "remained a tenuous but enduring link between the labor movement and the rubber workers."[136] In other industries in the mid-1920s, unionized workers sometimes engaged in very militant strikes. On May 1, 1926, for example, streetcar workers employed on interurban lines between Akron, Cleveland, Canton, and other centers struck in support of a claim for a wage increase of between seventeen and twenty-eight cents an hour, plus a reduction of the working day from ten to nine hours. The employers stood firm and the workers returned without any gains, but with loss of seniority rights, and the victimization of "ringleaders." Late in the strike, someone dynamited the tracks between Kent and Ravenna.[137]

By the early 1920s, the rubber companies had perfected their methods for keeping the unions out. Goodyear's Flying and Engineering Squadrons were a potent deterrent and the companies maintained swarms of spies. Two of the leading members of the 1921–23 strike committee were private detectives. Plant police forces kept armories bristling with weapons. From the early 1920s, Goodyear also employed "more than a hundred deputy sheriffs, all Klansmen, scattered through the shops so that they will know beforehand if anything is going to happen." According to the IWW, "the deputies work without pay from the companies," which, if true, suggests that they were paid from the public purse.[138] The welfare measures introduced after the 1913 strike also played a role in maintaining the open shop.

Following the brief slump of 1921, America entered into the great boom of the "Roaring Twenties" with its promise of permanent prosperity. Some workers, particularly Southerners, believed that the IA really served their interests. America's small farmers, particularly in the South, had never shared the prosperity of the boom years. Prices for agricultural products fell sharply after the 1918 Armistice and a rural depression lingered through the 1920s, forcing six million farmers off the land. The South, David M. Kennedy writes, was America's most rural region and had changed little since the end of Reconstruction in 1870, with outdated farming methods and little mechanization.[139] Many of the Southern immigrants had been brought up in abject poverty, with few modern amenities, few luxuries, and little hope that things would ever get better. For them, life and work in the city could seem like living the American Dream, at least during the great boom of the Roaring Twenties. For the first time in their lives, they would have cold and perhaps hot running water, flush toilets and electricity, buy their provisions in well-stocked grocery stores, and save for a refrigerator and a motorcar. David Kennedy writes eloquently of "country ways of life … untouched by modernity":

> The fifty million Americans who dwelt in what F. Scott Fitzgerald called 'that vast obscurity beyond the city' still moved between birth and death to the ancient rhythms of sun and season. More than forty-five million of them had no indoor plumbing in 1930, and almost none had electricity. They relieved themselves in chamber pots and outdoor latrines, cooked and heated on wood stoves, and lit their smoky houses with oil lamps…. [The mother of a future governor of Arkansas] could not do the family laundry until she had first boiled the guts of a freshly butchered hog to make lye soap … [and] sunset routinely settled a cloak of darkness and

> silence on that immense domain where the fields of the republic rolled on under the night.[140]

After the poverty of the hollows and hill farms, many incomers were grateful for the relatively high wages paid in Akron. An Akron Wobbly noted that they believed themselves "deeply indebted to the rubber companies who pay a 'living wage.'"[141] Nevertheless, some of the incomers did have previous experience of union struggles "back home" in Appalachia and later rose to prominence in the industrial union movement. One of these was Art Dockery, later vice-president of URW Local 5 at B. F. Goodrich. Before his arrival in Akron in 1919, Dockery, who was a preacher's son, had worked as a teenage lumberjack in North Carolina. When the boss imposed a twenty-five percent pay cut, Dockery and his buddies "all went home for their guns, took to a nearby hill, [and] not a log was lumbered, and the strike was won!"[142] Nevertheless, Southerners like Dockery emigrated to a greatly different world; from pre-modern rural villages to a city that epitomized capitalist modernity and sat at the center of a global industrial empire.

In 1927, Goodyear produced its one-hundred-millionth tire.[143] In 1935, the company employed upwards of forty thousand people in its factories and plantations around the world.[144] Firestone was in the same league. A news report in 1935 marveled at Harvey Firestone's influence over the nominally independent West African state of Liberia, where his firm had carved the huge Harbel plantation from the jungle.[145] Goodyear's Paul Litchfield announced that his company "spread all over the globe so that the sun never sets on the Goodyear factory."[146] Goodrich's massive Akron plant consisted of 116 separate buildings set on 165 acres on South Main. It was a city within a city" that boasted an internal electric transportation system, police and fire departments, a subway equal in length to the Holland Tunnel under the Hudson, and a power house that generated enough electricity to supply two hundred thousand households.[147] Fierce competition weeded out the smaller fry among the rubber firms. Marx had forecast some seventy years earlier that economic power would be concentrated into fewer and fewer hands—that the larger "capitals" would gobble up the smaller—and this was borne out in Akron. By 1937, apart from the Big Three rubber firms (Goodyear,

Goodrich, and Firestone) only the Mohawk, General Tire, and Seiberling companies had survived and once thriving firms such as Swinehart, Marathon, Mammoth & Star, and Portage Tire & Rubber had perished.[148] Akron seemed firmly under the thumb of the rubber barons.

11.

The Klan, Racism, and Labor in Akron

The decade following the end of the Great War was a lean time for organized labor in Akron. The slump of 1921–22 was relatively short-lived. Trade picked up and America plunged headlong into the Roaring Twenties. With the economy booming, full employment returned to Akron. The huge influx of Southerners that had begun during World War I profoundly altered the composition of the city's working class. Between 1910 and 1920 an estimated one hundred thousand white immigrants made their way north to Akron from the hollows, hill farms, and impoverished towns of Appalachia.[1] This helped turn the city into a bastion of the "American Nativist" Ku Klux Klan. Much of the Akron establishment supported this ugly radicalism of the right,[2] some doubtless because they knew that it diverted working-class dissatisfaction that might otherwise have benefited the unions and the Left. Yet before the Civil War, Akron had been an important way station on the "underground railroad" that spirited escaped slaves to freedom in Canada. The city had witnessed Sojourner Truth's celebrated peroration "Ain't I a Woman?" in which she called for equal rights for women and justice for Black people,[3] and it had been home to John Brown. In 1900, however, even before the mass influx of white Southerners, Akron witnessed an ugly race riot, in which a drunken racist mob, egged on by local grandees and sensational newspaper headlines, had burned down city hall and besieged the downtown police station.[4] The mass migration of the Southern white population dimmed the prospects for independent working-class organization in the city, at least in this period. It also put paid to any hope of resurrecting the city's socialist organizations, already battered by repression and internecine feuds.

Racism was rampant across 1920s America. It hindered the development of working-class consciousness and inhibited the growth of militant labor organization. Some nineteenth-century American labor unions barred Black laborers from membership, but others took a progressive stand. In the 1880s, the masthead of the Akron *Labor Unionist* proudly proclaimed its support for all workers "without Regard to Creed, Color, Nation or Party."[5] By the 1920s, such an inclusively class-conscious outlook died under the weight of the 1913 defeat, boomtown conditions, and mass migration. The Red Scare of 1918–19 had catapulted the US into the frenzy of state and vigilante violence that eclipses the McCarthyism of the 1950s. Across America, mobs targeted Blacks as well as white leftists. The number of lynchings and race riots soared between 1918 and 1922[6] and anti-immigrant hysteria led in 1924 to the passage of the racist Johnson-Reed Act. The huge influx of white Southerners during the boom years did nothing to improve race relations in the city. Many of the incomers regarded Catholics, Jews, leftists, and foreign immigrants as threats to the American way of life and had been raised to believe that Black people were their natural inferiors. Unfortunately, but not surprisingly, the American Federation of Labor joined the anti-immigrant chorus.[7]

Racism predated the influx of white Southerners. Historically, Akron's white community regarded Black people, whether free or not, as inferior. Hiram Bowen, an early proprietor of the *Summit Beacon,* opposed the extension of the "Peculiar Institution" (slavery) to the North but supported its retention in the Old South.[8] On the eve of the Civil War, the *Beacon* approved Illinois Senator Stephen Douglas's argument,

> [t]he slavery question was a matter of political economy. People bought where they could purchase cheapest, and sold where they could get the best prices—so in regard to the

> employment of negro [sic] labor; where it was cheapest, it would be employed; where white labor was cheapest, slave labor would be excluded.[9]

Racial injustice had the full weight of the law behind it. The Ohio Black Acts of 1804 and 1807 stripped Black Americans of many of their civil rights, making it illegal to harbor runaway slaves or for Black children to attend the public school system. Blacks could not testify against whites in court.[10] In 1845, when a more liberal Ohio Senate voted to allow Blacks to testify, there was a storm of public outrage and the lower house voted down the bill.[11] Nor did the passage of the Thirteenth, Fourteenth, and Fifteenth amendments to the US Constitution end the racist machinations of Ohio lawmakers. In theory, by 1900 Black citizens were legally equal to whites,[12] but in practice they occupied an intermediate space between slaves and free men. In that period, Akron's Black community kept a low profile. They were often bystanders in the debates between their white partisans and racist detractors.

Ohio had never been a slave state, and despite an eight-fold increase in their number between 1910 and 1919,[13] there were few people of color in Akron. John Lee Maples estimates their number at 494 out of a total population of almost 70,000 in 1910, and 5,580 out of just over 208,000 in 1920.[14] By 1938, there were 12,000 Black residents in Akron.[15] This climbed to 14,000 in 1940[16] and to around 20,000 in 1947.[17] Black people endured a color bar in employment, housing, and education. Jim Crow-style segregation was the norm in restaurants, bars, cinemas, and other places of entertainment in Akron. Most local government jobs were "whites-only" preserves. In 1910, a meeting of local people of color and supporters called for the city to hire Black police officers,[18] but it was not until 1922 that the city appointed a token Black officer.[19] The white socialist Chalmers Stewart ironically recalled the Colonial Theater in East Mill Street—a landmark during his childhood in the 1920s—as "a fine old piece of Americana, complete with [what many whites called] 'nigger heaven,' the topmost tier with a continuous bench, no individual seats."[20] The Black community lived in segregated slum districts, and when Goodyear built its model Goodyear Heights housing precinct, they did not allow their Black employees to purchase houses.[21] If Black employees attempted to move into better housing, they risked eviction or worse at the hands of mobs.[22]

The city's manufacturers maintained a strict color bar, with Black laborers restricted to menial of unskilled positions. Left-wing gummers agitated for equality in the rubber mills, but they were out of step with the views of many of their workmates. In 1937 for instance, a Communist pamphlet attacked the "Jim-Crow conditions" prevailing in the Goodyear plant. Black workers were barred from the main plant canteen, forced by the management "to eat in that dirty little hole in the wall called the Mill-room cafeteria."[23] Black workers were called "boys" regardless of age.[24] James Turner started work at Firestone in 1934 and, despite his education and high intelligence, he was assigned to the lowly yard gang, one of the most "distasteful" jobs in the plant. In winter, Turner and his fellow Black laborers dug the pipeline from the plant's water supply, often up to their knees in freezing water in subzero weather. In summer, they cleaned the heater pits in sweltering temperatures. Turner was later "promoted" to janitor and mill room operative before being hired as a full-timer by the United Rubber Workers.[25] Firms such as Ohio Brass at Barberton refused to hire Black laborers for any type of work, even the most unskilled,[26] and Goodyear's in-house welfare schemes were segregated, with a separate "Goodyear Colored Club."[27] The rubber baron Harvey Firestone agreed with his notoriously racist friend Henry Ford that Black people were inferior human beings, and in 1915, he attended a so-called "Race-Betterment Conference" in San Francisco.[28] The same was true of the other corporations.[29] George Bernard Shaw pithily summed up the basis for the racial division of labor: "[t]he American white relegates the black to the rank of shoeshine boy; and he concludes from this that the black is good for nothing but shining shoes."[30]

For many of the Southern immigrants, the "degraded nature" of Blacks was self-evident, but as the writer Octave Mannoni has shown, assumptions of racial superiority are often laced with a strong dose of sexual fear.[31] There were few Blacks in the city, and many whites were determined that it should remain that way. The Ku Klux Klan found Akron fertile soil for its poisonous doctrines. It quietly recruited members and when it revealed itself publicly in the early 1920s, it was strong enough to take over control of the city.[32] In May 1922, Klansmen staged a monster rally in the Goodyear Hall, replete with the usual tomfoolery of burning crosses, white hoods, and pseudo-medieval titles.[33] David "Old Man" Curtiss Stephenson, the "Grand Dragon" of the Indiana Klans, whipped up the crowd and a seventy-five-piece band provided them with foot-tapping entertainment.[34] By 1925, Klavern No. 27 boasted fifty-two thousand members,[35] and even if this is an exaggeration, it was still the "Invisible Empire's" largest affiliate.[36]

While the bulk of the Akron Klan's foot soldiers were white working-class Southerners, local notables provided the leadership. These included the Rev. Dr. Howard S. MacAyeal, who used his influence as a *Beacon* columnist to take over the Akron school board. Judge Ernest E. Zesiger and Goodrich manager Joe Hanan both served as Exalted Cyclops of the klavern.[37] By 1924, anyone with political aspirations found it expedient to join. Recruits included Mayor D. C. Rybolt, and the Summit County sheriff, Chris Weaver.[38] The Klansmen placed their friends in key administrative positions and infiltrated the City Police Department. The local National Guard was nicknamed "the Grand Dragon's Guard" because of Klan control.[39] Mayor Rybolt hid his face behind a hood at rallies but was recognizable by his "peculiar gait."

The Klan's torchlight rallies and spectacular cross-burnings were thrilling politics-as-entertainment for the gullible and poorly educated. On one occasion, a 3,400-strong procession of hooded Klansmen paraded on horseback through the city streets and burned a fifty-two-foot high cross in the city's fairgrounds.[40] They set ablaze a giant cross on the steps of City Courthouse to mark July 4, 1925, rigging it with explosives timed to detonate at intervals throughout the evening. Eventually, the Akron Klan overreached itself. Reverting to brutal form, Klansmen threatened anyone who dared question its activities.[41] Power also bred corruption. Sheriff Weaver, for instance, sold confiscated bootleg liquor on the sly and fell out with Klan rivals[42] over the division of spoils. Maples considers the July 4 Independence Day parade to have been "the absolute pinnacle of the Klan's power in Akron."[43] Afterwards, a Citizens' Committee of one hundred drove the Klan from the school board.[44] Men such as Rybolt who had joined the Klan to further their own interests slipped away. The Klan's influence declined sharply, but it never completely disappeared. It had fed from a deep trough of racism, which far from drained, was overflowing. Thereafter, Jim Crow continued as before in every area of life, with the city's Black population relegated to menial jobs, substandard housing, and subjected to racial insults and humiliations on a daily basis. Even after the apogee of Klan power, many of the rubber companies' plant police were Klansmen.[45] Harley Anthony, who worked at Goodrich during the 1920s, claimed there were thousands of Klansmen in the rubber mills, many of them supervisors who gave preference to fellow Kluxers.[46] Unionists and leftists of all stripes had to keep their heads down in such a hostile environment, because the Klan was virulently anti-union and anti-socialist. It was also hostile to Jews, Catholics, and Blacks, and worked with the city's business moguls to keep the factories white, all-American, Protestant, and loyal to free enterprise.

In such conditions, Black dissatisfaction with life in "the City of Opportunity" grew. In 1917, the first chapter of the National Association for the Advancement of Colored People (NAACP) opened in Akron, with "Cap" Herring serving as its first president.[47] While the support of white liberals and socialists was welcome, the Black community realized that self-emancipation was the road to freedom and equality. Four years after the arrival of the NAACP, a small meeting convened in a basement in Newton Street to form a chapter of Marcus Garvey's United Negro Improvement Association (UNIA),[48] with M. P. Winbush as president. The UNIA regarded the NAACP as too timid but did make common cause with it against the Ku Klux Klan. The UNIA held many of its early meetings in the city's Second Baptist Church, but in 1922, it secured its own premises at 1103 Bellows Street, and in May 1922, Marcus Garvey spoke to supporters in the Perkins Auditorium,[49] and at subsequent mass meetings in the Second Baptist Church.[50] When the Liberian government opposed his plan to resettle millions of American and Caribbean Blacks, Garvey explained this was because it was "influenced by England and France and by an American rubber company, which had received a large concession" for a plantation.[51] The firm was Akron's Firestone Tire & Rubber, which became the effective neocolonial overlord of the African state.[52] After Garvey's arrest and imprisonment on charges of mail fraud orchestrated by FBI chief J. Edgar Hoover, the UNIA vice-president, William L. Sherrill, spoke in Akron against Garvey's persecution by J. Edgar Hoover.[53] Although Sherrill was a brilliant orator,[54] and the UNIA's message was powerful, the organization declined in importance after Garvey's deportation to the West Indies. His utopian "Back to Africa" plan was impractical,[55] but his message of Black self-emancipation is timeless.

Meanwhile, Akron's rubber corporations were churning out an ever-greater volume of goods for ever-bigger profits. Goodrich's after-tax profit for the first half of 1928 came to $5 million, while Goodyear made $18.5 million profit in the first nine months of the same year. J. D. Tew, the President of B. F. Goodrich, forecast that production in his Akron plant would rise by fifteen percent in 1929.[56] Real estate prices climbed to record highs with land in Akron's Main Street valued at $14,500 a foot,[57] which translates to anything between $207,000 and over $1 million in today's values.[58] Many people assumed that the boom would be endless, but some prudent souls urged caution. Charles Landon Knight, the proprietor of the *Akron Beacon Journal,* warned, "Practically the whole American public has gone mad on the stock market and herein lies a grave danger … we are riding for a fall."[59] He was correct. Akron's social and economic history was to enter a new period. At the end of the 1920s, the city's labor movement was only just surviving, kept alive by a small group of leftwing activists in the Central Labor Union. Their great dream was to organize the giant rubber mills. It seemed an unattainable dream but was to come sooner than the city's unionists perhaps expected.

12.

From the American Dream to a Nightmare

World trade virtually collapsed following the Wall Street Crash of October 1929, and hard times returned to Akron with a severity unseen since the 1890s. Tens of thousands of the city's workers lost their jobs and those who kept them were careful not to jeopardize their employment in any way. By 1932, sixty percent of the city's workforce were jobless.[1] It was the darkest period of the century. Some people took their own lives. Many retreated into numb despair, focusing on scraping up the next meal or finding the money to pay their rent. Others heeded the clarion call of the city's communists to organize to demand relief and fight back against evictions. Surprisingly, some workers took industrial action even as the factories were turning employees out into the street. There was also a trickle of gummers into the AFL rubber workers' union, which had been a largely paper organization for many years. The city's establishment responded to all signs of militancy with a heavy and sometimes brutal hand.

The Great Crash surprised most Americans, including President Herbert Hoover, who claimed that in the summer of 1928, "We in America are nearer to the final triumph over poverty than ever before in the history of any land."[2] Prescient observers such as the *Beacon Journal*'s

Charles Knight, however, had warned that it was coming. All the signs of impending collapse were there. Even before the crash, rubber prices had been steadily falling—from thirty-eight cents a pound in February 1928 to seventeen cents a pound in November of that year. After the crash, prices went into free fall. In December 1930, rubber was selling at nine cents a pound, and the Akron rubber corporations put their African and Asian plantations in mothballs. The production of cars and buses slumped by forty percent, and thousands of dealers were bankrupted. In 1929, Firestone made a net cash loss of $3.25 million—an enormous sum for the times. Tire production plummeted from around thirteen million items in 1929 to just over seven million in 1932. With trade stagnant, tens of thousands of Akron's workers were once again unemployed. Firestone cut its workforce from 11,925 to 9,648, and most employees were put on short hours with the plant running two, five-hour shifts per day five days a week.[3] The *Beacon Journal* reported that in November 1930, there were twenty thousand jobless men and an undisclosed number of unemployed women in the city. Akron's economy did not hit rock bottom immediately after the Great Crash; profits and production continued on an irregular downward spiral. Across America, unemployment grew from 4.5 million in 1930 to 13 million in 1933.[4] Goodyear still turned a profit of almost $10 million in 1930, probably because it had existing contracts to fill, but in 1931, it made less than $5.5 million. On March 9, 1933, the Seiberling, Firestone, and the Falls rubber companies suspended all production. Goodyear was working two days a week. At the end of the month, the rubber plants returned to working five days a week,[5] but this was still nowhere near the seven-day, four-rotating shifts of the boom years. At this time, Akron was virtually a one-industry town and the knock-on effects of rubber's woes affected almost the entire population.

The consequences were catastrophic for the working class. When the Great Depression began, unemployment compensation did not exist, and the jobless depended on charity. Father Boeke of St. Paul's in Firestone Park, for example, stored potatoes and second-hand clothing in his church basement for distribution to the poorest families. He saved people from starvation, but charity, no matter how well meant, was no substitute for the right to a living income, and a guaranteed income became a central demand of leftist agitators.

The *Beacon*'s star reporter John Botzum reported a scene of abject misery in the Akron employment offices on E. Buchtel Avenue. One young rubber worker had sold his furniture, and his wife had gone home to her mother. An agency worker said that the young man came in every day, desperate for work, but "now he looks like a bum." Some young women entered the office, trying to look brave. "Refined and cultured," they had worked as nurses. "The saddest cases," Botzum wrote, "are the widows who have children to feed and clothe."[6]

Numbers of unemployed men made a precarious living by selling apples in the street.[7] Southerners who could do so went back to Appalachia to wait out the slump on marginal farms. Milk consumption plummeted from 107,757,000 pints in 1930 to 62,660,437 pints the following year,[8] doubtless with an increase in the incidence of rickets in children.

Some citizens were so despondent that they took their own lives. The North Hill viaduct was a convenient place for suicide. A twenty-year-old who leapt to his death in 1931 had a bit of paper in his pocket on which he had scrawled, "I'm sorry."[9] Stanley Mikolajczyk, a fifty-year-old unemployed rubber worker, also jumped off the bridge,[10] but shooting was more prevalent. Men were twice as likely as women to commit suicide, and the foreign-born were twice as likely to kill themselves as the native-born. Poor people living in downtown precincts or close to the big factories were also over-represented.[11] In 1936, a twenty-eight-year-old Akron mother tried to kill herself by cutting off her tongue. She was, a journalist reported, "anemic, undernourished," and "too tired to live."[12]

By 1933, one quarter of American workers—almost thirteen million—were unemployed, up from 4.5 million in 1930.[13] In May 1933, the city of Akron declared itself bankrupt. Large numbers of police, teachers, and other employees lost their jobs, and garbage collection was suspended. Schools shut down and all but three fire stations closed, leaving "the bankrupt city ... with fifteen policemen and thirty firemen to guard its property and lives." The following year, Mayor C. Nelson Sparks told the Senate Labor Committee that forty-six percent of the Akron population lived in households without an employed breadwinner.[14] City employees' salaries were cut by fifteen percent, and then by twenty-five percent, and in September 1934 pay envelopes contained only scrip or IOUs. The city did not climb out of debt until September 1937.[15]

It would be wrong to view Akron's working-class population purely as helpless victims. Many of them fought back tenaciously against the system responsible for their miseries. Radicals of one type or another led these movements of resistance. These included members of the Socialist, Communist, and Trotskyist parties, along with Wobblies; unaffiliated radicals such as Wilmer Tate, the Secretary of the Central Labor Union; his friend James McCartan of the Typographers' Union; and the Barberton union firebrand Francis Gerhart. At a time when the unemployed depended on charity, the radicals spearheaded campaigns for public relief and public works schemes.

Communists were the largest organized left-wing force in Akron, but party organizer David Williamson's claim that there were two thousand Communists in the city in 1930 was a wild exaggeration.[16] Another Communist organizer, Jim Keller, estimated that when he arrived in late 1935, there were around ninety party members in Summit County, and this rings true.[17] Williamson's inflated claim may have been designed to lure potential members into joining what they imagined was a more powerful organization. However, what the party lacked in numbers it made up for in energy, dedication, and iron discipline.

By this time, the Communist Party, like its sister organizations around the world in the Comintern, had been thoroughly "Bolshevized" in the image of Stalin's Russian party. The Comintern or Communist International, with its headquarters in Moscow, had been set up to foment revolution around the world. By the late 1920s, it had become an instrument of Soviet foreign policy, controlled from the top down by operatives of the Russian Communist Party. In the process, these operatives subordinated the interests of the world working class to those of an increasingly brutal bureaucratic ruling caste in the USSR.[18] In 1922, when the authoritarian tendencies of the Soviet leaders had not fully developed, the German-Polish revolutionist Rosa Luxemburg warned against those leaders "mak[ing] a virtue of necessity and freez[ing] into a complete theoretical system all the tactics forced upon them by fatal circumstances..." She added, ominously in hindsight, against "recommend[ing] them to the international proletariat as a model for socialist tactics."[19]

With full-blown Stalinism, "recommendations" became prescriptions. The Comintern would tolerate no other model of party or state bar a single-party, totalitarian dictatorship.

The Communist Party of America, which emerged after the Socialist Party splintered in 1919, was by this stage a cadre party. Members were expected to devote their lives to agitation and propaganda under the party leadership's direction. Obeying a nationwide directive issued following the Great Crash, the Akron Communists organized an Unemployed Council and a branch of the Trade Union Unity League, which had replaced the earlier Trade Union Educational League. The police and city authorities regarded Communist activity as a sinister "un-American" plot and did not hesitate to resort to unconstitutional methods to suppress the party's activities. State and private forces had crushed left-wing organizations during the Red Scare following World War I and the Akron establishment was determined that they would not rise again.

Akron also had large ex-servicemen's organizations,[20] which often provided strong-arm men to attack the "Reds." In 1930, for instance, they threatened a counter-demonstration against the Communist May Day rally in Perkins Square, but their intervention was not required, given the large numbers of police sent to break up the gathering.[21] Although the party professed pacific intentions, Akron police chief Frank Boss had prepared his officers—and public opinion—for violent confrontation. Officers arrested a Garfield High School student for distributing "crudely lettered handbills" at the Goodrich gates, claiming that the Communists paid him to do it.

The party called for a general strike on May Day, 1930, hoping that the city's "Negroes" in particular would heed the call,[22] but the appeal was unheeded. This was hardly surprising, given that the rubber mills and other large enterprises were nonunion and sympathetic workers were fearful of losing their jobs by responding to the call of a small and publicly reviled organization. Many others had taken a strong dose of anti-Communism—not the least because of the activities of the Klan, which still enjoyed considerable support, particularly among Southern incomers.

Nothing the Communists were doing was an incitement to violence, and in theory, the US Bill of Rights guaranteed all citizens the right to free speech, freedom of the press, and freedom of association and assembly. However, as permits to distribute handbills were required under a city ordinance, the authorities simply denied permission, claiming that they feared public disturbances. The Communists ignored this and continued to organize for the rally. The police arrested six men "for smearing red chalk appeals on factory sidewalks" and grabbed three women who had been "illegally" distributing handbills. Frank Boss declared that he would not tolerate disorder, or "flaunting of the red flag."

The scene had been set for violent confrontation, which happened when one hundred marchers set off along South Main and Exchange Streets. Chief Boss had mobilized "every available policeman in Akron" and these lay in waiting for the marchers. When the marchers reached the Goodrich gates on South Main, mounted officers charged them, swinging nightsticks. A police motorcyclist knocked party organizer David Williamson down and other officers trampled him, as he lay injured on the ground. The parade scattered, leaving the street littered with torn placards and handbills. Several women in red sashes were "roughly handled" and five people were arrested, some of them for "inciting a riot." Two teenagers were arrested for "disorderly conduct by noise"—namely for singing the "Internationale," the socialist anthem. It was a police riot, but Judge J. Earl Cox, who later became chairman of the Summit County Democratic Party, jailed the arrested marchers.[23]

Anna Myers, the feisty sixteen-year-old leader of the Akron Communist children's chorus, was defiant. "You fools," she told the police: "this is what makes Communists." She was right. The party did not back down, and the numbers attending the Unemployed Council rallies increased. In January 1931, the Communists led a procession through a blizzard to City Hall to demand better conditions for the unemployed. The following month saw a five-hundred-strong procession of so-called "malcontents" march on City Hall to demand the creation of an emergency fund to provide the city's unemployed with a minimum payment of $15 per week. A contingent of gummers organized by the Rubber Workers' Industrial League joined the march.

The League's importance should not be overstated. It was a "Red" union: an instrument of the party, with only minor support in the rubber mills, but it was significant that a number of rubber workers had risked dismissal by marching. The police did not always have their way. The city's Safety Director, Ross Walker, hated Communists. He had banned the parade and previously sent police to break up "mixed [race] dances" but this time, the city council overruled him. Mayor Weil met a delegation to discuss their demands, which included the provision of unemployment pay, an end to evictions and a ban on cutting off utilities such as water, gas, and electricity.[24] In the winter of 1931, seven children had starved to death in Tuscarawas County, just south of Akron.[25] The Unemployed Council had organized "gas squads" to turn gas back on when the company turned it off.[26] By this stage, people were desperate and one suspects they would have joined any protest regardless of who organized it. In the event, only the radical left were willing and capable of organizing resistance to horrible conditions.

Many Americans have scant respect or tolerance for Communists and are reluctant to give them credit for anything, but participation in the Unemployed Council's activities required great courage, and its struggle did yield some positive results. After one Council rally in Barberton, the streets ran red with marchers' blood. Howard Wolf describes how

> [c]ompletely losing his head, [Barberton] Mayor Seney A. Decker ... swore in an army of punch-drunk prizefighters, hulking ex-convicts and frenzied super-patriots and sent them out to break up the next Communist meeting with clubs and tear gas while the suburban city's police stood around and indulged in hearty belly laughs. Four or five were seriously injured by the clubbers and hundreds of men, women and children living in the vicinity were gassed.

Decker's lurid tale of Red violence did not square with the facts. The injured included Frank Demshaw, a "120-pound war veteran photographer for the *Beacon Journal,* and a volunteer assistant who had been holding his flashlight apparatus." They were not Communists or Unemployed Council activists, but Decker's goons believed they were and considered them fair game for brutal violence. One of the goons was scapegoated and sent to jail, but Decker escaped scot-free.[27]

In April 1931, the Akron Unemployed Council sent an eighteen-strong contingent to join the first stage of the National Hunger March[28] on Washington, cheered on by young women in red bandannas as they left the city. The Akron marchers included two young mothers—Victoria Zebor and Nina Wilcox. They sang the "Internationale" and "Solidarity Forever" and ignored a hostile counter-demonstration by the American Legion as they passed though Barberton. The Akron Chamber of Commerce refused to help the marchers in any way.[29] Marchers had set off from five cities in Ohio and converged on the state capital, Columbus, in pouring rain. In December, the national march converged on Washington, DC, to present a list of demands to Congress. These included: the provision of unemployment insurance, a seven-hour workday with no cut in pay, a federal work program paying union wages, an end to racial discrimination in relief payments and an end to deportations of immigrant workers, support for the demands of the veterans and poor farmers, and for all funds earmarked for making war be used for unemployment relief.[30] One year later, Representative Ernest Lundeen of the Minnesota Farmer-Labor Party introduced the first unemployment insurance bill in Congress. This was the precursor of the Roosevelt administration's national unemployment compensation law. The courageous actions of Communists such as Akron's Victoria Zebor and Nina Wilcox had set the process in motion.

The Unemployed Council organized residents to resist the many evictions in Akron during this period. The police often responded violently, slugging activists as families sat out in the street with their pitiful belongings. In the summer of 1932, they charged Antonio Spagnola and John Bender with trespass for resisting eviction. In response, one hundred Communist sympathizers demonstrated outside the court. Earlier, a riot had broken out when the activists tried to prevent the eviction of a family at 297 Moon Street. Patrolman Emory Davis shot one of the demonstrators, so the crowd beat him up, prompting Mayor C. Nelson Sparks to fulminate that "radicals who take advantage of a condition of distress to incite riot and attendant disorder will not be tolerated in Akron and law and order will be maintained regardless of the consequences."[31] Sparks hated Communists and other radicals, claiming that they wished to nationalize women and that their Russian comrades were cannibals. As the depression ground on and class conflict intensified, his behavior became increasingly unhinged. Once, when addressing a meeting at the Goodyear Heights Church, he thumped the pulpit so vigorously that he tore the ligaments in his left arm.[32] The Unemployed Council ignored him and continued its anti-eviction fights, as in one instance in the winter of 1933 when the police fired tear gas at a protest on Kenmore Hill.[33] The Central Labor Union also took action to support bricklayers on unemployment relief work when Sparks attempted to pay them below the going rate.[34]

The Communist activists who led the unemployed protests were brave people. They professed a collectivist creed that challenged head-on the individualistic dogmas that many citizens regarded as the core of true Americanism. As the 1930s unfolded, reports of the horrors of Stalin's rule appeared to justify these attitudes, but the authorities tended to regard all leftists as beyond the pale. Akron's Communists defied baton-wielding police to exercise what were, on paper, their constitutional rights. The city's establishment believed that Communists merited brutal repression as "sinister" agitators motivated by an "evil" ideology. In truth, what motivated them was a burning anger against the injustice of class rule. *Beacon Journal* writer Ruth McKenney joined the Communist Party after witnessing manifest injustice and oppression during the course of her employment. One assignment led her to cover the Summit Beach Park Casino "walkathons," in which competing couples would dance for days of a time to see who could outlast the others to claim the first prize of $1,000 or the second of $500. The prospect of three free square meals a day during the ordeal was attractive, and "like so many racehorses, their diet ... [was] "carefully observed."[35] McKenney was a talented writer and her *Beacon Journal* account of the spectacle is heartbreaking:

> A stocky little girl in a blue sweater and orange running pants trotted desperately around a poorly lighted track on Tuesday night. Three thousand paying spectators yelled themselves hoarse at the spectacle, screaming epithets at the losers, as a jazz band played frenetically. Exhausted contestants stumbled and fell or dragged their semi-comatose partners round the ring. From time to time, white-coated attendants carried away unconscious contestants, leaving their partners sobbing.[36]

McKenney's account helped mobilize public opinion against the contests, and the city authorities closed them down shortly afterwards.[37]

Yet for all of its activists' bravery, dedication, and passion, the Communist Party's Stalinist ideology limited its appeal and, in the end, condemned it to political oblivion. Whereas the Socialist Party had been a broad, open, multi-tendency organization that prided itself on its democratic internal life and promised democratic rule should it come to power, the Communist Party was a hierarchical organization intolerant of dissent. The "party line" was always "correct" and members were bound to implement it no matter how it changed. In 1928, the Moscow-based Comintern imposed a new leadership on the American party and took away the members' right to present alternative policies before conferences. These dictatorial measures "coincided with a radical shift in Comintern strategy." The new leadership discarded the "united front" policy of working within the existing labor movement because,

> According to the Comintern's analysis of the 'third period,' capitalism was entering its terminal crisis ... [and] the only obstacle to imminent workers' revolution was the 'social-fascist' leaders of the social-democratic trade unions and political parties.

Therefore,

> Throughout the capitalist world, the Communist parties launched sectarian attacks on the social-democratic and reformist leaders, refusing ... all united action with the social-democratic parties and unions. The most tragic fruits of the 'third period' were gathered in Germany, where the Communists' refusal to press for united action with the Social Democrats against the rising tide of fascism allowed Hitler to take power and smash the oldest and best organized labor movement in the world without any significant resistance.[38]

While not as disastrous as in Germany, the results of the Comintern's ultra-leftism were pernicious for the American Communists, the Left as a whole, and for the working class they purported to lead.

Between 1928 and 1935, the party pursued ultra-left policies that isolated it from the working class it claimed to represent.

Ruth McKenney's claim that by 1930 Akron's Central Labor Union was "on its last legs"[39] hints at the party's ultra-sectarian politics at that time. It is certainly true that the labor movement was in bad shape. American union membership had declined from a peak of 5.1 million to 3.4 million in 1929.[40] The great slump had weakened the Akron CLU, but McKenney exaggerates its decline. In fact, there was a steady dribble of individual rubber workers into the AFL's rubber union at the time,[41] and the CLU's affiliates sometimes took militant action. Wilmer Tate, the CLU's secretary, was a dynamic organizer. Hailing from Iowa, this "red-haired giant," the descendant of Dutch and Irish immigrants, came to Akron with his family in 1916 and found work as a machinist. He joined the AFL Machinists' Union Akron local in 1918 and became its president[42] after his mentor, Sam Newman, moved to Washington to take up a national position. Like Newman, Tate was an old style socialist. Utterly incorruptible, he dedicated his life to the cause of labor and later became the respected "father of the CIO in Akron." The CLU had its share of narrow craft unionists, but Tate's allies such as James McCartan of the Typographers' Union shared his broader vision of industrial unionism.

Between 1928 and 1935, the Communist Party labeled people such as Tate and McCartan as "left social fascists" and refused to work within AFL unions. Party leader William Z. Foster claimed that the AFL President, William Green, was "already practically [an] open-Fascist." The AFL leaders were fascists, Foster claimed, because "they are the brazen defenders of capitalism,"[43] an outlandish claim that blinded the party's followers to threats from real fascists. "During the period of the formation of AFL federal locals in rubber in 1934," writes Milton Derber, "the Communists were actively boycotting and fighting them." Instead, the party leadership instructed its members to build alternative "revolutionary unions."[44] The vehicle for this sectarian policy was the misleadingly named "Trade Union Unity League." Where the party had any strength, the policy was immensely destructive of real "unity." On the ground in Akron, it meant that the party refused to make common cause with other leftists such as Socialists and Wobblies and thus weakened resistance. Party leaders attacked other leftists as "saboteurs" and even as spies and wreckers if they were Trotskyists.[45] As a loyal party member, Ruth McKenney dutifully followed the twists and turns of party policy and "forgot" that the party had recently anathematized socialists such as Wilmer Tate as left social fascists. After the Popular Front about-turn, she praised him as an honest militant who was instrumental in organizing Akron's rubber workers.[46]

The onset of the Great Depression did not completely stifle trade union militancy in Akron. In the months before the crash, for instance, a desperate struggle broke out between union projectionists and the owners of the city's movie houses. In those pretelevision days Akron supported a score or more cinemas, plus theaters, vaudeville, and dance halls, many of them clustered downtown on Howard Street.[47] The projectionists, who were members of the International Alliance of Theatrical Stage Employees (IATSE), walked off the job in April 1929 to support their demand for a pay raise. The employers refused to negotiate, fired union members, and brought in nonunion labor.

Three weeks later, passersby would have witnessed wild scenes as two thousand patrons fled the Riverview Park dance hall on the first night of the season. The dancers were fleeing from a barrage of stink bombs, let off by IATSE members fired by Riverview director Frank C. Buben, who had hired scab labor at his two movie theaters. While the stink bombing may have been relatively harmless, the dispute took a more sinister turn when another theater owner had his front door blown off its hinges. Three months after the start of the strike, a bomb exploded in the ticket booth of the Ideal Cinema at 244 Wooster Avenue and another nine cinemas were subsequently bombed. Just before Christmas 1930, the police arrested a striking projectionist.[48] The strike fizzled out shortly afterwards, and when the Southern Theater in Grant Street was bombed two years later, and there was a further spate of stink bombings, the police blamed mobsters rather than strikers.[49] This is very likely, given that organized criminals linked to the Al Capone gang in Chicago had targeted the union and the industry for takeover.[50]

It was against this turbulent background that sensational claims of a menacing Communist plot surfaced in Akron. The police alleged that the conspirators intended to sabotage the USS *Akron*, a US Navy

Zeppelin under construction at the city's huge Goodyear airdock. One March evening in 1931, the police arrested Paul F. Kassay—a thirty-seven-year-old Hungarian-born Goodyear mechanic—at his home near the Akron Municipal Airport. They charged him with conspiracy to commit sabotage under Ohio's 1919 Criminal Syndicalism Act. The court freed him on $40,000 bail, but Goodyear fired him despite the formal presumption of innocence. According to the prosecution, Kassay had intended to leave out some of the blimp framework's six-and-a-half million rivets and insert defective ones. Kassay, they alleged, would spit on rivets on cold days so that the frozen saliva would thaw in warmer weather and weaken the rivets. Supposedly, the spit would also create oxalic acid that would weaken the duralumin girders. According to assistant prosecutor George Hargreaves, Kassay was acting on the orders of an "international ring of communists." Even more sensationally, Hargreaves alleged that Kassay had planned to hide in the blimp's control car and wreck it on its maiden voyage.[51]

Many people were prepared to believe the charges, outlandish as they were. America at this stage was in the throes of another Red Scare orchestrated by Representative Hamilton Stuyvesant Fish III, who headed a Congressional Committee investigating Communist subversion. Fish took a keen interest in the trial,[52] and it may well have been at his urging that the Bureau of Investigation turned its attentions to the Zeppelin factory. The police told the court that they had searched Kassay's house and found "a considerable quantity of communistic literature, drawings of a zeppelin and some letters which may prove interesting." Hargreaves added that Kassay had claimed to be a friend of Bela Kun, the leader of the failed 1919 Hungarian revolution, and to have served as an officer in the Austro-Hungarian navy. Hargreaves painted Kassay as "a highly intelligent type and of a dangerous, fanatical nature." Two G-men had infiltrated the hangar with Goodyear's approval, posing as foreign Communist agents, and tried to worm their way into Kassay's confidence. Kassay was the first person tried under Ohio's criminal syndicalism law. He denied that he was a Communist and insisted that the case was "a dirty frame-up." He claimed that some of his coworkers resented his promotion to supervisor and were embittered when Goodyear exempted him from a general wage cut. He said that he distrusted the G-men and had strung them along to gather evidence against them. He insisted that he would never have sabotaged the airship and that his "lifetime ambition to be recognized as one of the best aircraft mechanics and engineers in the world ... [had been] ruined."[53] Judge Walter B. Wanamaker dismissed the charges and ruled that the criminal syndicalism law was contrary to freedom of speech and therefore unconstitutional. The police had not charged Kassay with "doing" anything, but with "saying" things, he pointed out. Given the febrile political climate, Kassay was lucky that Wanamaker was on the bench as the criminal syndicalism law provided for maximum penalties of ten years jail or a $5000 fine, or both. After the Ohio Supreme Court upheld Wanamaker's ruling, Kassay moved to California and faded into obscurity. The charges were farcical, but an innocent man had narrowly escaped draconian punishment. Even if Kassay were a Communist, it is difficult to think of any reason why he might wish to sabotage the airship.

Frederick Engels had argued long ago against industrial sabotage, noting that in the case of the Luddite machine-breakers in the early Industrial Revolution, "when the momentary end was attained, the whole weight of social power fell upon the unprotected evil-doers and punished them to its heart's content."[54] On yet another level, the trial showed that the Department of Justice would not shy away from framing up real or suspected radicals and was a warning to workers not to associate with them. If this were the case, it failed, because Akron was about to ride an unprecedented labor upsurge. Radicals would play an important role in the process.

13.

Industrial Unionism Comes to Town

Frederick Engels predicted that the formation of class consciousness in America would be telescoped into a fraction of the time it had taken in Europe. On the old continent, it had taken many years for the working class to realize that it formed a distinct and permanent class in capitalist society, and longer for this realization to translate into independent class organizations. However, Engels believed that

> [o]n the more favored soil of America, where no mediæval ruins bar the way, where history begins with the elements of modern bourgeois society as evolved in the seventeenth century, the working class passed through these two stages of its development within ten months.[1]

Over four decades later, Engels' forecast had failed to eventuate. In Akron, the giant rubber mills, which epitomized American mass production industry, remained defiantly nonunion, and the city's politics remained firmly in the grasp of the two capitalist parties. Unions did exist in Akron, but the craft-conscious American Federation of Labor had long before turned its back on the workers in the city's mass production industries. From the early 1930s, however, there was a spontaneous movement of gummers into the AFL rubber union. By 1933, helped by the Roosevelt administration's National Industrial Recovery Act

(NIRA), Wilmer Tate of the Central Labor Union and a core of militants inside the mills began to organize in earnest. They formed what Firestone unionist James Turner called "a kind of underground movement," which held its meetings in secret because of spies and quietly spread the union message on the factory floor, in bars, and other places frequented by the workers. Turner recalls wearing his union badge on the inside of his lapel because discovery meant summary dismissal and blacklisting out of the industry.

Eventually, members could wear their buttons openly and proudly,[2] but only after some of the most spectacular class battles in US history. By 1934, the activists had recruited up to forty thousand members into federal locals of the United Rubber Workers' of America. (Federal locals were controlled by the AFL leadership, which appointed organizers and determined policies irrespective of the members' wishes.) Instinctive industrial unionists, the local URW militants clashed with the craft-minded AFL leaders, who attempted to head off strike action at every opportunity, and who wished to separate workers organizationally according to their craft or occupation.[3] Disgusted with the vacillations of the Washington-based AFL leadership, many gummers left the union. Nevertheless, the activists prevailed. Rubber workers in a number of plants took strike action, and there were bitter disputes in a number of other industries in Summit County. In April 1935, local militants forced Bill Green, the AFL's President, to grant them a charter for an international union under local control.

Gummers going on shift in the hot summer of 1933 would have taken union handbills from a large, sandy-haired man standing at the factory gates. Wilmer Tate's face was familiar to many of them as a perennial union "agitator"—the Central Labor Union Secretary, for whom "the cause of labor is religion."[4] Despite the setbacks of 1921 and 1926, Tate had never given up hope of unionizing the mills, and as a socialist, he supported industrial-style organization. The passage of the Norris-La Guardia Act of 1932 and Roosevelt's NIRA in June 1933 made his job somewhat easier. Despite NIRA's Section 7 (a), which appeared to grant workers the right to unionize, organizing the unorganized was not plain sailing. In practice, the famous clause served company unions more than the AFL, and the two years of the Act's existence were a period of ferocious repression of independent unions.[5] Despite this, many unionists interpreted the clause to mean, "President Roosevelt wants you to organize." Doubtless, many believed it, but for the more sophisticated it was a convenient tactical ploy. Roosevelt's Labor Secretary Francis Perkins later admitted that her boss had only "a sort of distant sympathy for labor" and that his administration had only inserted the clause in the Act following AFL International President Bill Green's strenuous protests. According to Congress of Industrial Organizations chief John L. Lewis, "F. D. R. was not too friendly to Section 7 (a)."[6] By itself, NIRA and the subsequent Wagner Act could not substitute for autonomous working-class action, and by the end of the decade, Roosevelt had become an open strikebreaker.

Wilmer Tate was once feted as "the father of the CIO in Summit County," but few Akronites know of him today. He was a skilled worker, but as a socialist, he was a firm believer in the industrial form of union organization. A workaholic, he toiled up to eighteen hours a day at the CLU offices at 184 West Center Street. Indeed, he worked so hard and smoked so many cigarettes that in July 1935, he suffered his first heart attack despite his relatively young age.[7] A firebrand with a big booming voice, he was at the same time a bookish man who spent his spare time reading widely on economics and labor history,[8] including the works of Marx and Engels.[9] He was a natural leader and possessed "that air of conviction which draws men to him."[10] Tate had obtained the support of his rival, Frank N. Patino, the conservative Australian-born CLU President, for a union organizing drive in the rubber mills and had traveled to Washington, DC, to secure Bill Green's backing. His closest allies were James McCartan, a combative socialist with "a roaring voice," who headed up the Typographers' Union local,[11] and Francis Gerhart, the firebrand socialist President of the CLU in neighboring Barberton. Crucially, too, there was a solid core of union-minded workers inside the rubber mills—determined and intelligent men who had won the respect of their fellow workers.

Despite Section 7 (a), the rubber companies were determined to keep the open shop and Goodyear's Paul Litchfield claimed that the New Deal was influenced by "communistic" ideas.[12] The mills were swarming with spies and plant police, many of whom were members of the Ku Klux

Klan. Nevertheless, the CLU's recruiting drive was so successful that Bill Green sent an AFL general organizer, Coleman Claherty, to help induct the influx of new members into the URW's new federal locals. In late 1933, Claherty moved into the downtown Savings and Loans Building and impressed *Beacon* reporter Harry Harrison with his "air of business-like dignity." A former Cleveland blacksmith, Claherty had worked as an AFL organizer for twenty-five years and boasted that he had "many times fled" the "loaded shotguns of mine owners' Cossacks." He put the most positive spin on NIRA, telling Harrison "it's fair sailing now, for labor is protected by law of the national government."[13] In fact, the rubber corporations resisted the unions with every legal and extra-legal trick at their disposal, and they would simply defy the federal government if they could get away with it.[14] The news baron William Randolph Hearst declared that the New Deal was "a measure of state socialism" and "a menace to political rights and constitutional liberties."[15]

Nevertheless, gummers were flocking to the URW because wages and conditions in the rubber mills had been steadily declining for many years, even during the great boom. Future International Union President Leland S. Buckmaster, who worked for eighteen years as a tire builder at Firestone, said, "When I was laid off during the 1920 depression I was making $1.25 an hour. When I came back seven months later, I got 80 cents an hour for the same job. We didn't get a single raise in the eight or nine years before the big depression of 1929, and then things got worse."[16] Working conditions had also steadily deteriorated. The big corporations had introduced the Bedaux system in the 1920s and, according to an *Akron Times-Press* reporter, "the man with the stopwatch has become a symbol of Akron's rubber industry."[17] In his wake, well paid pace setters established production "norms" to force ever-increasing outputs from ever-smaller numbers of workers. Goodyear tire builder Haskell Jones recalled a fast worker who, twenty-seven-years old, and fit and strong, could turn out seventy good tires a day. Few of his colleagues could—or wanted to—match his output, especially the older men,[18] yet the stopwatch men insisted that it was the norm. From the employers' point of view, the speed-up was a huge success. A federal government report estimated that between 1921 and 1931, "the poundage and output per man in the [US] rubber industry tripled" and that 7,155 fewer workers produced twenty-one million more tires. In the same period, there was a net loss of 42,691 workers in the industry. Some of this was due to technological change such as the assembly line, which appeared in the 1930s,[19] but the workers knew from bitter experience that much of the increase was due to the speed-up.[20] The workers "cordially detested" Bedaux,[21] which they called the "rawhide" labor system,[22] and it was perhaps the main reason why so many were joining the URW. According to the Wolf brothers, the speed-up left gummers "broken at forty"[23] and condemned them to an early death. Union troubadour Joe Glazer relates a somber account of the effects of the Bedaux system on a Depression era rubber worker: "[he] told me that when he came out of the plant he would sit down at the curb and wait for the trolley. He said, 'Some days I was so tired from the speed-up I would have to wait for two or three street cars before I had the strength to get up from the curb and catch the next car for home.'"[24]

By January 1934, there were forty thousand union members in Akron, organized in seventy-five locals. This compared with five thousand one year earlier, most of them in craft unions outside of the rubber mills.[25] The city was on the verge of an enormous upsurge of "social unionism" that challenged the employers as never before and contrasted sharply with the "business unionism" espoused by the leaders of the American Federation of Labor. Contemporary labor activist Mark Dudzic explains social unionism thus:

> Social unionism, at its most fundamental, understands that workers are a class with interests that go beyond a particular bargaining relationship that they may have with an employer. It understands also that employers are part of a capitalist class [that] … seeks unrestricted, hegemonic control in all spheres of society. In practice, this understanding means that unions must align the interests and struggles of their members with those of the entire working class and contest capital for power in all social spheres. It is the old solidarity unionism—'an injury to one is an injury to all'—writ large.[26]

Militant strikes erupted in many different industries across Summit County, not just rubber. Seven hundred workers at the Diamond Match factory in Barberton walked off the job to force the company to comply with the NIRA match code, which would give significant pay increases to women workers. They stayed out for five weeks and won a signed contract. Match workers' leader Francis Gerhart announced that the factory was one hundred percent organized. Significantly, the strike won the support of many professionals and small businesspeople.[27] This was to be a feature of many other union struggles in this period and contrasted with widespread middle-class support for the employers during the 1913 IWW strike. The match strike was peaceful, but in April 1934, the Columbia Chemical Company at Barberton fired striking union members and brought in scabs and armed Pinkerton "detectives." Columbia backed down after a few days and recognized the union when the five hundred workers and their supporters responded with mass pickets. In the aftermath of the strike, the police charged two company gunmen with carrying concealed weapons.[28] Women workers had played a prominent part in the strike, even lying down in front of the gates to prevent scabs from driving into the plant.[29] The following month saw Akron bakers and bakery drivers walk off the job to demand an end to the open shop. Pickets turned back trucks bringing in bread from Cleveland and other centers. In the following months, there were lengthy strikes of machinists and chemical workers, along with tailors at the Enterprise Manufacturing plant in Akron.[30]

By May 1934, the *Beacon Journal* estimated that twenty-five thousand of the city's thirty thousand rubber workers had joined the URW.[31] Gummers at Mohawk Rubber and American Hard Rubber took strike action over union recognition,[32] and pressure was building up in the bigger plants for similar action. The *India Rubber World* lamented that while the Akron mills had been virtually strike free in the past, "times have changed and a clean record is broken" with over 175 recent strikes.[33] The rubber workers' mood was militant, but this contrasted sharply with the old-school AFL approach of general organizer Coleman Claherty. Claherty believed that employers and workers shared common interests and that given time, the rubber bosses would cooperate with the union. His approach was reflected in the wording on one union banner: "Goodrich local 18319 where labor and capital meet."[34] The idea was at best utopian, for the rubber moguls had never tolerated unions in the past, and despite 7 (a) they clung to the open shop. Paul Litchfield insisted that the Goodyear Industrial Assembly fulfilled NIRA requirements and catered for the needs of the workers in the plant. "Organized labor," he told a foremen's convention, "seizes upon one part of ... [NIRA] and endeavors to array class against class, and to turn it into governmental sanction for a great membership drive."[35] The clause, he claimed, had allowed agitators to fan the "dying embers of class consciousness" into roaring flames.[36] There was some truth in this, regardless of Roosevelt's real intentions.

The relationship between the AFL hierarchy and the rubber workers steadily deteriorated. The rank-and-file leadership in the mills were exceptional people. Daniel Nelson tells us that gummers such as Walter Kriebel, Rex Murray, and Sherman Dalrymple had "the ability to inspire confidence among their fellow workers." They were imbued with "a fierce antiauthoritarianism" that conflicted with the AFL's top-down, bureaucratic approach.[37]

Photographs show Dalrymple—the future URW international president—as a determined man with strong features, thick eyebrows, and a beaked nose.[38] He had enlisted as a private in the marines in the First World War and risen to the rank of first lieutenant. He had come to Akron in 1903 as a boy, but had also done stints as a logger and a grade school teacher in his native West Virginia.[39] Despite his high intelligence, he worked in the Goodrich curing pit,[40] one of the heaviest and dirtiest jobs in the industry.

Like Wilmer Tate, Dalrymple believed that mass production workers needed to organize on industrial rather than craft lines. Their approach is encapsulated in the rallying cry, "United We Stand, Divided We Fall." A resolution from the Columbia Chemical workers' local in Barberton to the AFL in 1935 indicates that under the influence of socialists such as Tate and Gerhart, class consciousness was taking root in Summit County. "Every man," the resolution declared, "can see the crying need for enlisting together not only as workers in a particular shop or factory *but as a class of workers*."[41] [Emphasis added.] The gummers must have been exasperated when, after paying their dues to the federal URW, Claherty directed them into "their" respective craft unions. Only production workers would remain in the URW, even though the rubber mill artisans themselves rejected the AFL's policy.[42] Three months after Claherty's arrival in the city, he removed Frederick L. Phillips and Clark

C. Culver as financial secretaries of the Goodrich and Goodyear locals because of their strong advocacy of industrial unionism.[43] It would be a mistake to think that the industrial union idea "suddenly emerge[d] full-blown from the heads of a few of the more aggressive AFL leaders like John L. Lewis."[44] John Borsos's observation that Barberton workers did not need the CIO to convert them to industrial unionism applies just as strongly to their fellow workers in nearby Akron.[45]

The URW membership and their local leaders were also impatient with what they saw as Claherty's overly cautious approach to winning union recognition and signed contracts. Increasingly, they took matters in their own hands. Workers at General Tire & Rubber voted on March 13, 1934, to strike if their grievances were not resolved. Claherty managed to restrain them but by April 1934, he could no longer ignore the rising demand for action, which forced him to convene a mass meeting of URW members from all of the city's locals. There was standing room only at the Akron Armory when Sherman Dalrymple called the meeting to order, remarking that it was the largest meeting of organized labor in the city's history. The old trouper Claherty could make a militant speech, and he did not disappoint that Sunday afternoon. Accompanied on the platform by John P. Frye, who was standing in for AFL International President William Green, and by Leo Kryzcki of the Clothing Workers' Union, Claherty rhetorically blasted the employers' refusal to negotiate.[46] Despite his fiery words, he did not dare allow a strike vote, even though to be successful such a motion had to obtain a seventy-five percent majority under the AFL's restrictive rules. Time, however, was running out for his "moderate" approach. Although the URW won National Labor Board ballots, thus qualifying as the bargaining agent for employees in the mills, the rubber companies appealed to the courts in what was a costly and time-consuming ploy, further irritating the rank and file.

On June 19, tire builders employed by General Tire & Rubber sat down at their machines and refused to work in protest at a further speed-up. This was the first sit-down strike in a wave of stay-ins that hit Akron over the next few years and probably the first in the union upsurge across America. Time and motion men had reappeared, and the company imposed new piecework rates pegged to new production norms set by the pacesetters. Soon the entire plant was at a standstill and almost all of the factory's 1,100 production workers were walking the picket lines. The strike was "unofficial" but the strikers' aims centered on URW recognition and the elimination of the Independent General Workers' Union, a "yellow" union that had recently appeared in the plant. Company President Bill O'Neil denied that he controlled the IGWU but the workers were not convinced as the outfit persistently tried to undermine the strike. General Rubber Local's Rex Murray estimated that his union represented one thousand of the plant's 1,100 production workers and that the IGWU had the support of half of one percent of the workforce.[47]

By the end of the month, negotiations had reached deadlock, despite the intervention of Ralph A. Lind, the regional labor board secretary. Claherty prevented other URW locals from launching sympathy strikes, but he did authorize a $1 levy to support the General Tire strikers. Under heavy pressure from the AFL hierarchy, the strikers returned to work without formal recognition of their union, but with General Tire's agreement to close down the yellow union. It was a partial victory, but it left many of the rank and file and their local leaders convinced that they could have won much more.[48] Gummers at Seiberling Tire & Rubber in Barberton also won a partial victory in December 1934. When the company refused to meet with the union, the workers in the plant voted by a four to one majority to take strike action. Fearful of losing market share to the bigger companies in the event of a strike, Seiberling negotiated. Management refused, however, to sign the verbal agreement, claiming that it "would serve no good purpose."[49]

In early 1934, Akron's big rubber employers began to prepare for all-out industrial war with the unions. Over in Los Angeles, Firestone fired the local URW leaders and ignored orders from the National Labor Relations Board for their reinstatement. In Akron itself, Firestone teamed up with Goodrich to hire Colonel Joseph J. Johnston to train supervisors and nonunion "Red Apples" for "guard duty." Johnston, whom unionists regarded as a freelance "scab-herder," had honed his military skills in the National Guard at public expense. Goodyear, too, began drilling its plant police and Flying Squadron in preparation for the looming showdown with the union.[50]

Company spies and goons were active, and a cottage industry of provocateurs emerged in Akron. In the summer of 1934, two Youngstown men smashed windows at South High School during a meeting of Firestone rubber workers, hoping to discredit the union. The authorities could not readily ignore damage to public property. Detective Norman Harper informed Judge Werner at the men's trial that they made money by attending union meetings and selling reports to the employers and had been brought in "to give Akron labor a black eye."[51] The police also arrested a stand-over man called Domenic Scianna and two associates for threatening union members.[52]

The industry had been experiencing a mini-boom, but in September 1934, it collapsed, leaving the companies with big stockpiles of tires. Large-scale layoffs and intensified speed-ups followed, prompting furious responses by the unionized gummers. For their part, the rubber firms sought to tie up the union's hands in interminable court proceedings. When Coleman Claherty called for fresh NLRB elections to determine who would represent the gummers, the rubber companies declared that they were unnecessary.[53] Two days before the scheduled elections, they sought to delay them with court injunctions, and because of this, Claherty reluctantly endorsed strike action to force the employers to recognize the union.[54] On March 27, 1935, he told a mass meeting that the union would ballot its members to determine if they supported strike action. The following day, the employers announced that the yellow unions would also organize a strike ballot. Given the loaded questions on the company union's ballot papers, it was not surprising that there was a resounding vote against a strike.[55] On April 1, the URW balloted its members and the result was diametrically opposed to the result of the yellow union ballot. Ninety percent of the Goodyear Local's members voted for strike action, along with two-thirds of the members at Firestone and Goodrich. The vote at the latter two plants narrowly failed to achieve the seventy-five percent majority demanded by the AFL's restrictive rules,[56] but it was a significant result given that the AFL hierarchy opposed strike action. Claherty worried that "[t]he situation in Akron is becoming tense and anything is liable to break loose most any time. But we will try to keep the situation in hand and if any action is taken, it will be taken in an orderly manner...."[57] As far as the local URW leaders were concerned, they had a moral mandate to strike regardless of the AFL's obstructive rules. Claherty himself noted that the Firestone strike vote failed by thirteen votes to achieve the seventy-five percent figure.[58]

In response to the URW strike vote, the new Summit County Sheriff, Jim Flower, threatened to break up any picket lines. He swore in one thousand special deputies—850 of whom were rubber company employees—and armed them with clubs and tear gas.[59] The Akron city authorities also hired extra police officers, swore in special deputies, and stockpiled tear gas and other weapons. According to the Trotskyist journalist B. J. Widick, the companies hired three thousand private "detectives" at this time and prepared to bring in strikebreakers from out of town.[60] They turned the rubber mills into veritable fortresses with high barbed wire fences and floodlighting around their perimeters. Firestone unionist James Turner later recalled that his employer had mounted machine guns atop factory buildings.[61] The Akron Chamber of Commerce teamed up with the Lions and Rotary clubs to organize vigilantes, no doubt recalling the part played by the Citizens' Welfare League in the defeat of the 1913 strike.[62] On the union side, autoworkers in Detroit and the Cleveland Federation of Labor and Metal Trades Council pledged their support for the URW.[63]

Alarmed by the tense situation, the National Labor Relations Board summoned representatives of the URW and the rubber companies to a conference in Washington, DC, in April. In a touch of low farce, the company representatives refused to sit in the same room as the union delegates, forcing the Federal Government's chief negotiator, Labor Secretary Frances Perkins, to shuttle from room to room bearing messages from the opposing sides. The employers only attended the meeting for public relations purposes, as was shown when Perkins conveyed a message to the URW in which they stated their willingness to meet with "chosen representatives" of the rubber workforce. It was a double cross and must have infuriated Perkins as much as the union, for the "representatives" they had in mind were the officers of the Goodyear Industrial Assembly and the other company unions. The conference ended inconclusively, and the NLRB elections were postponed indefinitely. Nevertheless, Bill Green agreed to call off strike action and presented the surrender to the union members as a victory.[64]

The members left the union in their droves, disgusted by Green's pusillanimity. So many left that a gummer called P. E. Pinegar wrote an angry letter to the *Beacon* editor. The unions, he claimed, "can now muster in dress parade only 228 in one and 268 in another with their treasuries as bare as Mother Hubbard's cupboard ... and they are going to stay that way until there is a leadership the workers can have confidence in."[65] Branko Widick reported that members of the Goodyear local "walked out, half-sick, half crying" from a report-back meeting, with an irate Goodrich worker demanding Claherty explain "where'd you get the guts to bring back that goddamned sell-out to us?" The increasingly conservative Goodyear Local President John House ruled a motion to repudiate the agreement out of order and "progressives went home as one goes to a funeral," Widick added.[66] Mohawk Tire & Rubber workers were so incensed that they barred Claherty from attending meetings of their local.[67] Emboldened by the union's reversals, the small India Tire company at Mogadore, which had earlier agreed to a closed shop, locked out its two hundred workers and declared the agreement null and void. Desperate to head off militancy, Claherty fell back on red-baiting, starting "a terrific red scare in an attempt to intimidate progressives." Taking her cue from the AFL, Labor Secretary Perkins ordered the Department of Justice to launch an investigation into leftist influence in the Akron mills. To their discredit, Goodrich Local President Sherman Dalrymple and CLU President Frank Patino joined in the witch hunt, writing redbaiting articles for the *Summit County Labor News*.[68] Wilmer Tate had warned Claherty that his behavior could not continue:

> The men think we're bastards, too. I tell you, I ain't going to sit through another meeting like the one last Sunday at Goodyear, with guys yelling for a strike all over the place and booing the very name of the AF of L. We got to do something. Conditions are terrible in the factories.[69]

At first glance, Green and Claherty's behavior is baffling. They must have known that the rubber companies were stalling. The Schechter Poultry Corporation had lodged an appeal in the Supreme Court against its 1934 conviction in a lower court for breaching NIRA rules, and the nation's employers were watching the case with keen interest. On May

27, 1935, the Supreme Court ruled NIRA was unconstitutional. Although the Roosevelt administration almost immediately replaced NIRA with the National Labor Relations (Wagner) Act and replaced the National Labor Board with National Labor Relations Board, the rubber companies had resisted the call for union recognition and used the breathing space to prepare for the inevitable showdown with the gummers.

The reason for Bill Green's behavior lay in his conservative social and religious philosophy. Born into a British immigrant coal mining family in Coshocton, Ohio, in 1873, Green went down the local mine at the age of sixteen when poverty prevented him from studying to become a Baptist minister. He worked as a Sunday school teacher, and his devout beliefs informed every aspect of his life, including his union activities. As a young man, he became a local union official and was elected International Secretary-Treasurer of the United Mine Workers of America in 1913. In 1924, he succeeded Samuel Gompers as President of the AFL Although he had been a working miner in an industry marked by savage conflict, he was no class warrior. A series of bitter strikes in the 1890s had convinced him to strive for "rational discourse with employers," and he firmly believed in the "power of Christian love to smooth and sweeten all relations between capital and labor."[70] Arguably, such "boundless optimism" blinded him to the reality of industrial relations in mass production industry. Alternatively, in the view of militant unionists, he was a bumbling "labor skate" whose privileged position led him to betray the interests of the workers he was elected to serve.

Green was used to getting his way, but he met his match when he clashed with the homegrown URW leaders, who had worked for decades in the Akron mills and knew from bitter experience that the rubber corporations would never willingly recognize unions. The clash was not a straight-out Left-Right fight. There were leftists in the URW leadership, but many of those who rose to prominence were conservative "practical" unionists who rejected Green's craft approach as unworkable, but shared his desire for orderly business unionism. Green was opposed to strikes and preached class harmony, but gummers such as Sherman Dalrymple had learned the hard way that "No capitalist concern is in business for the love of it. The motivating force is dollars, dollars, and more dollars."[71] The URW's local leaders believed that strike action was an essential weapon in the struggle to force the rubber barons to the negotiating table. The farcical outcome of the Washington conference also convinced them of the need to form their own democratically controlled International Union to replace the federal locals dominated by Green and Claherty. They were also determined that the union had to organize on industrial rather than craft lines to maximize its power.

Although most gummers had left the union in disgust, the core of URW activists did not abandon the fight. They caucused with Wilmer Tate and other progressives and demanded a charter as an International Union with their own elected officers. A URW convention was set for September 12 at Akron's Portage Hotel, and Claherty worked feverishly to organize as many small locals as he could in order to outvote the Akron bloc. One Youngstown local had less than a dozen members, but a disproportionate number of votes.[72] Despite these machinations, Green and Claherty lost vote after vote on the conference floor. A proposal to grant Green power to appoint the union's officers was lost by forty-four votes to nine, but Green remained adamant that the URW would not be an industrial union. The delegates had to accept the international union charter in its entirety, without amendment, he stated. The elections, however, returned only one Green supporter to the union board. The delegates elected Sherman Dalrymple as International President, with the New Englander Thomas Burns as vice-president, despite Green's ruling that financial support for the new union was conditional on accepting Claherty as president. The delegates also rejected a constitutional clause that would have barred "communists" from membership: indeed, the document specifically recognized the existence of class struggle and called for the abolishment of capitalism.

The rubber workers now had an international union under their own control. Writing after the conference, B. J. Widick opined that "earnest and sincere … officers were picked whose personal honesty is beyond question and who have the confidence of the rubber workers."[73] The new international leadership could now focus their energies on winning the union recognition and collective bargaining rights they were theoretically entitled to by federal law.[74] However, they had first to win back the confidence of the rank-and-file gummers. What one local union leader described as "the disgusting, vascillating [sic], dilatory and dissimulating policy of Claherty"[75] had seriously weakened the union. John D. House later estimated that the union's Akron membership fell from between thirty-five thousand and forty thousand in 1934 to a mere 3,080 in September 1935.[76] Widick reckoned that by March 1935, the Firestone local's membership had dwindled from eight thousand to less than two thousand.[77]

By the end of 1935, however, with Green and Claherty sidelined,[78] the rubber union was gaining strength. The same was true of unions in other industries. Another long struggle broke out in Barberton in September when members of the Operative Potters' Local 149 quit work at the Ohio Insulator works. The strikers' demands included a pay raise, improved ventilation, elimination of the Bedaux system, and a stop to enforced contributions to the Barberton "Community Fund," which was administered by the employers and their right-wing allies and distributed "virulently anti-union" literature in local schools.[79] The strike was peaceful but after nine weeks, on the night of November 22, Colonel Joe Johnston and a band of strikebreakers drove at high speed through the picket line. The strikers retaliated by throwing rocks, and a bloody battle broke out in which Johnston's men discharged tear gas at the pickets and injured a number of innocent bystanders, some of them in their own homes. During the mêlée, Johnston was himself struck by a brick. Summit County Sheriff Flower—described by Branko Widick as "a big burly brute"—ordered the union to lift the picket line. When they refused, his men fired tear gas at point blank range into the pickets' ranks and wielded their billy clubs savagely. Vicious fights broke out intermittently throughout the day. The workers threw up barricades, and a mass picket reinforced by unionists from across Summit County closed down the plant. When the Barberton CLU threatened a general strike, Johnston and his scabs disappeared and Flower backed off. After four weeks, the strike ended.[80]

The Barberton strikes were significant because they attracted wide community support and because workers from other factories across the region were willing to come to the assistance of their fellows. This was an alternative form of community-based unionism very different to the top-down business unionism propounded by the AFL hierarchy. A radical social movement was springing up in Summit County, built by the workingmen and women themselves. Even Akron's housemaids formed a union.[81] The unions were involved in all kinds of community activities, including dances, talent shows, card parties, baseball games, bowling tournaments, boxing and wrestling matches, picnics and so on, seven nights a week.[82] John Borsos considers that the Ohio Insulator strike "energized the entire region."[83] High school students were also caught up in the wave of radicalization. The novelist Burr McCloskey recalled organizing a United Students' Alliance while at Central High School in 1937, and seeking, unsuccessfully, to affiliate the Alliance with the Central Labor Union. McCloskey's greatest coup was getting the entire student body to walk out, although he admitted that he had "cheated a little" by "ringing the fire bell" and then telling his classmates that they were on strike.[84] McCloskey later worked at Firestone, an experience he used to write a nightmarish novel whose anti-hero is a tire builder.[85]

The radical ferment also helped to produce a number of leftwing activists and writers, including the Third World debt campaigner Susan George, who grew up in an affluent Akron family in the 1930s and '40s.[86] The charismatic anti-Vietnam War activist Carl Oglesby also hailed from Akron, albeit from "the other side of the tracks." According to Mike Davis, who knew him in Students for a Democratic Society, Oglesby wore a beard "because his face was cratered from a poor-white childhood." His parents were Southerners who had made the trek to Akron, where his father was a rubber worker.[87] The famed inventor Stan Ovshinsky also grew up in Akron, the son of poor Russian immigrants who were members of a small Jewish socialist circle in the city.[88] Ovshinsky began his working life as a machinist at B. F. Goodrich. In 1940, at the age of eighteen, Ovshinsky represented the URW Goodrich Local on the CIO's Akron Industrial Union Council. He remained a "Debsian" socialist until the end of his life,[89] and was involved with the postwar United Labor Party with the leftwing historian Gabriel Kolko.[90]

Meanwhile, fresh trouble was brewing in the 1930s rubber industry. A price war had broken out, with the big companies slashing the retail price of tires in order to gain greater market share and drive out competitors. Naturally, cheaper tires were made possible by cutting wages and speeding up production.[91] Thus, in October 1935, Goodyear's Cliff Slusser took advantage of the continuing weakness of the Goodyear URW local to move against the six-hour working day. Tire builder Haskell Jones recalled that the company first tried to do this by stealth. The foremen asked, "You want to work a couple hours over?" Most workers agreed because following the Depression, "everything they had was worn out," including clothing and furniture. When the gummers discovered that the extra hours would be paid at single time, they were incensed at "the dirty bastards."[92] The shorter working day had been introduced because of the strain of production work on the gummers' health—particularly that of heavy tire builders and pit workers—and now, coupled with the eternal speed-up, they found the threat of the longer day intolerable. Jones later recalled the terrible strain on the sixty- and sixty-five-year-olds, who "couldn't figure they could ever work eight hours again."[93] The longer week also threatened the jobs of around 1,200 workers in the plant. As a sweetener, the company promised a $3 pay raise, but one irate tire builder wrote to the *Beacon Journal* to complain that the increase was "not what it is cracked up to be." It meant he would be working the extra time for eight cents an hour.[94]

To the management's amazement, such was the depth of feeling that the Goodyear Industrial Assembly's "lower house" voted unanimously to reject the eight-hour day. Just a few months before, a journalist had written a puff piece for the *Atlantic Monthly* claiming that "the Goodyear set-up in employee relations is unique in American industry ... [and if] the proof of the pudding is in the eating, one can say that the Goodyear plan has succeeded."[95] In fact, the Assembly would soon be defunct as Paul Litchfield vetoed its demand to retain the six-hour day and thus exposed it as a toothless tool of management. Shortly afterwards, the Assembly came to heel and dropped its opposition to the longer day.[96] The URW complained to the National Labor Relations Board, which rebuked management, demanded the retention of the six-hour day, and agreed that ending it would lead to huge job losses.[97]

For the URW, the tide was turning. The gummers began renewing their membership and in November, the union staged its biggest mass meeting since the fall of 1933.[98] When Goodyear management announced cuts to the piecework rates of truck tire builders, one 150-strong shift responded with a brief, spontaneous sit-down strike. Startled by this development, the company promised to review the cuts and when it appeared that they might not do so, the men arriving for morning shift staged a further, one-hour sit-down. The situation was resolved by compromise, which Goodyear Local President House admitted was "better, but not entirely satisfactory."[99] The sit-downs were not the first in Akron's history,[100] but they foreshadowed an extraordinary upsurge of strikes, go-slows, and sit-downs that was to erupt in the New Year. Akron was on the verge of all-out class war and the rubber companies had brought it on themselves. One imagines Frederick Engels' ghost looking on with approval at these exciting, but belated, developments.

14.

A City in Radical Ferment

The AFL's fifty-fifth annual convention, held in Atlantic City on October 19, 1935, famously descended into "a roaring riot and a three blow fistfight" between John L. Lewis of the United Mineworkers and William L. Hutcheson of the Carpenters.[1] Lewis swung the first punch after Hutcheson continually interrupted a rubber workers' delegate from Barberton with points of order, called Lewis a "bastard," and told him to shut up.[2] After the fracas had died down, President Bill Green denied the young rubber worker the floor.[3] The previous Wednesday, the craft union advocates had inflicted an "overwhelming defeat" on their industrial opponents,[4] ignoring a vintage speech by Lewis in which he excoriated the AFL for its continued failure to organize workers in mass production industry. The Federation, Lewis charged, "is still tinkering with this job in the great rubber stronghold of Akron in the same inefficient manner as was the case some twenty or more years ago and with no more result and no more hope."[5] Despite the vote, the conservatives could not hold back the industrial union tide. Summit County's mass production workers were already convinced of the need to organize industrially and the gummers had won their independence, but Lewis's words were electrifying nonetheless.

On January 19, 1936, Lewis stormed into Akron as the standard-bearer of the newly formed Committee for Industrial Organization[6] and delivered a rousing speech to a mass meeting of rubber workers. On the platform with him at the Akron Armory were John Brophy, chair of the CIO, and Sherman Dalrymple and Thomas Burns of the URW. Lewis's speech was a call to arms. "We only ask to let the industrial unions go where craft unions have failed," he said to thunderous applause. Next, he turned his rhetorical guns on the rubber corporations, declaring, "We're partners in theory and enemies in fact." This industry, he boomed, "has taken untold millions of dollars for its stockholders and yet it has been a daily struggle for workers to make ends meet."[7] In contrast to the meager earnings of the gummers, Goodyear President Litchfield took home $81,000 a year.[8] Lewis's speech was "a battle cry," but it only reinforced what the gummers themselves already knew.[9] Now, with the promise of heavyweight assistance from Lewis and the CIO, the URW could force the recalcitrant corporations to the negotiating table. The workers poured back into the union. According to Dalrymple, by March 1936, the Goodyear local alone had increased its membership by fifteen hundred percent.[10] Several huge strikes, many of them sit-downs, broke out in the rubber and other industries. Two of the largest strikes were those at Goodyear in 1936 and Firestone in 1937. Akron became a union town. The union upsurge could also be seen as a revolt of the white Southerners, the long despised "snakes," "hillbillies," and "crackers," who had made Akron their home. Diverted from the labor movement in the 1920s by the reactionary message of the Ku Klux Klan, they now appeared to have achieved the class consciousness necessary to build and sustain an industrial labor movement. If Akron was a microcosm of America, it seemed that the nation's labor movement was finally fulfilling the promise noted back in the nineteenth century by Marx, Engels, and other leftwing observers.

The union victories were never a foregone conclusion. The powerful rubber corporations had hunkered down for confrontation, with barbed wire fences, floodlighting, and stockpiles of tear gas, arms, and ammunition.[11] Sherman Dalrymple announced that three hundred Goodyear supervisors and Flying Squad members had been sworn in as special deputies after "intensive training in military tactics, including the use of gas guns.""[12] Spies and Klansmen still infested the factories. The National Service Corporation of Youngstown had attempted to infiltrate the Firestone local, and General Tire hired out-of-town thugs to beat up its workers.[13] The La Follette Senate hearings revealed that General Tire had spent $14,000, Goodrich over $7,000, and Firestone nearly $2,000 on spies and professional strikebreakers such as Colonel Joe Johnston.[14] In labor cost equivalents, these sums translate into millions of dollars today. For Chalmers K. Stewart,

> the strikes were a first-hand confirmation of what had always been theoretically clear to us—that the capitalist class was prepared to use all means—fink agencies, scabs, police, goons, tear gas, city officials, and schools, even to the point of killing—if that was deemed necessary to preserve the alleged rights of 'private property' and corporate profits.[15]

A further problem for the unions was that although the Depression had temporarily eased, there were still large numbers of jobless people desperate for jobs, particularly as the companies deliberately maintained a large "reserve army of labor."

To counter these threats, the workers hit on the sit-down strike. Rubber workers in Mansfield, Ohio, used the tactic in May 1934,[16] and workers led by Rex Murray at Akron's General Tire & Rubber staged a sit-down shortly afterwards. There had also been a brief sit-down at Goodyear in late 1935. The tactic was stunningly effective as small numbers of militants in key departments could bring production to a standstill across whole factories and prevent scabs from taking their jobs. Employers were reluctant to evict the strikers forcibly in case of damage to valuable machinery. Stay-in strikes were the opposite of sabotage, of which most workers disapproved, but they were also a frontal challenge to private property, which was sacred in many Americans' eyes, including the more conservative union leaders. Ruth McKenney credits Alex Eigenmatt (or Eigenmacht), who had witnessed "inside strikes" back in his native Yugoslavia, with bringing the idea to Akron,[17] but another explanation is that rubber workers simply sat down on the diamond during a ball game until a replacement was found for the umpire, who was a hated nonunionist.[18] Truck tire builders at Firestone took up the tactic with gusto, sitting-in for three days from January 31 to February 1, 1936, to force the company to lift the suspension of a union committeeman, Clay Dicks, who had been provoked into a fist fight outside the plant gates by a pace setter. The sit-down caught both plant superintendent W. R. Murphy and the local union leaders by surprise. At 2:00 a.m., the tire builders stopped the belt. The sit-down spread rapidly around Plant No. 1 and paralyzed other departments as they ran out of materials. With Plant No. 2 poised to join the sit-down, management agreed to reinstate Dicks and to begin negotiations on wage rates. Firestone also agreed to compensate the strikers for half of time lost.[19]

Inspired by the Firestone sit-down's success, somewhere between one hundred and 250 nonunion workers in the Goodyear pit sat down the following day for six hours to protest a ten percent pay cut. The company refused to back down, so the strikers joined the URW, spurning the Industrial Assembly, which had tried to mediate the dispute. Just over a week later, a sit-down of Goodrich workers forced management to rescind a pay cut and reimburse the workers for some of the time lost. Five days later, workers in Goodyear Plant 2 sat down to demand the reinstatement of the six-hour day and refused to work despite threats from gun thugs roaming the factory. The company locked the strikers in and fired them but reinstated them when the URW intervened and persuaded them to leave the plant. By this time, the whole factory was seething with rebellion.[20] Despite its refusal to grant concessions, Goodyear publicly announced an $800,000 profit increase for 1935 over 1934, bringing its admitted total to $5.5 million.[21]

February 18, 1936, dawned frigid and blustery over the Goodyear factories in East Akron, and the temperature fell to nine degrees below zero Fahrenheit. A *Beacon* reporter sketched the scene:

> Bitter cold wind sweeps down along the Little Cuyahoga River across S. Martha av., where Goodyear workers shiver on the picket lines.... Little groups of pickets huddle around blazing embers in metal drum.... The men around them stomp their feet to keep from freezing ... "[22]

Fifteen thousand Goodyear workers had started an immense strike that was to last for thirty-three days. They commenced the strike without direction from their inept local union leaders—rank-and-file militants, including leftists, took control, shaped the strike demands, and organized for a protracted struggle. A pugnacious Southerner called Skip O'Harra brandished the Stars and Stripes and led his friends out into the blizzard to begin picketing. Soon sixty picket lines marched in chain fashion, blocking every gate into the vast factory in what was possibly the longest picket line in American history. B. J. Widick, whom the *Beacon* fired for supporting the strikers, wrote, "Pickets took charge of traffic, closed liquor stores, and generally ran East Akron under direction of a special strike committee."[23] Members of the Cooks' and Waitresses' Union set up soup kitchens to feed the pickets. Two thousand gummers from other firms joined their Goodyear brothers and sisters on the picket lines.[24] The strikers blocked off the eighteen-mile perimeter of the mammoth plant with its 160 gates and erected some three hundred tar-paper shanties to protect them from the elements. James Turner believes it was "probably the longest picket line in the history of the labor movement in this country."[25] The plant police filmed them from inside the gates, ostensibly to keep the company executives informed,[26] but more likely to record "evidence" for future victimization.

The strikers' demands included: the continuation of the six-hour day, no layoffs, no wage cuts, an end to the speed-up, and a signed agreement with URW Goodyear Local President John House, who had initially called the walk-off "an outlaw strike"[27] but was forced to be more supportive by rank and file pressure. He told the press, "The Goodyear factory is down. If they want to reopen, they can call us and negotiate an agreement with us." A company spokesperson announced that "Our position has not changed. We are still looking to the forces of government to protect us in our operations and our employes [sic] who want to work against mob rule."[28] Goodyear insisted that the Industrial Assembly represented the gummers, although the strikers vastly outnumbered the firm's putative fifteen hundred "loyalists" (who included Klansmen, remnants of the IA, and Flying Squadron men).

On the sixth day of the strike, despite Bill Green's reservations, the AFL made the strike official. On February 24, Summit County Sheriff Jim Flower read an injunction to the strikers, ordering them to lift the pickets. He deputized one thousand men to assist his regular forces, but the strikers defied him. Wilmer Tate, who had ousted the conservative Frank Patino as Central Labor Union President, warned that any attempt to break the picket would trigger a citywide general strike. The CLU elected a fifteen-strong action committee and gave it full power to do "anything they advise to help the Goodyear strikers."[29] Up to ten thousand workers from across the city and its environs gathered to defend the pickets. On March 7, the city police threatened to break the picket line but backed off when thousands of unionists again turned out to block them. As had been the case in the 1913 strike, women were prominent in the struggle. Rose Pesotta, the New York garment workers' leader, who had been seconded to the Goodyear strike as a CIO organizer, wrote a strong feminist article in the *United Rubber Worker* praising the role played by women in the strike. Women's place, she asserted, was not in the home but in the paid workforce and the union.[30]

Goodyear President Paul Litchfield swore that he would never sign an agreement with the URW,[31] "even if a vote of employees shows that a majority wish to be represented by the union."[32] However, less than a week later, with the strike nearing its third week and Goodyear losing vast profits and market share, he decided to negotiate—or was perhaps directed to do so by shareholders. On the other hand, ex-mayor Sparks, a far-right hothead, launched a five-thousand-strong "Law and Order League" armed with clubs and blackjacks. Modeled on the vigilantes who had helped to break the 1913 IWW strike, the League was bankrolled by Goodyear to the tune of $15,000.[33] In incendiary radio broadcasts, Sparks threatened to "crack heads," run "agitators" out of town, and forcibly reopen the plant. Unlike in 1913, it was empty bluster. Wilmer Tate derided Sparks as a "Little Mussolini,"[34] and Branko Widick jeered in the *United Rubber Worker* that "the sparks of fascism failed to ignite."[35] There was little stomach in the city's middle and business classes for violent confrontation despite Goodyear's intransigence and Sparks' bellicose posturing. The *Beacon Journal* editorialized against vigilantism,[36] and Governor Martin L. Davey refused to call out the National Guard to break the picket lines.

Sparks later told the Congressional Dies Committee that the Communist Party had organized the strike,[37] but Communist organizer Jim Keller later revealed that there was only one party member at Goodyear when the strike began,[38] and the *Daily Worker* described it as "a largely spontaneous uprising of workers."[39] Later, however, the party gave credence to Sparks' allegations by claiming to have been the prime mover for the strike,[40] and in 1954, a former party member told the House

Un-American Activities Committee that Akron Communist organizer James Keller was the "chief strategist of the Goodyear strike."[41] The party certainly exaggerated its size and importance, however. John Williamson claims that between 1933 and 1935, "almost alone, the Communists fought on to restore [working-class] confidence. Even our people were downcast by the number of defeats." One should treat the claim with extreme caution, although Communists certainly were very active in Akron, particularly in organizing the unemployed. Until 1935–36, however, the Communist Party was stuck in the sectarian "Third Period" rut, and this greatly limited its appeal. Isolated from the labor movement mainstream, it wasted its energies attempting to form "red" unions under its control. By the time of the Goodyear strike, however, the Communist Party changed course and began to court socialists and other progressives in a new "popular front" strategy. The party closed down its red unions and urged workers to join the AFL unions. They would have done so without the advice. As Milton Derber points out, "[by the time the party line had changed to permit the Communists to enter the mainstream of the labor movement, they were substantially discredited among the tire builders."[42]

The URW's international leadership scoffed at Communist claims to have organized the Goodyear strike,[43] but although party organizers greatly exaggerated its influence, its militants did play a prominent role. This was particularly true of the early days when conservative Local President John House was dithering about whether to call on the international union to make the strike official. Although Keller's later account of the strike is marred by grave distortions, he, along with party sympathizers Eric Spitzer and Bob Gamble, were active behind the scenes.[44] Keller claimed to have led the Goodyear strike and to have recruited 125 gummers to the party by the end of it. Most left shortly afterwards, he admits, attributing this to "lack of training in the science of Marxism-Leninism."[45] On the other hand, the party's critics claim that on more than one occasion the pickets "made a bonfire" of its literature.[46] Socialists such as Powers Hapgood, Wilmer Tate, Leo Krzycki, and McAllister Coleman, along with the anarchist Rose Pesotta, played prominent roles in the strike, and the Trotskyist journalist Branko Widick took charge of the union's publicity. Nevertheless, despite the radicals' important contribution, the strike could not have succeeded without the solidarity of the "ordinary" gummers and the widespread sympathy of the general population. The Communist Party's initial assessment that the strike was a spontaneous eruption is accurate.

By March, the dispute had reached stalemate. With neither side prepared to concede defeat, Labor Secretary Frances Perkins charged her assistant, Edward F. McGrady, a former AFL vice-president, with the hopeless task of settling the dispute. A mass meeting howled down his proposal that they return to work and submit their claims to arbitration. Finally, at a further meeting held in the Akron Armory on March 21, the strikers agreed to return to work after negotiation of a settlement by the union.[47] The vote was not unanimous. Goodyear steadfastly refused to recognize the URW, or to disband the "yellow" union, and declined to sign a formal contract. Nevertheless, the verbal agreement was, in the opinion of the local CP organizer Jim Keller, "the real McCoy"—the best settlement that could be reached, particularly as public support for the strikers was waning.

Some militants, including those the Communists reviled as "Trotskyites," disputed this view, which Keller shared with the conservative John House.[48] The militants pointed to the donation of some $25,000 worth of foodstuffs to the union by small merchants,[49] and to the *Beacon Journal*'s studied rejection of Nelson Sparks' rabblerousing. According to the *United Rubber Worker*, "Goodyear officials began to realize that the entire city was with the strikers in their demands for a just settlement." This seems an accurate assessment, for when the URW staged a mass victory parade through the city streets downtown shoppers cheered the procession.[50]

Despite the reservations of a portion of the membership, the settlement was a partial victory over the most obdurate of the Big Three corporations. There would be no victimizations or abrogation of service records, and management agreed to negotiate with URW representatives. Goodyear had to notify the union of any proposed changes to wage rates. In a thirty-six-hour week, workers in the tube division would work six shifts of six hours each, and the workers had to ratify any change in the departments affected. Elsewhere the maximum working week would not exceed forty hours, and lists of layoffs were to be made available to the union.[51] The agreement paved the way for the formal recognition of the union in 1941 and for an eventual closed shop.[52]

Goodyear only grudgingly accepted the settlement. Two months after the strike ended, they had thirty-one union members briefly jailed on charges of riot. It was a clear provocation, and the judge later dismissed the charges.[53] The following month, company goons savagely beat the union's International President, Sherman Dalrymple during an organizing drive at Goodyear's Gadsden plant in Alabama. The firm's claim to "genuinely regret" the beating[54] was undermined by Goodyear vice-president Slusser's threat that any union organizer who went to Gadsden would "get his head knocked off"[55] and by the deployment of the Klan and the fascist Silvershirts against unionists. The union too had its share of hard men, some of whom who frog-marched supervisors and "Red Apples" (company loyalists) into "bullpens" during the sit-down strikes.

The settlement did not end the sit-down wave. Goodyear workers in Akron staged a further nineteen sit-downs in the three months following the end of the big strike and between March and December 1936, there were no fewer than fifty-two sit-downs in the Akron industry as a whole. The tactic was so effective that in February 1939 the US Supreme Court—ever the willing tool of big business—declared it illegal in the Fansteel case.[56] Many top union leaders—including Sherman Dalrymple—were also critical of the tactic, which they regarded as anarchic and an impediment to orderly collective bargaining.[57] The Akron locals did not agree with him, and the issue was to contribute to a bitter schism with the URW's international officials. Ironically, the *India Rubber Journal,* which acted as an employers' mouthpiece, blamed the leadership for leading the workers astray and "inflaming [them] with hatred … against the employers…." The result would be, the *Journal* warned, "unemployment in a ruined city."[58]

The buoyant mood of Summit County's working class in the aftermath of the Goodyear strike was demonstrated when at least ten thousand and possibly as many as twenty thousand Akron and Barberton union members joined a May Day procession that snaked for one-and-half miles through the city streets. The parade ended at Grace Park in a mass meeting chaired by the Mohawk Rubber URW local president and addressed by the Wilmer Tate and Francis Gerhart, along with Joseph Schlossberg of the Amalgamated Clothing Workers' Union and the Flint UAW's Maurice Sugar, the author of the defiant song "Sit-Down."[59]

All speakers called for the union offensive to continue and for the creation of a labor party.[60] Women had always been employed in the rubber mills, and they often played a prominent role in union struggles. In August 1936, for instance, the predominantly female workforce at the L. E. Shunk Latex Products factory struck work to protest layoffs, set up picket lines and armed themselves with "little clubs" to deter strikebreakers.[61]

Meanwhile, scores of strikes broke out in other industries across the Akron district, most of them centering on the demand for union recognition and signed contracts. Simultaneously with the Goodyear strike, five hundred workers at the Columbia Chemical plant in Barberton occupied their plant in support of a pipefitters' wage claim. The most spectacular struggle of all broke out in neighboring Kent, thirteen miles away over the Portage County line, as the Goodyear strike was ending. Five years earlier, the Black & Decker Company had begun the manufacture of fractional horsepower electric motors in the town.

In March 1936, International Association of Machinists' members at the factory stopped work to back their demands for a thirty-six-hour week, a ten percent pay increase, and union recognition. The strike was peaceful until early on June 18, when a convoy of scabs crashed into the factory, firing shotguns and teargas at a skeleton picket line.[62] The La Follette Senate civil liberties committee later revealed that National Metal Trades Association (NMTA) chief Homer D. Sayre had hired the strikebreakers through a Cleveland detective agency, and that sixteen of the forty-six scabs had criminal records for offences including robbery, assault, and illegal possession of bombs. Their leading light was Louis "Babe" Triscaro, a well-known Cleveland boxer who had served time for armed holdup. The strikebreakers toted an astounding arsenal of weapons, including shotguns, rifles, revolvers, gas guns, tear gas "jumpers," brass knuckles, and ammunition. Their fusillade at the factory gates had badly injured a number of pickets, including fifty-year old Tony Pudloski, who was shot in the leg; W. A. Gray, who received buckshot wounds to the face; and James Pomphrette, who was "severely gassed." The stunt massively backfired. Shortly afterwards "a howling, roaring and booing crowd of several thousand union men from Summit and Portage counties" laid siege to the strikebreakers holed up in the plant.[63] Chalmers Stewart, who was Akron Teachers' Union President at the time, later recalled an extraordinary scene:

> The plant was ... besieged by men armed with hunting rifles. Windows at the plant had all been shot out. Water from the plant water tank was arching to the ground out of bullet holes. The police abandoned the streets ... strikebreakers ... had crashed the picket line, which included women, in big vans. That's when the men got out their rifles and laid siege to the plant.[64]

Rolling gunfire echoed round the town for five hours as the armed workers, many of them from the rubber mills, attacked the strikebreakers inside the plant from behind a 150-foot swathe of no-man's land. Cars jammed the neighboring streets, and Kent's industries closed down as union members flocked to the picket lines. One scab crawled out through a window and fled to Ravenna, leaving the others cowering inside.[65] Fourteen hours after they had crashed into the Black & Decker plant, National Guardsmen escorted the forty-six scabs, their faces white with fear, past the angry pickets. Supporters from Akron burned a scab truck in the parking lot next at the Kent City Hall.[66] The police had wisely stayed in their quarters. If the editorials in the Kent *Courier-Tribune* are a gauge, local opinion was firmly behind the strikers and placed the blame for the uproar firmly on the employers. As Stewart remarked, "The difference between this encounter and those in Akron at the time was here, for a change, the workers were not clubbed, tear gassed and arrested by the cops."[67]

Implausibly, NMTA chief Homer Sayre told the press that his association's objective was "to promote harmonious relations" between labor and capital. The strike ended on June 29 in a union victory, securing a forty-hour week, layoffs by seniority, a five percent pay raise, and union recognition. The strikers were jubilant. The company disbanded the yellow union, and its former members enrolled in the Machinists' union. In the brief hiatus between the settlement and resumption of work, the workers occupied themselves with "neglected fishing, lawns that needed mowing, work that had been put off until the strike was settled."[68] The police later charged the scabs with assault with intent to wound for firing on and gassing the pickets, but later quietly dropped the charges.[69] Sayre was never prosecuted, despite having orchestrated the violence.

Meanwhile, relations between the Summit County industrial unionists and the Washington-based AFL leaders steadily worsened. The Central Labor Union became the site of brewing confrontation. In February 1936, Wilmer Tate defeated Frank Patino of the Bricklayers' Union in the elections for CLU President by 65 votes to 49.[70] Patino did not accept defeat graciously. Matters came to a head at a "tumultuous meeting" of the CLU on July 10, with Patino's building trades group denouncing an alleged Communist takeover. Tate's offence in Patino's eyes was to have called for Bill Green and John Lewis to negotiate over the place of the Committee for Industrial Unionism in the AFL[71]

In November, the AFL suspended the URW and nine other international CIO unions.[72] When Akron bus drivers, office workers, and grocery clerks voted to switch to the CIO, the local AFL organizer H. A. Bradley declared, "We're not going to sit back like a lot of ninnies and let them raid our unions." He was not at this stage thinking of suspending or outlawing the CLU, he added, but the time was coming as Tate had refused to purge the CIO unions from the body.[73] Shortly afterwards, Bill Green expelled ten URW Akron locals,[74] and in September Bradley "stalked into Akron's Central Labor Union, removed Tate from the presidency, canceled all democratic rights, and appointed himself as chairman of the council." Thirty-seven out of forty-five Council affiliates withdrew in protest and formed an opposition caucus[75] in protest at the actions of the man they called "a little Caesar." Tate insisted that he would not be driven from the labor movement and that "even the rank and file of the building trades unions whose racketeering business agents supported [his expulsion] … are against it."[76]

Shortly afterwards, Tate was expelled from his own union, the International Association of Machinists. He pointed out that Arthur O. Wharton, the IAM's autocratic International President, had not dared to request that Tate's own local do his bidding.[77] Wharton was an AFL official of the type Tate described as "brass hats," which caused Bill Green to throw an extended tantrum when he met a delegation of Akron unionists. According to Bruce Minton of *New Masses,* a Communist-aligned magazine, Wharton had earlier written to an IAM, local in Pittsburgh stating imperiously that "The Grand Lodge officers of the machinists do not take orders from the rank and file."[78] The CIO immediately hired Tate as a general organizer. The AFL formally expelled the URW in May 1938, but given that Frank Grillo claimed a membership of over forty thousand in the Akron region,[79] it had little cause to worry. When the AFL revoked the CLU's forty-year-old charter, the CIO formed the Akron Industrial Union Council, headed by Wilmer Tate, to coordinate its powerful affiliates.[80] Tate and his supporters did, however, do everything in their power to maintain unity of the CIO and AFL rank and file in the city.[81]

By the end of the decade, Summit County's workers were still pouring into the CIO unions. The new federation's policy of building alternative unions to some ineffectual AFL organizations sparked intense rivalry, despite the temporary rapprochement following a police riot at Goodyear. This was the case in the city's public transit industry, where the new CIO Transport Workers' Union pushed aside the weak AFL local and, after a series of militant strikes, secured large wage increases for drivers and other classifications. The split was particularly acrimonious in the building industry, where some the AFL unions were little more than rackets. When the press asked about workers having to buy jobs and pay kickbacks to officials, general organizer Bradley "laughed heartily" and dismissed the allegations as unworthy of comment.

The evidence suggests otherwise. Shortly afterwards, "leisurely burglars" broke into the CIO's Akron offices and stole the safe and four hundred dollars in cash. The burglary came as no surprise, as the CIO's United Construction Workers' Union was "poaching" disgruntled tradesmen away from the AFL at the time. In late 1940, gangsters bombed power shovels on three small construction sites and fled, leaving the body of a local man called Robert C. Floyd in the debris. The police arrested Floyd's brother Tilford and an accomplice called Harry J. Jones for the crime. The pair were officials of AFL Operating Engineers' Local 18, and Jones was vice-president of the Ohio State Federation of Labor. Bradley foolishly defended the bombers—whom he had sponsored for union positions despite their substantial criminal records—claiming they had been framed-up to discredit the AFL.[82] Floyd confessed, and they served long sentences in the Ohio State Penitentiary for the bombings. Although Daniel Nelson describes Bradley as "a shadowy figure,"[83] he was the most prominent AFL figure in the city, and Bill Green later appointed him as founding International President of the International Chemical Workers' Union.[84] There is no suggestion that Bradley condoned the bombings, but he does not appear to have made any real effort to cleanse the AFL locals of gangster elements.

Nevertheless, despite such ructions, the AFL-CIO split was never popular among Summit County's unionists. Wilmer Tate insisted that the rank-and-file would support any moves for industrial peace and in 1942, the rival federations organized a joint Labor Day rally at Summit Beach Park. John Borsos also claims that members of the rival federations cooperated at the grassroots level in Barberton, not surprising given that the socialist Francis Gerhart led the AFL Match Workers' local in the town. Such local initiatives mirrored moves for reconciliation at a national level, for in 1944 unity negotiations began between the AFL's Bill Green and Philip Murray of the CIO. While re-amalgamation made sense for many reasons, the CIO's drift back to a more bureaucratic-conservative modus operandi made it much easier.

By 1937, Firestone was the only Akron rubber firm to have avoided signing an industrial agreement of some kind with the URW. The company had been hit by several sit-down strikes, but these were sectional in nature. At the beginning of March that year, the big dispute that the company had been preparing for since 1934 broke out. Firestone decided to punish the union for holding a recruiting drive and for staging short stoppages, including a sit-down strike,[85] and insisted that it would negotiate only with the company union, the Employees' Conference Plan.[86] The strike began haphazardly, probably against the wishes of the conservative local union president, Leland S. Buckmaster—"an old schoolmarm type" according to Bruce Meyer[87]—but it was to last for eight weeks and end in a comprehensive victory for the union.[88] The strike began in the Firestone No. 2 plant on March 2 when the company locked out two thousand tire department workers, some of whom had been involved in the sit-down strike. Buckmaster told the press that he was confused about the reasons for the lock out, but the company claimed that the URW had tried to force some company unionists to join the URW. The following day, seven thousand URW members walked off the job in Plant No 1 to protest the lockout in the other plant. They set up picket lines, but the union leadership disbanded them, hoping that negotiations would make them unnecessary. It was not to be. The union met all night with company representatives but neither side would budge from their positions. The union called a mass meeting in the Akron Armory to decide on a course of action, and the press reported that the huge room was "packed" with gummers. By this stage, Firestone's operations were at a standstill. Both main plants were shut and ten thousand employees were on strike or locked out. The strike, a *Beacon Journal* writer noted, was only one of many in America and in the Akron district as "strikes pop up like boils on the face of Uncle Sam," but it was one of the largest. By March 8, Buckmaster was still reluctant to say that a fully-fledged strike had broken out, but he did admit that "the men are refusing to work."

The strike had started chaotically, but the union eventually clarified its demands. Firstly, they insisted that Firestone recognize the URW as the sole bargaining agent for the workers. This meant the abolition of the company union. They also wanted a promise from the company to bargain in good faith on wages, hours, and working conditions, and "to incorporate the settlement in a signed agreement." The following day, the workers took a formal strike vote, carried supposedly by acclamation, although in fact by a majority of 2,665 to 93. Somewhat surprisingly, given the lengths it had gone to turn the factory into a fortress, the company made no preparations to start production. Nevertheless, the union threw up pickets around the six-mile perimeter of the plants to keep out strikebreakers. Union members were required for six-hour stints on the picket line at the times of their normal shifts. Acting swiftly, and with great discipline, they built thirty picket shanties, which eventually boasted stoves, electricity, and other conveniences, and gave them fanciful names such as "FDR," "Lewis," "Powder Puff," and "Mae West." The police announced that they would permit the shanties as long as they did not obstruct the streets, and the strike remained peaceful throughout the long weeks that followed. Even C. Nelson Sparks, the anti-union fire-eater who had threatened to unleash vigilantes against the Goodyear strikers the previous year, was in a conciliatory mood, urging mediation and not violence. The union began what turned into marathon negotiation sessions with management, but there was little desire on either side to compromise.

Curiously, company Chairman Harvey S. Firestone and President John W. Thomas delegated control to plant superintendent W. R. Murphy and remained at their winter houses in Florida throughout the strike. One gummer wrote to the *Beacon* to urge it to "push a little … [then Governor Martin] Davey might get Harvey out of his winter palace and back to Akron, where 40,000 people are suffering from his lock-out." Harvey Firestone, it transpired, was ill, but this does not explain Thomas's absence. Negotiations were fruitless. The union announced that its key demands were nonnegotiable, and John Thomas reaffirmed in a letter to the union that the company would never recognize the URW as the sole bargaining agent. The union signaled that it was digging in for a long struggle when it announced that it was making plans for a mass demonstration on Sunday April 4, some weeks hence. "We want to make it the largest labor parade in Akron's history," Buckmaster declared. The union also organized a mass meeting for strikers' wives and mothers. Held in the Majestic Theater on South Main, this gathering was addressed by union officials and Municipal Judge G. L. Patterson (a former NLRB official and Democrat mayoral candidate) and chaired by a striker's wife called Mary Stitzel.

On Sunday, April 4, the heavens smiled on the union. The sun shone brightly as the city's unionists turned out in huge numbers for the Firestone strikers' solidarity parade. Wilmer Tate took pride of place at the head of the march, which took an hour to pass Exchange Street on its way to Thornton Street. The police estimated the marchers to number twenty-five thousand, with twice that number of spectators lining the streets. Sherman Dalrymple claimed at least thirty thousand marchers. Whatever the number, it was probably the largest parade in the city's history. There were many thousands of gummers from all of Summit County's rubber plants, joined by others from CIO unions, including contingents of city and county workers, waterworks employees, barbers, bakers, and beauticians. Numbers of AFL craft unionists also marched in solidarity with the industrial unionists and a horse labeled "Roosevelt" pulled a cart mocking the "nine old men" of the Supreme Court, causing great merriment among the spectators. The parade was an impressive spectacle; Frank Grillo, the URW's International Secretary-Treasurer, observed that it "should show the companies we have the strength to command exclusive bargaining rights." This was indubitably the case, but superintendent Murphy still refused to back down on the key sticking point of de-recognition of the minuscule company union. Opponents of the strike organized a redbaiting letter writing campaign in the local press. An "Indignant Wife," outraged by the disrespect for the Supreme Court judges, wrote that she had told her husband she would divorce him unless he tore up his URW card. She claimed he obeyed. In a radio broadcast, Wilmer Tate decried what he called an organized effort to break the strikers' morale but was confident "stooges shall not destroy the unity of our ranks." The strike stretched into its seventh week and remained peaceful despite some tense moments when police rushed to the plant with "sirens screaming" for some reason that was never made clear.

The end of the strike came quickly when it dawned on the rubber companies that the union was not going to back down and would not compromise on its core demands. On April 28, 1937, the *Beacon*'s headline announced, "Goodyear and Goodrich Drop Support for Company Unions," the Industrial Assembly and the Cooperative Plan respectively. The companies gave no reasons for their sudden volte-face, but by this time, the URW claimed one hundred percent coverage at Goodrich and seventy-seven percent at Goodyear. The Big Three had evidently caucused together, for on the same day Firestone capitulated and agreed to most of the union's demands. The following morning, a huge meeting of gummers ratified the agreement. The signed agreement, which was to run until 1941, gave the URW sole bargaining rights and recognition. There was to be no discrimination or loss of seniority. The company also agreed to a standard thirty-six-hour week of six shifts of six hours a day and agreed to provide one week paid vacation after five years for all employees. The meeting ratified the agreement by at least 4,300 votes to two hundred. The union did not explain the "No" votes, but it is possible that a minority opposed a clause stipulating that there would be no strikes for the duration of the agreement. The clause, they probably feared, would take control away from the members and invest it in the leadership.[89]

The URW was ecstatic. "Union Whips Firestone!" Branko Widick enthused in a flaring *United Rubber Worker* headline.[90] And so they had. They had also "whipped" the other large corporations, which had faced up to the new industrial relations reality and abolished their company unions. The Firestone strike was one of the most successful campaigns of the newly formed Congress of Industrial Organizations, which was simultaneously waging a number of bitter disputes around the country. Conversely, the settlement was a bitter defeat for Harvey Firestone. Now sixty-six years of age, Firestone was an aggressive, self-made man, a close friend of Henry Ford and used to getting his way. If he had not have fallen ill, he might have returned to Akron and taken a tougher stance against the union. Although he claimed that he "had never felt better," he died on February 7 the following year. Shortly afterwards, his nemesis, Wilmer Tate, also fell ill and although his doctor told him to take a complete rest, he found it impossible to do so. He was to die young in 1944.

There is a certain symmetry in the lives of the industrial baron and that of the CIO leader. Both were Midwest farm boys. Both left the land and made their living in the city of Akron. Both were possessed of a work ethic so fierce that it probably shortened their lives. Both were gifted mechanically, Tate so much so that his bosses usually made him foreman despite his wishes, which always made him quit.[91] There any resemblance ends. The socialist Tate wanted a society of equals; whereas Firestone epitomized American individualism, Tate stood for collective solidarity. In their two persons is concentrated the essence of the great clash of social classes and philosophies. For Tate and his allies, the union was a fighting social movement, not just a business association along the lines approved by Bill Green of the AFL. The difference is highlighted in an anecdote related by James Turner, Black URW officer and later NAACP president in Akron. Turner recalled a fellow Firestone employee he called "Slim," who would hop slavishly when the foreman yelled, but who stopped jumping when he realized there was a union:

> This is what the union meant to many of us. Not dollars, not cents, but a sense of dignity, a sense of pride, and a sense of being a human being. Not hanging up your pride on a hat rack outside the door, and then coming to work....

Turner added that the strikes were sustained by "the whole community working together and particularly ... [by] the laboring people sticking together."[92]

Firestone striker Clarence Gregg leads victory cheers, Akron, 1937. Reprinted with permission of the *Akron Beacon Journal* and Ohio.com

The triumphant Firestone strikers cheered themselves hoarse and danced in the street outside the plant. A sound truck drove up, and thousands of men and women went through the steps of traditional Appalachian square dancing to the music of banjos, fiddles, and guitars. The choice of music and dance was not surprising because the great majority of Akron rubber workers and their families hailed from the South. Chalmers Stewart recalls "a city where more or less standard English was in constant struggle with various southern sub-species."[93] The Southerner Tom Jones, whose family worked in the mills, writes,

> it was the Southern whites, which were initially hired in the belief that they were not prone to unionize, [who] led the strike … with massive unemployment outside the walls of the rubber factories and stronger ties to the community their view of union membership was quite different…."[94]

If, as the Marxist historian Art Preis argues "the rise of the CIO was … the greatest event in modern American history,"[95] much of the drama was down to the poor southern immigrants who labored in the factories in Midwest cities like Akron. Industrial capitalism had blighted the lives of the mountain immigrants; befouled their rivers and forests and forced them from their houses; belittled their culture and sneered at their country ways, so there is something intensely satisfying about them using their traditional culture to celebrate a victory over a system that was so alien to their way of life. For many, too, the picket lines provided a practical education in the brute facts of ethnicity and class. The CIO organizer Rose Pesotta recalled that many of the rank and file strike leaders, including the fearless picket captain Skip O'Harra, were former Klansmen. A friendly striker's wife told her that the Klan was "A social and educational society … in the manner of explaining a local custom to an outsider." Many of the pickets initially disbelieved that Pesotta was Jewish and a leftist, but they came to respect and admire her courage and dedication—and to question their own prejudices as a result.[96] When Goodyear workers staged a sit-down to protest Sherman Dalrymple's bashing by company goons, the anti-union Klan burned a warning cross outside the plant. The workers promptly sat down again. Actions such as these were significant given that Akron had boasted a huge klavern of the hooded bigots. Led by local rich men, the Klan promoted the divide-and-rule summed up decades later in Lyndon Baines Johnson's folksy words: "If you can convince the lowest white man he's better than the best colored man, he won't notice you're picking his pocket. Hell, give him somebody to look down on, and he'll empty his pockets for you."[97] The union still had much work to do to overcome racism among its members, but as James Turner reminds us, whereas the AFL had been reluctant to take in women, minorities, and Blacks, the CIO was all-inclusive.[98]

However, despite the URW's formal commitment to racial equality, there is little doubt that huge numbers of white workers still supported the color bar or were too frightened to challenge their racist colleagues, managers, or supervisors. There were cases of "hate strikes" against the hiring of Black employees. In 1943, for example, white women employees struck over the hiring of two Black women in the sole and heel department of Seiberling Tire & Rubber at Barberton. The union denounced the women for violating "one of the most sacred principles of the United Rubber Workers of America, namely, our pledge of no discrimination against fellow workers on account of creed, color and nationality," and persuaded them to return to work alongside the Black women,[99] but one suspects that more often than not such incidents went unreported. It was not until 1955 that the first Black tire builder learned the trade—perhaps the most highly paid of the non-craftsman classifications in the rubber mills, Only with the passage of the Civil Rights Acts in the 1960s that there was any general improvement for Black workers in the mills, with the force of law behind it.[100] Looked at in this way, an all-inclusive, progressive class consciousness was as far away as it had ever been in Akron.

The establishment's response to multi-racial organizing by the city's leftists in the 1930s shows that racism was not the sole prerogative of poor white Southerners. Although some critics insist that Marxism subordinated the struggle for Black liberation to abstract class demands, this is unfair. Akron's white Communists and other leftwing radicals recognized the special, "double" nature of Black oppression, taking their point of departure from Marx, who had insisted that "Labor cannot emancipate itself in the white skin where in the black it is branded."[101] In 1921, the founding documents of the Workers' (Communist) Party recognized the special oppression of Black Americans over and above that of the white working class. That Stalinism had disfigured the American Communist Party by the late 1920s is undeniable, but this should not obscure the commitment of party members to ending racial oppression. In the early 1930s, Akron's Communists organized the city's unemployed on multi-racial lines. In February 1931, the party's unemployed activists protested "illegally" after the city's safety director, Ross Walker, refused permission for a mixed race dance in a council hall.[102]

Campaigning for equality and justice for people of color was radical business, but some Black community leaders craved respectability and sought to distance themselves from the Left. Incredibly, one Black community leader eulogized Harvey Firestone as "the benefactor" of Akron's Black community. Speaking to an audience of 1,400 Blacks and a sprinkling of invited white guests in 1938, the NAACP's Dr. George E. Haynes praised Firestone for "a new type of humanitarianism." One wonders if Haynes was aware that Firestone's Liberian plantations had impressed indigenous tribesmen into bonded labor.[103] Haynes warned his listeners to avoid leftists, despite their consistent support for racial equality. The Communist Party and the Farmer-Labor Party, for example, ran mixed-race slates for the city council, state, and county elections. In 1939, the Communist Party stood Fred W. Seibert and his Black running mate, Ben Atkins, for councilmen-at-large and they topped the poll in the poor, mainly Black Third Ward of Akron.[104] One of Haynes' guests in the Baptist Hall meeting was C. W. Seiberling, a member of the family that had created Goodyear Tire & Rubber, a Jim Crow factory. Seiberling praised Firestone, absurdly, as "the greatest friend of the Negro this city has ever produced."[105] The same evening, Emmer Lancaster, The University of Akron's first Black law graduate, revealed that the city's twelve-thousand-strong Black community was served by just six physicians, three dentists, and five lawyers.[106]

The radical ferment of Akron during the mid-1930s also impelled a number of the city's sons and daughters to volunteer to fight for the Spanish Republic against Franco's fascist insurgency. Indeed, some 150

"Ohio boys" joined the Abraham Lincoln Brigade, bound for Spain, not all of them Communists. They included Frank Cook, a coalminer who later became Akron organizer of the Young Communist League. Frank Lukas (or Lukaszewicz), who lived in Akron and Cleveland, worked as a printer and fought as a machine gunner with the Lincolns in Spain.[107] Charles Roffeld, who also appears to have hailed from Akron, was shell shocked when an Italian submarine torpedoed his ship, and he served afterwards in a noncombatant capacity.[108] The Akron gummer Steve Miletich, an organizer for the Young Communist League, died during the siege of Belchite in August 1937.[109]

Akron's Salaria Kee O'Reilly served as a nurse with the Lincolns in Spain in hospitals near Madrid and at Teruel. Late in life, she claimed that she "didn't know what a communist was" before she went to Spain,[110] but her NKVD dossier states that she joined the Middle Harlem local of the American Communist Party in 1935 and applied for a transfer to the Spanish CP in 1937.[111] Nevertheless, she was also a devout Catholic throughout her life.[112] In an unpublished memoir, she wrote that "Fascism and slavery and persecution and Jim Crow are just one and the same thing."[113] In all probability, she did join the party but was never a Stalinist hardliner.[114]

Salaria's life epitomizes the hardships faced by Akron's Black population. Despite considerable sacrifice, Salaria's family sent her to Akron's Central High School, but she transferred to the more liberal Akron West High School when she was excluded from Central High's basketball team because of her color.[115] After graduation, she applied to nursing training schools in Akron, Cleveland, and Detroit, all of which rejected her because of her color.[116] The Harlem Hospital Training School admitted her in 1930, possibly after intervention by Idabelle Firestone and Eleanor Roosevelt. Even then, she could not escape Jim Crow. The hospital employed both white and Black staff, but strictly segregated the dining facilities. Taking four colleagues with her, the rebellious Salaria sat down at a "whites only" table. The waiter refused to serve them, whereupon they stood up and pushed the table over. Eventually, the hospital management agreed to end the segregated dining rooms.[117]

Salaria Kea O'Reilly with photos on wall behind of her in International Brigade nurse's uniform. Reprinted with permission of the *Akron Beacon Journal* and Ohio.com

By the time she graduated in 1934, Salaria had acquired a militant social consciousness. She joined with a group of Harlem nurses and doctors to send medical supplies to help the Ethiopian people, who were resisting the Italian invasion.[118] After graduation, she took up Arnold Donewa's suggestion to go to Spain as a nurse with the International Brigades and sailed for Spain with eleven other doctors and nurses aboard the SS *Paris* on March 27, 1937. They were welcomed at the Catalan port of Portbou on April 3, by an enormous crowd of local people.[119] As the sole person of color aboard ship, she created a sensation when she arrived onshore.[120] Although Portbou was "an exquisite tropical Mediterranean port," any illusion of arriving in a peaceful idyll was soon lost. The team traveled to Madrid via Barcelona, both of which were under siege by Franco's fascist armies, and set up a field hospital at Villa Paz, a one-time summer home of the former king, Alfonso XIII.[121] The makeshift infirmary rapidly "filled with soldiers of every degree of injury and ailment [and] of almost every known race and tongue." The poet Langston Hughes described Kee as "one of the most competent nurses in that war-torn country."[122] The Republican soldiers' injuries were often horrific; their soldiers were outgunned.[123] More horrors were to come when Salaria's team moved to a field hospital at Teruel in April 1938. Salaria's team were sometimes operating for forty hours straight, often subsisting on beans and rancid oil. They were also in constant danger from fascist airplanes, which would deliberately target ambulances and hospitals.[124]

Kee also saw what the war meant for the poor people of Spain. On the first two mornings after the medical team's arrival, she witnessed villagers going to work in the fields. On the third day, aircraft destroyed their village. "No one went to the fields to work that day. Most of them were dead." The suffering of these Spanish peasants made her realize that oppression was not just due to race,[125] but that people were also oppressed because of class. "So many tragedies I shared with the Spanish people," she wrote. On several occasions, she helped dig out children from bombed buildings. Children's colonies outside Barcelona, she tells us, "were special targets" for the fascist planes.[126]

It was not just Franco's forces and their German and Italian allies who were responsible for the suffering of the Spanish people. After an artillery barrage at Teruel, Salaria's team picked up empty shell casings littering the ground. They were of American manufacture.[127] Firestone, Ford, General Motors, Studebaker, Du Pont, and Texaco supplied Franco's army with tires, trucks, ammunition, and gasoline on credit, much of it arriving aboard Nazi freighters.[128] Eventually it was Salaria's turn to suffer serious injury during an aerial bombardment, after which she returned home.[129]

After arriving at New York City in May 1938,[130] she toured the country, speaking out at countless public meetings, collecting funds for medical supplies, and agitating for the US government to lift its embargo on aid for the Republic. On Sunday 26 June, she spoke at the Second Baptist Church in Akron on the topic of "Behind the Spanish Battle Lines."[131] As Kathe Pollitt wrote many years later, "If anyone prevented the Loyalist defeat from being an entirely black mark in American history, it was the Lincoln Brigaders."[132] Akron can be proud of Salaria Kee's contribution to that redemption, which stands in stark contrast to Harvey Firestone's support for Franco.

Meanwhile, Goodyear and the local Republican establishment made one final effort to crush the URW using the methods they employed in Memphis and Gadsden. In late May 1938, the Akron police and plant guards brutally attacked union pickets and sympathizers on the street outside the Goodyear No. 1 plant in East Akron. Angered by company stalling on negotiations over grievances over seniority and "wage chiseling" in defiance of the Wagner Act, workers spontaneously downed tools and picketed the plant without waiting for their officials' approval. Determined to prevent a repeat of the 1936 strike, the Republican mayor, a local businessman called Lee D. Schroy, mobilized the city police force, and Goodyear massed its private police force at the factory gates. Up to four thousand unionists gathered on the street, but police captain Sam Williams ordered that no more than ten strikers could picket the plant gates.

Towards midnight on May 26, what the *Beacon Journal* described as "the bloodiest labor battle in Akron's history" erupted. When the strikers defied Williams' order to restrict the number of pickets, the captain commanded his officers to baton charge the crowd. They wielded their heavy nightsticks indiscriminately, but the workers fought back with fists and bricks. The strikers fell back but failed to disperse, whereupon the Goodyear guards began to discharge hundreds of rounds of tear gas directly into the crowds and onto shop awnings across the street. With up to a dozen rapid-fire gas guns firing constantly, the street soon filled with "a dense fog of thick, gray, sweetish-tasting gas [that] stung the eyes like acid and bit into the lungs," a *Beacon* man reported from the scene. Photographs show the Goodyear guards grinning as they discharged volley after volley of the gas bullets, each the size of ten-cent milk cans. The assault went on for several hours and with their blood lust up, they bombarded the union offices across the street. Over one hundred workers were taken to the hospital and a handful of police officers were injured in the fray.

According to Mayor Schroy and the *Beacon,* the affray was a mob riot, but URW International Vice-President Thomas F. Burns angrily dismissed the claim, and the union executive board voted unanimously to endorse what had begun as a wildcat. Although Mayor Schroy blustered the following day about law-and-order and threatened to send the entire police force to break any picket lines, cooler heads prevailed when all of the city's AFL unions fell in behind the CIO and joined them in a United Labor Defense Committee to coordinate resistance. The city's transportation workers and truck drivers voted to stage solidarity strikes, and irate unionists picketed City Hall in protest. The Goodyear workers were disorganized at the start of the strike, but now, with the city on the verge of a general strike, management agreed to immediate talks with the union to resolve the backlog of grievances, and Schroy backed away from further threats of violence. On May 31, Goodyear workers voted to call off the strike, and the dispute was settled without further mayhem.[133] One ominous development, however, was threats by the rubber companies to "decentralize" production to nonunion sites outside of Akron. During 1937, the companies had built new factories in half a dozen other places around America and expanded existing plants.[134] Naturally, these were at least initially nonunion sites. During a walk-off by ten thousand B. F. Goodrich workers just before the bloody battle at Goodyear, the company threatened to decentralize if the union rejected wage cuts and changes to seniority agreements.[135] It was a harbinger of things to come for Akron, for the US rubber industry—and indeed for American manufacturing industry as a whole. Nevertheless, the Akron working class had won some impressive victories. The giant rubber mills, which had been open shop bastions, had fallen before labor's offensive. Akron's working class, however, had reached a fork in the road. It could continue the forward march of militant social industrial unionism, or it could retreat into the timeworn patterns of the past.

15.

The Defeat of the Labor Party and Social Unionism in Akron

Although the world's first labor party appeared in 1827 in Philadelphia[1], and Akron artisans launched a similar organization in the following decade, America has never sustained a mass party of the working class. By the end of the First World War, the Socialist Party, which had begun with great promise, was a shadow of what it had been. America–including Akron—came closest to realizing the labor party dream during the industrial unionism upsurge of the 1930s, but the episode is today a largely forgotten historical footnote.[2]

In 1930s America, however, the triumph of industrial unionism gave fresh impetus to the labor party idea. This was particularly so in Akron and Summit County. The new class-based industrial unions only needed a small leap in consciousness for its members and supporters to see the need for complementary political organization. A later unionist summed this up in the slogan, "The bosses have two parties, we need one of our own!"[3] Yet supporters of the Farmer-Labor Party as the official political voice of labor were decisively defeated after a brief "civil war within labor's civil war" that also tamed the militant spirit of industrial unionism. The pressure for independent working-class political action was diverted safely into "Labor's Non-Partisan League," which Lief Davin argues

> was designed by its top leaders [including John L. Lewis] to be a transitional step toward today's complete alignment of organized labor with the Democrats [and therefore] to wean organized labor, especially the new CIO unions in the mass production industries, away from independent political action, away from a labor party for which so many were then clamoring.[4]

The historic defeat of the labor party project stemmed from the creeping bureaucratization of the CIO unions and their shift from social-industrial to "industrial-business unionism." Although more progressive than the Republicans, the Democratic Party is not and never was a labor party. The consequences of the Labor Party defeat can be felt to this day. "For many welfare scholars," argues sociologist Barry Eidlin, "the lack of a US labor party is key to explaining the high levels of poverty and inequality in the country."[5]

The Farmer-Labor Party (FLP) was born in Chicago in July 1920, and by the 1930s it had won a foothold in Akron and other Midwest centers. Its program included the eight-hour working day and the forty-hour week, the preservation of civil liberties and union rights, and the nationalization of major industries.[6] This stance brought it into sharp conflict with conservative forces in the unions and threatened the capitalist two-party duopoly. At the AFL's 1935 convention, conservatives narrowly headed off a motion to commit the federation to building a labor party,[7] but with millions of workers pouring into the new industrial unions, the labor party idea appeared to be gaining momentum. As the URW's Salvatore Camelio argued, "If [organized] labor is to survive, we must fight in the political field as well as the economic field .... we must take independent political action."[8]

The labor party idea was particularly strong in Akron. In 1934, the Akron Typographers' President James McCartan had stood for Congress as an independent labor candidate, pledging to "fight for the measures needed by the farmers, soldiers, and workers for their immediate relief and ultimate recovery." He advocated improved welfare for veterans, decent pensions for all, the nationalization of the banks, public ownership of utilities, and increased regulation of the economy. The economy's "fruits," he declared, were "millionaires and paupers, hunger in the midst of plenty, wars and pestilence."[9] On March 27, 1936, Akron's Central Labor Union (CLU) voted to support the Farmer-Labor Party,[10] and on 6–7 June, three hundred delegates from one hundred labor organizations met in the Akron Armory to begin organizing the party.[11] The convention elected CLU President Wilmer Tate as chair of the party's district executive board. Other prominent members included the URW's Luther L. Callahan, Lloyd Holmes, N. H. Eagles, and the Barberton CLU President Francis Gerhart. A number of Akron unions affiliated to the party, including the URW's Goodrich local. Resolutions demanded the immediate release of Tom Mooney, the Scottboro Boys, and "all other political prisoners," and the dropping of charges against the thirty-one rubber workers arrested following the recent Goodyear strike. The meeting also foreshadowed the creation of a statewide party.[12] Earlier, up to twenty thousand workers and their supporters from fifty local unions had marched in the 1936 Akron May Day parade, which snaked for one-and-half miles through the city streets. The speakers, who included Eagles, Tate, and Gerhart, along with the New York clothing workers' leader Joseph Schlossberg, and Detroit labor lawyer Maurice Sugar, urged the formation of a nationwide labor party.[13]

Conservative forces were determined to derail the project. Three months before the FLP's Akron convention, the Summit County Federation of Labor Clubs interviewed Republican and Democrat candidates to draw up a slate for the May primaries.[14] Led by J. Earl Cox—a Democrat who had run unsuccessfully for Akron mayor—and his colleague M. R. Crouch, the federation endorsed Roosevelt for president, and Martin L. Davey for Ohio governor, and refused support for the Farmer-Labor Party. The organizers also barred Jim Keller, the Akron Communist leader, from attending their April convention.[15] The federation's endorsement of Martin Davey dismayed FLP supporters, for the previous year the Governor had used the National Guard to break the Little Steel strike in Ohio. The Communists' (belated and short-lived) support for the FLP also gave the conservatives the pretext to redbait the party. Tate observed that Cox and Crouch were trying to "grab the tail of our kite" for an altogether different project.[16] Just how different was shown by keynote speaker Judge E. E. Zesiger's disingenuous claim that "the time is not yet right for the formation of a labor party."[17] Another adversary was bricklayers' union secretary Frank Patino, whom Tate had recently ousted from the CLU presidency. Patino doubled as chairman of the Ohio Republican Party's labor committee and was a close friend of Goodyear's virulently anti-union vice-president Cliff Slusser.[18] This local opposition was lackluster and insincere: Zesiger had been Exalted Cyclops in the Local Ku Klux Klan and had helped break the 1913 rubber strike, and Branko Widick dismissed Patino as "a hopeless, petty bureaucrat."[19] Ominously, however, formidable local and national figures were lining up against the labor party project.

On April 2, 1936, CIO leader John L. Lewis joined with Sidney Hillman of the Amalgamated Clothing Workers to announce the formation of the curiously named Labor's Non-Partisan League (LNPL). Hillman had been a socialist and his union had long endorsed the labor party idea, but he convinced a majority of his executive board members to throw the union's weight behind the Democrats. He argued that the Roosevelt administration's National Recovery Act and similar legislation had revived the union movement and that as the Supreme Court had recently declared the Act's predecessor unconstitutional, it was imperative that the labor movement should support Roosevelt's reelection.

Labor needed to block a reactionary, anti-union Republican administration and enable the Democrats to pass further pro-union legislation.[20] Further, given America's entrenched first-past-the-post voting system, support for a third party could take votes from Roosevelt and ensure a Republican victory. Lewis's vision was for a "reformed" capitalism, not its abolition or stringent regulation by a workers' party. Both men were seasoned political brawlers, and Lewis in particular had never shrunk from unsavory methods—including physical violence and stuffing ballot boxes—to maintain control of his own Mine Workers' Union. Nevertheless, as the standard-bearer of industrial unionism, he had enormous prestige. AFL President Bill Green was also implacably opposed to an independent party, so although the defeat of the labor party project was not inevitable, the odds were stacked against it.

Despite this, the Summit County FLP met in early June 1936 to nominate candidates for the November Congressional and other elections. Declaring "open warfare" on both Republicans and Democrats, the meeting nominated Wilmer Tate for Congress.[21] Midway through July, they elected a slate of candidates, including URW General Tire local President Rex Murray for Summit County sheriff, and a full ticket for the Ohio Senate that included James McCartan of the Typographers, L. L. Callahan of the Goodrich URW Local, and Mae Probst of the Union Buyers' Club. More than ninety Summit County organizations, including forty-two local unions and three central labor unions, backed the party. These included both CIO and AFL unions. The movement had also spread across the Portage County line. This, however, was the high-water mark for the party. In an ominous portent, the Akron CLU voted to withdraw support following a redbaiting campaign by conservative delegates.[22] The Communist Party did have some influence inside the FLP, but Wilmer Tate and James McCartan were old-style socialists, Luther Callahan was devoutly religious, and Rex Murray "though a fiery, militant unionist, was an anti-communist."[23]

On August 5, 1936, the national AFL leadership expelled ten CIO unions, including the URW. The rift between the craft and industrial unionists had widened into "civil war." However, although some writers portray the breach as a factional struggle between Left and Right, the reality was more complex. In fact, there was a "civil war within a civil war" inside the CIO. On the CIO's Left were class struggle militants such as Tate who favored the labor party and social unionism. On the Right, Lewis, Hillman, and their supporters stood for business-industrial unionism and an alliance with the Democratic Party. For the Socialist Party leader Norman Thomas, Labor's Non-Partisan League was "frankly a tail to the Democratic kite," but for Lewis and Hillman the radicals were dangerous utopians who jeopardized what organized labor had gained through the New Deal. Lukewarm FLP supporters drifted away, and the Communists proved to be fair-weather friends. Akron Communist leader John Williamson blithely informs us that "the Farmer-Labor Party became the broader and more powerful Labor's Non-Partisan League."[24] The Communist Party thus lurched from the sectarianism of the Third Period to the confused opportunism of the Popular Front, which meant they became uncritical cheerleaders for Roosevelt. One local Communist even imagined that Roosevelt might stand as a labor party candidate in 1940.[25] The Non-Partisan League was the negation of the FLP, not its complement.

The Communist Party reached the zenith of its influence in Summit County in the late 1930s and declined rapidly thereafter as members left, disillusioned with its Stalinist dogmatism. The party received its largest-ever vote in the 1939 Akron council elections, when Fred W. Seibert and Ben Atkins received 2,175 and 1,570 votes out of a total of almost seventy-five thousand.[26] They topped the poll in the poor, mainly Black Third Ward of Akron.[27] However, according to the *Beacon Journal*, by March 1941, the party's Summit County membership had dwindled to 250, down from four hundred two years earlier.

Although anti-Communist repression may have driven many out of the party, probably more left because they could not stomach the Stalinist dogmatism and the flip-flops of policy. In 1939, the Communist line changed again to conform to the expectations of the Stalin-Hitler Pact, but after the Nazi invasion of the USSR in 1941, the party became the most enthusiastic supporter of war against Hitler and opposed strikes no matter what the cause. The policy was to bring them into sharp conflict with non-Communist URW militants in Akron. According to the *Beacon*, by 1947, the party controlled only one local union in Akron—United Steelworkers Local 1159. Opponents sneered that the local's president, Amos Murphy, had been elected without the members knowing his politics. He was, however, reelected despite his employer attempting to fire him for being a "Red."[28]

Meanwhile, the naïveté of the Summit County FLP and the chicanery of local electoral officials greatly assisted the rightwing forces ranged against the labor party. The party had failed to participate in the April primaries and had to use the process of petition to get on the ballot. On September 1, the Ohio State Secretary invalidated the petitions for the party's three State Senatorial positions. While he did approve Tate's candidacy for the 14th Congressional District and that of the party's local government candidates, the party faced the uphill task of collecting two hundred thousand signatures in a matter of weeks to appear on the ballot with its "insignia." Five days later, the Summit County Board of Elections invalidated all of the FLP's candidates on the grounds that the party had submitted their names en bloc and not by individual petition.

Tate protested that he had followed the instructions of electoral staff, but the Board refused to reconsider its blatantly discriminatory ruling. The American Civil Liberties Union agreed to appeal the party's case in the Ohio Supreme Court, but by this stage, it was on the path to "utter destruction."[29]

Had the Akron labor movement united behind the FLP, it could have weathered the storm, learned from its mistakes, and built a formidable political machine. This, however, is "history in the subjunctive." The local "moderates," with heavyweight assistance from Lewis and Bill Green, were determined to crush the nascent party. On the one hand, the Akron CLU condemned the exclusion of the FLP from the ballot, but on the other, it endorsed the LNPL and praised Roosevelt as "Labor's friend."[30] Wilmer Tate did not share these illusions. On September 7, he attended a Labor Day picnic organized by the Summit County Federation of Labor Clubs, and listened with gritted teeth as M. R. Crouch and CIO general organizer Adolph Germer lavished praise on Roosevelt and studiously ignored mention of the FLP. Tate angrily "harangued the Republican and Democratic Congressional candidates to their faces." Both parties had the financial support of the rubber bosses, he thundered, "while my campaign is sponsored by the nickels and dimes of workers."[31] The center of gravity of American politics had not shifted much from the time when Akron's wealthier citizens bought the votes of their poorer neighbors with churns of eggnog and noggins of whiskey.

A major setback to the party's hopes was delivered in mid-September 1936 by the United Rubber Workers' national convention in Akron. Paradoxically, the URW had been forged in the heat of some of the most intense class struggles in American history. Akron's rubber workers had pioneered the sit-down strike as one of the most potent weapons in labor's arsenal. The impetus for action, however, had come from the rank-and-file gummers in defiance of conservative and bumbling AFL officials. Increasingly, too, the union's international leadership was shying away from militant action. The massive Goodyear strike had begun spontaneously, against the wishes of local union President John House, and was sustained by rank-and-file action. Sherman Dalrymple and most of the union's international board disapproved of "anarchic" behavior such as the sit-down strike. They listened attentively to complaints by Goodyear management about "more than a hundred incidents" of "wildcat" sit-downs throughout 1936. Dalrymple was "uncomfortable" about this and John L. Lewis had sent general organizer Allan Haywood as a "troubleshooter" to help restore order.

These simmering tensions exploded at the URW national convention, where the two most contentious issues were the sit-down tactic and the labor party project. While the radicals did support the use of grievance procedures to resolve disputes, they refused to condemn the sit-down tactic outright as the conservatives demanded. The battle on the convention floor was a straight Left-Right fight in which the Right emerged victorious as "a budding permanent bureaucracy in the ascendant."[32] The Left faced a barrage of points of order and the delegates only voted by a narrow margin to allow the Socialist Party leader Norman Thomas to address the convention. The international executive board had learned to use the "parliamentary" tactics and redbaiting previously employed against them by Bill Green and the AFL hierarchy. The convention condemned the sit-down tactic and rejected the labor party project. It affirmed support for orderly collective bargaining and threw support behind Labor's Non-Partisan League and the reelection of Roosevelt and the Democrats. In vain, the Left pointed out that the Democrats had broken strikes and set the police on picket lines. In Gadsden, Alabama, for example, both Republicans and Democrats had approved the violent repression of workers in the local Goodyear plant. In reply, officials such as Dalrymple, House and Buckmaster stressed the importance of the National Recovery Act in union revival. Dalrymple temporarily vacated the chair to lead the opposition to the labor party.

Support for the FLP was lost 61 votes to 39, and the convention even declined to endorse the principles of the party, with some delegates claiming they would drive members from the union. What was clear, however, was that the Akron locals supported the FLP while the rest of the country's locals and the national leadership with the exception of New England's Salvatore Camelio did not. The Akron URW locals remained industrially militant, and support for a labor party remained strong in the city into the 1950s,[33] but this never translated into an organization. A brief candle of hope had sputtered out in a dark political landscape.

The final blow to the labor party dream fell at the CIO's first national convention, which met in Pittsburgh in November 1938. The convention affirmed support for the Non-Partisan League (i.e. the Democrats) and voted down a motion to support the labor party project. The majority position ignored Roosevelt's steadily growing hostility to militant labor action, as evidenced by his declaration of "a plague on both your houses" after police gunned down striking steelworkers in the 1937 Memorial Day massacre. Although the CIO had begun as a massive upsurge of rank-and-file workers, John L. Lewis and other central leaders were political and social conservatives. For them, a party "based on class, anticapitalist in nature and with an aggressive radical-populist program" was anathema.[34] They were industrial unionists but apart from their rejection of craft unionism, they were in agreement with the AFL on almost everything else. Indeed, Lewis was a Republican.

On October 7, the Ohio Supreme Court unanimously upheld the Board of Elections exclusion of the Summit County FLP's nominees from all positions on the ballot.[35] Tate asked for a re-hearing but it was clear that the labor party was doomed. Many Summit County AFL and CIO unions campaigned energetically for Roosevelt. The URW alone distributed thirty thousand FDR buttons to its members and, according to the *Beacon,* some workers complained that they were forced to wear them.[36] Roosevelt romped home to a huge victory in the elections, and although support for a labor party remained strong in the URW's Akron locals, the FLP was dead as an organized political force. Curiously, in the summer of 1940, John L. Lewis gave an impassioned pro-third party speech to the Townsend Old Age Pension convention in St. Louis. He argued for a new party "based on a coalition of labor, poor farmers and Negroes [sic], dedicated to fighting for the interests of the common people."[37] By this time, it was too late, even if the mercurial Lewis had been serious. Mass support for such a party had dissipated and Lewis soon transferred his support to Wendell Willkie, the corporate executive who had won the Republican nomination for president.[38] The CIO overwhelmingly endorsed Roosevelt's reelection.

Although CIO leaders such as Lewis and Sherman Dalrymple recognized the need to organize the workers in mass production industry on an industrial basis, they were determined to control the process from above, to restrict union activity to wages and conditions, and to clamp down on militancy. They were business-industrial unionists who shared Roosevelt's fear of a leftward movement of the working class. Unions were not to be vehicles of class struggle and social change, but partners of the capitalists. The workers were to be obedient members of a sectional interest group organized for the orderly negotiation of contracts with employers. There was no room in this view for independent political organization. The workers movement in Akron and America as a whole had missed a great historical opportunity, headed off by leaders who were little different in the final analysis from Samuel Gompers and Bill Green. The Second World War was looming, and the conflict would further strengthen the rightward course of the labor movement. Although it is undeniable that Section 7 (a) of NIRA and the subsequent Wagner Act had helped American workers to organize, by 1938 the New Deal was running out of steam. In 1939, there were still ten million unemployed and millions earned less than forty cents an hour. Despite strong support for Roosevelt's reelection, the Republicans enjoyed a surge in the 1938 elections and proceeded to kill off many New Deal programs.[39] The Labor Party had been stillborn and the two-party duopoly continued without challenge.

16.

The Second World War and Akron Labor

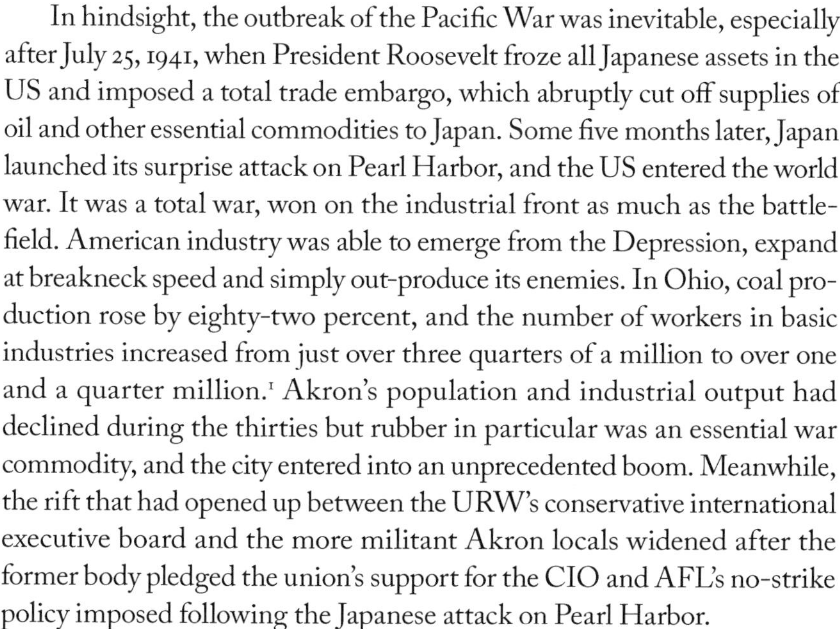

In hindsight, the outbreak of the Pacific War was inevitable, especially after July 25, 1941, when President Roosevelt froze all Japanese assets in the US and imposed a total trade embargo, which abruptly cut off supplies of oil and other essential commodities to Japan. Some five months later, Japan launched its surprise attack on Pearl Harbor, and the US entered the world war. It was a total war, won on the industrial front as much as the battlefield. American industry was able to emerge from the Depression, expand at breakneck speed and simply out-produce its enemies. In Ohio, coal production rose by eighty-two percent, and the number of workers in basic industries increased from just over three quarters of a million to over one and a quarter million.[1] Akron's population and industrial output had declined during the thirties but rubber in particular was an essential war commodity, and the city entered into an unprecedented boom. Meanwhile, the rift that had opened up between the URW's conservative international executive board and the more militant Akron locals widened after the former body pledged the union's support for the CIO and AFL's no-strike policy imposed following the Japanese attack on Pearl Harbor.

Despite widespread isolationist sentiment[2]—spearheaded by the CIO's John L. Lewis—the federal government and big business had been quietly preparing for conflict with Japan. The war drive created an immense profit bonanza for the rubber corporations and other sectors of the industrial economy. Lenin's quip that while "war is a terrible thing" it is also "a terribly profitable thing"[3] proved as true of World War II as the Great War. In January 1946, editors of the *New Republic* calculated that, "war profits—after deduction of war taxes—have been the greatest in history."[4] US corporate profits soared from $6.4 billion in 1940 to $10.8 billion in 1944 as President Roosevelt entered into a close alliance with the "economic royalists" he had once criticized.[5] Federal government spending soared from $9 billion in 1940 to $100 billion on 1945. Belief in laissez-faire economics was almost a religion in America, despite the fact that there was a long history of government intervention in the economy ranging from the Homestead Act of 1862 to the introduction of tariffs on foreign imports, labor regulation, and the use of force to break strikes. The pressures generated by the war further hardened the bureaucratic tendencies in the CIO unions and drove them further to the Right.

Lavish government subsidies and war contracts provided American industry with colossal profits. At the same time, with government connivance, business took advantage of the unions' "no strike" policy to attack wages and conditions. The drive towards war had far-reaching consequences for American labor. In mid-1940, Roosevelt embarked upon an ambitious plan to harness American industrial power for the looming conflict and signaled that he would not tolerate militant union action no matter what the cause. In 1941, two million strikers were involved in over four thousand strikes across the country, and some labor leaders were hostile to the war drive.

Roosevelt's labor policy was two pronged. Firstly, in March 1941, he set up the National Defense Mediation Board, a tripartite body to arbitrate disputes and prevent strikes. Secondly, he used force to break strikes in defense industries, such as in June 1941 at the North American Aviation plant in Inglewood, California, where he sent in federal troops. In the same month, at the request of Dan Tobin, the corrupt Teamsters' president and boss of the Democratic Party's labor committee, Roosevelt charged twenty-nine Trotskyist militants, including the leaders of the Minneapolis Teamsters' Union, with breach of the Smith Act, which made it a criminal offense to advocate the overthrow of the government.

Applying it to the Trotskyists was drawing a long legal bow. Their real "crime" was taking AFL Teamsters' Local Union 544 into the CIO and speaking out against the government's war plans.[6] *Akron Beacon Journal* columnist Westbrook Pegler applauded the arrests, but the city's Civil Liberties Defense Committee held a public protest meeting, addressed by Martin Rollins from Local 544,[7] and the URW's Akron locals denounced the imprisonment of the Minneapolis militants.[8] However, given that the CIO leadership had hitched labor's cart to the Democratic Party horse, it was restricted to ineffectual protest at the arrests and subsequent convictions and prison sentences.

At a specially convened conference held in Washington, DC, after the attack on Pearl Harbor, business and government representatives demanded the CIO and AFL's agreement to a total ban on strikes for the duration of the war against the Axis. Both federations dutifully fell into line, and the URW's international executive board followed suit without consulting the membership. On January 12, 1942, the federal government set up the War Labor Board to arbitrate any industrial disputes that might arise, but it worked at glacial speed and rarely found in the unions' favor. After Pearl Harbor, public anti-war sentiment faded rapidly to the pro-Axis fringes—according to Studs Terkel, most Americans believed the conflict "was a just war if there is any such animal."[9] Pollsters "found that the war's popularity only increased as the death toll mounted.[10]

While acknowledging that the conflict was "a war against an enemy of unspeakable evil," the leftist historian Howard Zinn poses pertinent questions about the less savory war aims of the Allied powers.[11] While this is not the place to discuss these matters in depth, it is arguable that the imperatives of the gummers and others who provided the labor for "the great arsenal of democracy" differed qualitatively from the motives of capitalist politicians, government bureaucrats, and captains of American industry. It would be far-fetched, for example, to claim that Akron's Harvey Firestone harbored any anti-imperialist or anti-fascist sentiment. During the Spanish Civil War, Firestone and other US corporations provided Franco's fascists—Hitler's allies—with tires, oil, and vehicles on credit while denying them to the Republic. Firestone's advertisements in the Francoist zones gloated, "Victory smiles on the best. The glorious

Nationalist [i.e. fascist] army always wins on the field of battle. Firestone Tires has its nineteenth consecutive victory in the Indianapolis 500."[12]

Likewise, it is also impossible to reconcile Firestone's use of forced labor in Liberia with the principles of the Atlantic Charter. Firestone's behavior was in stark contrast to that of Akron gummer Steve Miletich, who died fighting Franco's fascists in the siege of Belchite, and of Akron's Salaria Kee O'Reilly, who was wounded while serving as a volunteer nurse for the Spanish Republic.

Rubber is essential for modern military power,[13] and after Pearl Harbor Akron's gummers were prepared to work hard for the defeat of the Axis. For them, the conflict was a people's war against fascism. Many American workers and their union leaders also believed that labor should make a truce with management for the duration of the war; that "we're all in this together" and must sacrifice equally for victory. This was the message of the top CIO leaders, who promoted industry union councils and other bodies to increase war production.[14]

Most vociferous of all to win the war at all costs—at least after the Nazi invasion of the Soviet Union in June 1941—was the Communist Party. They had flipped from their characterization of F. D. R. as a Mussolini-style fascist at the start of the New Deal[15] and their initial view of the war as an imperialist conflict. The flip-flops of the party's line had alienated many militant unionists. In June 1945, for instance, B. F. Goodrich URW Local 5 condemned the activities of George F. Boyer, who was an executive board member of the Goodyear Local 2 and led a twenty-strong Communist caucus in the plant. A resolution moved by Local 5 leader George Bass condemned "the sinister and treacherous methods of Boyer and his group [which are] typical of the party line followers of Earl Browder and his gang of union wreckers who are the worst enemies of the labor movement within its ranks." Boyer had opposed a strike vote endorsed by a huge mass meeting.[16] Although the party's national membership swelled to 75,000 by the end of the war,[17] many unionists would have agreed with the "rubber workers' troubadour" Joe Glazer's satirical song "Our Line's Been Changed Again."[18]

For his part, CIO President Philip Murray, a staunch Roosevelt ally, appealed for fair play by the government and employers:

> Mr. President, I ask you in the spirit of justice … to sit down and ponder just a little more than you have, the need of giving labor in America a chance … [and] I ask you, Mr. American Businessman, to mete out to labor more than you have—more of the things to which they are entitled.[19]

Neither were listening, and this was not lost on the more militant union leaders. These included the officials of Akron's URW locals, who agreed that the Axis had to be defeated, but warned that the corporations would take advantage of the no-strike policy to degrade wages and conditions. In the Deep South, the Akron rubber corporations were meting out appalling violence to unionists, not "the things to which [workers] … were entitled." To expect these economic royalists to respect the workers if the unions eschewed the right to strike was magical thinking. The rubber corporations were also planning to take the industry out of Akron and into hitherto non-union territory. The threat of "decentralization" of work to non-union shops had always hung over the Akron unions. In 1936, the *United Rubber Worker* warned, "We must organize 100 percent. Otherwise the rubber barons will take work from Akron gum miners and force it upon unorganized workers whom they exploit ruthlessly."[20] In Alabama, Goodyear used shocking violence and employed the fascist Silvershirts and the Ku Klux Klan to intimidate unionists. They even beat up Sherman Dalrymple "while the local sheriff watched and mildly remonstrated."[21] The URW had forced the Big Three to negotiate in Akron, but little had changed in the South since Goodyear vice-president Cliff Slusser warned that anyone trying to organize his Gadsden, Alabama plant would leave on a stretcher.[22] Firestone's Memphis plant was another case in point. Wages and working conditions were appalling, and the company consciously segmented the workforce on racial lines. Black laborers performed the hardest jobs for the lowest pay and received routine insult and worse.

In mid-1940, a genial thirty-six-year-old Akron URW organizer called George Bass traveled south to begin organizing the Memphis plant. Bass had left his native Tennessee in 1919 to work in the Akron mills,[23] so as a Southerner he was a natural choice for the Memphis assignment. Working secretly, he recruited a considerable number of

Memphis gummers, most of them Blacks, but when he emerged into the open, he was subjected to "a nightmarish series of violent attacks," firstly by the police and then by Firestone goons. A seventy-five-strong mob of thugs wielding pipes, blackjacks, brass knuckles, sticks, knives, "and at least one pistol" attacked Bass and a local unionist. Frank McAllister, the southern secretary of the Workers' Defense League, remarked that, "if the Federal Government doesn't do something about the reign of terror in Memphis, they may as well haul down the American flag over the city hall there and replace it with the Nazi Swastika." Firestone had fired up the thugs by redbaiting the URW and stressing that the union's anti-racist policies would erode white privilege. To their eternal discredit, the city's AFL unions colluded with the company.[24] Six months later, Akron URW organizer John House was hospitalized after five Goodyear thugs beat him with lengths of insulated wire in the union's Gadsden office.[25] Years later, Bass still bore the scars from the bashing by Firestone's thugs.[26]

It is worth recalling that America fought the Axis with its own military segregated on racial lines and that the Red Cross maintained segregated "white" and "black" blood banks for the troops. At home in Akron, too, Jim Crow prevailed. Seven months after Pearl Harbor, Herbert A. Davidson, a Black physician in Akron, summed up the frustrations of his fellow citizens of color thus: "We Negroes in America are tired of begging. We want decent jobs that will enable us to pay our own way. We are tired of charity, W.P.A. and relief … We want to work and live decently; we want to get out of the slums. We are human and we have human desires and aspirations."[27] Years later, the Black Akron nurse Salaria Kee O'Reilly—a so-called "premature anti-fascist"—remembered her time as a volunteer with the International Brigades in Spain as, "the only time that people really respected me for what I was and for what I could do."[28] The University of Akron Archives holds a collection of threatening, racist letters sent to Dr. Davidson during this period.[29]

Davidson, a pediatrician, was an indefatigable fighter for racial equality, trade union rights, and democracy. He was well aware of the connection between sickness and poor working and living conditions. At the beginning of the Second World War, there were about twelve thousand Black residents in Akron. Their numbers climbed to approximately twenty thousand by 1947, but there was only a slight increase in the housing available in overcrowded "negro residential areas."[30] Davidson was an implacable foe of fascism, but he campaigned tirelessly to expose the hypocrisy of those who espoused the cause of democracy yet accepted America maintaining a Jim Crow army and segregated employment in war industries. His wartime scrapbook contains fascinating snapshots of race relations in the city during the war years. In 1942, Davidson mocked the oxymoronic claim of a local pseudo-intellectual that "intelligent discrimination is a good thing." "Would intelligent discrimination keep a white soldier ... from diving in the same shell hole with a Negro in time of danger?" Davidson demanded.[31] When racists tried to whip up hysteria by labeling Blacks as a potential fifth column, Davidson retorted, "You cannot discriminate against the Negro socially, economically, and politically and expect to retain his loving regard." "Negroes want jobs on [war] production in the factories," he added, but "today the doors are slammed in their faces. It is little wonder that with the cries of 'job shortage' ringing in their ears, Negroes are cynical about this being a 'war of democracy.'"[32] He was ruefully indignant that some Polish refugees from Hitler had "the audacity to practice fascism here" by discriminating against Black people in Akron housing projects.[33] Ohio Governor John Bricker had set up an Advisory Committee on the Employment Problems of the Negro in 1940 but it was disbanded after two years and had "accomplished little."[34]

The class struggle continued despite the outbreak of war. The *raison d'être* of capitalism is to reproduce capital, and it will take advantage of any weakness to maximize profits. This dynamic was not constrained by the appeals of labor leaders such as Philip Murray or by Roosevelt's half-hearted attempts at arbitration. As Sherman Dalrymple put it in a 1936 radio broadcast: "No capitalist concern is in business for the love of it. The motivating force is dollars, dollars, and more dollars."[35] Abandoning the right to strike in the face of some of the country's most ruthless employers was akin to a boxer agreeing to tie his hands while facing a dirty fighter armed with a cudgel. Not surprisingly given his harrowing experiences in Memphis, George Bass was to become an implacable foe of his union's wartime no-strike pledge. In 1943, there was speculation that Bass would follow John L. Lewis back to the AFL after Lewis called his members out on strike, but if Bass did entertain the idea, he decided to stick with the CIO.[36]

The war drive had sparked a colossal boom in Akron, reversing "a sorry picture" of "declining production figures, slumping employment totals and diminishing industrial income" in 1939, noted the *Beacon*.[37] In 1942, the *Encyclopedia Britannica* described Akron as a "city of phenomenal growth."[38] The city's population, which had declined from 255,040 in 1930[39] to around 243,000 in 1940, grew by 30,000 by 1944.[40] Most of the growth was due to the massive expansion of the city's rubber industry, which by 1941 employed 60,000 workers; a thirty per cent increase over the previous year.[41] By late 1941, the city had $600 million worth of defense contracts and Chamber of Commerce secretary Harry Bennett predicted that Akron's war orders could soon reach $2.4 billion under current contemplated Lend-Lease and US defense orders.[42] These figures translate in income values in 2017 dollars to $37 billion and $148 billion.[43] The demand for rubber war goods rose from three million synthetic tires in mid-1943 to eighteen million the following year, and Akron was producing sixty per cent of these.[44] The URW claimed that the US rubber industry's profits grew from $43,279,000 in 1936–39 to $307,368,000 in 1943, and continued to soar thereafter.[45] By March 1942, B. F. Goodrich had "amassed a net profit of 40.6 percent over and above the previous year," but "a further $6 million of clear profit went into the company's contingency fund and was not distributed to stockholders." The union calculated that Goodrich's after-tax profits were up 138.6 per cent over 1941.[46] This was in line with an unprecedented profit bonanza for US business. Writing in January 1946, *The New Republic*'s George Soule quantified the boom:

> The United States Department of Commerce estimates that the profits of all corporations in the United States, after deduction of taxes (including excess-profits taxes), were $8.5 billion in 1941, $8.7 billion in 1942, $9.8 billion in 1943 and $9.9 in 1944. In 1944 they were more than twice as large as in 1939, the last year in which World War II did not affect profits, and were $3 billion higher than in 1929, the greatest year of business boom hitherto experienced in this country. These estimates, say the

> government statisticians, may be too low, since they are based on the records of the larger concerns, and it is believed that the smaller ones made even greater advances.

Moreover, the federal government "virtually guaranteed contractors against loss by paying for their investments in war equipment."[47] This was certainly true of the synthetic rubber plants built in Akron during the war.

The war boom rapidly exhausted the region's labor supply. In November 1942, Akron's war manpower director forecast a looming shortage of twenty-three thousand workers as the corporations now had enough war contracts to keep industry at "boom production pace for the next five years."[48] Even after VJ Day in 1945, the *Beacon Journal* reported "the greatest job-shopping spree in the history of the rubber industry ... as the tire companies search frantically for about 5,000 men to enable them to reach peak production." They would hire "virtually anyone" but still reported a huge shortfall.[49] The rubber firms' first response to the crisis, in 1942, was to demand the lengthening of working hours, but the union initially refused to agree, pointing out that many people in the city were either unemployed or precariously employed. "Put them back to work first," said the URW's Luther Callahan. "Then, if there is a shortage of labor, we will do whatever is necessary for the welfare of the country." According to the union, there were still three thousand workers laid off at Goodrich and up to twenty-five hundred at Firestone.[50] Paranoia on the part of management and the FBI caused the rubber mills to fire several hundred "aliens"—many of them actually citizens of anti-Axis countries—following Pearl Harbor, but union pressure forced their reinstatement.[51]

The URW also denounced the rubber companies' discriminatory hiring practices, which denied many work because of "age, sex, color, size, education, lack of experience, or just plain bureaucratic red tape."[52] Jim Crow personnel policies continued to exclude Black workers from the better-paid, skilled jobs even when there were huge numbers of unfilled vacancies in those classifications. Some of the union's members were determined to maintain the color bar. In mid-1944, for instance, curing room workers at Goodrich struck work to protest the hiring of Blacks. Ringleader Jake Ratzer told the boss that "the people in Dept. 6565 did not intend for there to be any nigger sweat in the curing room when their sons returned from the service, and that they did not intend to work with niggers...." Ratzer added that he believed Firestone segregated Black people in separate departments, and that this should be the case at Goodrich. Ratzer and two others were summoned to a special executive board meeting and disciplined.[53] Nevertheless, while workers on the first and third shifts had walked off the job, those on the second shift, led by Chester Barr "vigorously applied our [union] principles and oath in action." The union pointed out that it was only when Black laborers were kept out of unions that standards were threatened, and that it was folly to split workers of different races.[54]

URW Local 5 also welcomed new women workers at B. F. Goodrich and declared somewhat optimistically that the "day is past when employers can discriminate against women in hiring." Moreover, declared the union newsletter, "We want these sister union workers to understand that our union stands for that great principle of progressive unionism: EQUAL PAY FOR WOMEN!"[55] [Capital letters in the original.] According to the War Manpower Commission, "as few as one in ten women applying for a job actually got it, with many told that they lacked experience, were 'a little too old,' that they 'didn't look like a good factory worker,' or that they were too thin or too fat, and so forth.'"[56] Nevertheless, following a citywide door-to-door survey, the authorities began preliminary action to recruit twenty thousand local women for war work.[57] Pressure from the unions and government agencies forced the rubber mills to take on thousands of women.[58] The War Job Enrollment Center on East Market Street placed full-page advertisements in the press exhorting people to apply for rubber jobs. One of these declared, "Women who have never done a day's work in their lives [sic] are finding new thrills in war work. Physically handicapped men and women are learning new usefulness as they help turn out the weapons of Victory...."[59]

The government directed workers in nonessential industries into war work and additional labor was brought from as far away as Mexico and the Caribbean. By the end of 1942, the mills were hiring over two thousand extra workers each week and one year later, the Akron workforce had grown to 117,000, of which some 64,000 worked in the rubber mills.[60] By late 1943, some 131,000 people worked in the Akron defense industries.[61] In the same month, the URW caved in to pressure and agreed to lengthen the working day from six hours to eight for the duration of the war.[62] As in the First World War, the vast expansion of jobs and industry created an acute housing shortage—and exorbitant rents. A WPA survey conducted in late 1941 revealed a habitable rental vacancy rate of half of one percent, and a federal study reported that Akron's housing situation was the worst in country.[63] Once again, landlords rented out beds on a rotating shift basis, families lived in shanties and dilapidated trailers, and warehouses and other vacant properties were converted to accommodate the influx of workers. The War Manpower Commission also asked residents to make room in their houses for those desperate for accommodation.[64]

The labor shortage had some positives for the city's working class. Overtime was plentiful, and this compensated to some degree for frozen hourly pay rates, but CIO organizer Paul Fessenden reported that fatigue from working long hours led to an increase in accident rates. In Summit County, these rose from 1966 in January–February 1941 to 2709 for the same period in 1942. "Labor hoarding" (maintaining a large workforce in a nonessential industry) exacerbated the problem. This was an unforeseen consequence of the federal government's policy of freezing workers in their jobs.[65] In September 1941, Goodyear signed its first ever contract with the URW, marking an end to a six-year fight by the union for recognition. The contract restricted the Flying Squadron's numbers to two per cent of the workforce and set minimum pay rates of sixty-five cents per hour for women and eighty-five cents for men.[66]

As the war dragged on, however, tensions built up over frozen pay rates and spiraling living costs, which cut workers' pay in real terms at a time when the corporations were making fabulous profits. The workers supported the war effort but did not see why they should lose hard-won conditions and see their unions sidelined. Thus, in Barberton there were sixteen major strikes during the war plus a number of shorter wildcats.[67] One of these strikes broke out at the Pittsburgh Valve division of Pitcairn, where ninety-five percent of production was war related. Wilmer Tate, now a CIO steel industry organizer, told the press that while the strike was unauthorized, it "resulted from a long series of differences with the company over pay reductions and indiscriminate firings of workers."[68]

Women wildcat strikers speak with man in military uniform, Akron 1942. Reprinted with permission of the *Akron Beacon Journal* and Ohio.com

There were many wildcats in Akron during the war years, some of them sit-downs and thus doubly illegal. Bruce Meyer has counted twenty-four wildcat strikes at the General Tire plant alone between August 1943 and January 1944.[69] One sit-down broke out in October 1942 at Goodyear when the company attempted to cut women's piecework rates. The company backed down, but the union's international officers disowned the women, and the press lambasted them as "unpatriotic." Local union officials tacitly supported the women, and the Local 5 publication *The Airbag,* which was distributed to members serving in the armed forces, reported the strike sympathetically.[70] The Goodyear Local's conservative president, John House, had lost his position to the more radical G. V. Wheeler in a Local 2 runoff election in late 1940.[71] The incident highlights the continuing animosity between the union's international executive board and the URW's militant local union officials, who were opposed to the no-strike policy. Meanwhile, according to the *CIO News*, corporate profits in 1942 were four hundred percent above those in 1939 and corporate executives had granted themselves huge pay hikes, some up to 218 percent over 1941 levels.[72]

The rift was to widen spectacularly in 1943–44 following a long-running dispute between the workers and B. F. Goodrich. In early 1942, URW Local 5 presented management with a claim for a ten percent raise, claiming that its members had suffered a ten to fifteen percent wage cut in real terms over the previous year. Goodrich executive T. G. Graham claimed that a pay raise "cannot be justified at this time," and that the War Labor Board (WLB) had advised him not to grant increases.[73] Bound by the no-strike policy, the union had little bargaining power, so angry rank-and-file members petitioned the WLB for redress, probably on the advice of their local union officers. Seven months after lodging the claim, the Local had not received a reply. The WLB did eventually refer the claim to a specially convened panel, which finally recommended an eight-cent-an-hour increase for the Goodrich gummers. The WLB reduced this to three cents and the union responded angrily, claiming that inflation had so ravaged gummers' wages that the purchasing power of $100 in 1939 had fallen to $78 in 1940, $69 in 1941, $60 in 1942, and $43 in 1943.[74]

In late May 1943, fifty thousand Akron gummers walked off the job for five days in a spontaneous protest at the yearlong delay and the "endless run-around" given to grievance committees "every time they have tried to meet with company representatives." So solid was the strike across the rubber mills that mass picketing was only necessary at the "comparatively poorly organized" Goodyear plants. The Trotskyist *Militant* reported that women picket captains were prominent in the strike and that the men obeyed their orders without question: the radical social unionist spirit was clearly still alive among rank-and-file gummers in the city. On the Firestone picket, the paper added, "Negro workers were especially noticeable ... [and] this was not accidental since the Firestone local has carried on a militant fight for equal rights in the plant." At a huge mass meeting in the Goodrich union hall, the workers voted to give the Board until June 16 to reconsider its decision to offer the paltry three cents an hour raise. Local 5 President George Bass threatened:

"We'll give them another dose of the same medicine, and next time it will be fully authorized by the [Local] executive board." International President Sherman Dalrymple had tried to stop the strike but could not defend the WLB's offer.[75] The strike outraged President Roosevelt, who declared that it was "a defiance of the war labor board, a challenge to government by law and a blow against the effective prosecution of the war."[76] However, although the *Beacon Journal* editorialized about "inflationary" wage demands, and demanded that the government "punish the guilty,"[77] its labor reporter Harold Lengs admitted that the majority of gummers would have been satisfied with the eight-cent raise proposed by the panel of inquiry and there would not have been strike action.[78] Thereafter, there were almost daily stoppages in some Akron plants.[79]

The Eighth International Convention of the URW was held in Toronto on September 20, 1943. Some twenty-two hundred Local 5 members had met previously to elect their delegates and had voted overwhelmingly to submit resolutions to rescind the no-strike policy, campaign against the Smith-Connally Act, withdraw union representatives from the War Labor Board, and promote better race relations. According to a report in *The Airbag,* the members were incensed by an attempt by management to undercut even the three cents an hour raise authorized by the WLB.[80] The resolutions did not carry, and for the first time in many years Local 5 did not gain representation on the International Executive Board. The newsletter reported that Sherman Dalrymple had "indicated bluntly that he expects to be 'a damned sight tougher' next year in enforcing action against locals and/or individual members engaging in work stoppages, for whatever cause."[81] On November 11, *The Airbag* reported that Local 5's officers had been reelected with "the largest vote in the history of the local."[82] Clearly, a showdown between the Akron locals and the international executive board was fast approaching.

In January 1944, under extreme pressure from the government, the press and the CIO's top leadership, an exasperated Sherman Dalrymple expelled seventy-two General Tire & Rubber band room workers, members of URW Local 9, without a hearing for staging an illegal sitdown.[83] Two of those expelled, Howard Haas and Raymond Sullivan, were former Local 9 presidents. They had been off-shift and had not participated in the stoppage, but their offense in Dalrymple's eyes was to advocate for their expelled colleagues and engage in "disruptive activities." The sit-downers lost their jobs as a result and a number of them, including Haas, were drafted into the armed forces. Sixty-two were however, reinstated after an appeal. The General Tire Local itself was placed in receivership after the membership "almost unanimously condemned Dalrymple's actions.[84]

Goodrich Local 5's officers hit back hard against what they considered arbitrary and illegal action by Dalrymple. A proposal to expel Dalrymple from Local 5 was endorsed by 1,419 votes to 626. The Akron CIO Industrial Union Council also condemned the band room workers expulsions as "hasty, ill-advised, illegal and unconstitutional" and upheld Dalrymple's expulsion on "nine counts of having violated the union's constitution," claiming that management had supplied most of Dalrymple's evidence. The URW's international executive board retaliated by directing Local 5 to reinstate Dalrymple.[85] Although the Local had no choice but to comply, the international board was increasingly powerless to stop wildcats. Indeed, short stoppages broke out at Seiberling Rubber and Goodyear just hours after they ordered Dalrymple's reinstatement.

J. Penfield Seiberling attacked the sit-downers as unpatriotic, revealing that just days before the strike in his plant, a former employee serving as a turret gunner in a US bomber was killed in action.[86] Tragic though the death was, the union could claim that many of its members in uniform wrote letters to *The Airbag* urging them to maintain pressure to maintain wages and conditions and "not to let the employers take advantage of the war to undermine the union." Indeed, "one soldier, Ralph Squires ... wrote that 'many men feel there's a strong need for a union in the army.'"[87] Local CIO chief Wilmer Tate had a son on active service in the army, but he too did not agree that the corporations should be allowed to use the war as a pretext to attack wages and conditions. Local 5 President George Bass also had a son in the Pacific, and a brother who was a Japanese POW.[88]

The international executive's reinstatement of Dalrymple into Local 5 did not end the dispute, for the local's officers referred the matter to the URW's international convention, which was held at the Park Central Hotel in New York City over five days in September 1944. The convention was a torrid affair. In his opening address the CIO's president, Philip Murray, made an impassioned plea to maintain the no-strike pledge. "I have always said," he told delegates, "that I will never violate a pledge or disregard a commitment made to my fellow men, my neighbors, and to our soldiers and sailors."[89] Spearheading the opposition to the union's incumbent international executive board was Akron's URW Local 5, which moved resolutions to rescind the no-strike pledge, reinstate the General Tire wildcatters and their two supporters, and uphold Dalrymple's expulsion from the Goodrich local. The convention coincided with a sit-down back in the Goodyear No. 2 plant in Akron, where tire builders struck against cuts to piecework rates.[90] The Akron militants also stood a team against the incumbents on the international board. Sherman Dalrymple had been elected unopposed four times before, but Local 5's George Bass opposed him now for International president. G. V. Wheeler from the Goodyear Local 2 stood against Leland S. Buckmaster for vice-president and "Ike" Watson of Local 7 stood against William Lanning for the position of Secretary-Treasurer. It was clear from the outset, however, that the incumbents would prevail, given that they had the support of most URW locals outside of Summit County—including thirty new locals added because of vast wartime expansion.[91] Dalrymple was reelected by 795 to 394 votes. Wheeler received 422 votes and Watson 370.

Nevertheless, the opposition put up a spirited fight. One Local 5 delegate compared the no-strike pledge to the hated yellow-dog contracts that had once stymied union organization, and Ike Watson told delegates that the pledge "gives flag-wavers a chance to tie workers' hands in order to frisk their pockets." A Local 5 delegate denied there was any "equality of sacrifice" between workers and the corporations. Instead, there were "violations of contracts, firing of union militants, break-down of collective bargaining, wage and job freeze, Smith-Connally,[92] and with prices and profits sky-high." Dalrymple admitted that these outrages were happening but could only counsel patience. The convention reaffirmed the no-strike pledge by 783 votes to 375. There had been talk of submitting the matter to a referendum of the members, but nothing came of this. Probably, it would have duplicated the vote on the conference floor, with Akron members outvoted by their more conservative fellows in other centers. The international board and their supporters had prevailed, but they sensed that they had to bend a little if differences were not to become irrevocable. Local 5's Howard Haas's commander had given him leave to attend the convention, and he spoke in favor of a compromise resolution moved by George Bass, which reinstated all suspended or expelled members with all rights and recognized Dalrymple's reinstatement into Local 5. The resolution received overwhelming support and at the end of the convention, Haas, who was in army uniform, shook hands with Dalrymple.[93] Although the wildcats did not stop, the delegates had preserved the URW's unity and after the end of the war, the no-strike pledge was no longer an issue.

The Convention also reelected the URW's International officers, defeating the Akron locals' nominees by a substantial majority.[94] Dalrymple's supporters organized an opposition slate in Akron itself, sparking a bitter factional row. At Local 5's regular business meeting held on November 16, 1944, Dalrymple's man John Saylor defeated George Bass for the presidency by 3,102 votes to 2,396. Jack Delaney also beat the incumbent for treasurer by an even larger margin, and Art Dockery was ousted as vice-president. There were allegations and counter-allegations of ballot irregularities and threats, and the locks were changed on the Local's office doors. When Goodrich tire-builders staged a wildcat in June 1945, the Local's new leaders refused to support them over the objections of George Bass and others.[95] On October 7, 1945, however, a letter from Charles E. Lanning, the secretary-treasurer of the International Union, announced the lifting of the no-strike pledge and the following month the Local's "old guard" were reelected.[96] It is significant that the labor party question was no longer raised as a point of dispute within the union. Intraunion disagreements had been almost solely over the issue of the wartime no-strike clause.

Akron, like America as a whole, received the news of Japan's surrender with unrestrained joy. The *Beacon* announced the Japanese surrender in flaring headlines and huge crowds converged on downtown streets to celebrate the hard won victory.[97] If they thought of the future, they probably did so with optimism: a "people's war" surely demanded a peace for the people; one of peace and prosperity. The war had been a watershed and a new period in world and American history was beginning. The

American people craved a return to normal life, but as the historians Kern and Wilson point out, "After so much tumult and change it was unclear what 'normal' meant.[98] The same tensions that had riven society before the outbreak of war continued, and new ones arose.

In September 1945, just weeks after VJ Day, Sherman Dalrymple resigned from his post as URW International president, which he had held continuously since the union gained its independence from Bill Green and Coleman Claherty over a decade before. Rumors had been circulating that he intended to accept a lucrative position in personnel with one of the large rubber firms, but this was undoubtedly malicious scuttlebutt. As a *Beacon* journalist observed, "it is his conviction that no man can conscientiously be on the union side of the labor fence one time and on the management side another."[99]

Dalrymple was scrupulously honest. His salary and possessions were modest, for unlike many old guard AFL officials, he had not used his position to line his pockets at the members' expense. He had, as the saying goes, paid his dues, standing with the union even in the darkest times. Goodyear thugs had viciously beaten him in Alabama. His family back in West Virginia had battled poverty before moving to Akron. He had suffered personal tragedies; his young wife died after an appendectomy in 1916 and his five-year-old daughter perished in a fire on a neighbor's property shortly after. He performed one of the dirtiest and hottest jobs at "the Goodrich," wrestling with heavy steel tire molds in the Pit. He was self-effacing to an astonishing degree. He had joined the Marines as a private in 1917 and served twenty-two months in France, including at the horrific battle in the Bellau Woods, and had been honorably discharged as a second lieutenant. He had received several citations for bravery, but seldom spoke of it. Once, he had "put the clamps on a URWA publicity man who was going to publicize" his gallantry to counter anti-union charges by a veterans' organization. Although he gave no hint of his plans after the resignation, he and his wife sold their modest Akron house and moved to Los Angeles.[100]

We can only speculate about the reasons for his resignation. He was not forced out, but he must have been uncomfortably aware that he was no longer popular among the gummers in his adopted hometown. In February 1946, the *Beacon Journal* announced that he had accepted the position of western director of the CIO Railroad Workers' Organizing Committee, based in Los Angeles. (The committee aimed to recruit members in non-union railroad shops and did not conflict with the established railroad brotherhoods.)[101] Dalrymple was not a natural bureaucrat, so he must have welcomed the chance to do what he did best—organizing the unorganized at the grass roots.

Less than a year before Dalrymple's resignation, Wilmer Tate—"the father of the CIO in Summit County"—had died after a long illness. He was fifty-nine years old. Tate was well to the left of the conservative Dalrymple, but although he had never been a member of the URW, he had been indispensable in its creation as an industrial union. The *Beacon Journal* was no friend of militant labor—nor of Tate's socialist beliefs—but it marked his death with a gracious tribute: "To the list of those who believed in a cause so strongly that they were willing to sacrifice their health and hasten their death should be added the name of Wilmer P. Tate." The URW owed much to him, the obituary continued. He had "a gift for picturesque language and a mind that absorbed economic, social and political information" and he "never quibbled about giving the facts whether or not they favored his side."[102]

Tate's death and Dalrymple's departure marked the end of an era for Akron labor. Despite their differences over matters such as the no-strike pledge and the labor party question, they had both been instrumental in building a powerful labor movement in the city. It had been a hard-fought, at times brutal, struggle; one that had won better wages and conditions, and—most importantly, a sense of dignity and respect—for the city's working class. Yet for all of his honesty and personal sacrifice, Dalrymple had also contributed to forcing a radical, social union movement back into the business union mold, and he had been instrumental in killing off the labor party project in Summit County.

17.

The Great Unfinished Business of the American Working Class

The Second World War ended less than 140 years after the Pennsylvanian backwoodsman Daniel Haines squatted at the site of what became Akron,[1] and a little more than a century after Akron's artisans formed permanent unions and stood candidates for public office. Union secretary Mr. E. N. Bangs and his fellow carpenters and joiners could not have known what the future held for their modest frontier village. Should one of them have fallen asleep like Rip van Winkle and awoken in 1945,[2] he would not have recognized his hometown. "A huge page in the history of society," as Frederick Jackson Turner puts it, would have been turned.[3] Not even the early nineteenth century factories of New England or the "dark Satanic mills" of the British industrial revolution could compare with the giant rubber mills that turned Akron's skies to darkness at noon. Wageworkers had formed a small proportion of Akron's population, most of whom were self-employed, but in 1945, the overwhelming majority of Akron's almost quarter of a million people were working class. Yet what had become of the political ambitions of Mr. Bangs and his fellow workmen? While we have no way of knowing exactly what ideas these early mechanics held, we do know that one of them denounced "those purse-proud, lordly aristocrats who produce nothing and consume all, and who grow rich upon the labor and toil of the industrial classes."[4] It is likely, therefore, that our Ohioan Rip van Winkle would have expected such anti-capitalist sentiments to have borne fruit in the form of a large working-class party, and perhaps in a more equitable and just society. He would have been sorely disappointed.

Assembling large numbers of human beings in Akron and employing them in huge factories and workshops had certainly created a working class—people who lived by selling their labor power. "Economic conditions" wrote Marx, "transformed the mass of the people of the country into workers. The combination of capital ... created for this mass a common situation [with] common interests." However, this structural change did not in Akron—or in America as a whole—automatically translate into class consciousness as Marx predicted. As this survey of the city's labor history has shown, the city's workers often rose up, went on strike, occupied their factories, and walked some of the longest picket lines in human history. Yet despite this rollercoaster of struggle, the development of a thoroughgoing class consciousness was blocked. In 1945, Akron's working class was "a class as against capital, but not yet [a class] *for itself*." [Emphasis added.] Marx considered that "the struggle of class against class is a political struggle,"[5] but periodic attempts at creating independent political organization in Akron failed, and the vast movement for social unionism in the 1930s succumbed to business unionism. The task for socialists had been, as Eric Hobsbawm put it in an essay on Gramsci, "to make a hitherto subaltern class capable of hegemony, [to] believe in itself as a potential ruling class."[6] They did not succeed.

Such is the strength of establishment ideology that many, if not most Americans deny the existence of social class. Alternatively, many people see themselves as middle class, although their relationship with Capital places them firmly in the working class. Werner Sombart's gloomy observations made over a century ago still hold today, although the reasons for it are rather more complicated than he thought. Examples throughout this book have shown that the living standards of Akron workers were not as high as Sombart believed those of American workers to be. Moreover, any improvements were due to the action of the workers themselves though their unions. Even when employers "freely" increased pay, they did so to head off union organization. Capitalist welfare, such as that which existed in Akron's rubber mills, was designed to achieve the same end, and to block state welfare legislation.

Akron's earliest unionists organized on a craft basis. Their numbers were small, and most were artisans. It made sense for them to organize on a craft union basis, but they possessed enough class consciousness to see the need to organize politically as well as industrially. Nevertheless, none of Akron's nineteenth-century labor parties survived for long. The established capitalist parties were quick to steal the milder parts of their platforms. Later in the century, a further problem was the hostility of the American Federation of Labor to industrial unionism and political action. By the early 1890s, the AFL had vanquished the Knights of Labor, who for all their inconsistencies, had tried to organize workers on a class basis and were prepared to act politically as well as industrially. The AFL was either indifferent or opposed to organizing the workers in mass production industry, and some of its affiliates excluded people of color from membership. Socialists such as Cleveland's Max L. Hayes fought inside the AFL unions for inclusive, mass unionism, but they were outnumbered.

Akron, like industrial northeast America as a whole, experienced large-scale immigration, both from overseas and from the South, and this cut across the development of an inclusive class consciousness. Foreign immigrants created what David M. Kennedy has called "a polyglot archipelago in a predominantly Anglo-Protestant sea." Working in menial and precarious employment and often speaking little English, foreign-born workers tended to form expatriate communities and faced hostility from the "native born." Many found life in America so hard that they returned to their countries of origin.[7] Akron also received tens of thousands of WASP Southerners, and vast numbers of them were wedded to the Jim Crow system. Many felt the same about Jews and Catholics, particularly immigrants, as they did about Black people. Colorblind working-class unity is not an optional extra for a genuinely progressive union movement: it must be a core principle. Racism certainly existed in Akron before the First World War—when the Ohio Federation of Labor operated a color bar[8]—but the huge influx of white Southerners brought with them virulent white nationalist ideas that saw the rise of the Ku Klux Klan in the city and set back labor organization.

Paradoxically, white Southerners later became the backbone of Akron's organized working class, but in 1945, racism was still a big problem in the city. At that time, around twelve thousand Blacks lived in Akron. Their contribution to the war effort had been disproportionately large, but they remained largely unrecognized, and their wages and living conditions lagged far behind those of the white population. Three years after the war ended, the Black population had increased by a further six thousand to eight thousand according to one estimate, but there had only been a slight increase in the amount of available housing.[9] They were still overrepresented in menial occupations, and the median annual income for Black men stood at $2,201 compared with $3,084 for white men. Black female workers took home on average $872 per annum, although they were better off than their sisters in nearby Canton who made $665.[10] Until the 1950s, there were virtually no white-collar jobs for Black people in Akron and it was not until 1956 that the city hired its first Black bus driver.[11] The poet Rita Dove's father worked in the rubber mills from 1944 and studied chemistry at night, gaining his first degree in 1947 and his master's in 1953. All of his white classmates got good jobs in the industry, but Dove continued in menial jobs. Only when the movement for civil rights gained momentum in the early 1960s did Goodyear hire him as a chemist.[12]

His case highlights the color bar that existed at every level in industry. Otis Spurling noted that when he started at Firestone in 1944, Black people "were not allowed to go further than the mill room, the pit, and [the] janitorial service...." He was laid off in 1954, despite vacancies for tire builders, and when he was hired as a tire builder the following year, white laborers refused to work with him. When he refused to back down, they still refused to talk to him. Black workers were the last hired and the first fired, and Goodyear policy was not to employ them in responsible positions.[13] Salaria Kee O'Reilly's white Irish-born husband John, whom she had met in the International Brigades in Spain, bitterly regretted moving to Akron. It was, he complained, "a Hell Hole of bigotry and prejudice."[14] Such bleak facts indicate that the Akron working class had not yet cohered into a "class for itself" but was still divided along racial/ethnic fault lines and lacked the inclusive class consciousness necessary to build an American labor party and break out of the business union mode.

According to a well-known 1920s union song,

> When I ply my needle, trowel or pick,
> I'm a decent sheeny, wop or mick,
> But when I strike, I'm a Bolshevik,
> I'm labor![15]

The song's intent was of course hortatory. Akron's workers had made common cause across ethnic lines on a number of occasions. The best white unionists worked hard to educate their fellow workers against racial bigotry. Bruce Nelson writes of how Black workers at a CIO-sponsored dance in Akron "declared that they were never so well-treated," and that white girls had competed with each other to dance with them.[16] Photographs taken during the 1913 IWW strike show Italian workers on the picket lines, but CIO organizer Rose Pesotta recalled 1936 Goodyear strikers' surprise when she told them she was Jewish. In another instance, however, white strikers had delighted in making a Black strikebreaker "dance," and one wonders whether his greatest sin in their eyes was to be Black or a scab. Sailors on slave ships had made their charges "dance" in their chains, and slavery was still fresh in human memory in America.

Akron, too, experienced the mushroom growth of a boomtown, with huge waves of newcomers and high labor turnover rates. In their relationship with Capital, they were a working class, but it was a working class in flux and ferment: not one that had coalesced culturally from common experience into body with a sense of solidarity and common purpose. The working class of, say, 1925 did not have the same cultural composition as the class of 1912–13, which had voted Socialist and joined the great IWW strike in the rubber mills.

The 1913 strike was something of a watershed in Akron's labor history. Beginning as a spontaneous walk-off over onerous working conditions, it soon lined class against class in Akron. American capitalists have often dealt brutally with strikers, and Akron was no different. The strikers faced a hostile alliance of manufacturers, police, courts, vigilante gangs, and local authorities, and with the IWW and Socialist locals

Flashlight photo of group of workers in wet area of Goodyear plant, Akron 1913. Courtesy of the Goodyear Collection, University of Akron Archives.

infested with spies and isolated from the broader labor movement, the strike collapsed. Labor activist Jim McCartan adds that the strikers were starved back to work. Despite the Wobblies' reputation for wild-eyed and violent radicalism, the IWW local had acted as a conventional union during the strike, but instead of rallying behind it, the AFL sent two organizers—Carl Wyatt and John L. Lewis—to set up a rival union. The battle demonstrated the truth of Marx's opinion that "the struggle of class against class is a political struggle," but the Socialist Party shortly afterwards was torn asunder by the State repression of the Red Scare years, and internal battles that saw it split three ways. The Socialist Party never regained the influence it had won before the Great War, and the Communist Party, deformed as it was by Stalinism, could never hope to win the allegiance of the city's working class, despite the courage and dedication of its members.

Akron came closest to building a militant social union movement and its corollary of a labor party in the 1930s. The city's gummers threw off the AFL's craft union embrace and the URW became a bastion of the Congress of Industrial Organizations. Although Summit County was home to as Wilmer Tate, Jim McCartan and Francis Gerhart—socialist militants who never lost sight of the vision of industrial unions in the city's mass production industries—the impetus that forced the big corporations to recognize the unions came from below. In the cases of Goodyear in 1936 and Firestone in 1937, for example, rank-and-file gummers initiated huge strikes without waiting for permission from union officialdom. Rank-and-file workers also initiated most, if not all of the sit-down strikes that engulfed the big factories and the URW's international leadership detested them perhaps as much as the employers themselves. By the mid-1930s, Akron was famous as a union town. It was possible for workers to spend their leisure time at union functions such as picnics, dances, sports events and the like. Goodrich URW Local 5 reckoned that its hall had been used "for meetings and various forms of entertainment" 549 times in 1938. "Let us double that in 1939," exhorted the local's newsletter. A fish fry held early in the following year was so successful that people had to be turned away.[17] The unions had given workers a sense of purpose, hope for better things, and their struggles, as the URW's James Turner reminds us, were as much for respect as for dollars and cents.

In 1945, almost a century and a half after Akron workers formed their first unions, the city's workers had organized in industrial unions set up after bitter struggle with some of the nation's most implacably hostile employers, including the Big Three rubber companies, which were among the world's first multinational corporations with operations spanning the globe. In 1950, the city's rubber mills employed at least forty-four thousand people.[18] The URW had signed agreements and grievance procedures, seniority, and some measure of control over work tempos. This, however, was the high tide of union achievement and power in Akron. Even in the early 1930s, the rubber corporations had made ominous noises about "decentralization." Capital will always seek the best conditions for its maximum reproduction and shortly afterwards it began to shift to low wage, non-union sites far from Akron, such as at Memphis and Gadsden.

The Akron workers had been driven by a fierce anti-authoritarianism, but by the late 1930s, their unions were succumbing to bureaucratization. Union officials wanted an orderly process of collective bargaining, not what they saw as a wild insurgency from below. Over the strenuous objections of the big Akron locals, the URW's international leaders—supported by newer out-of-town locals—banned use of the sit-down strike. At the same time, they voted down support for the fledgling Farmer-Labor Party and threw union support behind Roosevelt and the Democrats. Their reasoning was no different to that of the AFL leaders from whom they had ostensibly broken. The craft unions' politics had seldom risen above those of Samuel Gompers, whose watchword was "reward your friends, punish your enemies,"[19] and who resolutely rejected all forms of socialism. Roosevelt—the CIO and URW leaders reasoned—was labor's friend, so they would throw their support behind him rather than take the logical next step of forming their own party to fight for working-class interests. Shortly afterwards, the CIO's first convention delivered the coup-de-grâce to the labor party project. As the Marxist writer George Novack put it: "Even though they captained a far more dynamic and highly developed movement, the general policies and ideological equipment of the top-ranking CIO leaders were little better than those of the old-line AFL bureaucrats." "John L. Lewis," Novack continues, "carried over into the new movement the basic outlook he had absorbed in the old ..."[20] That basic outlook was top-down, business unionism, albeit stripped of its craft prescription and with support for one of America's two capitalist parties. Shortly afterwards, Roosevelt emerged as an open strikebreaker, and this was entirely in keeping with the history of cooperation between the State and Capital to suppress independent working-class activity. As David Sessions reminds us,

> [f]or most of American history, politicians and courts have given employers nearly unrestricted control over the terms of work, and they have offered the resources of the state—above all the military and the police—to enforce those terms.[21]

Labor had lost a crucial opportunity to launch its own party, and it has not had the chance to do so again. Leftists attempted to set up a branch of the United Labor Party in the city in the 1950s, but it soon folded because it lacked the support of organized labor. In addition, the postwar Red Scare was raging, and leftists of all stripes were persecuted by the authorities—with the cooperation of AFL-CIO officialdom. According to an ex-member, Gabriel Kolko, "its founders were disparate" and included leftists of different types, "most [of whom] had bourgeois backgrounds and were college educated."[22]

The year 1945 was the high water mark for union membership in America, peaking at 35.5 percent of the non-agricultural workforce.[23] Today it is a third of that. Given that the great majority of Akron's workers toiled in the rubber mills where there was a virtual closed shop, the city's union density in that period was much higher than the national average. With the end of the war, the city's labor movement—and that of America as a whole—entered into a new period. Although some observers predicted that a new economic slump would follow the end of the war, the economy entered into what Eric Hobsbawm semi-ironically called the "Golden Age" of the long postwar boom. In 1946, the URW signed a joint collective bargaining agreement with the country's "Big Four" corporations: Goodyear, Goodrich, Firestone, and the East Coast-based US Rubber, and gummers enjoyed some of the highest wages and best conditions of American manufacturing workers.[24] This came at a price. The radical, democratic, and anti-capitalist unionism of the 1930s was effectively dead. Industrial business unionism prevailed, with power taken from the shop floor. In 1955, the CIO and the AFL re-amalgamated under the presidency of the crusty old bureaucrat George Meany, who boasted that he had never been on strike.[25] In 1955, the AFL and the CIO reunited without much fuss. Akron's Wilmer Tate had always stood for a united union movement, but the chances are that he would have agreed with Mike Quill, of the CIO's New York transit workers' union, who observed bitterly that the CIO had given in to the AFL's "Three Rs" of "Racism, Raiding, and Racketeering."[26] The URW's Akron locals held out the trend. Wildcats continued, and shop-floor resistance to national three-year contracts meant that annual contracts continued until the 1960s. Nevertheless, the social unionism of the 1930s was a thing of the past.

While there were periodic economic downswings, industry was in an upwards long wave, which some people believed would be permanent, and it was possible for business union leaders to extract concessions from management. By the 1970s, however, "stagflation" had set in and during the 1980s, Akron—like many other Midwestern manufacturing cities—went into a tailspin of deindustrialization. This was the "rustbelt era" of dead factories and accelerated urban decay.

Akron unionist Noah Carmichael was a child in Goodyear Heights during the tail end of the boom years. He recalls that his grandfather, who worked for General Tire & Rubber as a chemist, was raised in a poverty-stricken family, but as a Korean War veteran was able to gain an education under the GI Bill and raise a family in comfort and security. By the 1980s, however, the idea of working for the same company for thirty to forty years and being able to retire with dignity was "a New Deal era ghost." Carmichael "saw firsthand ... what has been echoed in so many other cities ... a somewhat rapid descent into boarded up shops, stores, and houses, all with the familiar gray-faded, flaking plywood window covers."[27]

The rubber mills, which had once employed around sixty thousand workers who enjoyed "high wages, permanent jobs, and generous pensions and health-care benefits," fell silent.[28] As the local journalists Steve Love and David Giffels wrote, "By 1983, there were virtually no tire-building jobs in Akron."[29] In 1986, Chalmers K. Stewart wrote, "The factories ... have vanished. Whole areas in Akron have been bulldozed flat, reminding one of Germany as the building started after the armies had passed by. Weeds ... push up through the rubble." Forty-four percent of the city's children were on some form of relief, and there were only 2,250 URW members left.[30]

That it was the end of a distinct period in Akron's industrial history was underlined by the death of George Bass. Bass, who had led the militant opposition to the URW's international leadership, died in a Middlebury nursing home, aged sixty-seven, in 1976. He had come to Akron as a child with his family from Tennessee and started work as a hose builder at the Goodrich when he was seventeen. He had lived through sixty-one years of the ups and downs and bitterly fought struggles of Akron's working class, and had the scars from thirty-one stitches inflicted by Firestone goons on his head to prove it. For Bass and his fellow workers and retirees, the period must have been bewildering.[31] For people left in precincts next to the former rubber plants, it must have been as in Si Kahn's sadly beautiful song "Aragon Mill":

There's no children at all,
In those narrow empty streets,
Since the mill has closed down
It's so quiet I can't sleep.[32]

The rubber workers fought back tenaciously in this melancholy industrial climate. In 1995, following an unsuccessful ten-month strike against Bridgestone-Firestone, the URW voted to merge with the Steelworkers' Union, an admission of its depleted bargaining power. Today, Akron's gummers are represented by the Rubber and Plastics Conference of the Steelworkers.[33] Their numbers are a fraction of what they were in union's heyday. Only Goodyear still maintains a presence in "Rubber's Home Town," but with three thousand workers, the factory is a shadow of what it once was. In fact, the rubber corporations had threatened to move out of Akron as early as the 1930s. When they did so, they were following the logic inherent in capitalism. First, they "decentralized" to low-wage areas of the US, and much later moved "offshore" to take advantage of even cheaper, non-union Third World labor forces. As early as 1938, the URW's John House had suggested that "world unions" were needed to organize against footloose multinational corporations.[34] Noah Carmichael sums up what decentralization meant for the Akron working class: "Everyone had to shift from industrial jobs, to working in health care, to the university, or go into lower paying service jobs. Not everyone was able to make the transition. Even the ones who did found themselves in need of more education and training for jobs that offered less pay, less benefits, and less job security than the previously unionized industrial jobs."[35]

Although the nature of the work on offer in Akron has largely changed, the imperative to unionize remains as strong as ever. Business unionism has proved unequal to the task of maintaining and expanding union power, but the message of 1930s solidarity unionism—of organizing from below—is timeless. Moreover, experience has highlighted the shortcomings of American individualist, anti-statist ideology and points to collectivist solutions. In comparison with other rich countries, the American social welfare and health system is grossly stunted. Bernie Sanders reminds us that today, "nearly 80% of [American] workers live from paycheck to paycheck—hoping they don't get sick or their car doesn't break down." Over thirty million Americans have no health insurance; one in five cannot afford the medicine prescribed by doctors. Over forty million Americans live in poverty, but 0.1 percent of the population owns almost as much wealth as the bottom ninety percent. Black families are eleven times worse off on average than white families.[36] The 1930s industrial pioneers took on a system that denied countless millions their basic rights, and Akron's labor movement was prominent in those struggles. We can only speculate about "what might have been" had the workers of Summit County and America built a labor party, but if labor's fortunes are to be revived, arguably it will require a revival of the spirit of 1930s social unionism, and that will mean revisiting the labor party idea. As Jason Schulman writes:

> The establishment of a labor party may have to wait until a genuinely new mass union movement arises—and with it the radical political currents that once flourished in the United States. But [Mark] Dudzic is right: whatever the difficulties, however delayed its birth, 'a labor party remains the great unfinished business of the US working class.'[37]

The ghosts of Akron's early labor pioneers would doubtless agree.

Notes

PREFACE

1. Paraphrased in Harry Belafonte and Michael Shnayerson, *My Story: A Memoir of Art, Race and Defiance* (New York: Vintage Books, 2012), 328.

2. William F. Warde, "American Philosophy and the Labor Movement," *International Socialist Review,* Vol. 23, No. 2 (Spring 1962): 2. Article available at Marxists Internet Archive, https://www.marxists.org/archive/novack/1962/xx/philosophy.htm. Warde was Novack's nom de plume.

3. Belafonte and Shnayerson, *My Story,* 328.

INTRODUCTION

1. There has never been a full-length study of the Akron labor movement, although a number of books and theses cover specific aspects of it. These include Dan Nelson's *American Rubber Workers & Organized Labor, 1900–1941* (Princeton, NJ: Princeton University Press, 1988), and unpublished theses by Rosswurm and Shrake, [Kevin Michael Rosswurm, "A Strike in the Rubber City: Rubber Workers, Akron, and the IWW, 1913" (master's thesis, Kent State University, 1975) and Richard W. Shrake II, "Working Class Politics in Akron, Ohio, 1936: The United Rubber Workers and the Failure of the Farmer Labor Party" (master's thesis, The University of Akron, 1974)]. Ruth McKenney's passionate, fictionalized account of the city's labor struggles in the 1930s provides us with an invaluable snapshot of the city during the mass labor upsurge of the 1930s. (Ruth McKenney, *Industrial Valley* (New York: Greenwood Press, 1968). The best general history remains Karl Grismer's *Akron and Summit County* (Akron, OH: Summit County Historical Society, c. 1951).

2. Werner Sombart, *Why Is There No Socialism in The United States?* (New York: Macmillan, 1976).

3. See, for example, Seymour Martin Lipset and Gary Wolfe Marks, *It Didn't Happen Here: Why Socialism Failed in the United States* (New York and London: W. W. Norton, 2000).

4. For instance, Jason Schulman, "Where Is Our Labor Party?" *Jacobin,* December 15, 2016, https://jacobinmag.com/2016/12/where-is-our-labor-party.

5. Cited in Meany's obituary in *The Washington Post,* January 11, 1980 and in Art Preis, *Labor's Giant Step: Twenty Years of the CIO* (New York: Pathfinder Press, 1964), 85.

6. Frederick Engels, preface to the American Edition of *The Condition of the Working Class in England* (New York: John W. Lovell, 1887), https://www.marxists.org/archive/marx/works/1887/01/26.htm.

7. Karl Kautsky, "Socialist Agitation Among Farmers in America," *International Socialist Review,* Vol. 3 (September 1902): 148, https://www.marxists.org/archive/kautsky/1902/09/farmers.htm.

8. V. I. Lenin, "The Results and Significance of the US Presidential Elections," *Collected Works,* Vol. 18 (Moscow: Progress Publishers, 1974), 402.

9. Leon Trotsky, "On the Labor Party Question in America," *Militant,* June 11, 1932. Available at Marxist Internet Archive, https://www.marxists.org/archive/trotsky/1932/xx/lp.htm.

10. See Robin Archer, *Why Is There No Labor Party in The United States?* (Princeton, NJ: Princeton University Press, 2010).

11. Derek Selden, "What Happened to the Labor Party?" Interview with Mark Dudzic, *Jacobin,* November 11, 2015, https://www.jacobinmag.com/2015/10/tony-mazzochi-mark-dudzic-us-labor-party-wto-nafta-globalization-democrats-union/.

12. Sombart, *Why Is There No Socialism,* 56.

13. Thomas C. Reeves, *Twentieth Century America: A Brief History* (New York: Oxford University Press, 2000), 48.

14. Seymour Martin Lipset, "Why Socialism Failed in the United States," American Enterprise Institute Bradley Lecture Series, October 2, 2000, https://www.aei.org/research-products/speech/why-socialism-failed-in-the-united-states/.

15. Leon Trotsky, *My Life: An Attempt at Autobiography* (Mineola, NY: Dover Publications, 2007), 272.

16. Michael Harrington, "Our Fifty Million Poor: Forgotten Men of the Affluent Society," *Commentary,* July 1959xhttps://www.commentarymagazine.com/articles/our-fifty-million-poorforgotten-men-of-the-affluent-society/.

17. Reeves, *Twentieth Century America,* 12.

18. See Louis Hartz, *The Liberal Tradition in America: An Interpretation of American Political Thought Since the Revolution* (New York: Harcourt, Brace, 1955).

19. Thomas Paine, *Common Sense; Addressed to the Inhabitants of America* (Philadelphia: W. & T. Bradford, 1775), 6, https://www.gutenberg.org/files/147/147-h/147-h.htm.

20. Robert Sobel, "Essays, Paper & Addresses. Coolidge and American Business," Calvin Coolidge Presidential Foundation, https://www.coolidgefoundation.org/resources/essays-papers-addresses-35/.

21. Leon Trotsky, *The Living Thoughts of Karl Marx* (New York: Longmans, Green, 1939), 34.

22. See, for instance, Julie Green, *Pure and Simple Politics: The American Federation of Labor and Political Activism, 1881–1917* (New York: Cambridge University Press, 1998).

23. Justin McCarthy, "Less Than Half in US Would Vote for a Socialist President," *Gallup,* https://news.gallup.com/poll/254120/less-half-vote-socialist-president.aspx. However, according to an Axios poll, sixty-one percent of people aged 18–24 had a favorable response to the word *socialism.* Felix Salmon, "Gen Z Prefers 'Socialism' to 'Capitalism,' *Axios,* January 28, 2019, https://www.axios.com/socialism-capitalism-poll-generation-z-preference-1ffb8800–0ce5–4368–8a6f-de3b82662347.html.

24. Mike Davis, "Why the US Working Class is Different," *New Left Review,* Vol 1, No. 123 (September–October 1980): 18–19.

25. American women did not win the right to vote until 1920.

26. Kautsky "Socialist Agitation Among Farmers in America."

27. Robert Michels, trans. Eden and Cedar Paul, with an introduction by Seymour Martin Lipset, *Political Parties: A Sociological Study of the Oligarchic Tendencies of Modern Democracy* (New York: Free Press, 1962).

28. Archer, *Why Is There No Labor Party in the United States?* In Britain, too, the drive to form the Labour Party came from general labor unions.

29. For a history of the AWU written by its early leader, see W. G. Spence, *History of the AWU,* undated edition (Melbourne: Melbourne University Press, 2013). The AWU, like the AFL, did not admit "colored" workers.

30. Davis, "Why the US Working Class is Different," 7–8. The allusion is to E. P. Thompson, The Making of the English Working Class (New York: Vintage Books, 1966), which argues that class is a cultural as well as structural phenomenon.

31. Ibid, 3.

CHAPTER 1

1. An American attempt to imitate the Irish accent.

2. Karl Marx and Frederick Engels, "Manifesto of the Communist Party," in Karl Marx and Frederick Engels, *Selected Works,* (Moscow: Progress Publishers, 1969), 114.

3. Karl Marx, trans. Eden and Cedar Paul, *Capital,* Vol. 1 (London and New York: Everyman's Library, 1974), 734.

4. Samuel A. Lane, *Fifty Years and Over of Akron and Summit County* (Akron, OH: Beacon Job Department, 1892), ch. 1, Kindle.

5. Peter Way, *Common Labour: Workers and the Digging of North American Canals, 1780–1860,* (Cambridge: Cambridge University Press, 1993), 4.

6. Thompson, *The Making of the English Working Class,* 10.

7. Wandering landless laborers in the Irish language.

8. John Tully, *Crooked Deals and Broken Treaties: How American Indians Were Displaced by White Settlers in the Cuyahoga Valley* (New York: Monthly Review Press, 2016), 36.

9. Frederick Jackson Turner, *The Frontier in American History* (New York: Henry Holt, 1953), 136.

10. Robert A. Wheeler, ed., Document Four. "George Washington on the Strategic Importance of the Cuyahoga River, 1786," letter to Richard Butler, Mount Vernon, January 10, 1788 in *Visions of the Western Reserve: Public and Private Documents of Northeastern Ohio, 1750–1860* (Columbus: Ohio State University Press, 2000), 51.

11. MeasuringWorth.com, https://www.measuringworth.com.

12. Robert E. Wright, "Origins of Commercial Banking in the United States, 1781–1830," Economic History Association, https://eh.net/encyclopedia/origins-of-commercial-banking-in-the-united-states-1781–1830/.

13. Construction laborers.

14. Way, *Common Labour,* 49 and O. W. Petersen, *The Jorgen Petersen Family,* (Akron, OH: O. W. Petersen, 1972), 3.

15. See, for instance, Karl Frederick Geiser, *Redemptioners and Indentured Servants in the Colony and Commonwealth of Pennsylvania, Supplement to the Yale Review, Vol. X, No. 2* (August 1901).

16. *Redemptioners* was the name given to the mainly German bonded laborers who were purchased by "soul drivers" from ships' masters in American ports for resale inland.

17. Kerby A. Miller, *Emigrants and Exiles: Ireland and the Irish Exodus to North America* (New York: Oxford University Press, 1985), 103–105.

18. Jim Tully, *Shanty Irish,* (Kent, OH: Black Squirrel Books, 2009), 14.

19. James S. Jackson, "Tracing Catholic History in Summit County," *ABJ,* July 29, 1978.

20. Estelle M. Stewart and Jesse Chester Bowen, "History of Wages in the United States from Colonial Times to 1928," Bulletin of the United States Bureau of Labor Statistics, Oct. 1939, 56, https://fraser.stlouisfed.org/title/4067.

21. Ryan Dearinger, *The Filth of Progress: Immigration, Americans, and the Building of Canals and Railroads in the West* (Oakland, CA: University of California Press, 2016), ch. 2, eBook Academic Collection (EBSCOhost).

22. Tully, *Shanty Irish,* 13.

23. MeasuringWorth.com, https://www.measuringworth.com.

24. *ABJ,* September 29, 1974.

25. Petersen, *Jorgen Petersen Family,* 3.

26. Tully, *Crooked Deals and Broken Treaties,* 36.

27. Marx, *Capital,* Vol. 1, 734.

28. *Akron Beacon Journal,* (*ABJ*), June 23, 1931.

29. William Donohue Ellis, *The Cuyahoga* (New York and Chicago: Holt, Rinehart and Wilson, 1966), 113.

30. Raymond Boryczka and Lorin Lee Cary, *No Strength Without Union: An Illustrated History of Ohio Workers, 1803–1980* (Columbus: Ohio Historical Society, 1980), 12.

31. Ellis, *The Cuyahoga,* 114.

32. Cited in Dearinger, *The Filth of Progress,* ch. 2.

33. Marx, *Capital,* Vol. 1, 734.

34. Cited in Ronald Shaw, *Canals for A Nation: The Canal Era in the United States, 1790–1860* (Lexington, KY: University of Kentucky Press, 2014), 171.

35. "Life Expectancy by Age, 1850–2011," Infoplease, 2017, https://www.infoplease.com/us/mortality/life-expectancy-age-1850–2011.

36. Augustus Porter, cited in Henry Howe, "Summit County Description and Stories, 1847," Document Twenty-Four in Wheeler, *Visions,* 318.

37. Boryczka and Cary, *No Strength Without Union,* 12–13.

38. *ABJ,* September 29, 1974.

39. Calculated using MeasuringWorth.com, http://www.measuringworth.com/uscompare/relativevalue.php.

40. Stewart and Bowen, *History of Wages in the United States,* 139.

41. Ellis, *The Cuyahoga,* 113.

42. Boryczka and Cary, *No Strength Without Union,* 13.

43. Stewart and Bowen, *History of Wages,* 137.

44. Kent State University Special Collections. The Richard Howe Collection. Box 2. Cash Account Book, March-December, 1827.

45. "Zerah Hawley: A Critical View of the Reserve in the Early 1820s," Document Twelve in Wheeler, *Visions,* 148, 161–62.

46. Ibid, "Emily Nash: A Girl's View of Growing Up on the Frontier, 1812–1820," Document Eleven.

47. Boryczka and Cary, *No Strength Without Union,* 14.

48. Ibid.

49. See for instance Thomas Desmond Williams, ed., *Secret Societies in Ireland* (Dublin and New York: Gill and Macmillan, 1973).

50. Boryczka and Cary, *No Strength Without Union,* 12–14.

51. See Dearinger, *The Filth of Progress,* ch. 2; Way, *Common Labour,* 200; and Jay M. Perry, "The Irish Laborer Feuds on Indiana's Canals and Railroads in the 1830s," *Indiana Magazine of History,* Vol. 109, Issue 3 (September 2013): 224–256.

52. Thompson, *The Making of the English Working Class,* 10.

53. White adult males who had resided in the State of Ohio for at least one year and who had paid taxes, could vote. Given that many canal laborers were illiterate, spoke little English, and had not enjoyed the suffrage back in Ireland, it is unlikely that they would have voted.

54. Murray Powers, "History of the Catholic Church in Summit County from origin to '76." Typescript, St Paul's Parish, Akron, Ohio, 1976. Copy in archives of Ohio Historical Society, Columbus, Ohio.

55. Way, *Common Labour*, 271.

56. Ibid, 272.

57. Powers, "History of the Catholic Church," 1–2. Also James S. Jackson, "Tracing Catholic History in Summit County."

58. Ronald D. Reid, "Youngstown and the P&O Canal," (Mahoning County Historical Society, undated). Kent State University Special Collections, Kent, Ohio. Richard Howe Collection, Box 2, Folder 27.

59. For a discussion of the effects of the canal and other infrastructural improvements on Ohio, see Kevin F. Kern and Gregory S. Wilson, *Ohio: A History of the Buckeye State* (Malden, MA: John Wiley and Sons, 2014), 167–176.

60. Frances McGovern, *Written on the Hills: the Making of the Akron Landscape*, (Akron, OH: The University of Akron Press, 1996), 3.

61. Dearinger, *The Filth of Progress*, ch. 2.

CHAPTER 2

1. Howard Wolf, "The *Akron Beacon Journal:* The First 100 Years." (Unpublished typescript, *Akron Beacon Journal* archives, c. 1939), 130.

2. From 45,365 in 1800 to 581,434 in 1820 with a further increase to almost one million in 1830. US Census Bureau, "Resident Population of Apportionment of US House of Representatives, Ohio." https://wwwcensus.gov/dmd/www/resapport/states/ohio.pdf

3. In 1810 there were only 13 towns in the US with a population greater than 8,000; in 1820, 13; in 1830, 26; and in 1840, 44. Helen L. Sumner, "Citizenship," in John Rogers Commons et al, *History of Labour in the United States, Vol. 1*, Part Two, 176. By 1830, less than forty percent of the American population lived in towns with populations larger than 8,000. By 1900, this had increased to 33.1%. See A. M. Simons, *The American Farmer* (Chicago: Charles H. Kerr, 1906), 63.

4. D. Griffiths Jr., *Two Years Residence in the New Settlements of Ohio, North America* (Ann Arbor, Michigan, University Microfilms, 1966), 33.

5. William Cahn, *A Pictorial History of American Labor* (New York: Crown Publishers, 1972), 28.

6. *ABJ,* December 18, 1928.

7. Curtis P. Nettels, *The Emergence of a National Economy,* 1775–1815, *The Economic History of the United States, Vol. III* (New York: Holt, Rinehart and Winston, 1962), 281.

8. Wolf, "The *Akron Beacon Journal,*" 1.

9. Ibid, 2.

10. Herman Fetzer, ed., *A Centennial History of Akron* (Akron, OH: Summit County Historical Society, 1925), 40.

11. Cited in Lane, *Fifty Years and Over,* ch. LIV.

12. Thomas Hardy, ed. Sarah E. Maier, *Tess of the d'Urbervilles* (Toronto: Broadview Literary Texts, 1996), 51.

13. See E. P. Thompson, "Time, Work-Discipline, and Industrial Capitalism," *Past and Present,* no. 38 (December 1967): 56–97.

14. Lane, Fifty Years, ch. LIV. Egg-nog is a sweet alcoholic beverage made of eggs, sugar, cream, milk, whiskey, and spices. In 1754, William Hogarth satirized the drunken corruption of English elections in a series of four oil paintings entitled "The Humours of an Election."

15. David J. Saposs, "Colonial and Federal Beginnings (to 1827)" in Commons et al, eds., *History of Labour in the United States, Vol. 1,* Part One, 173.

16. Steven F. Hipple, "Self-Employment in the United States," *Monthly Labor Review,* Bureau of Labor Statistics, https://www.bls.gov/opub/mlr/2010/09/art2full.pdf.

17. Around four-fifths of the free American population was self-employed in the early years of the nineteenth century. See Harry Braverman, *Labor and Monopoly Capital: The Degradation of Work in the Twentieth Century, 25th Anniversary Edition* (New York: Monthly Review Press, 1998), 36. Also bear in mind that approximately one-quarter of the workforce were black slaves. See Stanley Lebergott, "Labor Force and Employment, 1800–1960," in Dorothy S. Brady, ed., *Output, Employment and Productivity in the United States after 1800* (Washington, DC: National Bureau of Economic Research, 1966), 118.

18. Guillaume Tell Poussin, trans. Edmund L. Du Barry, first American Edition, *The United States: Its Power and Progress* (Philadelphia: Lippincott, Grambo, 1851), 472.

19. Ray Allen Billington, *Land of Savagery, Land of Promise: The European Image of the American Frontier in the Nineteenth Century* (New York: W. W. Norton, 1981), 253.

20. See Tully, *Crooked Deals and Broken Treaties.*

21. Commons, "Introduction" to Commons et al, History of Labour, Vol. 1, 3.

22. On the origins of "pure and simple" unionism, see for instance Samuel Gompers, *Seventy Years of Life and Labor, Volume 1* (New York: Dutton, 1925) and Green, *Pure and Simple Politics.*

23. Marx rendered these transactions as C–M–C as opposed to capitalist production for profit, which he rendered as M–C–M. See Marx, *Capital,* Vol. 1, 131.

24. Foster Rhea Dulles, *Labor in America: A History* (New York: Thomas Y. Crowell, 1949), 20.

25. John Chester Miller, *The First Frontier: Life in Colonial America* (New York: University Press of America, 1986), 1.

26. For a general discussion, see Philip Yale Nicholson, *Labor's Story in the United States* (Philadelphia: Temple University Press, 2004), 30.

27. "Notes of the Secret Debates."

28. Cahn, *A Pictorial History,* 22.

29. Cited in Estelle M. Stewart and J. C. Bowen, History of Wages in the United States From Colonial Times to 1928, Part 1, Revision of Bulletin No. 499 With Supplement, 1929–1933 (Washington, DC: United States Department of Labor, Bureau of Labor Statistics, 1934), 26.

30. "Thomas Kelly: A Manx Immigrant in the Western Reserve, 1828," Document Sixteen in Wheeler, *Visions,*199.

31. Ibid. "David Griffiths, Jr.: A Welsh Clergyman in Northeastern Ohio, 1835," Document Eighteen, 218.

32. Lane, *Fifty Years and Over,* ch. LIV.

33. Sumner, "Citizenship," 174.

34. D. B. Warden, *A Statistical, Political, and Historical Account of the United States* (Edinburgh: 1819), cited in Stewart and Bowen, 57.

35. Lane, *Fifty Years and Over,* ch. LIV.

36. Mary Ritter Beard, *The American Labor Movement* (New York: Arno and *New York Times,* 1969), 12.

37. Thomas R. Brooks, *Toil and Trouble: A History of American Labor, Second Edition* (New York: Dell Publishing, 1971), 11.

38. Nevertheless, as Marx explains, the form of circulation of commodities introduced by the merchant-capitalist became the "general formula of capital": M–C–M. See Marx, *Capital,* 141.

39. Frederic L. Paxson, *History of the American Frontier* (Boston & New York: Houghton Mifflin, 1924), 228.

40. Saposs, "Colonial and Federal Beginnings," 101.

41. Karl Marx and Friedrich Engels, Letter 209, Engels to Sorge, Correspondence, 1846–1895 (New York: International Publishers, 1936), 467. Marx repeated the claim in *Grundisse* (Harmondsworth: Penguin Books, 1973), 884.

42. Nettels, *The Emergence of a National Economy, Vol. II,* 138–139.

43. The laws included the Navigation and Iron Acts, which allowed the colonies to trade only with the Mother Country and forbade the manufacture of finished iron goods in the colonies. See, for example, Douglass C. North and Robert Paul Thomas, eds., *The Growth of the American Economy to 1860* (Columbia: University of South Carolina Press, 1968) and A. C. Bining, *British Regulation of the Colonial Iron Trade* (Philadelphia: University of Philadelphia Press, 1933).

44. Turner, *The Frontier in American History,* 11.

45. Brooks, *Toil and Trouble,* 13.

46. One should not overestimate the size of such associations. for in 1836 only two or three percent of the American nonagricultural workforce were union members. See Daniel Nelson, *Shifting Fortunes: The Rise and Decline of American Labor, From the 1820s to the Present* (Chicago: Ivan R. Dee, 1997), 4.

47. *Summit Beacon,* October 12, 1841.

48. Constitution and By-Laws of the Akron Mechanics' Association. Adopted July 1, 1846 and revised August 19, 1846.

49. The Locofocos, more accurately the Equal Rights Party, were a working-class breakaway from the Democratic Party's Tammany machine. The soubriquet stems from their use of Locofoco friction matches to light candles after their rivals extinguished the lights in a meeting hall. See, for instance, Edwin G. Burrows and Mike Wallace, *Gotham: A History of New York City to 1898* (New York: Oxford University Press, 1998), 609.

50. C. R. McLean and Wilbur C. Ammon, unpublished and untitled typescript. WPA Writers' Project, Akron, Ohio. No date and no pagination. Western Reserve Historical Society Library and Archives, Cleveland, Ohio. MSS.2970.

51. Cited in Kathleen L. Endres, *Akron's "Better Half": Women's Clubs and the Humanization of the City, 1825–1925* (Akron, OH: The University of Akron Press, 2006), 17.

52. *Summit Beacon,* November 23, 1842.

53. Lane, *Fifty Years and Over,* ch. LIV.

54. *ABJ,* November 27, 1907.

55. See Stewart and Bowen, *A History of Wages,* 13, 71.

56. Lane, *Fifty Years and Over,* ch. LIV.

57. *Summit Beacon,* April 17, 1850.

58. Alexis de Tocqueville, trans. Henry Reeve, revised by Francis Bowen and abridged with an introduction by Patrick Renshaw, *Democracy in America* (Ware, Herts: Wordsworth Classics, 1998), 256.

59. See, for instance, Nancy Isenberg, *White Trash: The 400-Year Untold History of Class in America* (New York: Viking, 2016).

60. See "Notes of the Secret Debates of the Federal Convention of 1787, Taken by Robert Yates, Chief Justice of the State of New York, and One of the Delegates to the Said Convention," Yale Law School Avalon Project, Documents in Law, History and Diplomacy, https://avalon.law.yale.edu/18th_century/yates.asp.

61. Speech at Constitutional Convention, 1787, cited in Noam Chomsky, ed. Peter R. Mitchell and John Schoeffel, *Understanding Power: The Indispensable Chomsky* (London: Vintage Books, 2003), 315.

62. *Akron Times-Press,* March 24, 1935.

63. Fetzer, *A Centennial History,* 51.

64. Wolf, "The *Akron Beacon Journal,*" 74.

65. *ABJ,* March 3, 1935.

66. Chester W. Wright, *Economic History of the United States, First Edition* (New York: McGraw-Hill, 1941), 402.

67. *ABJ,* November 27, 1907.

68. Ibid.

69. In a later period, the socialist labor leader Eugene V. Debs, while opposed to prohibition, campaigned against alcoholic overindulgence, which he attributed to social conditions. See, for instance, Eugene Debs, "On Liquor and Prohibition," *Terre Haute Star,* February 2, 1916, https://www.marxists.org/archive/debs/works/1916/0202-debs-liquorandprohibition.pdf.

70. "Emily Nash: A Girl's View of Growing Up on the Frontier, 1812–1820," in Wheeler, ed., *Visions,* 136–137.

71. Wolf, "The *Akron Beacon Journal,*"195–196.

72. *Summit Beacon,* June 4, 1851 and *ABJ,* February 12, 1961.

73. Sojourner Truth, "Ain't I A Woman?" December 1851. Modern History Sourcebook. Fordham University, http://sourcebooks.fordham.edu/mod/sotruth-woman-asp.

74. *Akron Daily Beacon,* October 24, 1872. The 1872 female servant wage translates into $42.40 in today's purchasing power. Calculated using Measuring Worth.com.

75. Stewart and Bowen, *A History of Wages,* 115–116.

76. Ibid, 116.

77. *Summit Beacon,* April 12, 1854.

78. Ibid, April 26, 1851.

79. See Endres, *Akron's "Better Half,"* 28.

80. Ibid.

81. J. David Hacker, "A Census-Based Count of the Civil War Dead," *Civil War History,* Vol. 57, No. 4, (December 2011).

82. Kern and Wilson, *Ohio: A History,* 216.

83. Louis Hacker, *The Triumph of American Capitalism: The Development of Forces in American History to the End of the Nineteenth Century* (New York: Columbia University Press, 1940), 373.

84. See, for instance, Ralph Adreano, ed., *The Economic Impact of the Civil War* (Cambridge. MA: Schenkman Publishing, 1962), and Gerald D, Nash, ed., *Issues in American Economic History* (Lexington, MA: D. C. Heath, 1980).

85. See Charles Post, "The American Road to Capitalism," *New Left Review,* Vol. 1, No.33 (May–June, 1982): 30–51.

86. See, for instance, Robert C. Allen, "International Competition in Iron and Steel, 1850–1913," *Journal of Economic History,* Vol. 29, No.4 (December 1979): 911–937.

CHAPTER 3

1. Brooks, *Toil and Trouble,* 38.

2. Reeves, *Twentieth Century America,* 2–3. A simple calculation using MeasuringWorth.com shows that these sums are eye-watering, even in today's values.

3. Kern and Wilson, *Ohio: A History,* 237.

4. "Ferdinand Schumacher," *Ohio History Central,* http://www.ohiohistorycentral.org/index.php?title=Ferdinand_Schumacher&rec=333.

5. Wolf, "The *Akron Beacon Journal,*" 167, 192.

6. *Summit Beacon,* November 22, 1872, and February 15, and 16, 1871.

7. *New York Times,* November 22, 1903.

8. Mark Twain and Charles Dudley Warner, *The Gilded Age A Tale of To-Day, Two Vols.* (New York: P. F. Collier & Son, 1873), https://www.questia.com/read/1364401/the-gilded-age-a-tale-of-today.

9. *ABJ,* December 15, 1864.

10. Ibid, December 26, 1867.

11. Ibid, July 23, 1890.

12. Figures adapted from Stanley Lebergott, "Labor Force and Employment, 1800–1960" in Dorothy S. Brady ed., *Output, Employment, and Productivity in the United States after 1800* (Washington, DC: National Bureau of Economic Research, 1966), 120, http://www.nber.org/chapters/c1567.

13. Braverman, *Labor and Monopoly Capital,* 36.

14. Figures from Nelson, *Shifting Fortunes,* 4.

15. *Daily Graphic,* June 28, 1888, cited in the *ABJ,* May 23, 1981.

16. *ABJ,* June 24, 1990.

17. Ibid, December 22, 1869.

18. For a business history of B. F. Goodrich, see Mansel G. Blackford and K. Austin Kerr, *B. F. Goodrich: Tradition and Transformation, 1870–1995* (Columbus: Ohio State University Press, 1996).

19. Wolf, "The *Akron Beacon Journal,*" 315.

20. Isaac Lippincott, *Economic Development of the United States* (New York: Appleton, 1927), 548.

21. Both statements are widely quoted. See, for instance, Michael J. Sandel, *America in Search of a Public Philosophy* (Cambridge, MA: Harvard University Press, 1998), 199.

22. Boryczka and Cary, *No Strength Without Union,* 79.

23. Michael Pierce, "Martin Foran and the Creation of Cleveland's Labor Movement," Warren Van Tine and Michael Pierce, eds., *Builders of Ohio: A Biographical History* (Columbus: Ohio State University Press, 2003), 173.

24. *Summit Beacon,* November 22, 1860.

25. *Akron Daily Beacon,* July 12, 1872.

26. Ibid, numerous editions, July, August and September 1872.

27. Ibid, July 12, 1872.

28. Ibid, June 24, July 12, and July 16, 1872.

29. By the Akron Porcelain and Plastics Company in Akron and Barberton, founded in 1890.

30. *Summit County Beacon,* April 6, 1853.

31. "Unity History," GMB Stoke Unity S75, www.gmbstokeunity.org.uk/unity-history/branch@gmbstokeunity.org.uk. https://www.gmbstokeunity.org.uk/history-of-gmb/.

32. See Martin Crawford, "Back to the Future? The Potters' Emigration Society and the Historians," *Labour History Review,* Vol. 76, Issue 2 (August 2011): 81–103.

33. Braverman, *Labor and Monopoly Capitalism,* 32.

34. M. C. Kennedy, PhD diss. cited in Braverman, *Labor and Monopoly Capital,* 307, n.

35. See Akron Porcelain & Plastics Co., Celebrating 125 Years: Five Generations Help to Build Akron Porcelain & Plastics, Chapter One, "Molding a Legacy 1828–1890," http://www.akronporcelain.com/History/Akronchapter1.pdf

36. Eric Hobsbawm, *Labour's Turning Point, 1880–1900: Extracts from Contemporary Sources,* Second Ed. (Brighton: Harvester Press, 1974), 4.

37. The tendency was noted as early as 1776 by Adam Smith, who famously described the splintering of skills in needle and pin production during the British Industrial Revolution. See Adam Smith, *The Wealth of Nations, Book I,* Chapter 1, "On the Division of Labour." Available at the Marxists Internet Archive, https://www.marxists.org/reference/archive/smith-adam/works/wealth-of-nations/book01/ch01.htm. Marx elaborated on Smith's work. See Marx, *Capital,* Vol.1, 351–359.

38. *Akron Daily Democrat,* March 3, 1894.

39. Information in the preceding paragraph, save for that from Wolf, is taken from C. Dean Blair, *The Potters and Potteries of Summit County, 1828–1915,* (Akron, OH: Summit County Historical Society, 1966), 1–16.

40. *ABJ,* April 30, 1976.

41. *Summit County Beacon,* January 20, 1875.

42. Ibid, December 27, 1876.

43. Ibid, December 5, 1877.

44. *Akron Daily Democrat,* March 3, 1894.

45. Blair, *The Potters and Potteries of Summit County,* 6.

46. *Akron Daily Democrat,* June 6, 1876.

47. For an account of the national strike, see Jeremy Brecher, *Strike! Revised, Expanded, and Updated Edition,* (Oakland, CA: PM Press, 2014), 11–32. For a lurid contemporary account, see James Dabney McCabe (writing as Edward Winslow Martin), *The History of the Great Riots,* (Philadelphia: National Publishing, 1877).

48. *Summit County Beacon,* August 1, 1877.

49. Ibid.

50. Ibid.

51. *Akron Beacon Journal,* March 19, and May 7, 1881.

52. Ibid, July 12, 1890.

53. Ibid, July 23, 1868.

54. Ibid, January 20, 1872.

55. Daniel Webster Brown Papers, University of Akron Archives (UAA).

56. *Daily Beacon,* February 19, March 20, and April 23, 1889 and April 22, 1890.

57. Teddy Sawyer, "Labor Organizations," in Scott Dix Kenfield, ed., *Akron and Summit County Ohio, 1825–1928, Vol. 1.* (Chicago and Akron: S. J. Clarke, 1928), 698.

58. Howard Wolf, "The *Akron Beacon Journal.*"

59. John E. Borsos, "Talking Union: The Labor Movement in Barberton, Ohio, 1891–1991" (PhD diss., University of Indiana, February 1992), 38–39.

60. *Summit Beacon,* August 1, 1861.

61. UAA, Summit County Historical Society Box A1, Barber, O.C. Biography.

62. John Borsos, "'We Make You This Appeal in the Name of Every Union Man and Woman in Barberton': Solidarity Unionism in Barberton, Ohio, 1933–41," in Staughton Lynd, ed., *"We Are All Leaders": The Alternative Unionism of the Early 1930s* (Urbana and Chicago: University of Illinois Press, 1996), 238.

63. Brown Papers. Brown and O. C. Barber were related by marriage.

64. *The People,* November 12, 1909.

65. *Akron Daily Beacon,* March 28, 1885.

66. Ibid.

67. Letter to the Editor, *Daily Beacon,* March 30, 1885.

68. *Daily Beacon,* April 6, 1885.

69. See, for instance, Louise Raw, *Striking a Light: The Bryant and May Matchwomen and Their Place in Labour History* (London: Continuum, 2009).

70. *Daily Beacon,* March 30, 1885.

71. Borsos, "Talking Union," 39.

72. *Daily Beacon,* April 6, 1885.

73. Borsos, "We Make You This Appeal," 240.

74. Borsos, "Talking Union," 401–402.

75. "Timeline of Beacon Journal History," *Akron Beacon Journal,* Wednesday, February 22, 2017, http://www.ohio.com/lifestyle/timeline-of-beacon-journal-history-1.524070.

76. *The Labor Unionist,* September 1, 1883.

77. Boryzcka and Cary, *No Strength Without Union,* 82.

78. Ohio History Central, *Knights of Labor,* www.ohiohistorycentral.org/w/Knights_of_Labor.

79. *Summit County Beacon,* April 23, September 3, and December 10, 1879.

80. Ibid, January 26, 1881.

81. Ibid, February 21, 1883.

82. Friedrich Engels, Preface to the American Edition (1887), *Condition of the Working Class in England,* (Panther, 1969), 4.

83. Brecher, *Strike!,* 33.

84. Brooks, *Toil and Trouble,* 42.

85. The Constitution of the KL, 1878, http://sageamericanhistory.net/gildedage/documents/KofLaborConst.html.

86. *Stark County Democrat,* June 23, 1883.

87. *Summit County Beacon,* January 30, 1886.

88. Ibid, September 18, 1886.

89. *McHenry Plaindealer,* April 14, 1886.

90. *The Labor Unionist,* September 1, 1883.

91. *Statesman Journal* (Salem, Oregon), May 12, 1895.

92. The "Locofocos" originated as a radical faction of the Democratic Party in New York City but formed their own short-lived Equal Rights Party in 1835.

93. Brooks, *Toil and Trouble,* 54.

94. *Summit County Beacon,* May 14, 1884, and September 1, 1886.

95. Ibid, March 10, 1887.

96. *Cincinnati Enquirer,* February 21, and 23, 1887. For an extended discussion of the national party, see Commons et al, *History of Labour in the United States, Vol. II* (Washington DC: Beard Books, 1918), 465–466.

97. *The Times* (Philadelphia), March 23, 1886.

98. *Sterling Standard,* March 18, 1886.

99. *Wheeling Daily Intelligencer,* March 12, 1886.

100. *Mower County Transcript,* January 14, 1887.

101. *Daily Beacon,* January 9, 19, and 22, 1886.

102. Ibid, February 19, 1886.

103. Ibid, April 20, 1886.

104. Numerous editions of the *Daily Beacon* carry articles on strikes and boycotts throughout the 1880s and into the 1890s.

105. Editorial, *Daily Beacon,* January 17, 1889.

106. *Daily Beacon,* January 22, 1890.

107. *The Labor Unionist,* September 1, 1883.

108. Ibid.

109. Ibid, "Convict Slave System."

110. Ibid.

111. *Daily Beacon,* May 1, 1886.

112. *Summit County Beacon,* January 16, 1889.

113. *Akron Daily Democrat,* February 2, 1895.

114. John D. House, "Birth of a Union," 2. Unpublished ms. 1978. Microfilm 1981, Ohio Historical Society, Columbus, Ohio.

115. *ABJ,* September 14, 1893.

116. Letter to the Editor, *Daily Beacon,* February 26, 1887.

117. Figures from David O. Whitten, "The Depression of 1893," Economic History Association, https://eh.net/encyclopedia/the-depression-of-1893.

118. The idea of a labor aristocracy is controversial, even among Marxists, and means a number of different things. It is used in this book to describe a comparatively privileged stratum of skilled workers in the working class. For an absorbing discussion of the phenomenon in the context of nineteenth-century England, see Jonathan Strauss, "Engels and the Theory of the Labor Aristocracy," *Links International Journal of Socialist Renewal,* links.org.au/node/45.

119. Cited in Susan Allyn Johnson, "Industrial Voyagers: A Case Study of Appalachian Migration to Akron, Ohio, 1900–1940" (PhD diss. Ohio State University, 2006), 54.

120. See, for instance, "Panic of 1893," Ohio History Central, www.ohiohistorycentral.org/w/Panic_of_1893.

121. David O. Whitten, "The Depression of 1893," *Economic History Association,* https://eh.net/encyclopedia/the-depression-of-1893.

122. In 1911, the German Marxist Karl Kautsky calculated that between 1815 and 1907, there had been crises of overproduction in the years 1815, 1825, 1836, 1847, 1857, 1866, 1873, 1882, 1891, 1895, 1900, and 1907. See Karl Kautsky, "Finance-Capital and Crises," *Social Democrat* XIV, London, July–September, 1911. Available at the Marxists Internet Archive, http://www.marxists.org/archive/kautsky/1911/xx/finance.htm.

123. Nelson, Shifting Fortunes, 4.

124. Letter to the editor, *ABJ,* March 10, 1887.

125. Ibid, April 25, 1896.

126. Ibid, February 15, 1933.

127. *Daily Beacon,* January 13, 1894.

128. Ibid, January 15, 1894.

129. Ibid, January 17, 1894.

130. *Los Angeles Herald,* May 3, 1894.

131. "Historical Background and Development of Social Security," *Social Security Administration* (US), https://www.ssa.gov/history/briefhistory3.html.

132. *Daily Beacon,* May 12, 1893.

133. Ibid, February 3, 1893.

134. Ibid, May 1, 1896.

135. Ibid, January 20, April 2, and April 5, 1896.

136. Ibid, January 14, 1896.

137. Ibid, March 16, 1897.

138. Boryczka and Cary, *No Strength Without Union,* 133.

139. *Summit County Journal,* March 9, 1899 and *Summit County Beacon,* March 10, 1899.

CHAPTER 4

1. George Orwell, "Down the Mine," http://orwell.ru/library/essays/mine/english/e_dtm

2. US Department of Commerce, Historical Statistics of the United States (Washington DC: US Government Printer, 1957), 355.

3. *Stark County Democrat,* August 14, 1876.

4. *Summit Beacon,* June 6, 1849.

5. See US Department of Labor, Bureau of Labor Statistics, "Number and Rate of Fatal Occupational Injuries, by Industry Sector, 2009. (Preliminary results)," (Washington DC: October 1, 2010), https://www.bls.gov/news.release/archives/cfoi_08192010.pdf.

6. *Summit Beacon,* July 25, 1849.

7. *Akron Daily Beacon,* December 12, 1872.

8. *Akron Times-Press,* March 24, 1935

9. *Akron Daily Beacon,* August 28, 1872.

10. Boryczka and Cary, *No Strength Without Union,* 65.

11. *Summit Beacon,* July 25, 1849.

12. Judy Anne Davis, *A History of Tallmadge Coal: A Tale of Woodchucks, Welshmen, and a Canal* (Stow, OH: Akron Public Library, 2006), 8, www.akronlibrary.org/images/Divisions/SpecColl/images/TallmadgeCoal-.pdf.

13. Bernard Mandel, "Jim McCartan, Rebel." Typescript Ohio Historical Society. File labeled "Jim McCartan Day."

14. Ibid.

15. James Green, *The Devil Is Here in These Hills: West Virginia's Coal Miners and Their Battle for Freedom* (New York: Atlantic Monthly Press, 2015), 23, 25.

16. Boryczka and Cary, No Strength Without Union, 66.

17. UMW(A) Preamble, January 25, 1890, http://ww.w.workerseducation.org/crutch/pamphlets/coal/coal_11.html.

18. This account is drawn from the *Daily Beacon,* August 28, 1872.

19. Ibid.

20. *Akron Daily Beacon,* November 24, 1873.

21. *Summit Beacon,* August 28, 1872.

22. See Georgius Agricola, De Re Metallica (trans. Herbert Clark Hoover and Lou Henry Hoover) (New York: Dover, 1950). (Originally published in Latin in 1556). Also Bernardino Ramazzini, trans. Wilmer Cave Wright, *De Morbis Artificum* (Chicago: University of Chicago Press, 1940).

23. See, for instance, A. M. Donoghue, "Occupational Health hazards in Mining: An Overview," *Occupational Medicine* 54 (2004): 283–289, and S. W. Fisher, "Health Hazards of Mining," British Journal of Independent Medicine 1 (3), (July 1944): 153–158.

24. *Daily Beacon,* January 20, 1871.

25. Ibid, January 18, July 9, August 26, 1871.

26. Ibid, July 6, 8, and 9, 1871.

27. Ibid, July 8, 1872.

28. Ibid, January 17, 1889.

29. Ibid, December 11, 1903.

30. *ABJ,* February 26, 1912.

31. See, for instance, Hugh D. Hindman, *Child Labor: An American History* (New York: M.E. Sharpe, 2002). Lewis W. Hines published haunting photographs of American child laborers. See "Child Labor in America, 1908–1912," www.historyplace.com/unitedstates/childlabor/.

32. See Robert Shogun, *The Battle of Blair Mountain: The Story of America's Largest Labor Uprising* (Boulder, Colorado: Westview Press, 2004).

33.*Akron Times-Press,* November 15, 1931. See also Cheri Goldner, "Welsh Ancestors of Summit County," *Past Pursuits: A Newsletter of the Special Collections Division of the Akron-Summit County Library,* Vol.7, No.2 (Akron: Summer 2008): 12, 4, http://www.akronlibrary.org/images/Divisions/SpecCol/images/PastPursuits/pursuits72.pdf.

34. Davis, *A History of Tallmadge Coal.*

35. Ronald L. Lewis, *Welsh Americans: A History of Assimilation in the Coalfields* (Chapel Hill, NC: University of North Carolina Press, 2008), 64.

36. Boryczka and Cary, *No Strength Without Union,* 66.

37. *Akron Daily Beacon,* May 26, 1874.

38. Preamble to 1890 UMWA Constitution.

39. Boryczka and Cary, *No Strength Without Union,* 66.

40. Ibid.

41. *Akron Daily Beacon,* September 30, 1870.

42. Davis, *A History of Tallmadge Coal,* 22.

43. *Stark County Democrat,* September 14, 1870.

44. *Summit County Beacon,* June 1, 1865.

45. *Akron Daily Beacon,* May 13, 1870.

46. Ibid, August 30, 1870.

47. UAA Summit County Historical Society, Box A1.

48. *Daily Beacon,* August 12, 1870.

49. Davis, *A History of Tallmadge Coal,* 22.

50. *Stark County Democrat,* November 10, 1870.

51. For a sympathetic treatment of a vilified union, see Anthony Bimba, *The Molly Maguires: The True Story of Labor's Martyred Pioneers in the Coalfields* (New York: International Publishers, 1992).

52. *Summit County Beacon,* June 7, 1876.

53. *Stark County Democrat,* July 27, 1876.

54. Ibid, May 1, 1876.

55. *Daily Beacon,* January 18, 1871.

56. The wave of strikes lasted from June to December and is the subject of numerous articles in the *Daily Beacon* at the time.

57. *Daily Beacon,* January 2, 1877.

58. Mandel, "Jim McCartan, Rebel."

59. *Akron Daily Beacon,* July 6, 7, 8, 13, 1880.

60. Ibid, July 6, 1880.

61. Ibid, May 21, 1890.

62. Ibid, April 25, 1896.

63. J. E. George, "The Coal Miners' Strike of 1897," *Quarterly Journal of Economics,* Vol. 12, No. 2 (January 1898): 186.

64. Akron *Daily Beacon,* January 26, 1898.

65. *Stark County Democrat,* August 14, 1876.

66. Davis, *A History of Tallmadge Coal,* 23–24.

67. Ann Harris, "Abandoned coal mines," Dept. Geological and Environmental Sciences, Youngstown State University, 2009, mines.ysu.edu/mines_by_county.php?state_Ohio&link=Summit.

68. Kristine Gill, "Abandoned Mines Pose Some Threat in Summit County," June 5, 2008, https://www.thesuburbanite.com/x61385611/Abandoned-mines-pose-some-threat-in-Summit-county.

69. Orwell, "Down the Mine."

70. Grismer, *Akron and Summit County,* (Akron, OH: Summit County Historical Society, c.1951), 377.

71. *ABJ,* February 19, 1941.

72. Ibid, November 13, 1945.

73. Ibid, February 25, 1946.

74. Austin, "Local Coal for the Akron-Canton Industrial District," 84, 86.

75. Ibid, 84.

76. Evelyn Gertrude Weston, "Wadsworth, Ohio: A Manufacturing Suburb of Akron, Ohio." (master's thesis, Department of Geography and Geology, Kent State University, Kent, Ohio, 1940). 8, 19.

77. Karl Marx and Frederick Engels, *The Communist Manifesto, in Selected Works, Vol. One* (Moscow: Progress Publishers, 1959), 115.

CHAPTER 5

1. Daniel Nelson, *Managers and Workers: Origins of the Twentieth-Century Factory System in the United States 1880–1920, Second Edition* (Madison: University of Wisconsin Press, 1995), Table 3, 8–9.

2. Wolf, "The *Akron Beacon Journal,*" 478.

3. *ABJ,* November 12, 1900.

4. Hugh Allen, *Rubber's Home Town: The Real-Life Story of Akron* (New York: Stratford House, 1949).

5. *Appeal to Reason,* July 25, 1914.

6. House, "Birth of a Union," 1978. 3.

7. In 1915, the US unemployment rate was 9.7 percent. This declined to 4.8 percent the following year, and fell to a low of 1.4 percent in 1918. The rate shot up again to 12 percent in 1920–21. Bureau of Labor Statistics, "The Life of American Workers in 1915," *Monthly Labor Review,* February 2016, https://www.bls.gov/opub/mlr/2016/article/the-life-of-american-workers-in-1915.htm.

8. Karl Marx and Frederick Engels, "Manifesto of the Communist Party," in Karl Marx and Frederick Engels, *Selected Works, Vol. 1* (Moscow: Progress Publishers, 1969), 114.

9. Cited in *Archie Green, Wobblies, Pile Butts, and Other Heroes: Laborlore Explorations* (Chicago: University of Illinois Press, 1993), 151.

10. University of Akron Archives (hereinafter UAA) B. F. Goodrich Files. Labor Relations Box D2, B. F. Goodrich D2–13, Wage Scale 1902.

11. Daniel Nelson, *American Rubber Workers,* 10.

12. Rosswurm, "A Strike in the Rubber City," 9–12.

13. Karl Grismer, *Akron and Summit County,* 365.

14. Ibid.

15. *International Socialist Review,* (*ISR)* Vol. XIII, No. 9, (March 1913).

16. House, "Birth of a Union," 3.

17. Marx and Engels, *Manifesto of the Communist Party,* 115.

18. Alfred Lief, *The Firestone Story: A History of the Firestone Tire & Rubber Company,* (New York: McGraw-Hill, 1951), 71.

19. *25 Years of the URW: A Quarter Century Panorama of Democratic Unionism* (Akron, OH: United Rubber, Cork, Linoleum and Plastic Workers of America, AFL-C.I.O, 1960). No page numbers.

20. *ISR,* (April 1913).

21. This would be worth around $1,920 in 2017. Calculated using MeausuringWorth.com, https://www.measuringworth.com/calculators/uscompare/relativevalue.php.

22. *Akron Press,* March 16, 1913.

23. House, "Birth of a Union," 3. More generally, see Kathleen L. Endres, *Rosie the Rubber Worker: Women Workers in Akron's Rubber Factories During World War II,* (Kent, OH: Kent State University Press, 2000).

24. *Akron Press,* March 11, 1913. Calculation of purchasing power today based on MeasuringWorth, https://www.measuringworth.com/calculators/uscompare /relativevalue.php.

25. *ISR,* (April 15, 1913).

26. *Akron Press,* March 17, 1913.

27. *Los Angeles Herald,* September 15, 1915.

28. Ann Schofield, "Rebel Girls and Union Maids: The Woman Question in the Journals of the AFL and the IWW," *Feminist Studies,* Vol. 9, No. 2 (Summer 1983), 336.

29. Mari Jo Buhle, *Women and American Socialism, 1870–1920* (Urbana & Chicago: University of Illinois Press, 1981), 150–151.

30. See Sally M. Miller, "For White Men Only: The Socialist Party of America and Issues of Gender, Ethnicity and Race," *Journal of the Gilded Age and Progressive Era,* Vol. 2, No. 3, New Perspectives on Socialism I, July 2003, 283–302.

31. *ABJ,* February 26, 1906.

32. Lief, *The Firestone Story,* 73.

33. Nelson, *Rubber Workers & Organized Labor,* 20.

34. Lief, *The Firestone Story,* 73.

35. *Appeal to Reason,* July 25, 1914.

36. Endres, *Rosie the Rubber Worker,* 25, 30, and Rosswurm, "A Strike in the Rubber City," 13.

37. This may have been the second sit-down strike in US labor history. See Rosswurm, "A Strike in the Rubber City," 19. Paul Litchfield mentions the strike in his *Industrial Voyage. My Life as an Industrial Lieutenant* (New York: Doubleday, 1954), 77.

38. *ABJ,* October 29, 1900.

39. House, "Birth of a Union," 2.

40. John Newton Thurber, *Rubber Workers' History (1935–1955),* (Akron, OH: Public Relations Dept., URCLPWA, 1956), 3–4; Nelson, Rubber Workers & Organized Labor, 12, 21; Alfred Winslow Jones, *Life, Liberty and Property: A*

Story of Conflict and a Measurement of Conflicting Rights (Philadelphia: J. B. Lippincott, 1941), 74; and *ISR,* (April 15, 1913).

41. *ABJ,* September 13, 1902.

42. Ibid.

43. Ibid, September 17, 1902.

44. Ibid, September 20, 1902.

45. Ibid, September 23, and September 24, 1902.

46. Ibid, October 10, and 25, December 6, 1902, and October 12, 1903.

47. Thurber, *Rubber Workers' History,* 3–4; Nelson, *Rubber Workers & Organized Labor,* 12, 21; and Jones, *Life, Liberty and Property,* 74.

48. House, "Birth of a Union," 2.

49. Rosswurm, "A Strike in the Rubber City," 23.

50. Howard and Ralph Wolf, *Rubber: A Story of Glory and Greed,* (New York: Covici-Friede, 1936), 499.

51. *Appeal to Reason,* May 6, 1911.

52. *ISR,* (April 15, 1913), 718.

53. Rosswurm, "A Strike in the Rubber City," 25, and *ABJ,* June 6, 1908.

54. *ABJ,* March 23, 1911.

55. Wolfs, *Rubber: A Story of Glory and Greed,* 499.

56. Ibid, 497–499.

57. *ABJ* May 27, 1908.

58. *Appeal to Reason,* July 25, 1914 and *ABJ,* April 19, 1911.

59. *ABJ,* June 3, 1914.

60. House, "Birth of a Union," 3.

61. Rosswurm, "A Strike in the Rubber City," 31–33.

62. Nelson, *Rubber Workers & Organized Labor,* 18.

63. Lief, *The Firestone Story,* 65.

64. *ISR,* (April 15, 1913).

65. Rosswurm, "A Strike in the Rubber City," 31.

66. *ISR,* (April 15, 1913).

67. Frederick Winslow Taylor, *Principles of Scientific Management,* 1911, http://melbecon.unimelb.edu/het/taylor/sciman.htm.

68. David Montgomery, *The Fall of the House of Labor: The Workplace, the State, and American Labor Activism, 1865–1925* (Cambridge: Cambridge University Press, 1989), 254.

69. See Charles D. Wrege and Amadeo G. Perroni, "Taylor's Pig Tale: A Historical Analysis of Frederick W. Taylor's Pig-Iron experiments," *Academy of Management Journal,* Vol. 17 (March 1974): 6–27. For a devastating critique of Taylorism, see Braverman, *Labor and Monopoly Capital,* 1998.

70. Taylor, *Principles of Scientific Management,* Chapter 1: "Fundamentals of Scientific Management."

71. V. I. Lenin, trans. Bernard Isaacs and Joe Fineberg, "The Taylor System—Man's Enslavement by the Machine," *Put Pravdy,* No. 35, March 13, 1914, https://www.marxists.org/archive/lenin/works/1914/mar/13.htm. However, after the October Revolution, Lenin viewed Taylorism more favorably and under Stalin, a separate caste of "socialist" managers enforced Taylorist methods. See John Bellamy Foster, "The Meaning of Work in Sustainable Society," *Monthly Review,* Vol. 69, No. 4 (September 2017), 1–14; Braverman, *Labor and Monopoly Capital,* 8–9; and Miklós Haraszti, *A Worker in a Workers' State* (New York: Penguin Books, 1977).

72. House, "Birth of a Union," 3.

73. Wolfs, *A Story of Glory and Greed,* 501.

74. *ISR* (April 15, 1913).

75. UAA Goodyear History Box 9. P.W. Litchfield, "Current Trends in Industry," address given November 20, 1929 in Boston Massachusetts to the New England Council, a local business association organized by New England state governors.

76. *ISR* (April 15, 1913).

77. *ABJ,* December 11, 1908.

78. "Life expectancy by Age, 1850–2011," Infoplease, https://www.infoplease.com/us/mortality/life-expectancy-age-1850–2011.

79. "Working Conditions in Factories," *Gale Encyclopedia of US Economic History,* ed. Thomas Riggs, 2nd ed., Vol. 3, 1484–1486. U.S. History in Context.

80. David Giffels, "Readin', Writin' and Route 21: The Road from West Virginia to Ohio" in Mari-Lynn Evans et al, eds., *The Appalachians: America's First and Last Frontier* (New York: Random House, 2004), 147.

81. The U.S Department of Labor warns that "Hydrogen sulfide gas causes a wide range of health effects. Workers are primarily exposed to hydrogen sulfide by breathing it. The effects depend on how much hydrogen sulfide you breathe and for how long. Exposure to very high concentrations can quickly lead to death." The effects of inhalation of the gas at various concentrations is described by the United States Department of Labor, Occupational Safety Health Administration. "Hydrogen Sulfide," https://www.osha.gov/SLTC/hydrogensulfide/hazards.html.

82. House, "Birth of a Union," 3.

83. Rosswurm, "A Strike in Rubber City," 35.

84. *Akron Press,* March 5, 1913.

85. University of Akron Archives (UAA). Goodyear Advertising Box 1.

86. Rosswurm, "A Strike in the Rubber City," 70–71.

87. Endres, *Rosie the Rubber Worker,* 99.

88. UAA URW Box 9–15. International Industrial Hygiene, Misc. K – P, before 1980 Box 2 of 2. See also P. J. Baxter and J. B. Werner, *Mortality in the British Rubber Industries,* 1967–76 (London: Health and Safety Executive, 1980).

89. International Agency for Research on Cancer, "Occupational Exposures in the Rubber-Manufacturing Industry," 2012, https://monographs.iarc.fr/wp-content/uploads/2018/06/mono100F-36.pdf.

90. See Sarah Levitt, "Manchester Mackintoshes: A History of the Rubberized Garment Trade" Textile History, 17 (1), 55 (1986), and "The Use of Bi-Sulphide of Carbon," *The India-Rubber and Gutta-Percha Trades Journal,* September 30, 1898.

91. UAA URW Box 9- 15. International Industrial Hygiene, Misc. K–P, before 1980 Box 2 of 2.

92. UAA URW Local 5 (B. F. Goodrich) B`ox A1, *The Airbag,* October 4, 1942.

93. Roger W. Shuy, "Language Call. Benny Come Home," January 6, 2007, http://itre.cis.upenn.edu/~myl/languagelog/archives/004012.html. Shuy reports that he had been recently approached by lawyers representing

workers who were suing their employers over diseases contracted by benzene use.

94. This is only one of a plethora of deleterious effects of aniline dyes on the human body. See Agency for Toxic Substances and Diseases Registry, ToxFAQs for Aniline, http://www.atsdr.cdc.gov/tfacts171.html.

95. Raw rubber becomes runny in hot weather and becomes hard and cracks in cold. The chemist Charles Goodyear discovered that if he heated rubber to high temperatures—a process he called vulcanization—these flaws can be rectified.

96. UAA, B. F. Goodrich NA1–1. Chronology of B. F. Goodrich (1870–1948).

97. Wolfs, Rubber: A Story of Glory and Greed.

98. UAA, B. F. Goodrich NA1–1. Chronology of B. F. Goodrich (1870–1948).

99. Endres, *Rosie the Rubber Worker,* 75.

100. Ibid, 89.

101. Joyce Dyer, *Gum-Dipped: A Daughter Remembers Rubber Town* (Akron, OH: The University of Akron Press, 2003), 95.

102. Roger W. Shuy, "Tireworker Terms," *American Speech,* (1964): 268–69.

103. UAA URW International Files Box 9-19. I.H. Heat Stress, Box 2 of 2.

104. US Department of Labor, Bureau of Labor Statistics, Industrial Poisons Used in the Rubber Industry (Washington, DC: Government Printing Office, 1915), https://fraser.stlouisfed.org/files/docs/publications/bls/bls_0179_1915.pdf.

105. Cited in Rosswurm, "A Strike in the Rubber City," 37.

106. US Department of Labor, Industrial Poisons, 56.

107. *ABJ,* July 4, 1913.

108. *ABJ,* December 2, 1912.

109. Nelson, *Rubber Workers & Organized Labor,* 23.

110. *Akron Press,* March 17, 1913.

111. *ISR* (April 15, 1913).

112. The average American hourly pay in 1909 was $3.80 according to Donald M. Fisk, "American Labor in the 20th Century," US Bureau of Labor Statistics, January 30, 2003, https://www.bls.gov/opub/mlr/cwc/american-labor-in-the-20th-century.pdf

113. Nelson, *Rubber Workers & Organized Labor,* 8.

114. Antonio Gramsci, "Taylorism and the Mechanisation of the Worker," *Selections from The Prison Notebooks* (London: Electric Book Company, 1999), 610, abahlali.org/files/Gramsci.pdf.

115. *ISR* (April 15, 1913).

116. Wolf, "The *Akron Beacon Journal*," 519.

117. Lief, *The Firestone Story*, 66."

CHAPTER 6

1. *Akron Beacon and Republican*, January 13, 1894.

2. *ABJ*, January 27, 1894.

3. Ibid, March 4, 1899.

4. *Akron Beacon and Republican*, August 6, 1897. See also the entry for Keinard in Michel Cordillot, *La Sociale en Amérique: dictionnaire bibliographique du mouvement social francophone aux Etats-Unis, 1848–1922*, Vol. 9 (Paris: Editions de l'Atelier, 2002), 243.

5. *ABJ*, March 3, May 5, and December 18, 1897.

6. Frederick Engels, Preface to the American edition of *The Condition of the Working Class in England* (Originally published 1887). Available at Marxists Internet Archive, https://www.marxists.org/archive/marx/works/1887/01/26.htm

7. Edward Bibbins Aveling and Eleanor Marx, *The Working Class Movement in America* (London: Swan Sonnenschein, 1891), 145–147.

8. Morris Hillquit, "Daniel De Leon and the 1899 Split of the SLP." Taken from Hillquit's *Loose Leaves from a Busy Life* (New York: Macmillan, 1934), 45–54. Available at Marxists Internet Archive, https://www.marxists.org/history/usa/parties/spusa/1934/0000-hillquit-ondeleon.pdf.

9. The SLP still exists and claims to be the world's second oldest Marxist party. It held its thirty-sixth National Convention at The University of Akron in 1983, but it has never been much more than a fringe phenomenon. The party's 1983 platform is available at https://www.marxists.org/history/usa/eam/slp/platform/plat1983.pdf.

10. So-called by De Leon because he said they were "jumping the party line." See Daniel De Leon and the Founding of American Socialism at https://www.marxist.com/daniel-de-leon-and-founding-of-american-socialism-1.htm.

11. Ibid, November 12, 1900.

12. For a recent re-evaluation of the SPA, see Paul Heideman, "The Rise and Fall of the Socialist Party of America," *Jacobin*, February 20, 2017, https://www.jacobinmag.com/2017/02/rise-and-fall-socialist-party-of-america.

13. *ABJ*, November 27, 1906.

14. Ibid, March 5, and September 4, 1902.

15. Ibid, September 9, and September 14, 1904.

16. Ibid, October 21, and November 10, 1910.

17. Heideman, "The Rise and Fall of the Socialist Party of America," 3.

18. *ABJ*, July 29, 1905.

19. Ibid, August 27, 1906.

20. Ibid, May 16, 1908.

21. Ibid, November 11, 1910.

22. *Mapping American Social Movements Through the 20th Century. Socialist Party of America History and Geography*. Pacific Northwest Labor and Civil Rights Projects, University of Washington, 2015, http://depts.washington.edu/moves/SP_intro.shtml.

23. For discussions of the Party's municipal successes, see Richard W. Judd, *Socialist Cities: Municipal Politics and the Grass Roots of American Socialism* (Albany, N.Y: State University of New York, 1989) and Arthur E. Matteo, "Socialist Municipal Administrations in the Progressive Era: A Case Study of Four Ohio Cities, 1911–1915," http://www.ohioacademyofhistory.org/wp-content/uploads/2013/04/DeMatteo.pdf.

24. William L. Abbott, *The American Labor Heritage* (Honolulu: University of Hawai'i Press, 1967), 32.

25. Wolf, "The *Akron Beacon Journal*," 516.

26. Jay Jennings, "Campaign Tactics of Eugene Debs in the 1912 Presidential Election," The Public Purpose, Vol. III, (2005): 65, https://www.american.edu/spa/publicpurpose/upload/Campaign-Tactics-of-Eugene-Debs-in-the-1912-Presidential-Campaign.pdf.

27. *ABJ*, May 27, and June 1, 1908. He polled only 4.54 percent of the vote according to Our Campaigns, https://www.ourcampaigns.com/CandidateDetail.html?CandidateID=185584.

28. *ABJ*, October 28, July 16, and October 29, 1908.

29. *Akron Press*, June 20, 1913.

30. Thus described in Ray Ginger, with an introduction by Mike Davis, *The Bending Cross: A Biography of Eugene V. Debs* (Chicago: Haymarket Books, 2007), 347.

31. Eugene V. Debs, "My Memorial Tribute," in Charles Baker, ed., "Marguerite Prevey in Memoriam," (Cleveland, OH: Charles Baker, 1925). Bound booklet, B p928m, in Ohio Historical Society Archives, Columbus, Ohio.

32. Ginger, *The Bending Cross,* 347.

33. Nelson, *American Rubber Workers,* 8.

34. Mabel D. Curry, "A Universal Mother," in "Marguerite Prevey in Memoriam."

35. *ABJ,* February 26, 1906.

36. US Department of Labor, Bureau of Labor Statistics, Summary of the Report on Condition of Woman and Child Wage Earners in the United States, Dec. 1915 (Washington, DC: Government Printing Office, 1916), 21–22, https://fraser.stlouisfed.org/files/docs/publications/bls_wis/bls_175_womeninindustry5.pdf.

37. Ibid, Charles Baker, "Mother Marguerite."

38. Ibid, George Fitzpatrick, "A Noble Friend."

CHAPTER 7

1. Hugh McAlister, *Steve Holworth of the Oldham Works: The Story of a Boy Who Chose a Career in the Rubber Industry* (Akron, OH: Saalfield Publishing, 1930), 138. McAlister was Margaret Alison Johansen's nom-de-plume. This is a thinly disguised, fictionalized account of the strike, written from a relentlessly anti-labor viewpoint.

2. Grismer, *Akron and Summit County,* 366.

3. *ISR* (April 1913), 712.

4. Lief, *The Firestone Story,* 66.

5. *ABJ,* February 13, 1913.

6. UAA, Goodyear History Box 2: W. D. Shilts, "The First Ten Years," Book 3, 1912–1916, 101. Bound typescript.

7. *ABJ,* February 13, 1913.

8. Grismer, *Akron and Summit County,* i.

9. John Tully, *The Devil's Milk: A Social History of Rubber* (New York: Monthly Review Press, 2011), 153.

10. A. S. McCormick, *The History of Medicine in Summit County, Ohio* (New York: Hobson Book Press, 1946), 48.

11. Litchfield, *Industrial Voyage,* 131.

12. UAA B. F. Goodrich Files, Labor Relations Box D2–16. Press clipping from unknown publication. "Wage List Shown by Rubber Strike," April 12, 1913.

13. McAlister, *Steve Holworth,* 138–146.

14. *ABJ,* April 2, 1935.

15. Ibid, February 24, 1913.

16. Ibid, February 28, 1913.

17. *Akron Press,* March 14, 1913.

18. *Solidarity,* August 13, and September 14, 1912.

19. Wolfs, *A Story of Glory and Greed,* 497.

20. UAA B. F. Goodrich Files. Box NA1–48, Reminiscences of David M. Goodrich.

21. *ABJ,* February 25, 1913.

22. See Joseph R. Conlin, *At the Point of Production: The Local History of the IWW,* (Westport, CT: Greenwood Press, 1981).

23. Grismer, *Akron and Summit County,* 365

24. Lief, *The Firestone Story,* 70.

25. Ibid, 89–90.

26. Wolfs, *Rubber: A Story of Glory and Greed,* 499.

27. Bryan D. Palmer, *James P. Cannon and the Origins of the American Revolutionary Left, 1890–1928* (Urbana and Chicago: University of Illinois Press, 2007), 61–63.

28. *Solidarity,* March 15, 1913.

29. Palmer, *James P. Cannon and the Origins,* 61–63.

30. *Akron Press,* February 18, 1913.

31. Ibid, February 25, 1913.

32. *ABJ,* February 17, 1913.

33. Harriman, "5-paragraph story." The author based this on reports in the paper from the time of the strike.

34. Shilts, "The First Ten Years," 101.

35. Litchfield, *Industrial Voyage,* p.131

36. *Appeal to Reason,* October 10, 1908.

37. Ibid, July 25, 1914.

38. *ISR* (April 15, 1913), 712, and Rosswurm, "A Strike in the Rubber City," 82.

39. *Appeal to Reason,* September 5, 1914.

40. Rosswurm, "A Strike in Rubber City," 78.

41. *ABJ,* March 8, 1913.

42. *Akron Press,* March 8, 1913.

43. *Appeal to Reason,* July 25, 1914.

44. Rosswurm, "A Strike in the Rubber City," 83.

45. *Akron Press,* March 10, 1913.

46. Rosswurm, "A Strike in Rubber City," 78–79 and Grismer, *Akron and Summit County,* 368.

47. *ISR* (April 15, 1913), 712.

48. *Appeal to Reason,* July 25, 1914.

49. James McCartan, undated fragment on the 1913 strike. Bowling Green State University (BGSU) Center for Archival Collections, MS 468 Sam Pollock Papers. Box 9, Personal Papers, Folder 16, James McCartan Correspondence.

50. Ibid, Folder 18 James McCartan: Literary productions, Walt Davis, unpublished article for *Labor Today,* January 7, 1963.

51. BGSU Center for Archival Collections, pOG 2563 Oral History Interview with Mr. Paul Sebestyen (Sebastian) on Akron's Rubber Strike and on general Ideological Background, July 8, 1969, by Roy Wortman, Department of History, Ohio State University, Columbus.

52. Akron Strike Bulletin. $15 is worth about $300 today.

53. Grismer, *Akron and Summit County,* 368.

54. Akron Strike Bulletin.

55. *Appeal to Reason,* July 2, 1914.

56. *Akron Press,* February 12, 1913.

57. Ibid, February 21. 1913.

58. Ibid, February 17. and 25, 1913.

59. *Appeal to Reason,* July 25, 1914.

60. *Akron Press,* March 11, 1913.

61. Akron Strike Bulletin.

62. Ohio Constitution [the 1851 Constitution with Amendments to 2015], https://www.legislature.ohio.gov/laws/ohio-constitution.

63. Rosswurm, "A Strike in the Rubber City," 83.

64. *Appeal to Reason,* July 25, 1914.

CHAPTER 8

1. Honoré de Balzac, "To the Reader," *The Elixir of Life* (New York: Windham Press, 2013).

2. Andrea Tone, *The Business of Benevolence: Industrial Paternalism in America* (Ithaca, NY: Cornell University Press, 1997), 22.

3. Cited in Palmer, *James P. Cannon and the Origins,* 399–400 n.

4. *Appeal to Reason,* July 25, 1914 and *ABJ,* January 16, 1914.

5. *ABJ,* October 31, 1914.

6. *Solidarity,* January 17, 1914.

7. *Appeal to Reason,* July 25, 1914.

8. Ibid and Rosswurm, "A Strike in the Rubber City," 92.

9. Nelson, *American Rubber Workers,* 30, 35.

10. *Appeal to Reason,* March 6, 1915.

11. Ibid, July 25, 1914.

12. Cited in Harry W. Laidler, *Boycotts and the Labor Struggle: Economic and Legal Aspects* (New York: John Lane, 1913), 290–293.

13. *Appeal to Reason,* July 25, 1914.

14. Nelson, *American Rubber Workers,* 35 and Rosswurm, "A Strike in the Rubber City," 65–66, 76.

15. *Akron Press,* February 17, 1913.

16. *Appeal to Reason,* July 25, 1914.

17. Nelson, *American Rubber Workers,* 26–29.

18. *Appeal to Reason,* July 25, 1914.

19. Rosswurm, "A Strike in the Rubber City," 56.

20. Nelson, *American Rubber Workers,* 29 and Rosswurm, "A Strike in the Rubber City," 56.

21. Ibid, 37.

22. *Akron Press,* March 24, 1913.

23. On the organization's origins among itinerant workers in the western states, see James P. Cannon, "The IWW" Available at Marxists Internet Archive, https://www.marxists.org/archive/cannon/works/1955/iww.htm.

24. UAA Goodyear History Box 2. Shilts History, 1912–1916. Unpublished bound typescript, 101.

25. Bowling Green State University, Center for Archival Collections, MS 468 Sam Pollock Papers, Box 9, Personal Papers, Folder 16 James McCartan Correspondence. James McCartan, undated fragment on the 1913 strike,

26. Rosswurm, "A Strike in the Rubber City," 54.

27. Ibid, 42.

28. *Akron Press,* May 2, 1913.

29. James McCartan undated fragment on the 1913 strike.

30. John Lee Maples, "The Akron, Ohio Ku Klux Klan, 1921–1928," (master's thesis, The University of Akron, 1974), 38.

31. Ibid, 87.

32. *Akron Press,* April 18, 1913.

33. IWW Akron Strike Bulletin.

34. Nelson, *American Rubber Workers,* 37.

35. Palmer, *James P. Cannon and the Origins,* 66.

36. *ABJ,* March 25, 1913.

37. Ibid, March 31, 1913.

38. Cited in Shilts History, 110–111.

39. 25 Years of the URW.

40. James McCartan, undated fragment on the 1913 strike.

41. Eric Loomis, *A History of America in Ten Strikes* (New York: The New Press, 2018), 7.

CHAPTER 9

1. See Nelson, *American Rubber Workers,* 42.

2. However, the Democratic Socialists of America, which has its roots in the Socialist Party, claimed a membership of 50,000 in 181 locals in 2018. (*New York Times,* April 20, 1918). There is an Akron DSA local.

3. The Knights are a "fraternal and secret society" organized like the Masons along Lodge lines.

4. *Appeal to Reason,* July 25, 1914.

5. *ABJ,* April 4, 1914.

6. *Akron Evening Times,* October 2, 1914.

7. *ABJ,* March 14, 1913.

8. *Akron Evening Times,* October 10, 1914.

9. *ABJ,* May 21, 1915.

10. Ibid, January 27, and April 28, 1915.

11. Dale Fetherling, *Mother Jones, The Miners' Angel* (Carbondale, ILL: Southern Illinois Press, 1974), 154.

12. The text of Wilson's 1915 "disloyalty" speech can be viewed in Lapham's Quarterly. https://www.laphamsquarterly.org/fear/hate-speech

13. Wolf, "The *Akron Beacon Journal,*" 588.

14. *ABJ,* August 2, 1934.

15. Ibid, February 26, and April 4, 1917.

16. Robert Justin Goldstein, *Political Repression in Modern America: From 1870 to 1976* (Chicago: University of Illinois Press, 2001), 121.

17. *ABJ,* May 30, and June 2, 1917.

18. Ibid, July 15, 1918.

19. Ginger, *The Bending Cross,* 355.

20. Bernard Mandel, "Jim McCartan, Rebel," pamphlet held by the Ohio Historical Society, Columbus.

21. Wolf, "The *Akron Beacon Journal,*" 593.

22. Chalmers K. Stewart, "The Past At Our Backs, 1910–1995. Akron-New York." Autobiographical Typescript held by the Tamiment Library, New York University.

23. *ABJ,* September 25, 1937.

24. *The Ohio Socialist,* January 1, 1919.

25. For an account of the meeting, see Ginger, *The Bending Cross,* 355–57.

26. Eugene V. Debs 'Canton Speech' (Chicago, ILL: Socialist Party of the United States, 1918).

27. Ibid, September 14, and 17, 1918.

28. *Cleveland Citizen,* August 24, 1918.

29. Theodore Kornweibel Jr., ed., *Federal Surveillance of Afro-Americans (1917–1925): The First World War, the Red Scare, and the Garvey Movement* (Frederick, MD: University Publications of America, 1985), ix.

30. Equal Justice Initiative. *Lynching in America: Confronting the Legacy of Racial Terror*, https://eji.org/reports/lynching-in-america.

31. Ann Hagedorn, *Savage Peace: Hope and Fear in America, 1919* (New York: Simon & Schuster, 2007), 25, 27.

32. *ABJ*, November 27, 1918.

33. Ibid, June 16, 1919.

34. Ibid, January 3, 1920.

35. Ibid, July 19. 1919.

36. *Cleveland Plain Dealer*, May 21, and July 17, 1919.

37. See, for instance, Joseph W. Sharts, "Communist Labor Heads Arrested! Infamous Freeman Act Used To Crush Political and Industrial Activity of Ohio Workers," *Miami Valley Socialist*, October 24, 1919, http://www.marxisthistory.org/history/usa/parties/cpusa/1919/1024-sharts-ohclparrests.pdf.

38. Mari Jo Buhle, Paul Buhle, and Dan Georgakas, eds., *Encyclopedia of the American Left, Second Edition* (New York: Oxford University Press, 1998), 182.

39. I have not been able to find figures for the Akron local, but out of 201 delegates who met in Cleveland's Acme Hall in October 1919, 170 went with the Communist Party of America, 28 stayed with the Socialist Party, and three opted for the Communist Labor Party. See *the Cleveland Citizen*, October 4, 1919.

40. *ABJ*, December 26, 1921.

41. *Plain Dealer*, March 3, 1927.

42. *ABJ*, March 8, 1921.

43. Ibid, July 11, 1919.

44. Ibid, July 18, 1919.

45. Ibid, May 2, 1921.

46. *Akron Evening Times*, January 22, 1920 and *ABJ*, February 17, 1920.

47. Sharts, "A Great Woman Passes.

48. Baker, "Mother Marguerite."

49. Curry, "Universal Mother."

50. Klara Zetkin, trans. Eden and Cedar Paul, "Through Dictatorship to Democracy" (Glasgow: Socialist Labour Press, 1926), https://www.marxists.org/archive/zetkin/1919/xx/dictdem.htm.

51. Baker, "Mother Marguerite."

52. Kirkpatrick, "A Noble Friend."

53. Reeves, *Twentieth Century America,* 85.

54. Alfred Winslow Jones, *Life, Liberty and Property: A Story of Conflict and a Measurement of Conflicting Rights* (Philadelphia: J. B. Lippincott, 1941), 305.

CHAPTER 10

1. *ABJ,* March 25. 1913.

2. *The Toiler,* September 3. 1920.

3. David M. Kennedy, *Freedom from Fear: The American People in Depression and War, 1929–1945* (New York: Oxford University Press, 1999). ch. 1. Kindle.

4. "A Strike in the Rubber City," 88.

5. *Appeal to Reason,* July 25. 1914.

6. Shilts, Book 3, 1912–1916, 102.

7. *Akron Press,* May 2. 1913.

8. Wolf, "The *Akron Beacon Journal,*" 519.

9. *ABJ,* February 10. 1913.

10. Henry Pfaff Oral History. An oral history interview with long-term Industrial Workers of the World (IWW) member Henry Pfaff, conducted in 1972. Book 17. Henry Pfaff Folio HD8066 B3, v. 17. Ann Allen, Roosevelt University Oral History Project in Labor History, https://libcom.org/history/1972-oral-history-interview-henry-pfaff.

11. *ABJ,* June 3, 1914.

12. John R. Vaughan, *Jottings of a Judge* (Akron, OH: Central Publishing, 1922), 8–9, 66.

13. Henry Pfaff Oral History.

14. Giffels, "Readin', Writin' and Route 21," 143.

15. Jones, *Life, Liberty and Property,* 57.

16. Grismer, *Akron and Summit County,* 378.

17. *ABJ,* August 9, 1970 and Chalmers K. Stewart, "Our Backs to the Past," 12–13.

18. Wolf, "The *Akron Beacon Journal*," 632.

19. *ABJ*, October 19, 1970.

20. Alan Woods, *First World War: A Marxist Analysis of the Great Slaughter*, Part Ten, The USA: War is Good for Business, *In Defence of Marxism*, April 2015, https://www.marxist.com/wwi-part-nine-usa-and-the-war.htm.

21. Wolf, "The *Akron Beacon Journal*," 557.

22. Lief, *The Firestone Story*, 92.

23. Ibid, 89.

24. Quentin J. Skrabec Jr., *Rubber: An American Industrial History*, (Jefferson, NC: McFarland, 2014), 116.

25. UAA Goodyear History Box 4. Address by E. J. Thomas, Goodyear President, to American Trading Company, October 29, 1947.

26. *Cleveland Plain Dealer*, August 29, 1915.

27. Kennedy, *Freedom From Fear*, ch. 1.

28. Wolf, "The *Akron Beacon Journal*," 557, 615.

29. Woods, "The U.S.A. and the War."

30. *ABJ*, January 4, 1921.

31. Wolf, "The *Akron Beacon Journal*," 623.

32. Ibid, 1.

33. Stewart, "The Past at Our Backs," 93.

34. C. R. McLean and Wilbur C. Ammon, Unpublished typescript, WPA Writers' Project, c.1938, no page numbers. Western Reserve Historical Society, Cleveland, MSS.2970.

35. Wolf, "The *Akron Beacon Journal*," 555.

36. *ABJ*, March 7, 1906.

37. Grismer, *Akron and Summit County*, 379.

38. McLean and Ammon, unpublished typescript. In 2014 values, the beds would cost somewhere between $17.70 and $473 per shift or around $53.10 per day.

39. *Akron Press*, February 5, 1913.

40. Ibid, March 9, 1913.

41. Ibid, June 20, and June 25, 1913.

42. *ABJ*, August 8, 1934.

43. Ibid, February 8, 1934.

44. Charles T. Nesbitt, "Akron's Public Health Problem," *The Ohio Public Health Journal,* (February 9, 1918): 87.

45. Dawn L. Corley, "Spanish Influenza in Summit County, Ohio, 1918–1920," (master's thesis, The University of Akron, May 1987), 65.

46. Cited in the *ABJ,* January 13, 1935.

47. Editorial, *Akron Daily Beacon,* January 3, 1878.

48. Wolf, "The *Akron Beacon Journal,*" 468–469.

49. Richard E. Mack, *Memoir of a Cold War Soldier* (Kent, OH: Kent State University Press, 2001), 3.

50. McGovern, *Written in the Hills,* 120.

51. UAA Summit County Historical Society. Box D3. Dixon G. Gale 1912–1954 Chief Sanitary Engineer, City of Akron, Papers.

52. Wolf, "The *Akron Beacon Journal,*" 450

53. Lief, *The Firestone Story,* 57.

54. Wolf, "The *Akron Beacon Journal,*" 581

55. Grismer, *Akron and Summit County,* 378.

56. Kennedy, *Freedom From Fear,* ch. 1.

57. Lief, *The Firestone Story,* 63.

58. *ABJ,* April 1, 1907.

59. Blackford and Kerr, *B. F. Goodrich,* 151.

60. Jeffrey Franks, email to author, April 11, 2014.

61. Kennedy, *Freedom From Fear,* ch. 1.

62. Reeves, *Twentieth Century America,* 4.

63. *ABJ,* April 11, 1905.

64. Ibid.

65. Leon J. Kamin, *The Science and Politics of IQ* (Harmondsworth: Penguin Books, 1974), 31.

66. Carl C. Brigham, *A Study of American Intelligence* (Princeton, NJ: Princeton University Press, 1923), 210.

67. David R. Roediger and Elizabeth D. Esch, *The Production of Difference: Race and the Management of Labor in US History* (New York: Oxford University Press, 2012).

68. Paul Spickard, *Almost All Aliens: Immigration, Race, and Colonialism in American History and Identity* (New York: Routledge, 2007), 2. See also Reeves, *Twentieth Century America,* 90–91.

69. McKenney, *Industrial Valley,* 105.

70. Mike Davis, "Why the US Working Class is Different," 18–19.

71. *Akron Press,* September 4, 1913.

72. *The Coagulator,* Class of 1929. Ginaven Collection, Akron-Summit County Library.

73. House, "Birth of a Union."

74. "*ABJ,* November 4, 1915.

75. Shilts, 121.

76. *The Industrial Pioneer: An Illustrated Labor Magazine,* August 1925.

77. *ABJ,* August 31, 1916.

78. Ibid, September 5, 6, and 7, 1916.

79. Ibid, October 1, 1919.

80. Nelson, *American Rubber Workers,* 71.

81. Wolf, "The *Akron Beacon Journal,*" 586.

82. *ABJ,* November 10, 1917 and March 28, 1918.

83. Wolf, "The *Akron Beacon Journal,*" 591.

84. *ABJ,* January 23, and June 10, 1918.

85. The *ABJ* published numerous articles on strikes in the industry in 1923. The report on Newman's attempt to form a union appeared on January 13, 1923.

86. Pfaff, Oral History.

87. House, "Birth of a Union."

88. Lief, *The Firestone Story,* 95–96.

89. Ibid, 77.

90. John Williamson, *Dangerous Scot: The Life and Work of an American "Undesirable"* (New York: International Publishers, 1969), 111.

91. Braverman, *Labor and Monopoly Capital,* 60, 104.

92. *Saturday Evening Post,* March 11, 1916.

93. House, "Birth of a Union," 3.

94. Tone, *The Business of Benevolence,* 2.

95. For the "labor control" approach to welfare capitalism, see Irving Bernstein, *The Lean Years: A History of the American Worker, 1920–1933* (Baltimore: Penguin Books, 1966).

96. Tone, *The Business of Benevolence,* 7–8.

97. *Industrial Pioneer,* August 1925.

98. Lief, *The Firestone Story,* 83. See also Clarice Finley Lewis, *A History of Firestone Park* (Akron, OH: Firestone Park Citizens' Council, 1986), and Kevan Delaney Frazier, "Model Industrial Subdivisions: Goodyear Heights and Firestone Park and the Town Planning Movement in Akron, Ohio, 1910–1920." (master's thesis, Kent State University, 1994).

99. Lief, *The Firestone Story,* 221.

100. Blackford and Kerr, *B. F. Goodrich,* 71.

101. *Literary Digest,* February 2, 1918.

102. *Goodyear: A Family Magazine,* May 1920.

103. Frazier, "Model Industrial Subdivisions," 6.

104. Tone, *The Business of Benevolence,* 52.

105. Ibid.

106. For an extended discussion of the attitude of the IWW, the Socialists, and the AFL, see Tone, *The Business of Benevolence,* 182–197.

107. A Rubber Worker, "Rubber Slavery in Akron." See also *Goodyear Tire & Rubber Company: A Study of the Labor Movement* (Akron, OH: Goodyear Tire & Rubber, 1920), 79–82.

108. House, "Birth of a Union," 3.

109. *Industrial Pioneer,* August 1925.

110. *The Toiler,* September 3, 1920.

111. Goodyear, *A Study of the Labor Movement,* 78.

112. *ABJ,* February 7, 1920.

113. *Industrial Pioneer,* August 1925.

114. Wolf, "The *Akron Beacon Journal,*" 623.

115. *ABJ,* January 4, 1921.

116. Ibid, September 7, 1921.

117. Ibid, January 8, 1934.

118. Ibid, May 10, 11, and 24, 1922.

119. Ibid, May 27, and 30, 1922.

120. Ibid, June ,7 and 13, 1922.

121. Ibid, December 5, 1922.

122. *Industrial Pioneer,* August 1925.

123. *ABJ,* December 26, and 29, 1922, and January 2, 3, 4, 8, and 9, 1923.

124. Ibid, January 13, 1923.

125. Ibid, December 14, and 20, 1923.

126. Blackford and Kerr, *B. F. Goodrich,* 87.

127. Ibid. For a discussion of the Bedaux system, see Steven Kreis, "The Diffusion of Scientific Management: The Bedaux Company in America and Britain, 1926–1945," in Daniel Nelson, ed., *A Mental Revolution: Scientific Management Since Taylor* (Columbus: Ohio State University Press, 1992).

128. *ABJ,* January 27, 1923.

129. Ibid, January 15, and 16, 1923. A brief biography of Conboy appears in the Samuel Gompers Papers, http://www.gompers.umd.edu/biographical%20 dictionary.pdf.

130. *ABJ,* January 15, and 22, 1923.

131. *Industrial Pioneer,* August 1925.

132. Ibid.

133. Nelson, *American Rubber Workers,* 96.

134. UAA, John D. House Papers, 1938 – Box 1.

135. Jack Wilson (Widick's pseudonym), "In a Billion Dollar Industry," *New International,* Vol. 2, No. 2, (March 1935), http://www.marxists,org/history/etol /newspaper/ni/vol02/no02/wilson-htm. The group appears to have had a local in Akron in 1926. See The Proletarian Party of America (1920–1930). Party History, http://www.marxisthistory.org/subject/usa/eam/proletarianparty.html.

136. Nelson, *American Rubber Workers,* 71.

137. *ABJ,* May 1, 24, and 26, 1926.

138. *Industrial Pioneer,* August 1925.

139. Kennedy, *Freedom from Fear,* ch. 1.

140. Ibid.

141. *Industrial Pioneer,* August 1925.

142. UAA URW Local 5 (B. F. Goodrich Files). Box A1, *The Airbag,* Newsletter of Local 5, Vol. 3, No. 8, October 18, 1944.

143. UAA, Goodyear History Box 4, Chronological data, Rubber History Book 4.

144. *The Wingfoot Clan,* May 8, 1935.

145. Arthur D. Howden Smith, "The Men who Run America," *Philadelphia Record,* November 22, 1935.

146. UAA Goodyear Files, Goodyear Labor (Personnel) Box 1. Notes for a talk by P. W. Litchfield, September 1934.

147. Western Reserve Historical Society, Cleveland. MSS.2970. C. R. McLean and Wilbur C. Ammon, unpublished typescript, undated.

148. Winslow Jones, *Life, Liberty and Property,* 41.

CHAPTER II

1. Maples, "The Akron, Ohio Ku Klux Klan," 112. Susan Allyn Johnson's thesis, "Industrial Voyagers" is an excellent work on Southern white migration.

2. The exception included of liberal religious leaders and Catholic priests. See Kern and Wilson, *Ohio: A History,* 361.

3. Sojourner Truth, speech delivered at the Women's Convention, Akron, Ohio, 1851. *Modern History Sourcebook,* http://www.fordham.edu/halsall/mod/sojtruth-woman.html.

4. The riot erupted following the arrest of an Black man for the kidnap and sexual molestation of a young white girl. Denied a fair trial, the suspect was later pardoned after serving many years of a lengthy prison term. See, for instance, Harry S. Quine, "The Darkest Night in Akron's History," in C.R. Quine, ed., *The Akron Riot of 1900* (Akron, OH: C. R. Quine, 1951). Also Shirla Robinson McClain, *The Contributions of Blacks in Akron: 1825–1975* (Akron, OH: Akron Gallery of Black History Curriculum Committee, 1996), 17, 70–72.

5. *The Labor Unionist,* September 1, 1883.

6. EJI, *Lynching in America.* The violence was epitomized by the massacre at Tulsa, Oklahoma in 1921, where racist mobs murdered hundreds of black citizens with impunity. See for instance Tulsa Race Massacre, History.com, https://www.history.com/topics/roaring-twenties/tulsa-race-massacre.

7. Reeves, *Twentieth Century America,* 91.

8. Wolf, "The *Akron Beacon Journal*," 111.

9. *Summit County Beacon*, October 25, 1860.

10. James H. Rodabaugh, "The Negro in Ohio," *The Journal of Negro History*, Vol.31, No.1 (January 1946): 15.

11. *Summit Beacon*, February 19, 1845.

12. Rodabaugh, "The Negro in Ohio," 19–20.

13. McClain, *The Contributions of Blacks in Akron*, 92. In 1802, there were only 500–600 Black people residing in all of Ohio. (Rodabaugh, "The Negro in Ohio," 13).

14. Maples, "The Akron, Ohio Ku Klux Klan, 1921–1928," 9.

15. *ABJ*, April 4, 1938.

16. Ibid, May 24, 1940.

17. Ibid, August 10, 1947.

18. Ibid, January 17, 1910.

19. "All America City. History of Akron." It was a token appointment, for the Lively Report, published almost half a century later in 1969, criticized the city's continuing failure to hire Black officers. See Report of the Akron Committee on Civil Disorders, Akron Ohio, April 16, 1969, http://www.ascpl.lib.oh.us/internetresources/sc/OnlineBooks/Commitee-Report-Civildisorders.pdf.

20. Stewart, "The Past at Our Backs."

21. White nonemployees were however welcome to apply. See Frazier, "Model Industrial Subdivisions," 50.

22. In the summer of 1913, for instance, a 125-strong white mob surrounded three North Hill residences occupied by Black people and ordered the occupants to leave. (*Akron Press*, August 13, 1913). In another incident, "a Negro was hung in effigy" in front of a house in a "white" neighborhood as a warning for the occupants to quit. The Black residents organized a mass meeting to protest at the mob's actions: a brave act in a city still haunted by the specter of the 1900 white race riot. (See McClain, *The Contributions of Blacks in Akron*, 95 and *Akron Press*, August 15, 1913). Most people from the Akron Black community had immigrated from the South, where lynching was commonplace, and mobs lynched at least fifteen Black people in Ohio between 1880 and 1940. See Equal Justice Initiative (EJI), *Lynching in America: Confronting the Legacy of Racial Terror*, https://eji.org/reports/lynching-in-america. See also Danny Lewis, "This Map Shows Over a Century of Documented Lynchings in the United States,"

Smithsonian.com, https://www.smithsonianmag.com/smart-news/map-shows-over-a-century-of-documented-lynchings-in-united-states-180961877/.

23. *The Goodyear Worker,* February 1937.

24. Ibid, 164–166.

25. Bowling Green State University Center for Archival Collections. MMS 922. Ohio Labor History Project 14.4.1 Mr. James Turner, Retired Fair Practices Director Rubber Workers International. Interview conducted December 4, 1975, by Carl Clausen, Ann Van Tine, and Patricia Curran in Akron, Ohio.

26. Borsos, *"Talking Union."*

27. Walter E. Klippert, *Reflections of a Rubber Planter: The Autobiography of an Inquisitive Person* (New York: Vintage Press, 1972), 34.

28. Kevin MacDonald, "Henry Ford and the Jewish Question," Review of Neil Baldwin, *Henry Ford and the Jews: the Mass Production of Hate* (New York: Public Affairs, 2001), http://www.kevinmacdonald.net/HenryFord-1.htm.

29. Maples, "The Akron, Ohio Ku Klux Klan," 48.

30. Cited in Andrew Bailey, ed., *First Philosophy: Fundamental Problems and Readings in Philosophy,* Second Edition (Peterborough ONT: Broadview Press, 2011), 860.

31. Octave Mannoni, *Prospero and Caliban: The Psychology of Colonization, Second Edition* (New York: Praeger: 1964).

32. Wolf, "The *Akron Beacon Journal,*" 632.

33. *ABJ,* May 23, 1922.

34. Wolf, "The *Akron Beacon Journal,*" 616.

35. Ibid, 2.

36. Ibid, 16.

37. Ibid.

38. Maples, "The Akron, Ohio Ku Klux Klan," 40.

39. Kymberli Hagelberg, *Wicked Akron: Tales of Rumrunners, Mobsters and Other Rubber City Rogues* (Charleston, SC: The History Press, 2010). Kindle.

40. Maples, "The Akron, Ohio Ku Klux Klan," 26.

41. Ibid, 30.

42. Ibid, 44.

43. Ibid, 95.

44. *Akron Times Press,* July 5, 1925.

45. *Industrial Pioneer,* August 1925. (Published by the IWW)

46. Boryczka and Cary, *No Strength Without Union,* 177.

47. All America City. History of Akron, http://www.ci.akron.oh.us/history/timeline/1900.htm.

48. I am indebted to Stephanie Sulik, a graduate student at the University of Arlington, Texas, for this information, and for drawing my attention to UNIA's activities in the city.

49. *ABJ,* May 11, 1922.

50. Ibid, August 19, 1924.

51. Ibid, September 1, 1924.

52. See Tully, *The Devil's Milk,* 194–98.

53. *ABJ,* March 7, 1925.

54. Ibid, April 2, 1923.

55. See James Ciment, *Another America: The Story of Liberia and the Former Slaves Who Ruled It* (New York: Hill and Wang, 2013).

56. *India Rubber World,* February 1, 1929.

57. Wolf, "The *Akron Beacon Journal,*" 687.

58. Calculated using MeasuringWorth.com, https://www.measuringworth.com/calculators/uscompare/relativevalue.php.

59. Wolf "The *Akron Beacon Journal,*" 691–94.

CHAPTER 12

1. Kern and Wilson, *Ohio: A History,* 379.

2. Cited in Kennedy, *Freedom From Fear,* ch.1.

3. Lief, *The Firestone Story,* 169, 177, 221–222.

4. Milton Derber, "Growth and Expansion," in Milton Derber and Edwin Young, eds., *Labor and the New Deal* (New York: Da Capo Press, 1972), 83.

5. McKenney, *Industrial Valley,* 13, 16, 75, 82.

6. *ABJ,* August 11, 1930.

7. Ibid, June 12, 1930.

8. Wolf, "*The Akron Beacon Journal,*" 54.

9. *ABJ,* April 12, 1970.

10. McKenney, *Industrial Valley,* 21.

11. *ABJ,* June 6, 1932.

12. Ibid, November 18, 1936.

13. Derber, "Growth and Expansion," 83.

14. McKenney, *Industrial Valley,* 87, 155.

15. *ABJ,* September 22, 1975.

16. Ibid, April 25, 1930.

17. Jim Keller, *A Veteran Communist Speaks: The Akron Rubber Strikes of 1936* (Chicago: Workers' Press, 1975), 9.

18. The "class nature" of the Soviet Union was the subject of perennial debates among leftists. Those who did not regard it as "socialist" debated whether it was a "degenerated workers' state," "state capitalist," or "bureaucratic-collectivist" and whether its obnoxious characteristics predated Stalin's rise to power.

19. Rosa Luxemburg, trans. Bertram Wolfe, *The Russian Revolution* (New York: Workers Age Publications, 1940), ch. 8, "Democracy and Dictatorship." Marxists Internet Archive, https://www.marxists.org/archive/luxemburg/1918/russian-revolution/index.htm.

20. McKenney, *Industrial Valley,* 22.

21. *ABJ,* April 22, 1930.

22. Ibid, April 29, 1930.

23. Ibid, May 1, 1930.

24. Ibid, February 25, 1931.

25. *ABJ,* January 2, 1931.

26. Derber, "Growth and Expansion," 88.

27. Wolf, "The *Akron Beacon Journal,*" 712.

28. Socialists and Communists were prominent among the national march organizers. Film of the march, taken by Pathé in Washington, DC, can be viewed at https://www.youtube.com/watch?v=teqB2x5nPfU.

29. *ABJ,* April 4, 1931.

30. See, for instance, Chris Mahin, "The First National Hunger March Confront the U.S. Congress," December 1, 2017, https://chilaborarts.wordpress.com/2017/12/01/6174/.

31. Ibid, August 16, 1932.

32. McKenney, *Industrial Valley,* 51.

33. Ibid, 65.

34. *ABJ,* February 12, 1932.

35. *ABJ,* September 19, 1933.

36. Ibid, December 13, 1933.

37. Ibid, December 15, 1933.

38. Charlie Post, "The Popular Front: Rethinking CPUSA History," *Solidarity,* July–August, 2018, https://solidarity-us.org/atc/63/p2363/. See also Fernando Claudin, *The Communist Movement: From Comintern to Cominform* (New York: Peregrine, 1975), 127–165.

39. McKenney, *Industrial Valley,* 63.

40. Boryczka and Cary, *No Strength Without Union,* 184.

41. Lief, *The Firestone Story,* 223.

42. McKenney, *Industrial Valley,* 93–94.

43. Toward Soviet America, Marxist Internet Archive, 2009, https://www.marxists.org/archive/foster/1932/toward/.

44. Milton Derber, "Growth and Expansion," in Milton Derber and Edwin Young, eds., *Labor and the New Deal* (New York" Da Capp Press, 1972), 105–106.

45. See for instance John Williamson, *Dangerous Scot.*

46. McKenney, *Industrial Valley,* 93–94.

47. *ABJ,* July 28, 1940.

48. Ibid, April 20, April 12, June 27, July 11, 13, and 29, 1929, and December 18, 1930.

49. Ibid, December 28, 1932.

50. See, for instance, Eric Hart, "A Brief History of IATSE," September 6, 2010, http://www.props.eric-hart.com/features/a-brief-history-of-iatse/. The mob's union activities are detailed in Michael Woodiwiss, *Organized Crime and American Power: A History* (Toronto: University of Toronto Press, 2001), 156–59.

51. *ABJ,* March 20, 26, and 29, December 12, 1931, and March 19, 2011. See also Wolf, "The *Akron Beacon Journal,*" 710–71111.

52. Ibid (Wolf), 710.

53. *ABJ,* March 21, 2011.

54. Friedrich Engels, *The Condition of the Working-Class in England in 1844* (Cambridge: Cambridge University Press, 2010), 214.

1. Frederick Engels, Preface to the American Edition, *The Condition of the Working Class in England* (New York: John W. Lovell, 1887), Marxists Internet Archive, https://www.marxists.org/archive/marx/works/1887/01/26.htm.

2. Ohio Labor History Project, 14.4.1. Interview with Mr. James Turner, retired Fair Practices Director Rubber Workers International, conducted on December 4, 1975, by Carl Clausen, Ann Van Tine, and Patricia Curran in Akron, Ohio. Archives, Library of the Ohio Historical Society, Columbus, Ohio.

3. Thus plumbers, for instance, would be placed in the Plumbers' Union, mechanics in the Machinists,' and carpenters in the carpenters.' Only production workers would be left in the URW

4. *ABJ,* September 4, 1933.

5. The Trotskyist labor historian Art Preis estimates that whereas the AFL's membership grew by 500,000 to 3,600,000 during the period of the Act, company unions increased their membership by fifty percent. See Preis, *Labor's Giant Step,* 15–16.

6. Ibid, 13. See also R.W. Fleming, "The Significance of the Wagner Act." In Milton Derber and Edwin Young, eds., *Labor and the New Deal* (New York: Da Capo Press, 1972), 128.

7. *ABJ,* July 18, 1935.

8. Ibid, November 19, 1939.

9. McKenney, *Industrial Valley,* 94–95.

10. *ABJ,* February 16, 1936.

11. Ibid, June 27, 1933 and McKenney, *Industrial Valley,* 93.

12. Litchfield, *Industrial Voyage,* 257.

13. *ABJ,* October 6, 1933.

14. Fleming, "the Significance of the Wagner Act," 126.

15. Cited in Reeves, *Twentieth Century America,* 108.

16. Cited in Joe Glazer, *Labor's Troubadour* (Urbana and Chicago: University of Illinois Press, 2002), 56.

17. *Akron Times-Press,* October 15, 1934.

18. Tom Jones, *On A Burning Deck: Return to Akron: An Oral History of the Great Migration, Vol. 2, 1920–1991* (New Braunfels, TX: Tom Jones, 2017), 145.

19. Nelson, *American Rubber Workers,* 84.

20. McKenney, *Industrial Valley,* 117–118.

21. *Akron Times-Press,* October 15, 1934.

22. Burr McCloskey, "I Appeal the Ruling of the Chair," in Alice and Staughton Lynd, eds., *Rank & File: Personal Histories of Working-Class Organizers* (Princeton, N.J: Princeton University Press, 1981), 150.

23. Wolfs, *Rubber: A Story of Glory and Greed,* 497.

24. Glazer, *Labor's Troubadour,* 57.

25. *ABJ,* January 20, 1934.

26. Derek Seldman, "What Happened to the Labor Party?" An interview with Mark Dudzic, *Jacobin*, November 11, 2015, https://www.jacobinmag.com/2015/10/tony-mazzochi-mark-dudzic-us-labor-party-wto-nafta-globalization-democrats-union/.

27. McKenney, *Industrial Valley,* 143 and Borsos, "'We Make You This Appeal," 249–250.

28. *ABJ* April 20–26, 1934.

29. Borsos, "'We Make You This Appeal'," 250.

30. *ABJ,* May 9, 10, 11, 12, and June 30, 1934.

31. Ibid, May 5, 1934.

32. Ibid, June 25, 1934.

33. *India Rubber World,* May 1, 1934.

34. McKenney, *Industrial Valley,* 122.

35. UAA "American industry and the state," talk delivered by P. W. Litchfield, October 27, 1934.

36. UAA, address delivered by P. W. Litchfield on the Forum of Liberty, Broadcast No. 3, November 1, 1934.

37. Nelson, *American Rubber Workers,* 119–21.

38. *ABJ,* November 22, 1934.

39. Ibid, February 13, 1944.

40. Winslow Jones, *Life, Liberty and Property,* 86.

41. Borsos, "'We Make You This Appeal'," 254.

42. *ABJ,* September 1, 1935.

43. Ibid, January 20, 1934.

44. Preis, *Labor's Giant Step,* 3.

45. Borsos, "'We Make You This Appeal'," 245. It is ironic that Bill Green had himself once advocated industrial unionism and had even moved resolutions at AFL conventions to restructure the Federation along industrial lines. See Craig Phelan, *William Green: Biography of a Labor Leader* (Albany, N.Y: State University of New York Press, 1989), 24.

46. *ABJ,* April 16, 1934.

47. Ibid, June 28, 1934.

48. Ibid, June 26, 28, and 30. Also McKenney, *Industrial Valley,* 166–169, 172.

49. UAA, URW International President Local Unions Box 4, V.E. Atkins, factory manager, notice "To the employees of the Seiberling Rubber Company," November 27, 1934 and letter from Coleman Claherty to Frank Morrison, AFL Secretary, January 7, 1935.

50. Nelson, *American Rubber Workers,* 153–158.

51. *ABJ,* July 30, 1934.

52. Ibid, July 31, 1934.

53. McKenney, *Industrial Valley,* 182.

54. Ibid, 188, 191.

55. *ABJ,* March 28, 1935.

56. UAA URW International President Local Unions, Box 1–5. Letter to H. T. Wilson from Coleman Claherty, January 14, 1935.

57. Ibid.

58. Ibid.

59. *ABJ,* April 1, 1935.

60. B. J. Widick (writing as Jack Wilson), *New Militant,* March 30, 1935.

61. Turner interview, Ohio Historical Society.

62. Nelson, *American Rubber Workers,* 154–15757.

63. *New Militant,* April 13, 1935.

64. McKenney, *Industrial Valley,* 196–19999.

65. *ABJ,* March 28, 1935.

66. *New Militant,* April 20, 1935.

67. Ibid, August 17, 1935,

68. Ibid, May 4, and June 29, 1935.

69. Boryczka and Cary, *No Strength Without Union,* 199.

70. Phelan, *William Green,* 1–5 and 24–26. See also William Green, AFL-CIO, America's Unions, https://aflcio.org/about/history/labor-history-people/william-green.

71. *ABJ,* February 28, 1936.

72. *New Militant,* August 10, 1935.

73. Ibid, September 21, 1935.

74. For accounts of the Washington conference that voted for an international union outside of Green's control, see *New Militant,* September 14, 21, and 31, 1935; McKenney, *Industrial Valley,* 205–217; and Nelson, *American Rubber Workers,* 164–170.

75. UAA, URW International President Local Unions, Box 1–5, letter from Norbert B. O'Donnell, chair of URW federal labor union #19007, Kelly Tire & Rubber, to William Green, October 30, 1934.

76. UAA, Summit County Historical Society Box 1, John D. House papers, 1938—unpublished typescript by House.

77. *New Militant,* March 2, 1935.

78. Claherty was finished in Akron. In 1941, he suffered a serious stroke and never regained his health. He died in a Cleveland nursing home in 1956. (*ABJ,* January 4, 1956).

79. Ibid, November 13, 1936.

80. For accounts of the Ohio Insulator strike, see McKenney, *Industrial Valley,* 230–242; Widick, *New Militant,* November 25, 1935; Borsos, "We Make You This Appeal," 255–258; and Borsos, "Talking Union," 164–167. Jim Keller, who was a Communist Party organizer in Summit County during the period, discusses the strike in his pamphlet *A Veteran Communist Speaks,* 14–15.

81. *ABJ,* July 8, 1933.

82. Nelson, *American Rubber Workers,* 145.

83. Borsos, "'We Make You This Appeal'," 255–58.

84. *ABJ,* October 21, 1979.

85. Burr McCloskey, *He Will Stay Till You Come: The Rise and Fall of Skinny Walker* (Durham, NC: Moore Publishing, 1978).

86. Susan George, personal email to author, June 4, 2009.

87. John Simkin, "Carl Oglesby," Spartacus Educational, spartacus-educational.com/JFKoglesby.htm.

88. Stewart, "Backs to the Past."

89. Stan Ovshinsky, personal email to author, May 22, 2009.

90. Kolko, personal email to author, April 17, 2009.

91. *New Militant,* October 8, 1935.

92. Jones, *On A Burning Deck,* 134–136.

93. Ibid, 135–136.

94. *ABJ,* October 28, 1935.

95. Arthur Pound, "An Industrial Republic: The Goodyear Programme for Employee Representation and Education," *Atlantic Monthly,* (March 1935), 385. [British spelling in the original.]

96. *ABJ,* November 6, 1935. See also Widick, *New Militant,* October 21, 1935.

97. *New Militant,* January 11, 1936.

98. Ibid, November 2, 1935.

99. *ABJ,* November 6, 8, and 9, 1935, and *New Militant,* November 16, 1935.

100. In 1900, Goodyear workers staged a spontaneous but unsuccessful sit-down against cuts to piecework rates. See Rosswurm, "A Strike in Rubber City," 19 and Litchfield, *Industrial Voyage,* 77.

CHAPTER 14

1. *Daily Illini,* October 19, 1935.

2. Steve Martin, "John L. Lewis, 'Speech at the Fifty-Fifth Annual Convention of the American Federation of Labor (16 October 1935)," *Voices of Democracy*, No. 8, 2013, 56, http://voicesofdemocracy.umd.edu/wp-content/uploads/2014/10/Lewis-Interpretive-Essay.pdf.

3. *Decatur Herald,* January 5, 1936.

4. *New York Times,* October 17, 1935.

5. Quoted in Martin, "John L. Lewis, Speech," 54. Lewis himself had played the craft union game in Akron in 1913, when he and Carl Wyatt had tried to set up an AFL union during the IWW strike.

6. Later the Congress of Industrial Organizations.

7. Ibid.

8. *ABJ*, January 20, 1936.

9. McKenney, *Industrial Valley*, 248.

10. University of Akron Archives (UAA) United Rubber Workers files. URW International President, Local Unions. Box 1–5. Dalrymple, URW President to H.T. Wilson, Local 26 in Oldtown, Maryland, March 18, 1936.

11. UAA URW International President Local Unions, Box 4. Letter from O.H. Boseley, Recording Secretary, Firestone Local 18321 (AFL) to Coleman Claherty, July 13, 1934.

12. *ABJ*, March 18, 1937.

13. UAA URW International President Local Unions Box 1–3. Rex Murray, Local Union 9, to Sherman Dalrymple, February 13, 1936.

14. *United Rubber Worker*, September 1936.

15. Stewart, letter to Burr McCloskey, May 3, 1988, in "The Past at Our Backs," 99.

16. Nelson, *American Rubber Workers*, 133.

17. McKenney, *Industrial Valley*, 251. Also Williamson, *Dangerous Scot*, 113.

18. Louis Adamic, *My America*, 1928–1938 (New York: Harper, 1938), 405. Unless there is a strong oral tradition or recorded labor history, the generations often have to reinvent methods of struggle, often spontaneously. There had been a brief sit-down at Goodyear in 1900, but this seems to have been forgotten. Pittsburgh iron puddlers and boilermakers may have carried out the first American sit-down in 1842. See the timeline in Aaron Brenner, Benjamin Day and Immanuel Ness, eds., *The Encyclopedia of Strikes in American* History (London and New York: Routledge, 2015).

19. *New Militant*, February 8, 1975.

20. For a detailed account of the sit-downs, see McKenney, *Industrial Valley*, 251–72.

21. *New Militant*, February 29, 1936.

22. *ABJ*, February 19, 1936.

23. *New Militant,* February 29, 1936.

24. Ibid.

25. Interview with James Turner, Ohio Labor History Project 14.4.1. Archives, Library of the Ohio Historical Society, Columbus Ohio.

26. *ABJ,* February 19, 1936.

27. *New Militant,* February 29, 1936.

28. *ABJ,* February 19, 1936.

29. *New Militant,* February 29, 1936.

30. *United Rubber Worker,* April 1936.

31. *ABJ* March 3, 1936.

32. Cited in *25 Years of the URW.*

33. Keller, *A Veteran Communist Speaks,* 25.

34. *ABJ,* March 16, 1936.

35. *United Rubber Worker,* April 1936.

36. *ABJ* March 16, 1936.

37. Ibid, November 20, 1936.

38. Keller, *A Veteran Communist Speaks,* 13. According to Keller, in 1935 the CP had a total membership of about 90 in Summit County, including thirty who worked in rubber plants. Most of the CP gummers were concentrated at Firestone and Goodrich.

39. *ABJ* November 20, 1938.

40. Keller, *A Veteran Communist Speaks,* 1.

41. Shrake, "Working Class Politics in Akron, Ohio, 1936," 20–21.

42. Derber, "Growth and Expansion," 106.

43. *ABJ,* November 20, 1938 and February 18, 1939. See also Jones, *Life, Liberty, and Property,* 303–304.

44. Keller, *A Veteran Communist Speaks,* 28–34.

45. Ibid, 1, 34, and 38.

46. *ABJ,* November 20, 1938.

47. Ibid, 21, 23 and 23, 1936.

48. Keller, *A Veteran Communist Speaks,* 34.

49. *United Rubber Worker,* April 1936.

50. Ibid.

51. Ibid.

52. URWA, 25 Years of the URW.

53. *United Rubber Worker,* May and December 1936.

54. Ibid, June 1936.

55. Gene L. Howard, *The History of the Rubber Workers in Gadsden, Alabama, 1933–1983* (East Gadsden, AL: URWA Local 12, 1983), 6. Also *ABJ,* June 10, 1936.

56. NLRB vs. Fansteel Metallurgical Corp., February 27, 1939.

57. John Newton Thurber, *Rubber Workers' History (1935–1955),* (Akron, OH: URWA, 1956), 12.

58. *India Rubber Journal,* October 31 and November 28, 1936.

59. A rendition is available online at https://www.youtube.com/watch?v=kVrxruRTtDA.

60. *ABJ,* May 4, 1936.

61. Kern and Wilson, *Ohio: A History,* 384.

62. *Courier-Tribune,* June 19, 1936.

63. Ibid. Also *ABJ,* June 18, and 19, 1936 and January 22, 1937.

64. Stewart, "The Past At Our Backs."

65. *Courier-Tribune,* June 19, 1936.

66. Ibid, June 23, 1936.

67. Stewart, "The Past At Our Backs," 10.

68. *Courier-Tribune,* June 30, 1936.

69. *ABJ,* January 22, 1937.

70. Ibid, February 14, 1936.

71. Ibid, June 1, 1936.

72. Ibid, November 17, 1936.

73. Ibid, June 1, 1937.

74. Ibid, June 28, 1937.

75. Bruce Minton, "Akron—Where Unity is Real," *New Masses,* February 22, 1938.

76. *ABJ,* September 28, 1937.

77. Ibid, December 25, 1937.

78. *New Masses,* February 22, 1938.

79. Ibid, June 28, 1937.

80. Ibid, January 1, 1938.

81. *New Masses,* February 22, 1938.

82. *ABJ,* December 8, 1940.

83. Nelson, *American Rubber Workers,* 230.

84. International Chemical Workers' Union, Local 901, 1937–1990. The Ward M. Canady Center for Special Collections, University of Toledo, https://www.utoledo.edu/library/canaday/findingaids1/mss-085.pdf.

85. Lief, *The Firestone Story,* 226.

86. *United Rubber Worker,* March 1937.

87. Bruce M. Meyer, *The Once and Future Union: The Rise and Fall of the United Rubber Workers, 1935–1995* (Akron, OH: The University of Akron Press, 2002), 82.

88. The *ABJ* published comprehensive daily reports on the strike between March 3, and May 1, 1937. The following account of the strike is based on those reports.

89. For a discussion of this point of view, see Staughton Lynd, Introduction, in Staughton Lynd, ed., *"We Are All Leaders": The Alternative Unionism of the Early 1930s* (Urbana and Chicago: University of Illinois Press, 1996).

90. *United Rubber Worker,* May 1937.

91. *ABJ,* November 19, 1939.

92. Interview with James Turner, Ohio Historical Society.

93. Stewart, "The Past at Our backs," 77.

94. Jones, *On A Burning Deck,* 132.

95. Preis, *Labor's Giant Step,* 3.

96. Rose Pesotta, ed. John Nicholas Breffa, *Bread Upon The Waters* (Ithaca, N.Y: I.L.R. Press, 1987), 198–199 and 211–212.

97. *Washington Post,* November 13, 1988.

98. Interview with James Turner, Ohio Historical Society.

99. John Borsos, "Talking Union," 236–237.

100. Steve Love and David Giffels, *Wheels of Fortune: The Story of Rubber in Akron* (Akron, OH: The University of Akron Press, 1999, 114–17.

101. Karl Marx, trans. Samuel Moore and Edward Aveling, *Capital: A Critique of Political Economy, Vol. 1,* Ch. 10, Section 7, 195. Available at Marxists Internet Archive, https://www.marxists.org/archive/marx/works/download/pdf/Capital-Volume-I.pdf. See David R. Roediger, "Labor in a White Skin and Working Class History" in *Towards the Abolition of Whiteness: Essays on Race, Politics, and Working Class History* (London: Verso, 1994).

102. *ABJ,* February 25, 1931.

103. See Akingbade, Harrison Ola. "The Liberian Problem of Forced Labor 1926–1940." *Africa: Rivista Trimestrale Di Studi E Documentazione Dell'Istituto Italiano per L'Africa E L'Oriente* Vol. 52, no. 2 (1997): 261–73, http://www.jstor.org/stable/40761169.

104. *ABJ,* November 9, 1939.

105. Ibid, April 4, 1938.

106. Ibid.

107. Taminent Library and Robert F. Wagner Labor Archives, New York University. ALBA 236 Box 1 Folder 9, Joe Brandt Scrapbooks. Brandt was the Cuyahoga County organizer of the Communist Party.

108. ALBA IB Archive (Moscow) Personnel files. File 974 Document No. 3, Roffeld, Charles.

109. Tully, *The Devil's Milk,* 342.

110. Taminent Library and Robert F. Wagner Labor Archives, New York University. "Good Fight," ALBA #216 General Bios. Her surname is sometimes spelled "Kea".

111. ALBA IB Archive (Moscow) Personnel Files, Fond 545 Opis 6, File No. 920, Document No. 6, Kee, Salaria. This is her secret NKVD file.

112. *Democrat and Chronicle,* November 12, 1938 and ALBA #216.

113. Salaria Kee Memoir Typescript. ALBA #1. Frederika Martin Papers SERIES I. Medical Personnel: Biographical Information 1936–1988. Box 9, Folder 33.

114. Ibid.

115. Joe Brandt Scrapbooks, ALBA 236 Box 1, Folder 1, fragment.

116. Cited in Frances Patai, "Heroines of the Good Fight: Testimonies of US Volunteer Nurses in the Spanish Civil War, 1936–1939," *Nursing History Review,* Vol. 3, (1995): 88.

117. Joe Brandt Scrapbooks, fragment.

118. Ibid.

119. Robin Kelley, *Race Rebels: Culture, Politics and the Black Working Class* (New York: Free Press, 1994), 133, and Salaria Kea unpublished memoir, "While Passing Through," excerpt in *Health and Medicine* (Spring, 1987): 11–13.

120. *Pittsburgh Courier,* January 8, 1938.

121. Brandt Scrapbook, fragment, and Salaria Kee Memoir Typescript.

122. *ABJ,* April 13, 1938.

123. *Democrat and Chronicle,* November 11, 1938.

124. ALBA VF Nurses. Mildred Rackley, "From a Hospital in Spain: American Nurses Write" Medical Bureau to Aid Spanish Democracy, 1937?.

125. Salaria Kee Memoir Typescript.

126. Kee, "While Passing Through," 13.

127. Joe Brandt scrapbook, fragment.

128. Adam Hochschild, *Spain in Our Hearts: Americans in the Spanish Civil War, 1936–1939* (Boston & New York: Houghton Mifflin Harcourt, 2016), ch. 14 and Dominic Tierney, *FDR and the Spanish Civil War: Neutrality and Commitment in the Struggle that Divided America* (Durham, NC: Duke University Press, 2007).

129. Kee, "While Passing Through," 13.

130. *ABJ,* May 12, 1938.

131. Ibid, June 24, 1938.

132. *Nation,* April 14, 1984.

133. This account draws on articles published in the *ABJ* between May 26, and June 2, 1938, and in the June 4, 1938 edition of *Socialist Appeal.*

134. *ABJ,* January 1, 1938.

135. *Socialist Appeal,* May 28, 1938.

CHAPTER 15

1. See for instance Dulles, *Labor in America: A History, 35–51,* and William L. Abbott, *The American Labor Heritage* (Honolulu: University of Hawai'i 1967), 8–12.

2. Eric Lief Davin, "The Very Last Hurrah? The Defeat of the Labor Party Idea, 1934–1936," in Staughton Lynd, ed., *"We Are All Leaders": The Alternative Unionism of the Early 1930s* (Urbana and Chicago: University of Illinois Press, 1996), 155–156. The most in-depth study is Shrake, "Working Class Politics in Akron," (master's thesis, The University of Akron, 1974).

3. Derek Seldeman, "Whatever Happened to the Labor Party?" Interview with Mark Dudzic, *Jacobin,* October 11, 2015, https://www.jacobinmag.com/2015/10/tony-mazzochi-mark-dudzic-us-labor-party-wto-nafta-globalization-democrats-union/.

4. Davin, "The Very Last Hurrah?" 122–123.

5. Barry Eidlin, "Why Is There No Labor Party in the United States? Political Articulation and the Canadian Comparison, 1932 to 1948," *American Sociological Review,* 1–29, (2016), https://journals.sagepub.com/doi/full/10.1177/0003122416643758.

6. Mari Jo Buhle, Paul Buhle, and Dan Georgakis, eds., *Encyclopedia of the American Left, 2nd Edition* (New York: Oxford University Press, 1998), 147.

7. Davin, "The Very Last Hurrah?" 131.

8. *ABJ,* September 17, 1936.

9. Bowling Green State University Center for Archival Collections. MS 468Sam Pollock Papers, Box 9, Personal Papers, Folder 22, 1934 Election Material, "A Workingman for Congress."

10. Shrake, "Working Class Politics," 33.

11. Ibid, 48.

12. *ABJ,* June 8, 1936.

13. Ibid, May 4, 1936.

14. Ibid, March 25 and April 27, 1936.

15. Ibid, May 4, 1936.

16. *ABJ,* May 22, 1936.

17. *Akron Times-Press,* April 6, 1936.

18. Shrake, "Working Class Politics in Akron," 57.

19. *New Militant,* February 29, 1936.

20. Davin, "The Very Last Hurrah?" 144–145.

21. *ABJ,* June 6 and 8, 1936

22. *Akron Times-Press,* July 10, 1936.

23. Shrake, "Working Class Politics," 56. Shrake's assessment is based on an interview he conducted with Murray in Cambridge, Ohio, in 1973, and was confirmed by Harry Eagle.

24. Williamson, *Dangerous Scot,* 1969.

25. Shrake, "Working Class Politics in Akron," 89.

26. *ABJ,* November 9, 1939.

27. Ibid, November 9, 1939.

28. Ibid, October 27, 1947.

29. Ibid, 59–63.

30. *Akron Times-Press,* August 28, 1936.

31. Ibid, September 8, 1936.

32. Shrake, "Working Class Politics in Akron," 69.

33. This account of the URW convention is based on Davin, *"The Very Last Hurrah?"* 150–151 and Shrake, "Working Class Politics in Akron," 67–99.

34. Shrake, "Working Class Politics," v.

35. *ABJ,* October 8, 1936.

36. Ibid, October 3, 1936.

37. Walter Jason, "John L. Lewis," *New International,* March–April 1950, Marxists Internet Archive, https://www.marxists.org/history/etol/newspape/ni/vol16/no02/jason.htm.

38. John L. Lewis, radio speech, October 25, 1940. Available online at Rand's Esoteric Otr, https://randsesotericotr.podbean.com/e/john-l-lewis-speech-october-25-1940/.

39. Reeves, *Twentieth Century America,* 115.

CHAPTER 16

1. Kern and Wilson, *Ohio: A History,* 390.

2. According to Thomas C. Reeves (*Twentieth Century America,* 115), in 1937 ninety-four percent of Americans favored isolationism.

3. V. I. Lenin, "May Day and the War". Notes for a speech or article written in April 1915. Published in *Proletarskaya Revolutsia,* No. 1, January 1929, https://www.marxists.org/archive/lenin/works/1915/apr/30.htm.

4. *The New Republic,* January 7, 1946.

5. Howard Zinn, History is a Weapon. *A People's History of the United States,* Ch. 16, "A People's War?" Online at https://www.historyisaweapon.com/defcon1/zinnpeopleswar.html.

6. See Preis, *Labor's Giant Step,* 91–143, and Albert Goldman, *In Defense of Socialism: The Official Court Record of Albert Goldman's Final Speech for Defense in the Famous Minneapolis Sedition Trial* (New York: Pioneer Publishers, 1944).

7. *ABJ,* June 21, and September 13, 1941.

8. For example, URW Local 5, minutes of regular business meeting, April 2, 1944. The Communist Party, which had opposed US entry into the war during the period of the Stalin-Hitler Pact, switched to uncritical support for the war after the Nazi invasion of the USSR. It endorsed the use of the Smith Act against the Trotskyists—something it later regretted when the same law was used against it during the Cold War.

9. Studs Terkel, *"The Good War": An Oral History of World War II* (Harmondsworth: Penguin Books, 1986), 15.

10. Donny Gluckstein, *A People's History of the Second World War: Resistance versus Empire* (London: Pluto Press, 2012). Kindle.

11. Howard Zinn, History As A Weapon, *A People's History of the United States,* Ch. 16. Online at https://www.historyisaweapon.com/zinnapeopleshistory.html.

12. Quoted in Dominic Tierney, *F. D. R. and the Spanish Civil War: Neutrality and Commitment in the Struggle that Divided America* (Durham, NC: Duke University Press, 2007), 68.

13. See Tully, *The Devil's Milk,* 319–330.

14. See, for instance, Arthur Herman, *Freedom's Forge: How American Business Produced Victory in World War II* (New York: Random House, 2012), 116, 160 and 231.

15. See Richard Hofstadter, *The Age of Reform: From Bryan to F. D. R.* (New York: Vintage Books, 1955), 327.

16. UAA URW Local 5, Box F-1. Minute Books. Minutes of regular business meeting, June 3, 1945. Browder was the general secretary of the Communist Party.

17. Reeves, *Twentieth Century America,* 85. The membership surge came about in large part because of admiration of the Soviet Union's war against the Nazis after 1941.

18. There is a YouTube video of Glazer and Bill Friedland singing the song at https://www.youtube.com/watch?v=t4CgFRgVoVQ.

19. Cited in Preis, *Labor's Giant Step,* 132.

20. *United Rubber Worker,* June 1936.

21. Tully, *The Devil's Milk,* 339.

22. Howard, *The History of the Rubber Workers in Gadsden,* and *United Rubber Worker,* June 1936.

23. Undated fragment, *ABJ* Archives.

24. Michael K. Honey, *Southern Labor and Black Civil Rights: Organizing Memphis* (Urbana and Chicago: University of Illinois Press, 1993), 154–161, 164.

25. Tully, *The Devil's Milk,* 340.

26. *The Airbag,* September 13, 1944.

27. *ABJ,* July 22, 1942.

28. John Gerassi, *The Premature Antifascists* (New York: Praeger, 1986), 198.

29. UAA, Dr. Herbert A. Davidson Papers.

30. Ibid, August 10, 1947.

31. Ibid, August 4, 1942.

32. Ibid, August 5, 1942.

33. *Afro-American,* May 23, 1942.

34. Kern and Wilson, *Ohio: A History,* 392.

35. *ABJ,* February 28, 1936.

36. Undated fragment in ABJ archives, date illegible.

37. *ABJ,* May 12, 1941.

38. Ibid, June 28, 1942.

39. Ibid, May 5, and May 26, 1940.

40. Ibid, February 25, 1944,

41. Ibid, October 8, 1941.

42. Ibid, September 24, 1941.

43. Calculated using Measuring.Worth.com, https://www.measuringworth.com/calculators/uscompare/relativevalue.php.

44. *ABJ,* June 22, 1943.

45. *United Rubber Worker,* April 1945.

46. Tully, *The Devil's Milk,* 334.

47. George Soule, "Profits by the Billion", *The New Republic,* January 7, 1946.

48. *ABJ,* November 1, 1942.

49. Ibid, August 26, 1945.

50. Cited in Tully, *The Devil's Milk,* 335.

51. *The Airbag,* February 1, 1942.

52. Tully, *The Devil's Milk,* 336.

53. URW Local 5, Box F2. Minutes of special executive board meeting, September 1, 1944.

54. *The Airbag,* September 13, 1944.

55. Ibid, October 18, 1942.

56. Tully, *The Devil's Milk,* 336.

57. *ABJ,* June 11, 1942.

58. For an absorbing account of Akron's women war workers, see Kathleen Endres' wonderful *Rosie the Rubber Worker,* ch.3.

59. *ABJ,* December 7, 1942.

60. Tully, *The Devil's Milk,* 333.

61. *ABJ,* June 22, 1943.

62. Ibid, October 3, 1942.

63. Ibid, December 4, 1941.

64. Ibid, October 15, 1942.

65. Ibid, June 11, 1942.

66. Ibid, September 29, 1941.

67. Borsos, "Talking Union", ch.4.

68. *ABJ,* July 21, 1942.

69. Meyer, *The Once and Future Union,* 73.

70. *The Airbag,* October 18, 1942.

71. *ABJ,* January 1, 1941.

72. Cited in *The Airbag,* September 6, 1942.

73. *The Airbag,* February 1, June 7, and September 6, 1942.

74. Ibid, February 18, 1942.

75. *The Militant,* June 5, 1943.

76. *ABJ* May 27, 1943.

77. Ibid.

78. Ibid, June 6, 1943.

79. Brecher, *Strike!,* 214.

80. *The Airbag,* August 19 and September 5, 1943.

81. Ibid, October 21, 1943.

82. Ibid, November 18, 1943.

83. *ABJ* January 8, 1944.

84. *The Airbag,* February 17, 1944.

85. *ABJ, A*pril 15, 1944.

86. Ibid.

87. Cited in Tully, *The Devil's Milk,* 338.

88. *The Airbag,* September 13, 1944.

89. *Daily News,* September 19, 1944.

90. *ABJ,* September 20, 1944.

91. Ibid, September 17, 1944.

92. The 1943 Smith-Connally Act, passed over Roosevelt's veto, gave the US President war-time powers to seize enterprises hit by strikes or lockouts and to prohibit strikes thereafter.

93. Information on the convention largely taken from *The Militant,* October 2, 1944.

94. *The Airbag,* October 18, 1944.

95. URW Local 5, minutes of regular business meetings, November 16 and December 21, 1944, January 18 and June 1945.

96. Ibid, minutes of regular business meetings, October 7 and November 18, 1945.

97. *ABJ,* September 2 and 3, 1945,

98. Kern and Wilson, *Ohio: A History,* 393.

99. *ABJ,* September 10, 1945.

100. Ibid, September 10 and 16, 1945.

101. Ibid, February 23, 1946.

102. Ibid, (editorial), December 2, 1944.

CHAPTER 17

1. Tully, *Crooked Deals and Broken Treaties,* 15–16.

2. Washington Irving's character only slept for twenty years, of course.

3. Turner, *The Frontier in American History*, 11.

4. *ABJ*, November 27, 1907.

5. All quotations in this paragraph are from Karl Marx, *The Poverty of Philosophy,* 79. Marxists Internet Archive https://www.marxists.org/archive/marx/works/download/pdf/Poverty-Philosophy.pdf.

6. E. J. Hobsbawm, "Gramsci and Political Theory," *Marxism Today,* (July 1977): 209, http://banmarchive.org.uk/collections/mt/pdf/07_77_205.pdf.

7. Kennedy, *Freedom From Fear,* ch. 1.

8. Kern and Wilson, *Ohio: A History,* 358.

9. *ABJ,* August 10, 1947.

10. Ibid, September 17, 1953.

11. Dyer, *Gum-Dipped,* 166.

12. Love and Giffels, *Wheels of Fortune,* 115–117.

13. Ibid, 113–114.

14. Letter from Pat (John) O'Reilly to Frederika Martin, August 8, 1984. Folder 29, Salaria Kee Correspondence. ALBA # 1 Frederika Martin papers. Series I Medical personnel: Biographical Information, 1936–1988, Box 9, Tamiment Library, Robert F. Wagner Labor Archives, New York University.

15. Samuel H. Friedman, "I'm Labor!" Available online at http://www.protestsonglyrics.net/Labor_Union_Songs/Im-Labor.phtml.

16. Bruce Nelson, *Divided We Stand: American Workers and the Struggle for Black Equality* (Princeton N.J. and Oxford: Princeton University Press, 2001), 198.

17. UAA URW Local 5 (B. F. Goodrich) Files. Box A1. *The Airbag,* March 1939 and April 1939.

18. Kern and Wilson, *Ohio: A History,* 298.

19. Cited in Melvyn Dubovsky and Warren Van Tine, eds., *Labor Leaders in America* (Urbana and Chicago: University of Illinois Press, 1987), 80.

20. Warde, "American Philosophy and the Labor Movement".

21. David Sessions, "America's Missing Labor Party", *The New Republic,* October 2, 2018.

22. Gabriel Kolko, personal correspondence with the author, April 17, 2009.

23. Gerald Mayer, "Union Membership Trends in the United States" (Washington, DC: Congressional Research Service, 2004), 29. Online at https://digitalcommons.ilr.cornell.edu/cgi/viewcontent.cgi?article=1176&context=key_workplace

24. For a summary of the post-war history of the URW, see John L. Woods, "Rubber Workers' Strikes', in Brenner, Day and Ness, eds., *An Encyclopedia of Strikes in American History,* Kindle Edition.

25. See, for instance, Meany's obituary in *The Washington Post,* January 11, 1980. Also Preis, *Labor's Giant Step,* 85,

26. Cited in Philip Yale Nicholson, *Labor's Story in the United States* (Philadelphia: Temple University Press, 2004), 262. 1980.

27. Noah Carmichael, personal communication to the author, November 16, 2019. Carmichael is Secretary-Treasurer of Bricklayers' Union Local 7 and an Ohio field agent for the union.

28. Tully, *The Devil's Milk,* 352.

29. Love and Giffels, *Wheels of Fortune,* xiv.

30. Stewart, "The Past At Our Backs".

31. Obituary, *ABJ,* 1976, exact date illegible.

32. From the song "Aragon Mill" by Si Kahn © Joe Hill Music LLC (ASCAP) Administered by: Reel Muzik Werks El Segundo, California.

33. See, for instance, Bruce Meyer, "It's a Merger: URW Votes to Join Steelworkers", *Rubber and Plastics News,* July 10, 1995, https://www.rubbernews.com/article/19950710/ISSUE/307109978/it39s-a-merger-urw-votes-to-join-steelworkers.

34. UAA Summit County Historical Society papers. John D. House papers, 1938— Box 1.

35. Carmichael.

36. Bernie Sanders, "Trump's Economy Is Good for Billionaires, Not for Working People," *The Guardian,* January 16, 2019, https://www.theguardian.com/us-news/2019/jan/16/trump-economy-billionaires-working-people?CMP=Share_iOSApp_Other.

37. Schulman, "Where Is Our Labor Party?" Mark Dudzic is a radical activist and labor party advocate.

Bibliography

BOOKS AND JOURNAL ARTICLES

Abbott, William L. *The American Labor Heritage.* Honolulu: University of Hawai'i Press, 1967.

Adamic, Louis. *My America, 1928–1938.* New York: Harper, 1938.Adreano, Ralph, ed. *The Economic Impact of the Civil War.* Cambridge, MA: Schenkman Publishing, 1962.

Agricola, Georgius, trans. Herbert Clark Hoover and Lou Henry Hoover. *De Re Metallica,* New York: Dover, 1950.

Akingbade, Harrison Ola. The Liberian Problem of Forced Labor 1926–1940. *Africa: Rivista Trimestrale Di Studi E Documentazione Dell'Istituto Italiano per L'Africa E L'Oriente* 52, no. 2, 1997: 261–73.

Allen, Hugh. *Rubber's Home Town: The Real-Life Story of Akron.* New York: Stratford House, 1949.

Allen, Robert C. "International Competition in Iron and Steel, 1850–1913." *Journal of Economic History,* Vol. 29, No.4 (December 1979): 911–937.

Archer, Robin. *Why Is There No Labor Party in The United States?* Princeton, NJ: Princeton University Press, 2010.

Aveling, Edward Bibbins, and Eleanor Marx. *The Working Class Movement in America.* London: Swan Sonnenschein, 1891.

Baker, Charles, ed. *Marguerite Prevey in Memoriam.* Cleveland: Charles Baker, 1925.

Balzac, Honoré de. *The Elixir of Life.* New York: Windham Press, 2013.

Baxter, P. J. and J. B. Werner. *Mortality in the British Rubber Industries, 1967–76.* London: Health and Safety Executive, 1980.

Beard, Mary Ritter. *The American Labor Movement.* New York: Arno and the *New York Times,* 1969.

Belafonte, Harry and Michael Shnayerson. *My Story: A Memoir of Art, Race and Defiance.* New York: Vintage Books, 2012.

Billington, Ray Allen. *Land of Savagery, Land of Promise: The European Image of the American Frontier in the Nineteenth Century.* New York: W. W. Norton, 1981.

Bimba, Anthony. *The Molly Maguires: The True Story of Labor's Martyred Pioneers in the Coalfields.* New York: International Publishers, 1992.

Bining, A. C. *British Regulation of the Colonial Iron Trade.* Philadelphia: University of Philadelphia Press, 1933.

Blackford, Mansel G., and K. Austin Kerr. *B. F. Goodrich: Tradition and Transformation, 1870–1995.* Columbus: Ohio State University Press, 1996.

Blair, C. Dean. *The Potters and Potteries of Summit County, 1828–1915.* Akron, OH: Summit County Historical Society, 1966.

Borsos, John. "'We make you this appeal in the name of every union man and woman in Barberton': Solidarity Unionism in Barberton, Ohio, 1933–41," in Staughton Lynd, ed. *"We Are All Leaders": The Alternative Unionism of the early 1930s.* Urbana and Chicago: University of Illinois Press, 1996.

Boryczka, Raymond and Lorin Lee Cary. *No Strength Without Union: An Illustrated History of Ohio Workers, 1803–1980.* Columbus: Ohio Historical Society, 1980.

Braverman, Harry. *Labor and Monopoly Capital: The Degradation of Work in the Twentieth Century,* 25th Anniversary Edition. New York: Monthly Review Press, 1998.

Brecher, Jeremy. *Strike!* Revised, Expanded, and Updated Edition. Oakland, CA: PM Press, 2014.

Brecht, Bertolt. "Questions From a Worker Who Reads," trans. Michael Hamburger. *Bertolt Brecht, Poems 1913–1956.* London: Methuen, 1976.

Brenner, Aaron, Benjamin Day and Immanuel Ness, eds. *The Encyclopedia of Strikes in American History.* London and New York: Routledge, 2015.

Brigham, Carl C. *A Study of American Intelligence.* Princeton, NJ: Princeton University Press, 1923.

Brooks, Thomas R. *Toil and Trouble: A History of American Labor,* Second Edition. New York: Dell Publishing, 1971.

Buhle, Mari Jo, Paul Buhle, and Dan Georgakas, eds. *Encyclopedia of the American Left,* Second Edition. New York: Oxford University Press, 1998.

Buhle, Mari Jo. *Women and American Socialism, 1870–1920.* Urbana & Chicago: University of Illinois Press, 1981.

Burrows, Edwin G. and Mike Wallace. *Gotham: A History of New York City to 1898.* New York: Oxford University Press, 1998.

Cahn, William. *A Pictorial History of American Labor.* New York: Crown Publishers, 1972.

Cardinal, Eric. "New England and the Western Reserve in the Nineteenth Century: Some Suggestions." *Western Reserve Studies: A Journal of Regional History and Culture* (1986): 13–14.

Chomsky, Noam, ed. Peter R. Mitchell and John Schoeffel. *Understanding Power: The Indispensable Chomsky.* London: Vintage Books, 2003.

Ciment, James. *Another America: The Story of Liberia and the Former Slaves Who Ruled It.* New York: Hill and Wang, 2013.

Claudin, Fernando. *The Communist Movement: From Comintern to Cominform.* New York: Peregrine, 1975.

Commons, John Rogers et al. *History of Labour in the United States,* Vol. II. Washington, DC: Beard Books, 1918.

Conlin, Joseph, R. *At the Point of Production: The Local History of the I.W.W.* Westport, CT: Greenwood Press, 1981.

Constantine, J. Robert, ed. *Gentle Rebel: Letters of Eugene Debs.* Urbana and Chicago: University of Illinois Press, 1995.

Cordillot, Michel. *La Sociale en Amérique: dictionnaire bibliographique du mouvement social francophone aux Etats-Unis, 1848–1922,* Vol. 9. Paris: Editions de l'Atelier, 2002.

Crawford, Martin. "Back to the Future? The Potters' Emigration Society and the Historians." *Labour History Review,* Vol. 76, Issue 2 (August 2011): 81–103.

Davin, Eric Lief. "The Very Last Hurrah? The Defeat of the Labor Party Idea, 1934–1936," in Staughton Lynd, ed., *"We Are All Leaders": The Alternative Unionism of the Early 1930s.* Urbana and Chicago: University of Illinois Press, 1996.

Davis, Mike. "Why the US Working Class is Different." *New Left Review.* Vol. 1, No. 123 (September–October 1980).

De Tocqueville, Alexis, trans. Henry Reeve, revised by Francis Bowen and abridged with an introduction by Patrick Renshaw. *Democracy in America.* Ware, UK: Wordsworth Classics, 1998.

Dearinger, Ryan. *The Filth of Progress: Immigration, Americans, and the Building of Canals and Railroads in the West.* Oakland: University of California Press, 2016.

Derber, Milton. "Growth and Expansion," in Milton Derber and Edwin Young, eds., *Labor and the New Deal.* New York: Da Capo Press, 1972.

Dick, William M. *Labor and Socialism in America: The Gompers Era.* Port Washington, NY: Kennikat, 1972.

Donoghue, A. M. "Occupational Health Hazards in Mining: An Overview." *Occupational Medicine,* Vol. 54 (2004): 283–289.

Dubovsky, Melvyn and Warren Van Tine, eds. *Labor Leaders in America.* Urbana and Chicago: University of Illinois Press, 1987.

Dulles, Foster Rhea. *Labor in America: A History.* New York: Thomas Y. Crowell, 1949.

Dyer, Joyce. *Gum-Dipped: A Daughter Remembers Rubber Town.* Akron, OH: The University of Akron Press, 2003.

Ellis, Willam Donohue. *The Cuyahoga.* New York and Chicago: Holt, Rinehart and Wilson, 1966.

Endres, Kathleen L. *Akron's "Better Half": Women's Clubs and the Humanization of the City, 1825–1925.* Akron, OH: The University of Akron Press, 2006.

Endres, Kathleen L. *Rosie the Rubber Worker: Women Workers in Akron's Rubber Factories During World War II.* Kent, OH: Kent State University Press, 2000.

Engels, Friedrich. *The Condition of the Working-Class in England in 1844.* Cambridge: Cambridge University Press, 2010.

Fetherling, Dale. *Mother Jones, The Miners' Angel.* Carbondale: Southern Illinois Press, 1974.

Fetzer, Herman, ed. *A Centennial History of Akron.* Akron, OH: Summit County Historical Society, 1925.

Fisher, S. W. "Health Hazards of Mining." *British Journal of Independent Medicine,* Vol. 1 No. 3 (July 1944): 153–158.

Fleming, R. W. "The Significance of the Wagner Act." In Milton Derber and Edwin Young, eds. *Labor and the New Deal.* New York: Da Capo Press, 1972.

Foster, John Bellamy. "The Meaning of Work in Sustainable Society." *Monthly Review,* Vol. 69, No. 4 (September 2017): 1–14.

Geiser, Karl Frederick. *Redemptioners and Indentured Servants in the Colony and Commonwealth of Pennsylvania.* Supplement to the *Yale Review,* Vol. X, No. 2 (August 1901).

George, J. E. "The Coal Miners' Strike of 1897." *The Quarterly Journal of Economics,* Vol. 12, No. 2 (January 1898).

Gerassi, John. *The Premature Antifascists.* New York: Praeger, 1986.

Giffels, David. "Readin,' Writin' and Route 21: The Road from West Virginia to Ohio." In *The Appalachians: America's First and Last Frontier,* edited by Mari-Lynn Evans et al. New York: Random House, 2004.

Ginger, Ray, with an introduction by Mike Davis. *The Bending Cross: A Biography of Eugene V. Debs.* Chicago: Haymarket Books, 2007.

Glazer, Joe. *Labor's Troubadour.* Urbana and Chicago: University of Illinois Press, 2002.

Gluckstein, Donny. *A People's History of the Second World War: Resistance versus Empire.* London: Pluto Press, 2012.

Gompers, Samuel. *Seventy Years of Life and Labor.* Volume 1. New York: Dutton, 1925.

Goodyear Tire & Rubber Company. *A Study of the Labor Movement.* Akron, OH: Goodyear Tire & Rubber, 1920.

Green, Archie. *Wobblies, Pile Butts, and Other Heroes: Laborlore Explorations.* Chicago: University of Illinois Press, 1993.

Green, James. *The Devil Is Here in These Hills: West Virginia's Coal Miners and Their Battle for Freedom.* New York: Atlantic Monthly Press, 2015.

Green, Julie. *Pure and Simple Politics: The American Federation of Labor and Political Activism, 1881–1917.* New York: Cambridge University Press, 1998.

Griffiths, D. Jr. *Two Years Residence in the New Settlements of Ohio, North America.* Ann Arbor, Michigan: University Microfilms, 1966.

Grismer, Karl H. *Akron and Summit County.* Akron, OH: Summit County Historical Society, 1952.

Hacker, J. David. "A Census-Based Count of the Civil War Dead." *Civil War History,* Vol. 57, No. 4 (December 2011).

Hacker, Louis. *The Triumph of American Capitalism: The Development of Forces in American History to the End of the Nineteenth Century.* New York: Columbia University Press, 1940.

Hagedorn, Ann. *Savage Peace: Hope and Fear in America, 1919.* New York: Simon & Schuster, 2007.

Hagelberg, Kymberli. *Wicked Akron: Tales of Rumrunners, Mobsters and Other Rubber City Rogues.* Charleston, SC: The History Press, 2010.

Haraszti, Miklós. *A Worker in a Workers' State.* New York: Penguin Books, 1977.

Hardy, Thomas, ed. Sarah E. Maier. *Tess of the d'Urbervilles.* Toronto: Broadview Literary Texts, 1996.

Hartz, Louis. *The Liberal Tradition in America: An Interpretation of American Political Thought Since the Revolution.* New York: Harcourt, Brace, 1955.

Herman, Arthur. *Freedom's Forge: How American Business Produced Victory in World War II.* New York: Random House, 2012.

Hindman, Hugh D. *Child Labor: An American History.* New York: M. E. Sharpe, 2002.

Hobsbawm, Eric. *Labour's Turning Point, 1880–1900: Extracts from Contemporary Sources,* Second Ed. Brighton: Harvester Press, 1974.

Hobsbawm, Eric. *Uncommon People: Resistance, Rebellion, and Jazz.* New York: The New Press, 1999.

Hochschild, Adam. *Spain in Our Hearts: Americans in the Spanish Civil War, 1936–1939.* Boston & New York: Houghton Mifflin Harcourt, 2016.

Hofstadter, Richard. *The Age of Reform: From Bryan to F. D. R.* New York: Vintage Books, 1955.

Honey, Michael K. *Southern Labor and Black Civil Rights: Organizing Memphis.* Urbana and Chicago: University of Illinois Press, 1993.

Howard, Gene L. *The History of the Rubber Workers in Gadsden, Alabama, 1933–1983.* East Gadsden, AL: URWA Local 12, 1983.

Isenberg, Nancy. *White Trash: The 400-Year Untold History of Class in America.* New York: Viking, 2016.

Jones, Alfred Winslow. *Life, Liberty and Property: A Story of Conflict and a Measurement of Conflicting Rights.* Philadelphia: J. B. Lippincott, 1941.

Jones, Tom. *On A Burning Deck: Return to Akron: An Oral History of the Great Migration Vol. 2, 1920–1991.* New Braunfels, TX: Tom Jones, 2017.

Judd, Richard W. *Socialist Cities: Municipal Politics and the Grass Roots of American Socialism.* Albany: State University of New York, 1989.

Kamin, Leon J. *The Science and Politics of IQ.* Harmondsworth: Penguin Books, 1974.

Kea, Salaria. "While Passing Through." *Health and Medicine* (Spring, 1987): 11–13.

Keller, Jim. *A Veteran Communist Speaks: The Akron Rubber Strikes of 1936.* Chicago: Workers' Press, 1975.

Kelley, Robin. *Race Rebels: Culture, Politics and the Black Working Class.* New York: Free Press, 1994.

Kennedy David M. *Freedom from Fear: The American People in Depression and War, 1929–1945.* New York: Oxford University Press, 1999.

Kern, Kevin F. and Gregory S. Wilson. *Ohio: A History of the Buckeye State.* Malden, MA: John Wiley and Sons, 2014.

Klippert, Walter E. *Reflections of a Rubber Planter: The Autobiography of an Inquisitive Person.* New York: Vintage Press, 1972.

Kornweibel, Theodore Jr., ed. *Federal Surveillance of Afro-Americans (1917–1925): The First World War, the Red Scare, and the Garvey Movement.* Frederick, MD: University Publications of America, 1985.

Kreis, Steven. "The Diffusion of Scientific Management: The Bedaux Company in America and Britain, 1926–1945." In *A Mental Revolution: Scientific Management Since Taylor,* edited by Daniel Nelson. Columbus: Ohio State University Press, 1992.

Laidler, Harry W. *Boycotts and the Labor Struggle: Economic and Legal Aspects.* New York: John Lane, 1913.

Lane, Samuel A. *Fifty Years and Over of Akron and Summit County.* Akron, OH: Beacon Job Department, 1892.

Lebergott, Stanley. "Labor Force and Employment, 1800–1960." In *Output, Employment and Productivity in the United States after 1800,* edited by Dorothy S. Brady. Washington, DC: National Bureau of Economic Research, 1966.

Lenin, V. I. "The Results and Significance of the U.S. Presidential Elections." *Collected Works,* Vol. 18. Moscow: Progress Publishers, 1974.

Levitt, Sarah, 1986. "Manchester Mackintoshes: A History of the Rubberized Garment Trade." *Textile History* Vol. 17, No. 1, (1986).

Lewis, Clarice Finlay. *A History of Firestone Park.* Akron, OH: Firestone Park Citizens' Council, 1986.

Lewis, Ronald L. *Welsh Americans: A History of Assimilation in the Coalfields.* Chapel Hill, NC: University of North Carolina Press, 2008.

Lief, Alfred. *The Firestone Story: A History of the Firestone Tire & Rubber Company.* New York: McGraw-Hill, 1951.

Lippincott, Isaac. *Economic Development of the United States.* New York: Appleton, 1927.

Lipset, Seymour Martin, and Gary Wolfe Marks. *It Didn't Happen Here: Why Socialism Failed in the United States.* New York and London: W. W. Norton, 2000.

Litchfield, Paul. *Industrial Voyage. My Life as an Industrial Lieutenant.* New York: Doubleday, 1954.

Love, Steve and David Giffels. *Wheels of Fortune: The Story of Rubber in Akron.* Akron, OH: The University of Akron Press, 1999.

Lynd, Staughton, ed. *"We Are All Leaders": The Alternative Unionism of the Early 1930s.* Urbana and Chicago: University of Illinois Press, 1996.

Mack, Richard E. *Memoir of a Cold War Soldier.* Kent, OH: Kent State University Press, 2001.

Marx, Karl and Frederick Engels. *Manifesto of the Communist Party,* in *Karl Marx and Frederick Engels, Selected Works,* Vol. 1. Moscow: Progress Publishers, 1969.

Marx, Karl and Friedrich Engels. *Correspondence, 1846–1895.* New York: International Publishers, 1936.

Marx, Karl, trans. Eden and Cedar Paul. *Capital,* Vol. 1, London and New York: Everyman's Library, 1972.

Marx, Karl. *Grundisse. H*armondsworth: Penguin Books, 1973.

McAlister, Hugh. *Steve Holworth of the Oldham Works: The Story of a Boy Who Chose a Career in the Rubber Industry.* Akron, OH: Saalfield Publishing, 1930.

McCabe, James Dabney (writing as Edward Winslow Martin). *The History of the Great Riots.* Philadelphia: National Publishing, 1877.

McClain, Shirla Robinson. *The Contributions of Blacks in Akron: 1825–1975.* Akron, OH: Akron Gallery of Black History Curriculum Committee, 1996.

McCloskey, Burr. "I Appeal the Ruling of the Chair." In *Rank & File: Personal Histories of Working-Class Organizers,* edited by Alice and Staughton Lynd. Princeton, NJ: Princeton University Press, 1981.

McCormick, A. S. *The History of Medicine in Summit County, Ohio.* New York: Hobson Book Press, 1946.

McGovern, Frances. *Written in the Hills: The Making of the Akron Landscape.* Akron, OH: The University of Akron Press, 1996.

McKenney, Ruth. *Industrial Valley.* New York: Greenwood Press, 1968.

McKenney, Ruth, with an introduction by Daniel Nelson. *Industrial Valley.* Ithaca, NY: Cornell University Press, 1992.

Meyer, Bruce M. *The Once and Future Union: The Rise and Fall of the United Rubber Workers, 1935–1995.* Akron, OH: The University of Akron Press, 2002.

Michels, Robert, trans. Eden and Cedar Paul, with an introduction by Seymour Martin Lipset. *Political Parties: A Sociological Study of the Oligarchic Tendencies of Modern Democracy.* New York: The Free Press, 1962.

Miller, John Chester. *The First Frontier: Life in Colonial America.* New York: University Press of America, 1986.

Miller, Kerby A. *Emigrants and Exiles: Ireland and the Irish Exodus to North America.* New York: Oxford University Press, 1985.

Miller, Sally M. "For White Men Only: The Socialist Party of America and Issues of Gender, Ethnicity and Race." *Journal of the Gilded Age and Progressive Era,* Vol. 2, No. 3, *New Perspectives on Socialism* I. (July 2003): 283–302.

Montgomery, David. *The Fall of the House of Labor: The Workplace, the State, and American Labor Activism, 1865–1925.* Cambridge: Cambridge University Press, 1989.

Nash, Gerald C., ed. *Issues in American Economic History.* Lexington, MA: D. C. Heath, 1980.

Nelson, Bruce. *Divided We Stand: American Workers and the Struggle for Black Equality.* Princeton, NJ and Oxford: Princeton University Press, 2001.

Nelson, Dan. *American Rubber Workers & Organized Labor, 1900–1941.* Princeton, NJ: Princeton University Press, 1988.

Nelson, Daniel. *Managers and Workers: Origins of the Twentieth-Century Factory System in the United States 1880–1920, Second Edition.* Madison: University of Wisconsin Press, 1995.

Nelson, Daniel. *Shifting Fortunes: The Rise and Decline of American Labor, From the 1820s to the Present.* Chicago: Ivan R. Dee, 1997.

Nesbitt, Charles T. "Akron's Public Health Problem." *The Ohio Public Health Journal.* (February 9, 1918).

Nettels, Curtis P. *The Emergence of a National Economy, 1775–1815, The Economic History of the United States, Vol. III.* New York: Holt, Rinehart and Winston, 1962.

Nicholson, Philip Yale. *Labor's Story in the United States.* Philadelphia: Temple University Press, 2004.

North, Douglass C. and Robert Paul Thomas, eds. *The Growth of the American Economy to 1860.* Columbia: University of South Carolina Press, 1968.

Palmer, Bryan D. *James P. Cannon and the Origins of the American Revolutionary Left, 1890–1928.* Urbana and Chicago: University of Illinois Press, 2007.

Patai, Frances. "Heroines of the Good Fight: Testimonies of U.S. Volunteer Nurses in the Spanish Civil War, 1936–1939." *Nursing History Review,* Vol. 3 (1995).

Paxson, Frederic L. *History of the American Frontier.* Boston & New York: Houghton Mifflin, 1924.

Perry, Jay M. "The Irish Laborer Feuds on Indiana's Canals and Railroads in the 1830s." *Indiana Magazine of History,* Vol. 109, Issue 3 (September 2013): 224–256.

Pesotta, Rose, ed. John Nicholas Breffa. *Bread Upon The Waters.* Ithaca, NY: ILR Press, 1987.

Petersen, O. W. *The Jorgen Petersen Family.* Akron, OH: O. W. Petersen, 1972.

Phelan, Craig. *William Green: Biography of a Labor Leader.* Albany: State University of New York Press, 1989.

Pierce, Michael. "Martin Foran and the Creation of Cleveland's Labor Movement." In *Builders of Ohio: A Biographical History,* edited by Warren Van Tine and Michael Pierce. Columbus: Ohio State University Press, 2003.

Post, Charles. "The American Road to Capitalism," *New Left Review,* Vol. 1, No.33 (May–June, 1982): 30–51.

Poussin, Guillaume Tell, trans. Edmund L. Du Barry. *The United States: Its Power and Progress,* First American Edition. Philadelphia: Lippincott, Grambo, 1851.

Preis, Art. *Labor's Giant Step: Twenty Years of the CIO.* New York: Pathfinder Press, 1964.

Quine, Harry S. "The Darkest Night in Akron's History," in C. R. Quine, ed. *The Akron Riot of 1900.* Akron, OH: C. R. Quine, 1951.

Ramazzini, Bernardino, trans. Wilmer Cave Wright. *De Morbis Artificum.* Chicago: University of Chicago Press, 1940.

Reeves, Thomas C. *Twentieth Century America: A Brief History.* New York: Oxford University Press, 2000.

Rodabaugh, James H. "The Negro in Ohio." *The Journal of Negro History,* Vol. 31, No.1 (January 1946).

Roediger, David R. and Elizabeth D. Esch. *The Production of Difference: Race and the Management of Labor in U.S. History.* New York: Oxford University Press, 2012.

Roediger, David R. "Labor in a White Skin and Working Class History." In *Towards the Abolition of Whiteness: Essays on Race, Politics, and Working Class History.* London: Verso, 1994.

Sandel, Michael J. *America in Search of a Public Philosophy.* Cambridge, MA: Harvard University Press, 1998.

Sawyer, Teddy. "Labor Organizations." In *Akron and Summit County Ohio, 1825–1928,* Vol. 1., edited by Scott Dix Kenfield. Chicago and Akron: S. J. Clarke, 1928.

Schofield, Ann. "Rebel Girls and Union Maids: The Woman Question in the Journals of the A.F.L. and the I.W.W." *Feminist Studies,* Vol. 9, No. 2 (Summer 1983), 336–358.

Sessions, David. "America's Missing Labor Party." *The New Republic,* October 2, 2018.

Shaw, Ronald. *Canals for a Nation: The Canal Era in the United States, 1790–1860.* Lexington: University of Kentucky Press, 2014.

Shogun, Robert. *The Battle of Blair Mountain: The Story of America's Largest Labor Uprising.* Boulder, CO: Westview Press, 2004.

Shuy, Roger W. "Tireworker Terms." *American Speech,* (1964): 268–269.

Simons, A. M. *The American Farmer.* Chicago: Charles H. Kerr, 1906.

Skrabec, Quentin J. Jr. *Rubber: An American Industrial History.* Jefferson, NC: McFarland, 2014.

Sombart, Werner, trans. P. M. Hocking and C. T. Husbands. *Why is There No Socialism in the United States?* London: Palgrave Macmillan, 1976.

Spickard, Paul. *Almost All Aliens: Immigration, Race, and Colonialism in American History and Identity.* New York: Routledge, 2007.

Stewart, Estelle M. and J. C. Bowen. *History of Wages in the United States From Colonial Times to 1928,* Part 1, Revision of Bulletin No. 499 With Supplement, 1929–1933. Washington, DC: United States Department of Labor, Bureau of Labor Statistics, 1934.

Terkel, Studs. *"The Good War": An Oral History of World War II.* Harmondsworth: Penguin Books, 1986.

Thompson, E. P. *The Making of the English Working Class.* New York: Vintage Books, 1966.

Thompson, E. P. "Time, Work-Discipline, and Industrial Capitalism," *Past and Present,* no. 38 (December 1967): 56–97.

Thurber, John Newton. *Rubber Workers' History (1935–1955).* Akron, OH: URWA, 1956.

Tierney, Dominic. *F. D. R. and the Spanish Civil War: Neutrality and Commitment in the Struggle that Divided America.* Durham, NC: Duke University Press, 2007.

Tone, Andrea. *The Business of Benevolence: Industrial Paternalism in America.* Ithaca, NY: Cornell University Press, 1997.

Trotsky, Leon. *My Life: An Attempt at Autobiography.* Mineola, NY: Dover Publications, 2007.

Trotsky, Leon. *The Living Thoughts of Karl Marx.* New York: Longmans, Green, 1939.

Tully, James. *Shanty Irish.* Kent, OH: Black Squirrel, 2009.

Tully, John. *Crooked Deals and Broken Treaties: How American Indians Were Displaced by White Settlers in the Cuyahoga Valley.* New York: Monthly Review Press, 2016.

Tully, John. *The Devil's Milk: A Social History of Rubber.* New York: Monthly Review Press, 2011.

Turner, Frederick Jackson. *The Frontier in American History.* New York: Henry Holt, 1953.

US Department of Commerce. *Historical Statistics of the United States.* Washington, DC: US Government Printer, 1957.

URWA. *25 Years of the U.R.W: A Quarter Century of Panorama of Democratic Unionism.* Akron, OH: United Rubber, Cork, Linoleum and Plastic Workers of America, AFL-CIO, 1960.

Van Tine, Warren and Michael Pierce, eds. *Builders of Ohio: A Biographical History.* Columbus: Ohio State University Press, 2003.

Vaughan, John R. *Jottings of a Judge.* Akron, OH: Central Publishing, 1922.

Warden, D. B. *A Statistical, Political, and Historical Account of the United States.* Edinburgh: 1819.

Way, Peter. *Common Labour: Workers and the Digging of North American Canals, 1780–1860.* Cambridge: Cambridge University Press, 1993.

Wheeler, Robert A., ed. *Visions of the Western Reserve: Public and Private Documents of Northeastern Ohio, 1750–1860.* Columbus: Ohio State University Press, 2000.

Williams, Thomas Desmond, ed. *Secret Societies in Ireland.* Dublin and New York: Gill and Macmillan, 1973.

Williamson, John. *Dangerous Scot: The Life and Work of an American "Undesirable."* New York: International Publishers, 1969.

Wolf, Howard and Ralph. *Rubber: A Story of Glory and Greed.* New York: Covici-Friede, 1936.

Woodiwiss, Michael. *Organized Crime and American Power: A History.* Toronto: University of Toronto Press, 2001.

Wrege, Charles D. and Amadeo G. Perroni. "Taylor's Pig Tale: A Historical Analysis of Frederick W. Taylor's Pig-Iron experiments." *Academy of Management Journal,* Vol. 17 (March 1974): 6–27.

Wright, Chester W. *Economic History of the United States,* First Edition. New York: McGraw-Hill, 1941.

UNPUBLISHED DISSERTATIONS

Borsos, John E. "Talking Union: The Labor Movement in Barberton, Ohio, 1891–1991." PhD diss. University of Indiana, February 1992.

Corley, Dawn L. "Spanish Influenza in Summit County, Ohio, 1918–1920." Master's Thesis. The University of Akron, May 1987.

Frazier, Kevan Delaney. "Model Industrial Subdivisions: Goodyear Heights and Firestone Park and the Town Planning Movement in Akron, Ohio, 1910–1920." Master's thesis. Kent State University, 1994.

Johnson, Susan Allyn. "Industrial Voyagers: A Case Study of Appalachian Migration to Akron, Ohio, 1900–1940." PhD diss. Ohio State University, 2006.

Maples, John Lee. "The Akron, Ohio Ku Klux Klan, 1921–1928." Master's Thesis. The University of Akron, 1974.

Rosswurm, Kevin Michael. "A Strike in the Rubber City: Rubber Workers, Akron, and the I.W.W., 1913." Master's Thesis. Kent State University, 1975.

Shrake, Richard W. II. "Working Class Politics in Akron, Ohio, 1936: The United Rubber Workers and the Failure of the Farmer Labor Party." Master's Thesis. The University of Akron, 1974.

Weston, Evelyn Gertrude. "Wadsworth, Ohio: A Manufacturing Suburb of Akron, Ohio." Master's Thesis. Kent State University, 1940.

ELECTRONIC SOURCES

Agency for Toxic Substances and Diseases Registry. ToxFAQs for Aniline. http://www.atsdr.cdc.gov/tfacts171.html.

Akron Porcelain & Plastics Co., Celebrating 125 Years: Five Generations Help to Build Akron Porcelain & Plastics, Chapter One, "Molding a Legacy 1828–1890." http://www.akronporcelain.com/History/Akronchapter1.pdf.

All America City. History of Akron. http://www.ci.akron.oh.us/history/timeline/1900.htm.

Bureau of Labor Statistics. "The Life of American Workers in 1915," *Monthly Labor Review,* February 2016. https://www.bls.gov/opub/mlr/2016/article/the-life-of-american-workers-in-1915.htm.

Cannon, James P. The IWW. https://www.marxists.org/archive/cannon/works/1955/iww.htm.

"Carl Oglesby." Spartacus Educational. spartacus-educational.com/JFKoglesby.htm.

Davis, Judy Anne. *A History of Tallmadge Coal: A Tale of Woodchucks, Welshmen, and a Canal* (Stow, OH: Akron Public Library, 2006). www.akronlibrary.org/images/Divisions/SpecColl/images/TallmadgeCoal-.pdf.

Debs, Eugene. "On Liquor and Prohibition," *Terre Haute Star,* February 2, 1916. https://www.marxists.org/archive/debs/works/1916/0202-debs-liquorand prohibition.pdf.

Debs, Eugene. This Is Our Year. https://www.marxists.org/archive/debs/works/1912/twoparties.htm.

Documents Related to FDR and Churchill. National Archives, Washington, DC. https://www.archives.gov/education/lessons/fdr-churchill.

Eidlin, Barry, "Why Is There No Labor Party in the United States? Political Articulation and the Canadian Comparison, 1932 to 1948," *American Sociological Review,* 1–29, 2016. https://journals.sagepub.com/doi/full/10.1177/0003122416643758.

Engels, Frederick. "The Industrial Proletariat." In The Condition of the Working Class in England. https://www.marxists.org/archive/marx/works/1845/condition-working-class/ch03.htm.

Engels, Frederick, Introduction to the American Edition of *The Condition of the Working Class in England* (New York: John W. Lovell, 1887). Marxists Internet Archive. https://www.marxists.org/archive/marx/works/1887/01/26.htm.

Equal Justice Initiative. *Lynching in America: Confronting the Legacy of Racial Terror.* https://eji.org/reports/lynching-in-america.

Ferdinand Schumacher. Ohio History Central. http://www.ohiohistorycentral.org/index.php?title=Ferdinand_Schumacher&rec=333.

Fisk, Donald M. "American Labor in the 20th Century." US Bureau of Labor Statistics, January 30, 2003. https://www.bls.gov/opub/mlr/cwc/american-labor-in-the-20th-century.pdf.

Goldner, Cheri. "Welsh Ancestors of Summit County," *Past Pursuits: A Newsletter of the Special Collections Division of the Akron-Summit County Library,* Vol.7, No.2 (Akron: Summer 2008): 12, 4. http://www.akronlibrary.org/internetresources/sc/pursuits/pursuits7-2.pdf.

Gramsci, Antonio. "Taylorism and the Mechanisation of the Worker," In *Selections from The Prison Notebooks* (London: Electric Book Company, 1999), 610. abahlali.org/files/Gramsci.pdf.

Hart, Eric. A Brief History of I.A.T.S.E., September 6, 2010. http://www.props.eric-hart.com/features/a-brief-history-of-iatse/.

Harrington, Michael. "Our Fifty Million Poor: Forgotten Men of the Affluent Society," *Commentary,* (July 1959). https://www.commentarymagazine.com/articles/our-fifty-million-poorforgotten-men-of-the-affluent-society/.

Heideman, Paul. "The Rise and Fall of the Socialist Party of America," *Jacobin,* February 20, 2017. https://www.jacobinmag.com/2017/02/rise-and-fall-socialist-party-of-america.

Hillquit, Morris. "Daniel De Leon and the 1899 Split of the SLP." Taken from Hillquit's *Loose Leaves from a Busy Life* (New York: Macmillan, 1934), 45–54, Marxists Internet Archive. https://www.marxists.org/history/usa/parties/spusa/1934/0000-hillquit-ondeleon.pdf.

Hipple, Steven F.. "Self-employment in the United States," *Monthly Labor Review,* Bureau of Labor Statistics. https://www.bls.gov/opub/mlr/2010/09/art2full.pdf.

Historical Background and Development of Social Security. Social Security Administration (US). https://www.ssa.gov/history/briefhistory3.html.

Hobsbawm, E. J. "Gramsci and Political Theory," *Marxism Today,* (July 1977), 205-213. Online at http://banmarchive.org.uk/collections/mt/pdf/07_77_205.pdf.

International Agency for Research on Cancer. Occupational Exposures in the Rubber-Manufacturing Industry, 2012. https://www.ncbi.nlm.nih.gov/books/NB304412/.https://monographs.iarc.fr/wp-content/uploads/2018/06/mono100F-36.pdf.

International Chemical Workers' Union, Local 901, 1937–1990. The Ward M. Canady Center for Special Collections, University of Toledo. https://www.utoledo.edu/library/canaday/findingaids1/mss-085.pdf.

Jennings, Jay. Campaign Tactics of Eugene Debs in the 1912 Presidential Election, *The Public Purpose,* Vol. III, (2005): 65. https://www.american.edu/spa/publicpurpose/upload/Campaign-Tactics-of-Eugene-Debs-in-the-1912-Presidential-Campaign.pdf.

Kautsky, Karl. Finance-Capital and Crises, *Social Democrat,* XIV London July–September, 1911. http://www.marxists.org/archive/kautsky/1911/xx/finance.htm.

Kautsky, Karl. "Socialist Agitation Among Farmers in America," *International Socialist Review,* Vol.3 (September 1902), 148, Marxists Internet Archive. https://www.marxists.org/archive/kautsky/1902/09/farmers.htm.

Lebergott, Stanley. Labor Force and Employment, 1800–1960 in Dorothy S. Brady ed., Output, Employment, and Productivity in the United States after 1800 (Washington, DC: National Bureau of Economic Research, 1966), 120. http://www.nber.org/chapters/c1567.

Lenin, V. I. May Day and the War. Notes for a speech or article written in April 1915. Published in *Proletarskaya Revolutsia,* No. 1, January 1929. https://www.marxists.org/archive/lenin/works/1915/apr/30.htm.

Lenin, V. I., trans. Bernard Isaacs and Joe Fineberg, "The Taylor System—Man's Enslavement by the Machine," *Put Pravdy,* No. 35, March 13, 1914. https://www.marxists.org/archive/lenin/works/1914/mar/13.htm.

Lewis, Danny. "This Map Shows Over a Century of Documented Lynchings in the United States." Smithsonian.com. https://www.smithsonianmag.com/smart-news/map-shows-over-a-century-of-documented-lynchings-in-united-states-180961877/.

Life Expectancy by Age, 1850–2011. Infoplease. https://www.infoplease.com/us/mortality/life-expectancy-age-1850-2011.

Lincoln, Abraham. Address before the Wisconsin Agricultural Society, September 30, 1859. http://www.abrahamlincolnonline.org/lincoln/speeches/fair.htm.

Lipset, Seymour Martin. "Why Socialism Failed in the United States." American Enterprise Institute Bradley Lecture Series. October 2, 2000. http://www.aei.org/publication/why-socialism-failed-in-the-united-states/.

Luxemburg, Rosa, trans. Bertram Wolfe. *The Russian Revolution* (New York: Workers Age Publications, 1940). Marxists Internet Archive. https://www.marxists.org/archive/luxemburg/1918/russian-revolution/index.htm.

MacDonald, Kevin. "Henry Ford and the Jewish Question." Review of Neil Baldwin, *Henry Ford and the Jews: The Mass Production of Hate* (New York: Public Affairs, 2001). http://www.kevinmacdonald.net/HenryFord-1.htm.

Mahin, Chris. The First National Hunger March Confront the US Congress, December 1, 2017. https://chilaborarts.wordpress.com/2017/12/01/6174/.

Mapping American Social Movements Through the 20th Century. Socialist Party of America History and Geography. Pacific Northwest Labor and Civil Rights Projects, University of Washington, 2015. http://depts.washington.edu/moves/SP_intro.shtml.

Martin, Steve, and John L. Lewis. 'Speech at the Fifty-Fifth Annual Convention of the American Federation of Labor (16 October 1935), Voices of Democracy, No. 8, 2013, 56. http://voicesofdemocracy.umd.edu/wp-content/uploads/2014/10/Lewis-Interpretive-Essay.pdf.

Marx, Karl. *The Poverty of Philosophy.* Marxists Internet Archive. https://www.marxists.org/archive/marx/works/download/pdf/Poverty-Philosophy.pdf.

Marx, Karl, trans. Samuel Moore and Edward Aveling. *Capital: A Critique of Political Economy,* Vol. I, Ch. 10, Section 7, 195. https://www.marxists.org/archive/marx/works/download/pdf/Capital-Volume-I.pdf.

Matteo, Arthur E. Socialist Municipal Administrations in the Progressive Era: A Case Study of Four Ohio Cities, 1911–1915. http://www.ohioacademyofhistory.org/wp-content/uploads/2013/04/DeMatteo.pdf.

Mayer, Gerald. Union Membership Trends in the United States (Washington DC: Congressional Research Service, 2004). https://digitalcommons.ilr.cornell.edu/cgi/viewcontent.cgi?article=1176&context=key_workplace.

MeasuringWorth.com. https://www.measuringworth.com/uscompare/relativevalue.php.

Moffatt, Mike. "Are Wars Good for the Economy?" https://www.thoughtco.com/are-wars-good-for-the-economy-1148174.

Notes of the Secret debates of the Federal Convention of 1787, Taken by Robert Yates, Chief Justice of the State of New York, and One of the delegates to the Said Convention. Yale Law School Avalon Project, Documents in Law, History and Diplomacy. Avalon.law.yale.edu/18th_century/yates.asp.

Ohio Constitution [the 1851 Constitution with Amendments to 2015]. https://www.legislature.ohio.gov/laws/ohio-constitution.

Ohio History Central. Knights of Labor. www.ohiohistorycentral.org/w/Knights_of_Labor.

Orwell, George. "Down the Mine." http://orwell.ru/library/essays/mine/english/e_dtm.

Our Campaigns. https://www.ourcampaigns.com/CandidateDetail.html?CandidateID=185584.

Paine, Thomas. *Common Sense; Addressed to the Inhabitants of America* (Philadelphia: W& T Bradford, 1775). Project Gutenberg. https://www.gutenberg.org/files/147/147-h/147-h.htm.

Panic of 1893. Ohio History Central. www.ohiohistorycentral.org/w/Panic_of_1893.

Post, Charlie. The Popular Front: Rethinking CPUSA History, *Solidarity,* July–August, 2018. https://solidarity-us.org/atc/63/p2363/.

Report of the Akron Committee on Civil Disorders, Akron Ohio, April 16, 1969. http://www.ascpl.lib.oh.us/internetresources/sc/OnlineBooks/Commitee-Report-Civildisorders.pdf.

Roediger, David and Elizabeth Esch. "One Symptom of Originality: Race and the Management of Labor in the United States." *Historical Materialism* (January 2009), 17, 4. https://doi.org/10.1163/146544609X12537556703034.

Sanders, Bernie. "Trump's Economy is Good for Billionaires, Not for Working People," *The Guardian,* January 16, 2019. https://www.theguardian.com/us-news/2019/jan/16/trump-economy-billionaires-working-people?CMP=Share_iOSApp_Other.

Schulman, Jason. "Where Is Our Labor Party?" *Jacobin,* (December 15, 2016). https://jacobinmag.com/2016/12/where-is-our-labor-party.

Seldman, Derek. "What Happened to the Labor Party?" An interview with Mark Dudzic, *Jacobin* October 11, 2015. https://www.jacobinmag.com/2015/10/tony-mazzochi-mark-dudzic-us-labor-party-wto-nafta-globalization-democrats-union/.

Sharts, Joseph W. "Communist Labor Heads Arrested! Infamous Freeman Act Used to Crush Political and Industrial Activity of Ohio Workers," *Miami Valley Socialist,* October 24, 1919. http://www.marxisthistory.org/history/usa/parties/cpusa/1919/1024-sharts-ohclparrests.pdf.

Shuy, Roger W. Language Call. Benny Come Home, January 6, 2007. http://itre.cis.upenn.edu/~myl/languagelog/archives/004012.html.

Smith, Adam. *The Wealth of Nations,* Book I, Chapter 1, "On the Division of Labour." https://www.marxists.org/reference/archive/smith-adam/works/wealth-of-nations/book01/ch01.htm.

Sobel, Robert. "Essays, Paper & Addresses. Coolidge and American Business," Calvin Coolidge Presidential Foundation. https://www.coolidgefoundation.org/resources/essays-papers-addresses-35/.

Strauss, Jonathan. "Engels and the Theory of the Labor Aristocracy," *Links International Journal of Socialist Renewal.* links.org.au/node/45.

Taylor, Frederick Winslow. *Principles of Scientific Management,* 1911. http://melbecon.unimelb.edu/het/taylor/sciman.htm.

The Atlantic Charter. https://www.archives.gov/files/education/lessons/fdr-churchill/images/atlantic-charter.gif.

The Constitution of the KL, 1878. http://sageamericanhistory.net/gildedage/documents/KofLaborConst.html.

The Proletarian Party of America (1920-1930). Party History. http://www.marxisthistory.org/subject/usa/eam/proletarianparty.html.

Timeline of *Beacon Journal* History, *Akron Beacon Journal*/Ohio.com, Wednesday, February 22, 2017. http://www.ohio.com/lifestyle/timeline-of-beacon-journal-history-1.524070.

Toward Soviet America. Marxist Internet Archive. 2009. https://www.marxists.org/archive/foster/1932/toward/.

Trotsky, Leon. "On the Labor Party Question in America," *The Militant,* Vol. V., No. 24, June 11, 1932. Marxist Internet Archive. https://www.marxists.org/archive/trotsky/1932/xx/lp.htm.

Truth, Sojourner, Ain't I A Woman? December 1851. Modern History Sourcebook. Fordham University. https://sourcebooks.fordham.edu/mod/sojtruth2.asp.

Twain, Mark, and Charles Dudley Warner, *The Gilded Age A Tale of To-Day,* Two Vols. (New York: P. F. Collier & Son, 1873). https://www.questia.com/read/1364401/the-gilded-age-a-tale-of-today.

UMW of A Preamble, January 25, 1890. https://ecology.iww.org/texts/IWW/Coal220/11?bot_test=1.

US Census Bureau Fact Sheet. 2006–2008 American Community Survey—3 Year Estimates. https://www.census.gov/programs-surveys/acs/technical-documentation/table-and-geography-changes/2008/3-year.html

US Census Bureau, Resident Population of Apportionment of US House of Representatives, Ohio. https://www.census.gov/dmd/www/resapport/states/ohio.pdf.

US Department of Labor, Bureau of Labor Statistics, Number and rate of fatal occupational injuries, by industry sector, 2009. (Preliminary results.), (Washington DC: October 1, 2010). https://www.bls.gov/news.release/archives/cfoi_08192010.pdf.

US Department of Labor, Bureau of Labor Statistics, *Industrial Poisons Used in the Rubber Industry* (Washington, DC: Government Printing Office, 1915). https://fraser.stlouisfed.org/files/docs/publications/bls/bls_0179_1915.pdf

US Department of Labor, Bureau of Labor Statistics, Summary of the Report on Condition of Woman and Child Wage Earners in the United States, Dec. 1915 (Washington, DC: Government Printing Office, 1916), 21–22. https://fraser.stlouisfed.org/files/docs/publications/bls_wis/bls_175_womeninindustry5.pdf.

US Department of Labor, Occupational Safety Health Administration. Hydrogen Sulfide. https://www.osha.gov/SLTC/hydrogensulfide/hazards.html.

Unity History, GMB Stoke Unity S75. www.gmbstokeunity.org.uk/unity-history/branch@gmbstokeunity.org.uk.

Warde, William F., "American Philosophy and the Labor Movement," *International Socialist Review,* Vol. 23, No. 2 (Spring 1962), 2. Marxists Internet Archive. https://www.marxists.org/archive/novack/1962/xx/philosophy.htm.

Whitten, David O., The Depression of 1893, EH.net, Economic History Association. https://eh.net/encyclopedia/the-depression-of-1893.

William Green, AFL-CIO, America's Unions. https://aflcio.org/about/history/labor-history-people/william-green.

Wilson, Jack, "In a Billion Dollar Industry," *New International,* Vol. 2, No. 2, (March 1935). http://www.marxists,org/history/etol/newspaper/ni/vol02/no02/wilson-htm.

Woods, Alan, "The U.S.A. and the War: War Is Good for Business." Part Nine. *First World War: A Marxist Analysis of the Great Slaughter.* In Defence of Marxism. https://www.marxist.com/wwi-part-nine-usa-and-the-war.htm.

Working Conditions in Factories, *Gale Encyclopedia of US Economic History,* ed. Thomas Riggs, 2nd ed., Vol. 3, 1484–1486. *US History in Context.*

Wright, Robert E., Origins of Commercial Banking in the United States, 1781–1830, Economic History Association, EH.Net. https://eh.net/encyclopedia/origins-of-commercial-banking-in-the-united-states-1781-1830/.

Zetkin, Klara, trans. Eden and Cedar Paul, *Through Dictatorship to Democracy* (Glasgow: Socialist Labour Press, 1926). https://www.marxists.org/archive/zetkin/1919/xx/dictdem.htm

Zinn, Howard, History is a Weapon. *A People's History of the United States,* Ch. 16, "A People's War?" https://www.historyisaweapon.com/defcon1/zinnpeopleswar.html.

Index

Printed in the United States
By Bookmasters